The Pattern Library

Little Acorn Books™

The Pattern Library
I-Z

• instruments • tools • pets • wild, exotic & domestic animals • maps • transportation • food • containers • vegetables •
• inventions • appliances • household objects • architecture • dinosaurs • plants • insects • sea creatures • and more. •

by Marilynn G. Barr

The Pattern Library

Volume Two • I - Z

LAB201412P
THE PATTERN LIBRARY • VOLUME TWO • I - Z

black and white, large illustrations in printable pattern format for:
• instruments • tools • pets • wild, exotic & domestic animals • maps • transportation • food • containers • vegetables •
• inventions • appliances • household objects • architecture • dinosaurs • plants • insects • sea creatures • and more. •

by Marilynn G. Barr

Published by: Little Acorn Books™
Originally published by: Monday Morning Books, Inc.

Entire contents copyright © 2014 Little Acorn Books™

Little Acorn Books
PO Box 8787
Greensboro, NC 27419-0787

Promoting Early Skills for a Lifetime™

Little Acorn Books™
is an imprint of Little Acorn Associates, Inc.

http://www.littleacornbooks.com

Permission is hereby granted to reproduce student materials in this book for non-commercial individual or classroom use. *School-wide or system-wide use is expressly prohibited.

ISBN 978-1-937257-63-7

Printed in the United States of America

The Pattern Library

Volume Two • I - Z

Table of Contents

I
- ibex 8
- ice cream (one scoop) 9
- ice cream (five scoops) 10
- ice (cube) 11
- iceskate (left) 12
- ice skate (right) 13
- ice skate (left, with pompom) 14
- ice skate (right, with pompom) 15
- Idaho, USA 16
- igloo 17
- Illinois, USA 18
- Indiana, USA 19
- indri 20
- ink (jar) 21
- Iowa, USA 22
- iron 23
- ivy (outline) 24

J
- jack 25
- jacks 26
- jack o' lantern 27
- jack o' lantern (outline) 28
- jack o' lantern (standard) 29
- jack o' lantern (with mask) 30
- jack rabbit 31
- jack-in-the-box 32
- jar 33
- jellybeans 34
- jellyfish 35
- jonquil 36
- jump rope 37
- jumper 38

K
- kangaroo (animated) 39
- kangaroo (outline) 40
- kangaroo (stylized) 41
- Kansas, USA 42
- Kentucky, USA 43
- kerchief 44
- kettle 45
- key 46
- king 47
- kinkajou 48
- kite (box) 49
- kite (standard) 50
- kitten 51
- knives (butter and steak) 52
- koala 53

L
- ladle (gravy) 54
- ladle (soup) 55
- ladybug 56
- lamb 57
- leaf (dogwood) 58
- leaf (hickory) 59
- leaf (ginkgo) 60
- leaf (maple) 61
- leaf (maple, outline) 62
- leaf (oak) 63
- leopard 64
- leprechaun 65
- leprechaun (torso) 66
- light bulb 67
- lion (head) 68
- lion (laying) 69
- lizard 70
- llama 71
- lobster 72
- lock 73
- lollipop (flat) 74
- lollipop (round) 75
- Louisiana, USA 76
- Louisiana Purchase 77
- lunch box 78
- lyre 79

M
- Maine, USA 80
- manatee 81
- mandolin 82
- madril 83
- Manitoba, Canada 84
- maracas 85
- Maryland, USA 86
- mask (tiger) 87
- masks 88
- Massachusetts, USA 89
- matches (closed book) 90
- matches (open book) 91
- menorah 92
- menorah (outline) 93
- Mexico 94
- Michigan, USA 95
- microscope 96
- Minnesota, USA 97
- Mississippi, USA 98
- Missouri, USA 99
- mitt (3D) 100
- mitt (plain) 101
- mitten (left) 102
- mitten (right) 103
- mittens 104
- monkey 105
- monster (head) 106
- Montana, USA 107
- moon 108
- moon (with night cap) 109
- moose 110
- mouse (animated) 111
- mouse (animated, waving) 112
- mouse (animated, winter) 113
- mushroom (bell-shaped) 114
- mushroom (conical) 115
- mushroom (convex) 116
- mushroom (convex with skirt) 117

The Pattern Library

TPL

Volume Two • I - Z

Table of Contents

N
narwhal 118
nautilus 119
Nebraska, USA 120
necklace 121
necktie 122
needle (sewing) 123
nest 124
nest (outline) 125
net (without handle) 126
Nevada, USA 127
New Brunswick, Canada 128
Newfoundland &
 Labrador, Canada 129
New Hampshire, USA 130
New Jersey, USA 131
New Mexico, USA 132
newspaper (folded) 133
New York, USA 134
newt 135
nickels 136
North America 137
North Carolina, USA 138
North Dakota, USA 139
Northern Territory & Nunavut,
 Canada 140
Nova Scotia, Canada 141

O
octopus (floating) 142
octopus (poster) 143
octopus (sitting) 144
Ohio, USA 145
okapi 146
Oklahoma, USA 147
onion (spring) 148
Ontario, Canada 149
orangutan 150
Oregon, USA 151
ornament (pear-shape) 152
ornament (round) 153
ostrich 154

otter 155
overalls 156
owl 157
ox (musk) 158

P
pail (handle down) 159
pail (handle up) 160
paintbrush (plain) 161
paintbrush (wide) 162
paintbrushes (art) 163
palette (outline) 164
palette (with paint daubs) 165
pan (frying) 166
papaya 167
paper plate 168
parchment (scroll) 169
parachute 170
parrot 171
paste (jar) 172
peanut 173
pear 174
peas 175
pens 176
pencil (short and stout) 177
pencil (standard) 178
penguin 179
penguin (animated with hat) .. 180
pennies 181
Pennsylvania, USA 182
pentagon (shape) 183
perch 184
pie 185
pig 186
pig (animated) 187
pig (outline) 188
piggy bank 189
pinecone 190
pink (crayon) 191
pitcher 192
planet (with ring) 193

platypus 194
pocket (with stitches) 195
pocket watch 196
poinsettia (with veins) 197
poinsettia (without veins) 198
pony 199
popsicle 200
pot (cooking) 201
potato 202
pretzel (twist) 203
Prince Edward Island,
 Canada 204
puffin 205
pumpkin 206
pumpkin 207
pumpkin 208
puppy 209
purple (crayon) 210
pushpin 211
pyramid 212

Q
quail (animated) 213
quail (stylized) 214
quarters 215
Quebec, Canada 216
queen 217
question mark 218
quetzal 219
quill (pen) 220
quilt 221
quiver 222

R
rabbit (animated, waving) 223
rabbit (animated, floppy ears) . 224
rabbit (chocolate) 225
rabbit (outline) 226
rabbit (stylized) 227
raccoon 228
raccoon (waving) 229
raindrop 230

The Pattern Library

TPL

Volume Two • I - Z

Table of Contents

ram 231	silver (crayon) 270	starfish 310
red (crayon) 232	skeleton 271	stocking (outline) 311
reindeer 233	skirt (pleated) 272	stomach 312
rhinoceros 234	skunk 273	strawberries 313
Rhode Island, USA 235	snail (animated) 274	submarine (1898) 314
rollerskate (left) 236	snail (oultine) 275	submarine 315
rollerskate (right) 237	snail (stylized) 276	suitcase 316
rollerskate (child, left) 238	snake 277	sun (animated) 317
rollerskate (child, right) 239	sneaker (left-high top) 278	swan 318
rooster (animated) 240	sneaker (right-high top) 279	**T**
rooster (stylized) 241	sneaker (outline-high top) ..280	tadpole 319
rose 242	snipe 281	tamborine 320
S	snowflake 282	tan (crayon) 321
safety pin (closed) 243	snowman 283	teacup 322
safety pin (open) 244	snowman (waving) 284	teacup and saucer 323
sailboat 245	sock (left) 285	teapot 324
sailboat(outline) 246	sock (right) 286	telephone (1940s) 325
salmon (Chinook) 247	sofa 287	telephone (push buttons) ...326
sand pail poster 248	sombrero 288	telephone (cordless) 327
Saskatchewan, Canada 249	South America 289	telephone (first) 328
satellite 250	South Carolina, USA 290	telephone (rotary dial) 329
scissors (closed) 251	South Dakota, USA 291	telephone (slimline) 330
scissors (open) 252	space shuttle 292	Tennessee, USA 331
scissors (tailor's) 253	space shuttle (in flight) 293	Texas, USA 332
screw (flathead) 254	spade (symbol) 294	thimble 333
screw (Phillips) 255	spade (tool) 295	tiger 334
screwdriver (flathead) 256	sphinx 296	tire 335
screwdrive (Phillips head) .257	spider 297	tire 336
seal (animated) 258	Spirit of St. Louis 298	tomato 337
seal (animated, wearing hat) .259	spool 299	tooth 338
seashell 260	spoon (flat) 300	tooth (molar) 339
shaker (salt) 261	spoon 301	toothbrush 340
ship (toy) 262	squirrel (animated) 302	toothpaste 341
shoe (left-buckle) 263	squirrel (stylized) 303	toucan 342
show (right-buckle) 264	squirrel (wearing sweater) ..304	toucan (outline) 343
shoe (left-loafer) 265	stage 305	tractor 344
show (right-loafer) 266	stagecoach 306	traffic signal 345
shopping bag 267	stapler 307	tree 346
shrew 268	star (five points) 308	tree (pine) 347
shuttlecock 269	star (six points) 309	triangle 348

The Pattern Library

Volume Two • I - Z

Table of Contents

tricycle 349	**V**	wheel (spoked) 412
trowel 350	vacuum cleaner (1908) 381	wheelbarrow 413
truck 351	vacuum cleaner (upright) 382	whip 414
trunk (storage) 352	Valentine candy box 383	whisk 415
trunk (tree) 353	van 384	whistle 416
tub 354	vase 385	White House, The, USA 417
tube (cardboard) 355	venus flytrap 386	wig 418
tulip 356	Vermont, USA 387	window 419
tuna 357	vest 388	Wisconsin, USA 420
turkey 358	vicuña 389	wolf (running) 421
turkey (hen) 359	viking 390	wolf (standing) 422
turkey (outline) 360	violin 391	wood (cut logs) 423
turkey (tom) 361	Virginia, USA 392	wreath (detailed) 424
tuquoise (crayon) 362	visor 393	wreath (plain) 425
turtle (animated) 363	volcano 394	Wyoming, USA 426
turtle (animated with hat) 364	vole 395	**X**
turtle (loggerhead) 365	volley ball 396	x-ray 427
turtle (outline) 366	vulture 397	xantusia 428
turtle (pet) 367	**W**	letter Xx 429
turtledove 368	wagon (covered) 398	xylophone 430
typewriter (1867) 369	wagon (toy) 399	**Y**
U	walrus 400	yak 431
umbrella (beach) 370	Washington, USA 401	yarn ball 432
umbrella (outline) 371	Washington, DC (District of	yawn 433
umbrella (rain) 372	Columbia, USA) 402	yo-yo 434
umpire 373	watermelon (wedge) 403	Yukon, Canada 435
underwear 374	watermelon (whole) 404	**Z**
unicycle 375	weasel 405	zebra 436
United Kingdom 376	web (spider) 406	zebu 437
United States of America 377	West Virginia, USA 407	zipper 438
USS Constitution 378	Western hemisphere 408	zither 439
urchin 379	whale (animated) 409	
Utah, USA 380	whale (humpback) 410	
	whale (outline) 411	

More patterns for letters A through H are featured in *The Pattern Library™ • Volume One*, LAB201411P.

The Pattern Library

Volume Two • I - Z

***The Pattern Libary*™**—is a two-volume treasury of large, black line illustrations in printable, pattern formats. This, **Volume Two** contains patterns for letters **I** through **Z**. It's a rich collection of illustrations from our image libraries and an invaluable resource for children, parents, teachers, crafters and anyone who requires blackline images for an infinite number or projects. Illustrations are labeled and easy-to-find as they appear alphabetically in the table of contents (pp. 3-6). Multiple versions of a given object or animal are also labeled accordingly in the table of contents.

Note: In most instances, patterns are listed by category or species names first with details, if any, in parenthesis:

lollipop (flat) - Volume 2, I-Z
lollipop (round) - Volume 2, I-Z
mouse (animated, winter) - Volume 2, I-Z
turtle (loggerhead) - Volume 2, I-Z

Patterns include a wide selection of items found around the house, around town, in recreational environments, domestic, wild, and exotic animals, musical instruments, tools, dwellings, containers, the vintage and the unique.

Decorate workstations, display and bulletin boards, take-home communications, work folders, book reports, book covers, scrapbooks, picture albums, stationary, desks, doors, windows, flags, paper bag lanterns, and daisy chains or embelish presentations.

Create activity sheets, picture word walls, flash cards, picture dictionaries, index fact cards, collages, matching card games, door knob hangers, signs, tags, labels, picture blocks, bag puppets, stick puppets, mobiles, flannel boards, and anything else you can imagine.

ibex

ice cream (one scoop)

ice cream (five scoops)

ice (cube)

iceskate (left)

ice skate (right)

ice skate (left, with pompom)

ice skate (right, with pompom)

Idaho, USA

North
West East
South

Maps are representations and boundaries are not exact.

igloo

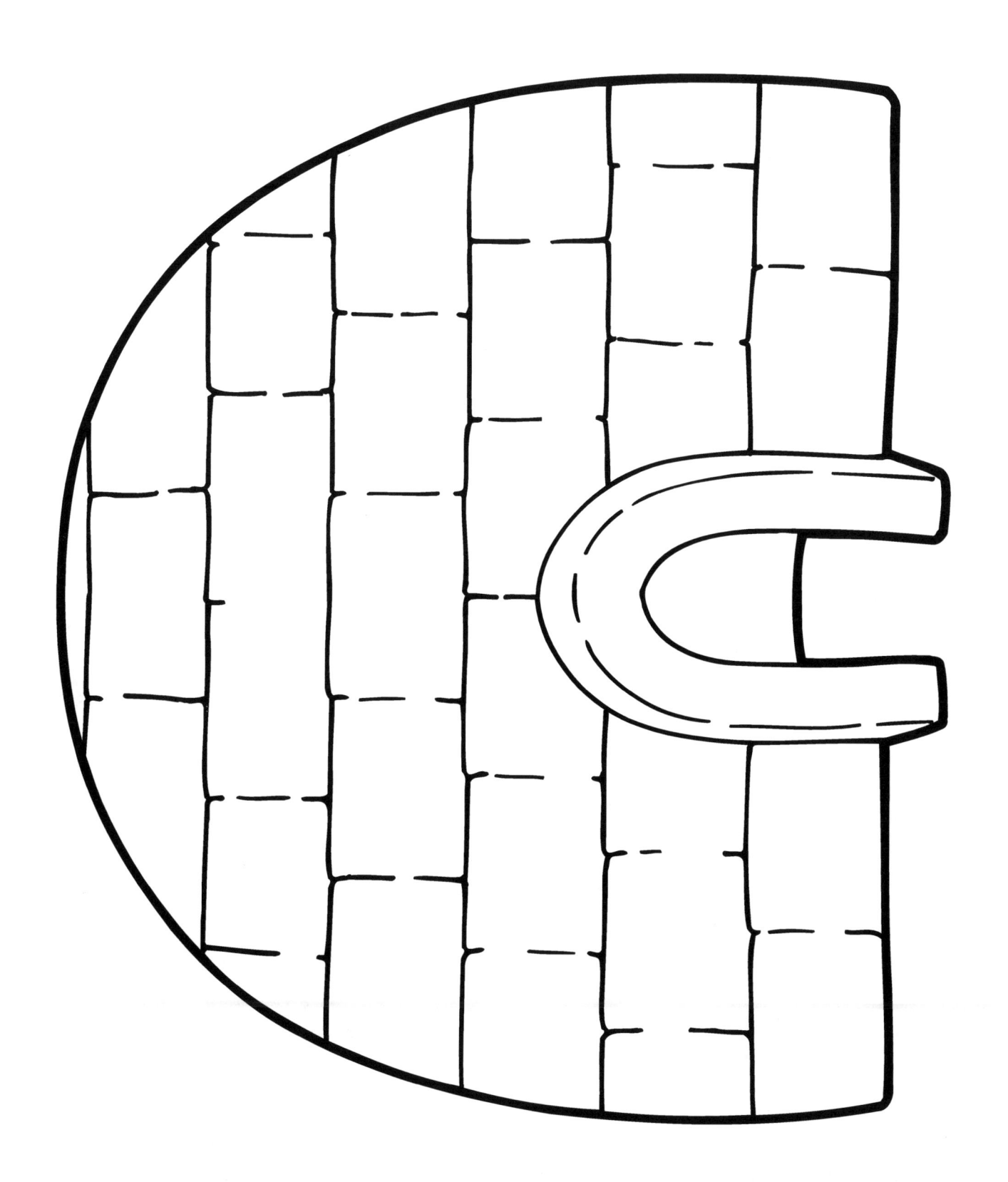

Illinois, USA

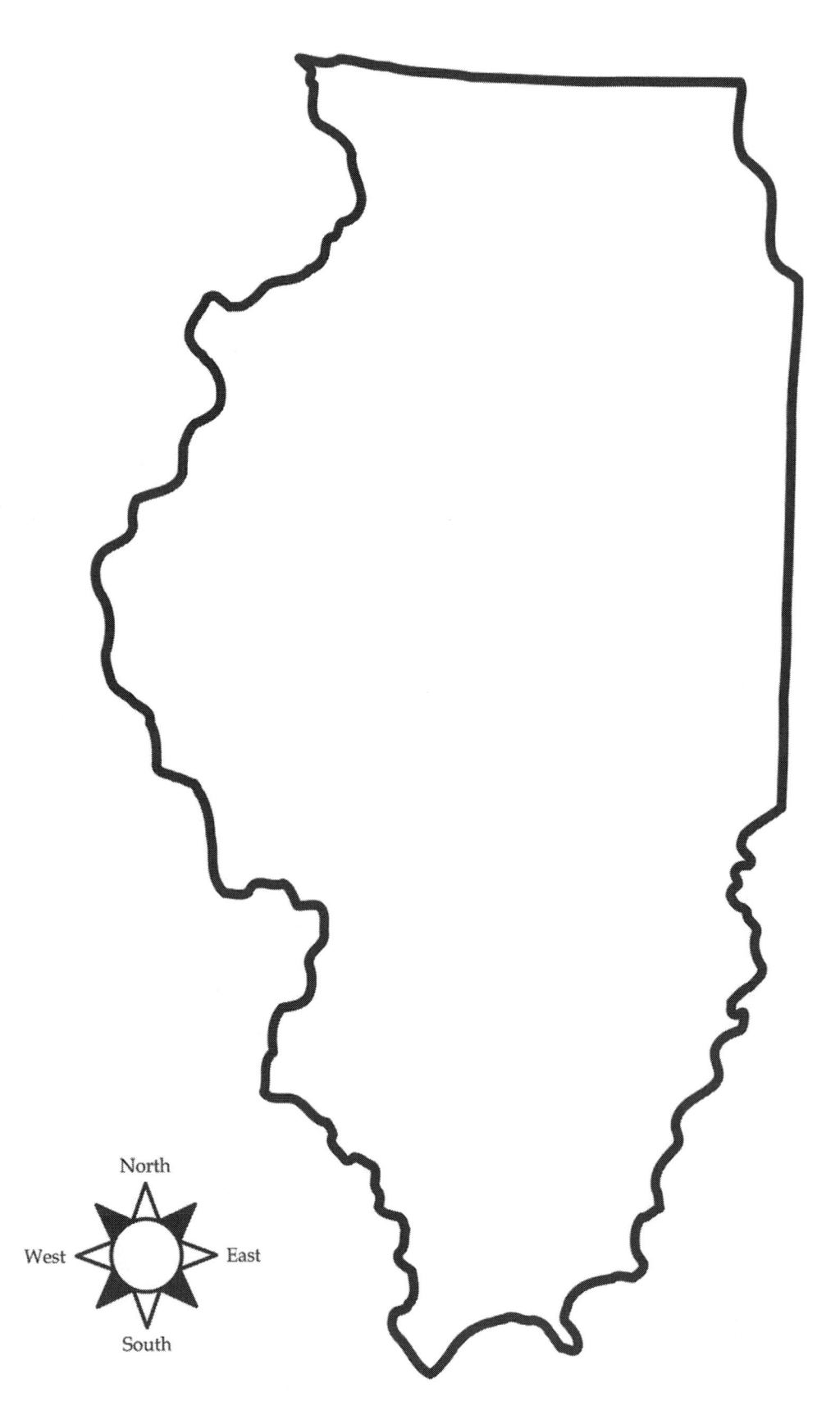

North
West East
South

Maps are representations and boundaries are not exact.

Indiana, USA

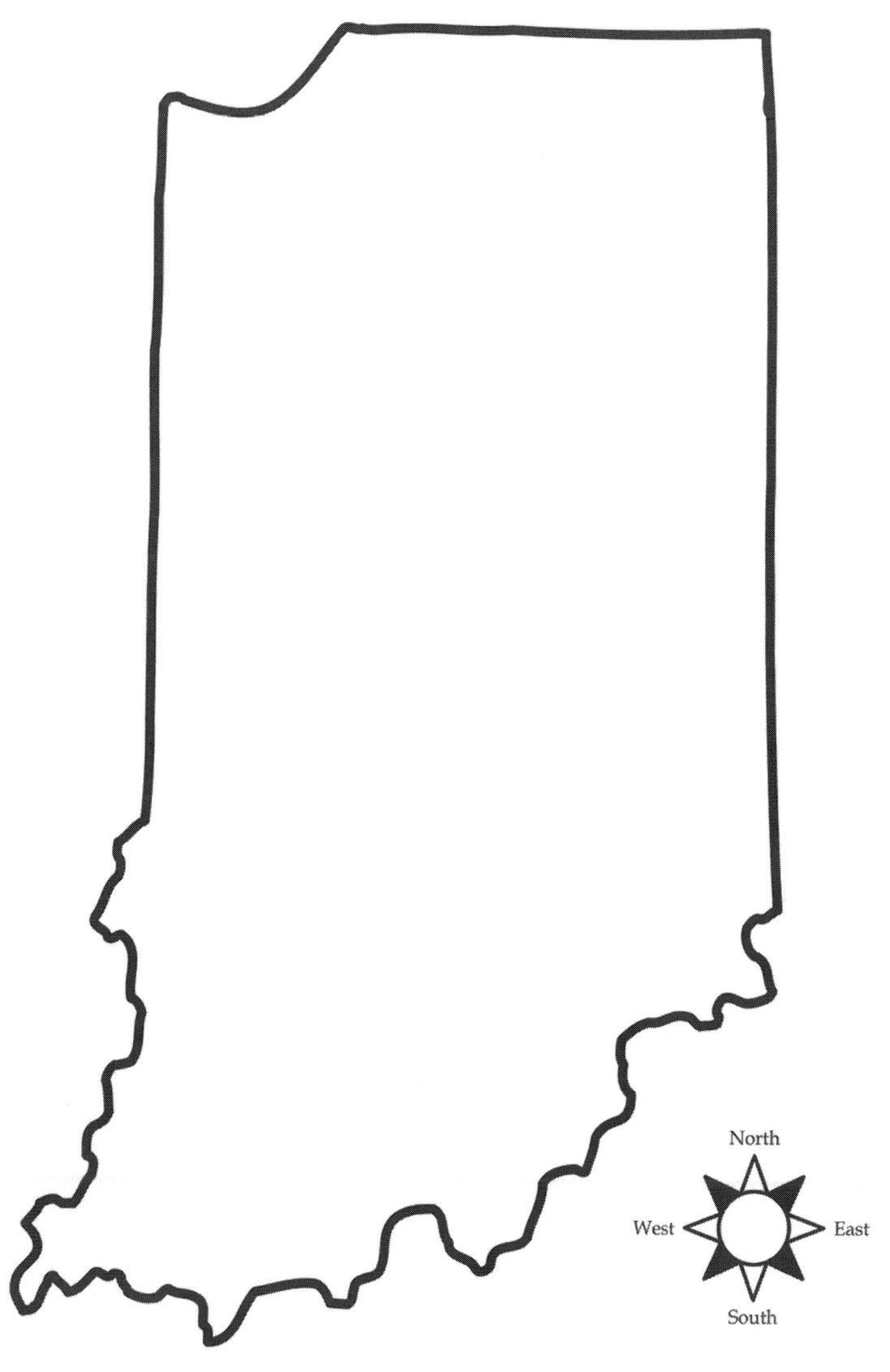

West — North — East — South

Maps are representations and boundaries are not exact.

LAB201412P • THE PATTERN LIBRARY • VOLUME TWO • I-Z • 978-1-937257-63-7 • © 2014 Little Acorn Books™

indri

ink (jar)

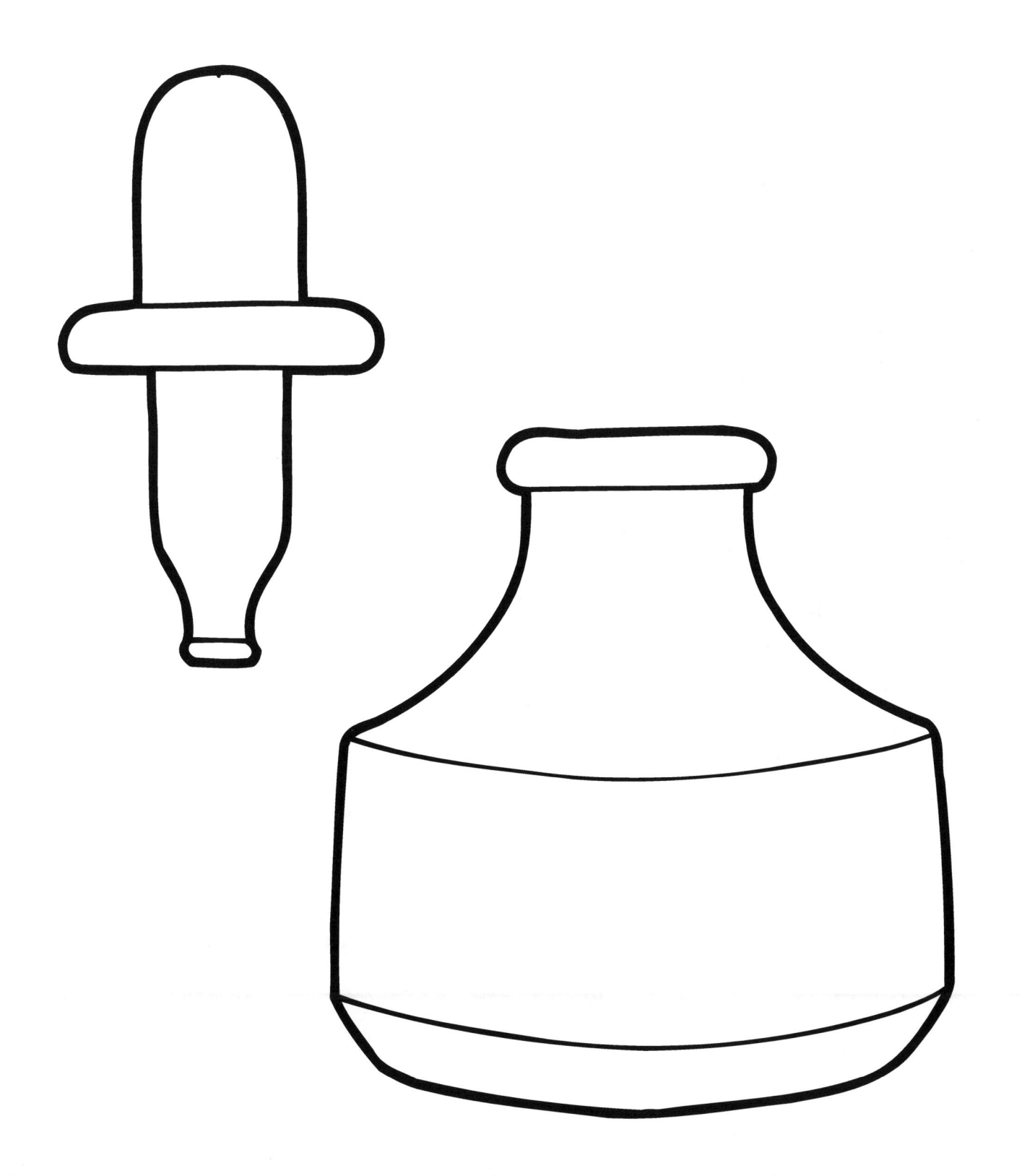

Iowa, USA

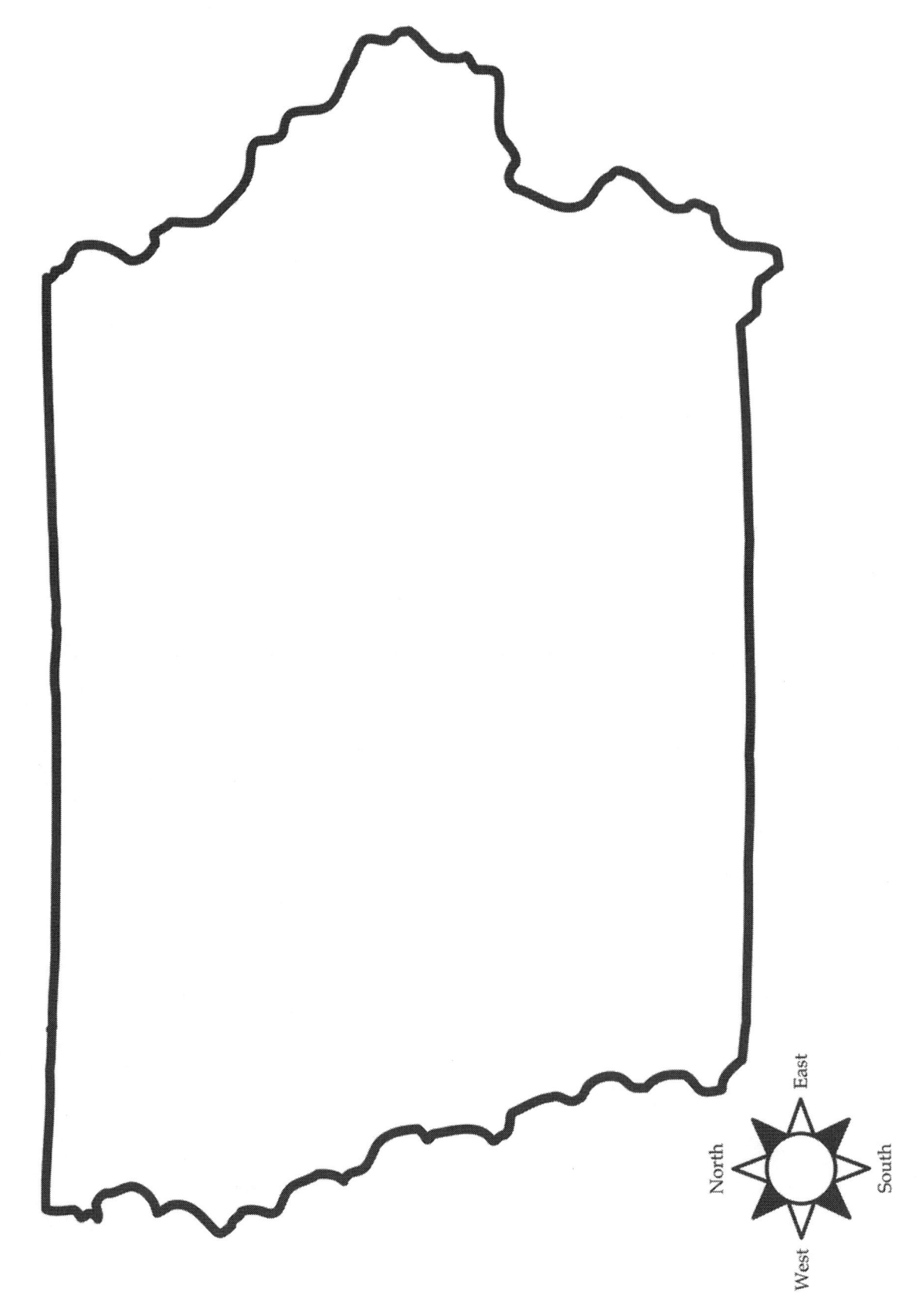

Maps are representations and boundaries are not exact.

iron

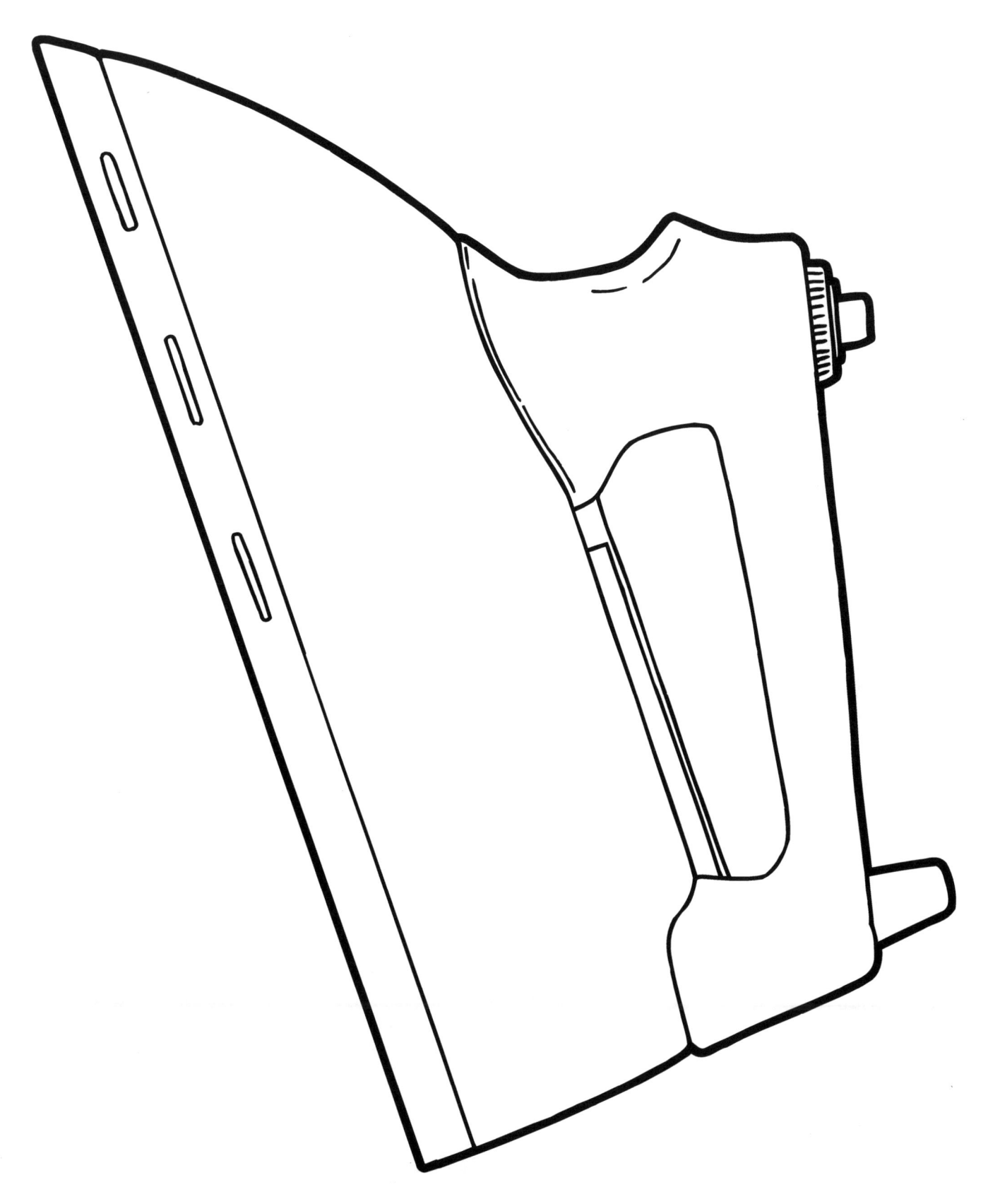

ivy (outline)

jack

jacks

jack o' lantern

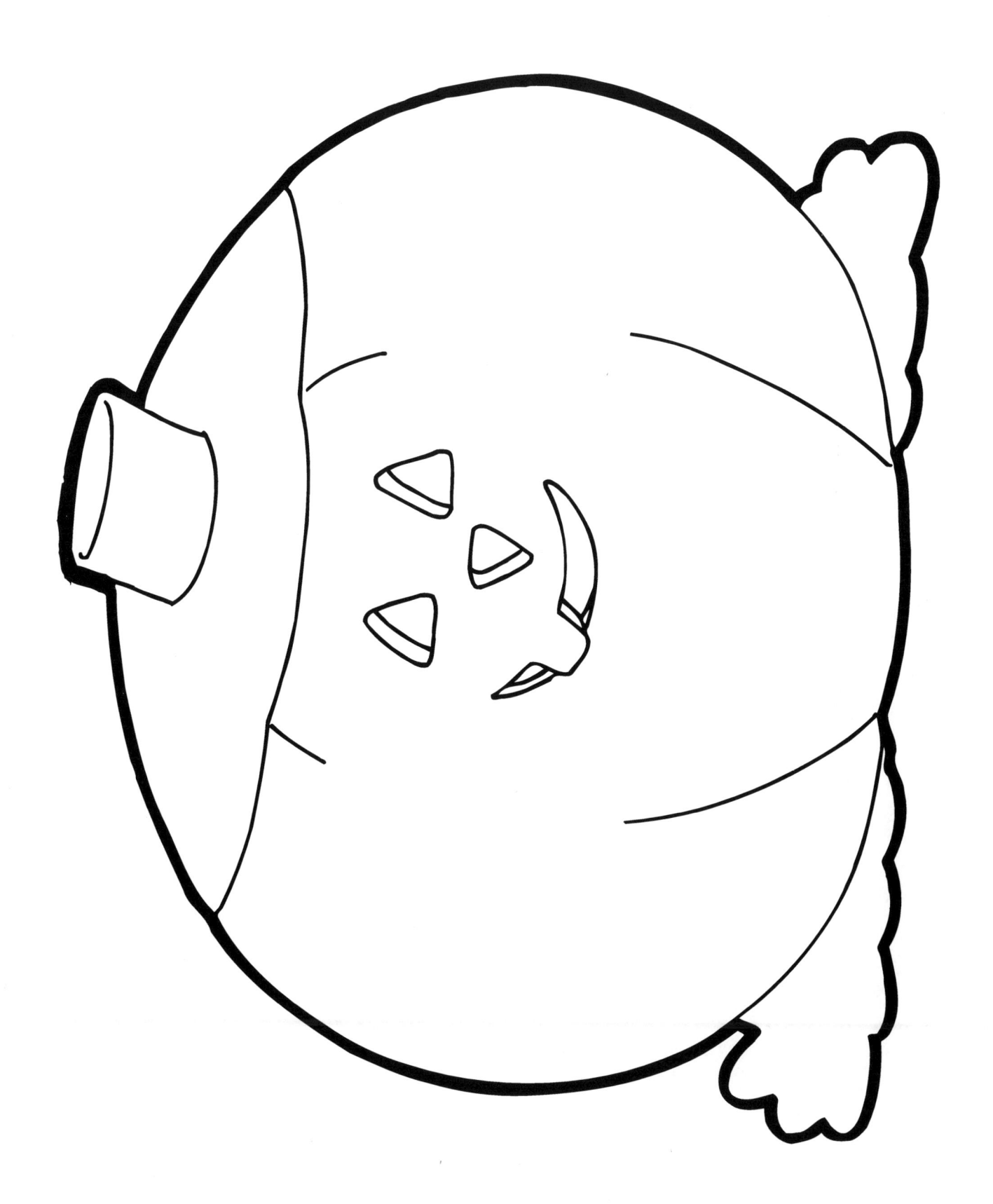

jack o' lantern (outline)

jack o' lantern (standard)

jack o' lantern (with mask)

jack rabbit

jack-in-the-box

jar

jellybeans

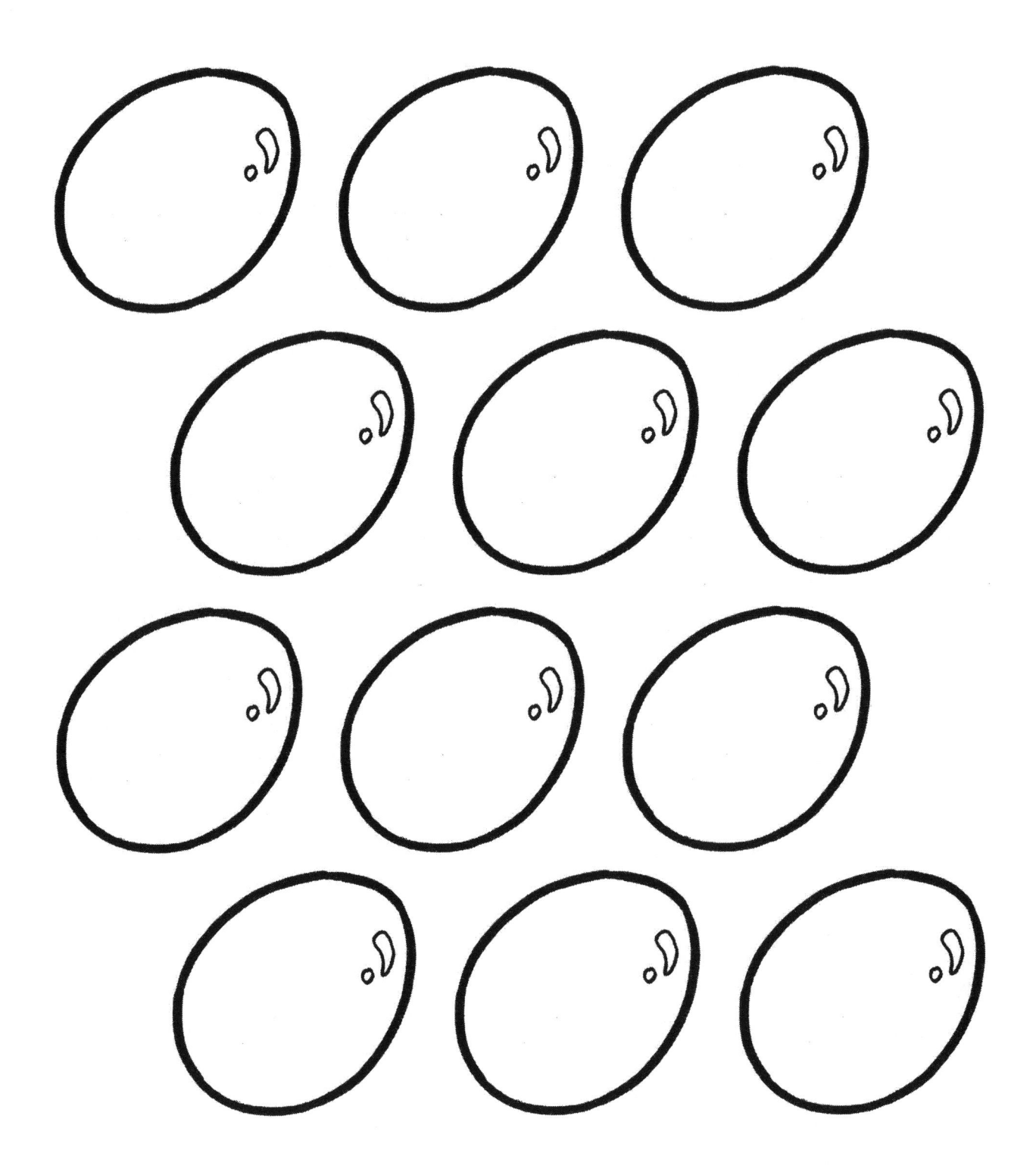

jellyfish

jonquil

jump rope

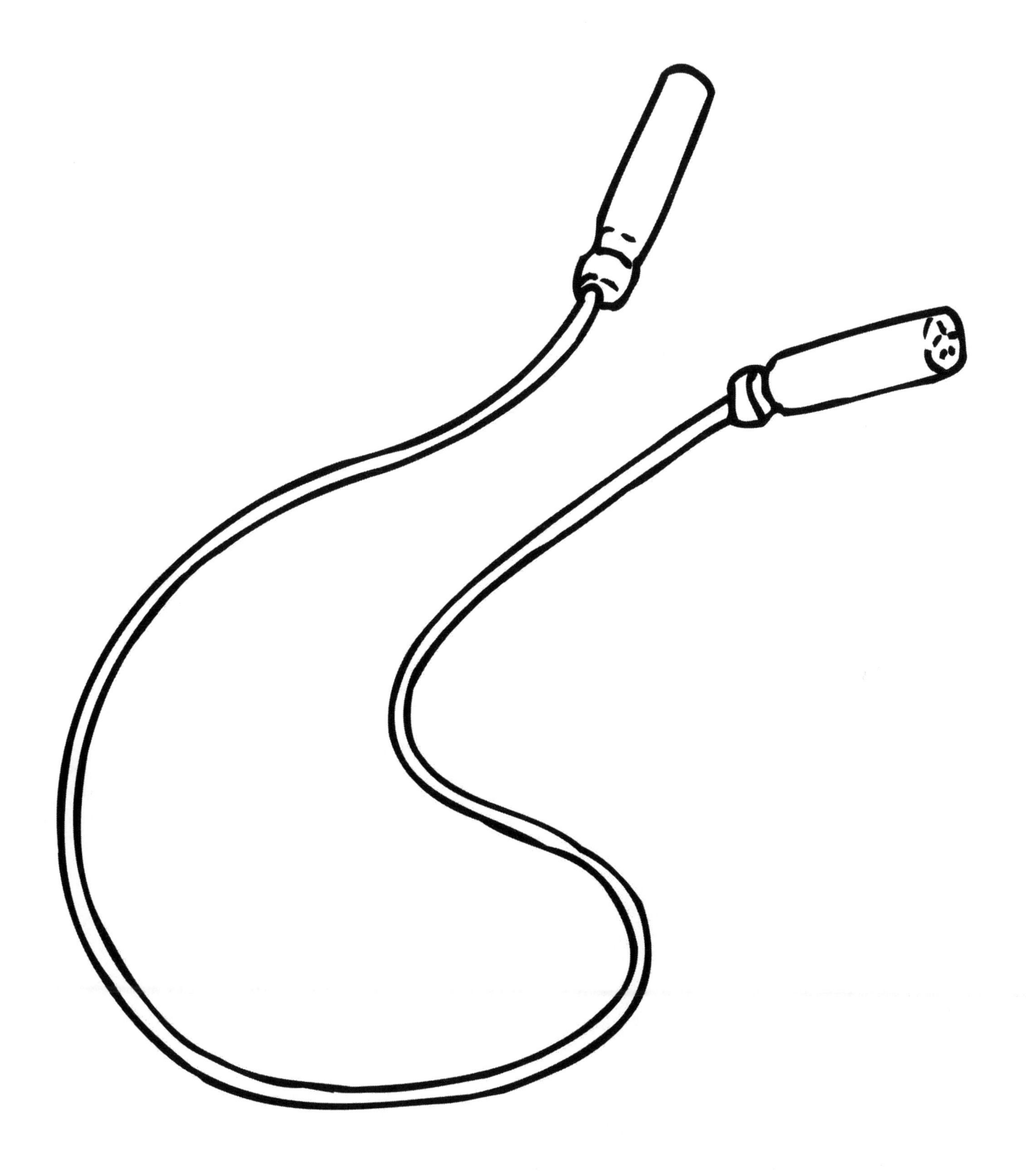

jumper

kangaroo (animated)

kangaroo (outline)

kangaroo (stylized)

Kansas, USA

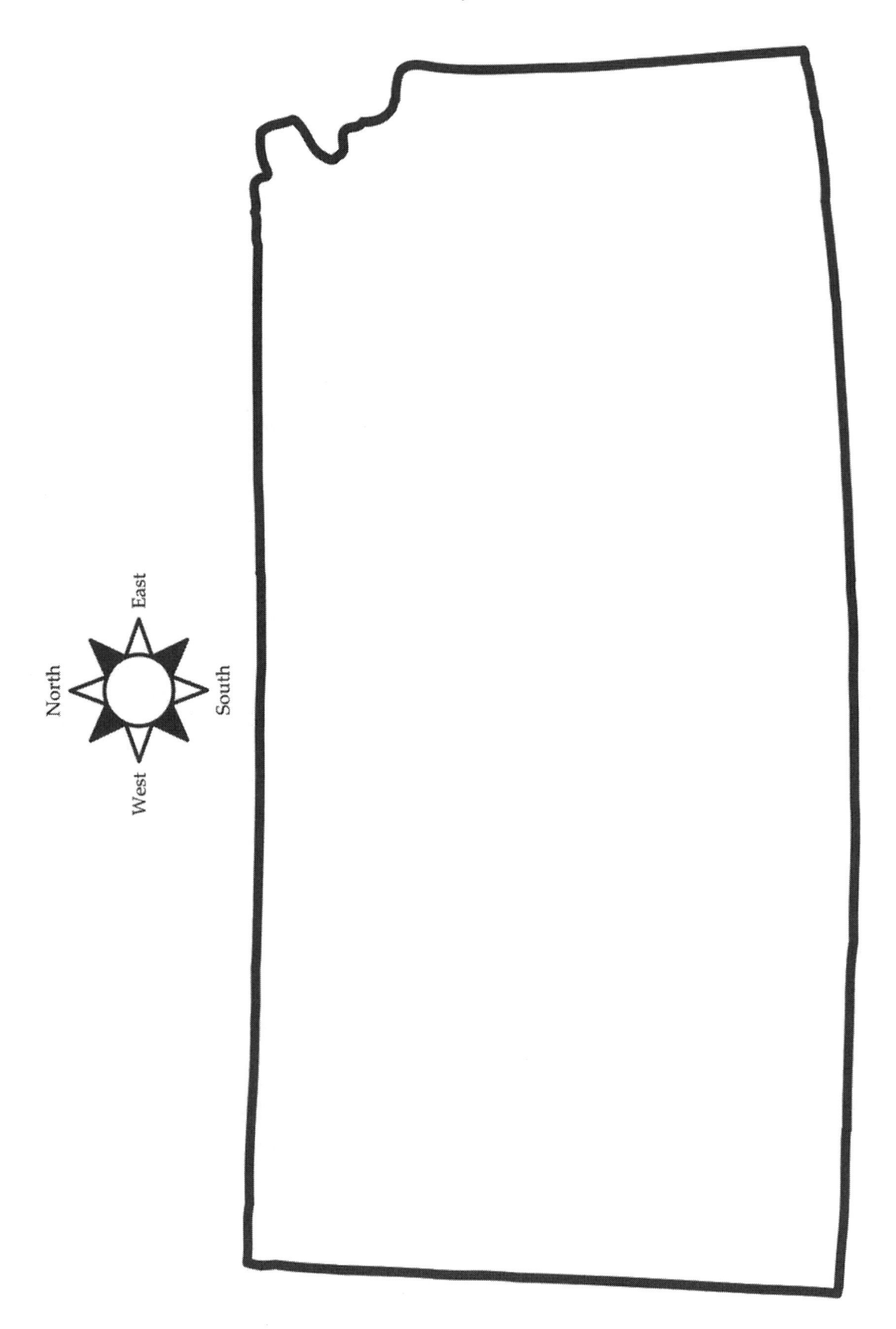

Maps are representations and boundaries are not exact.

Kentucky, USA

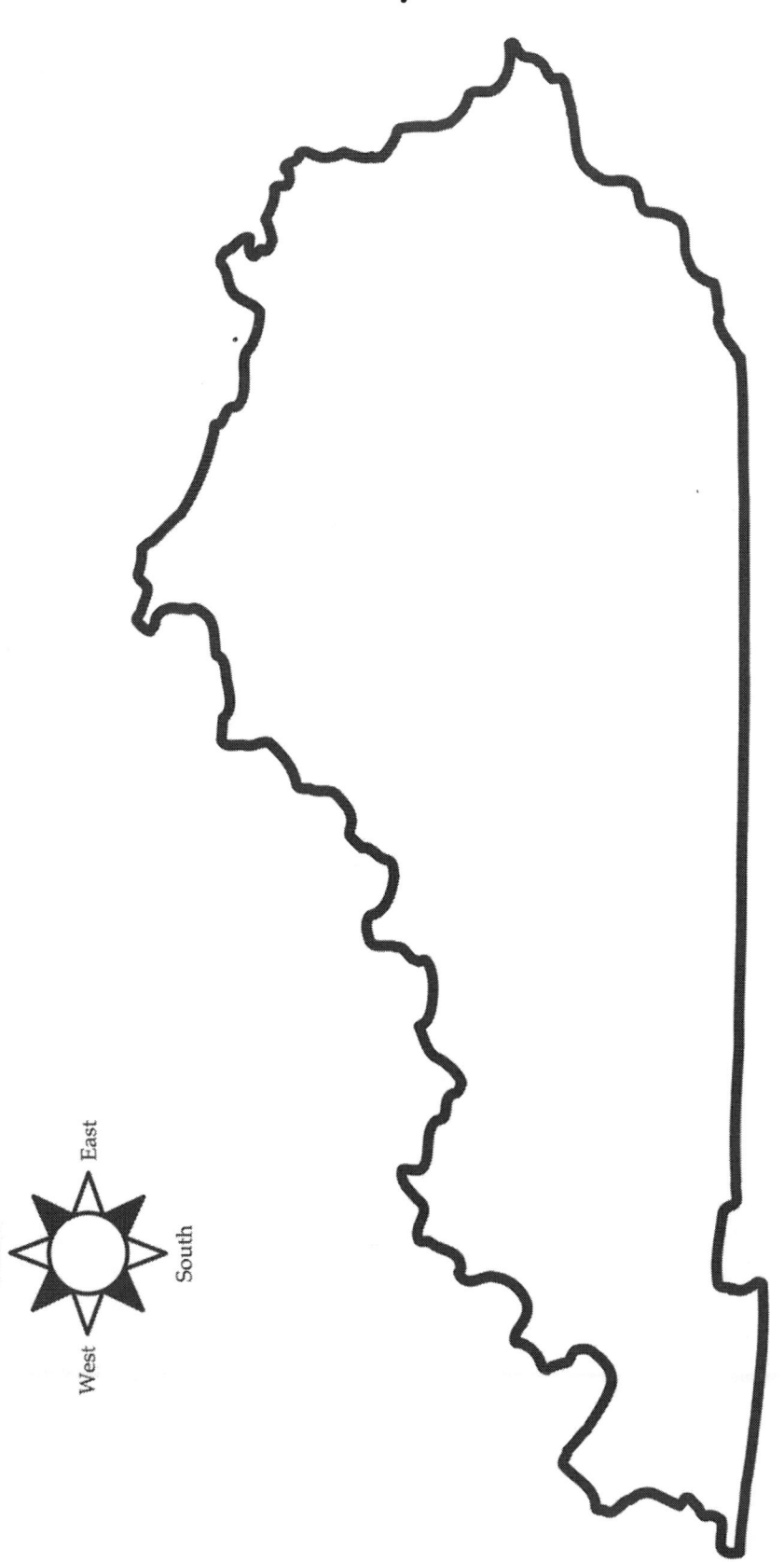

Maps are representations and boundaries are not exact.

kerchief

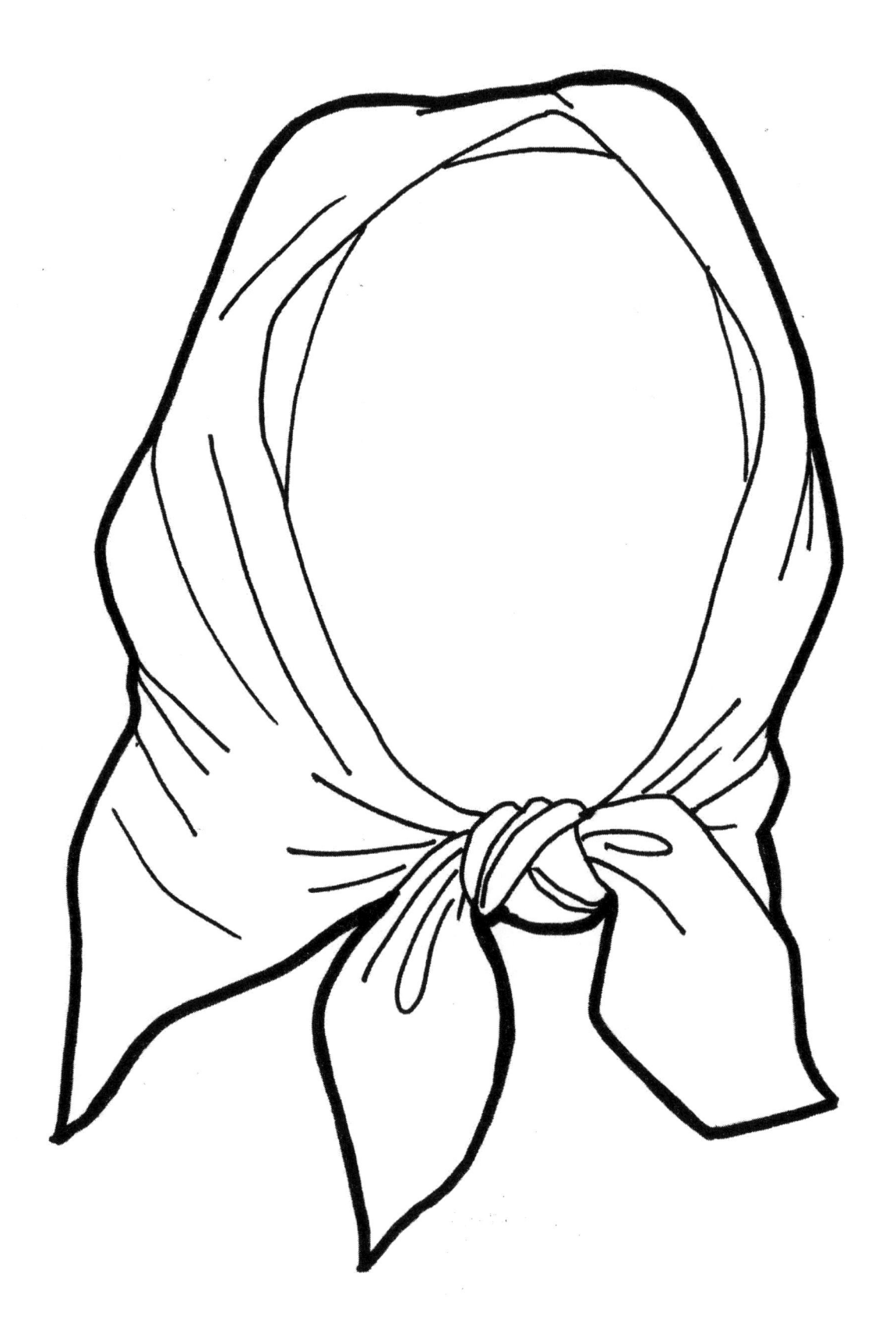

kettle

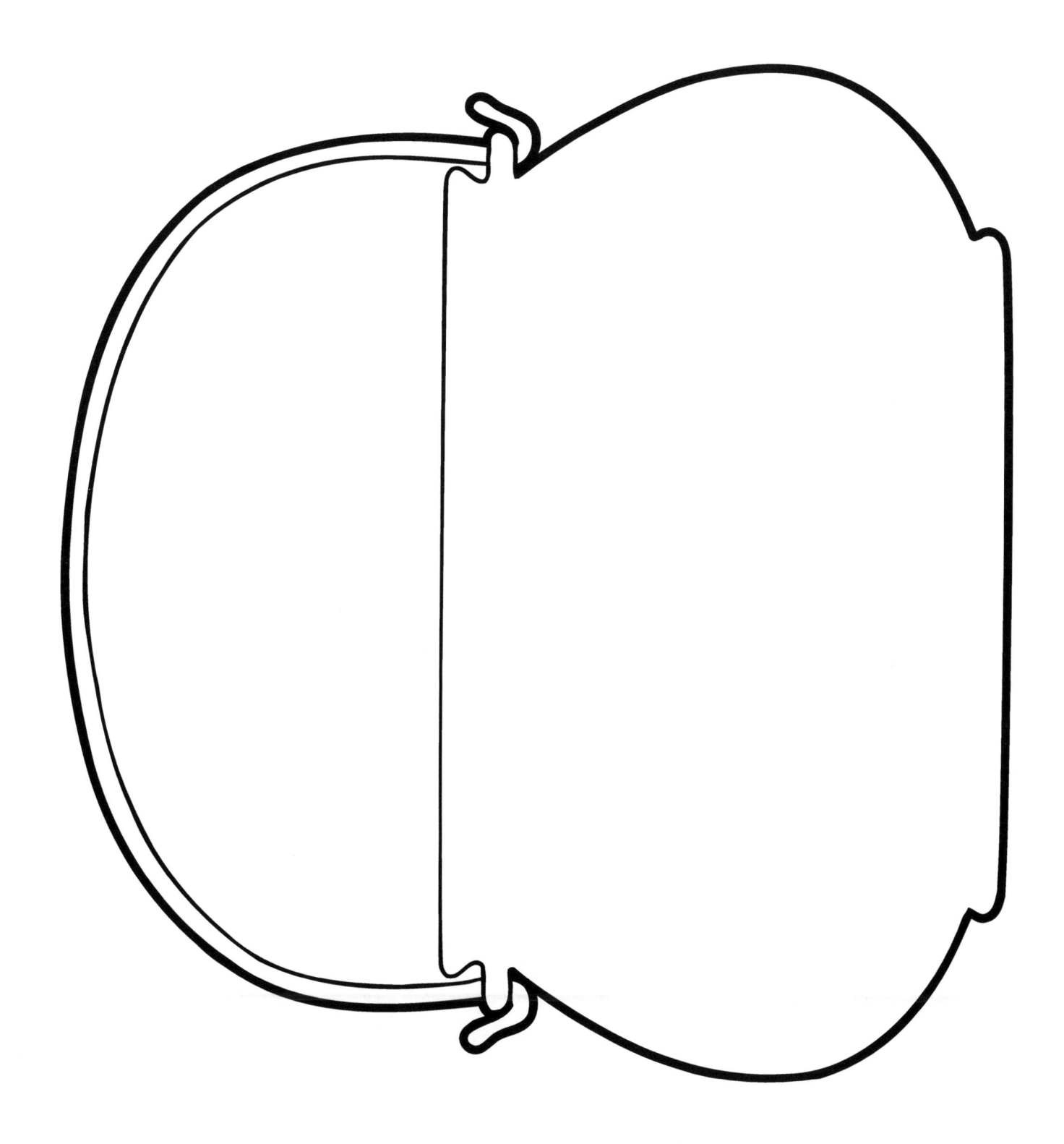

key

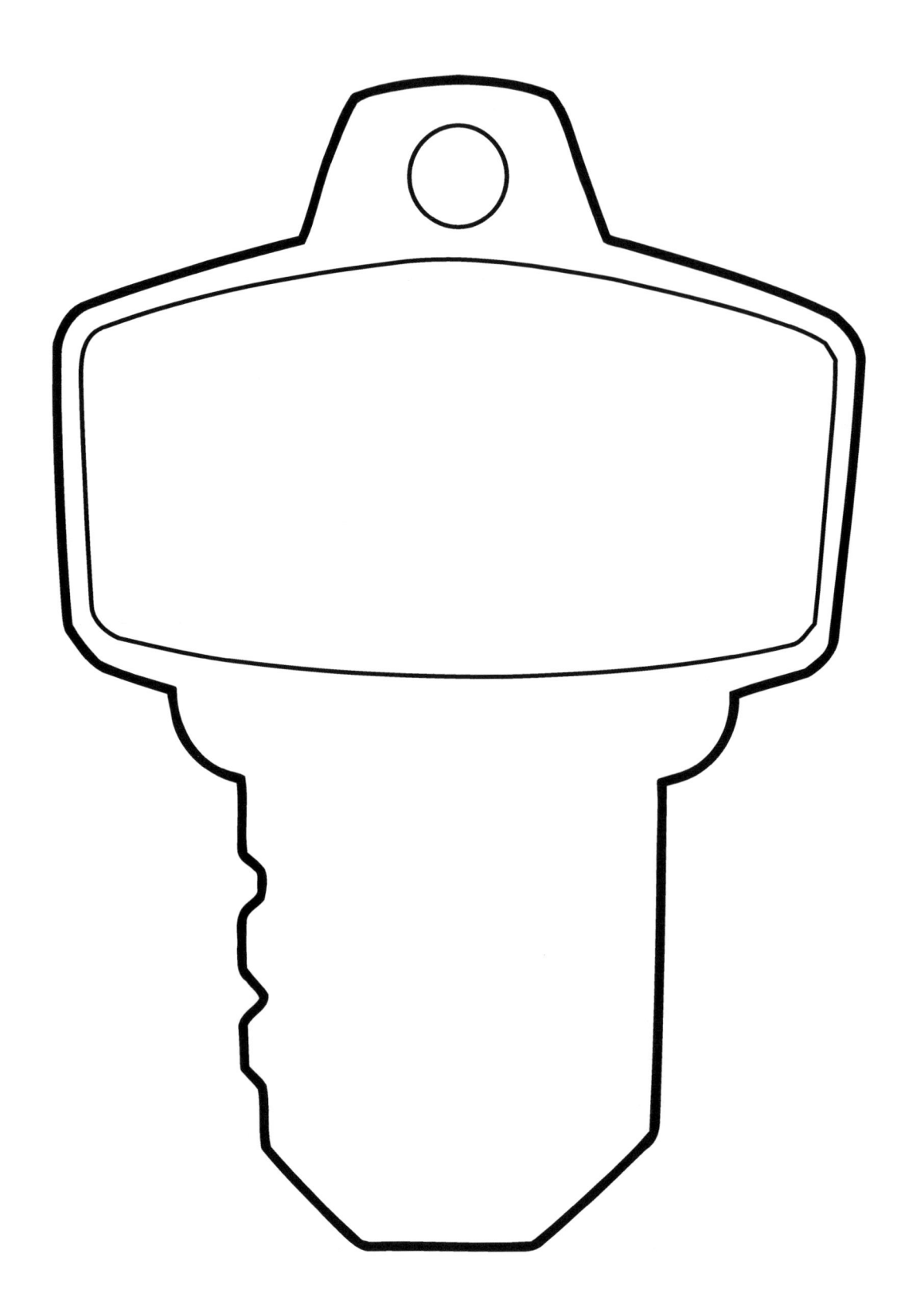

king

kinkajou

kite (box)

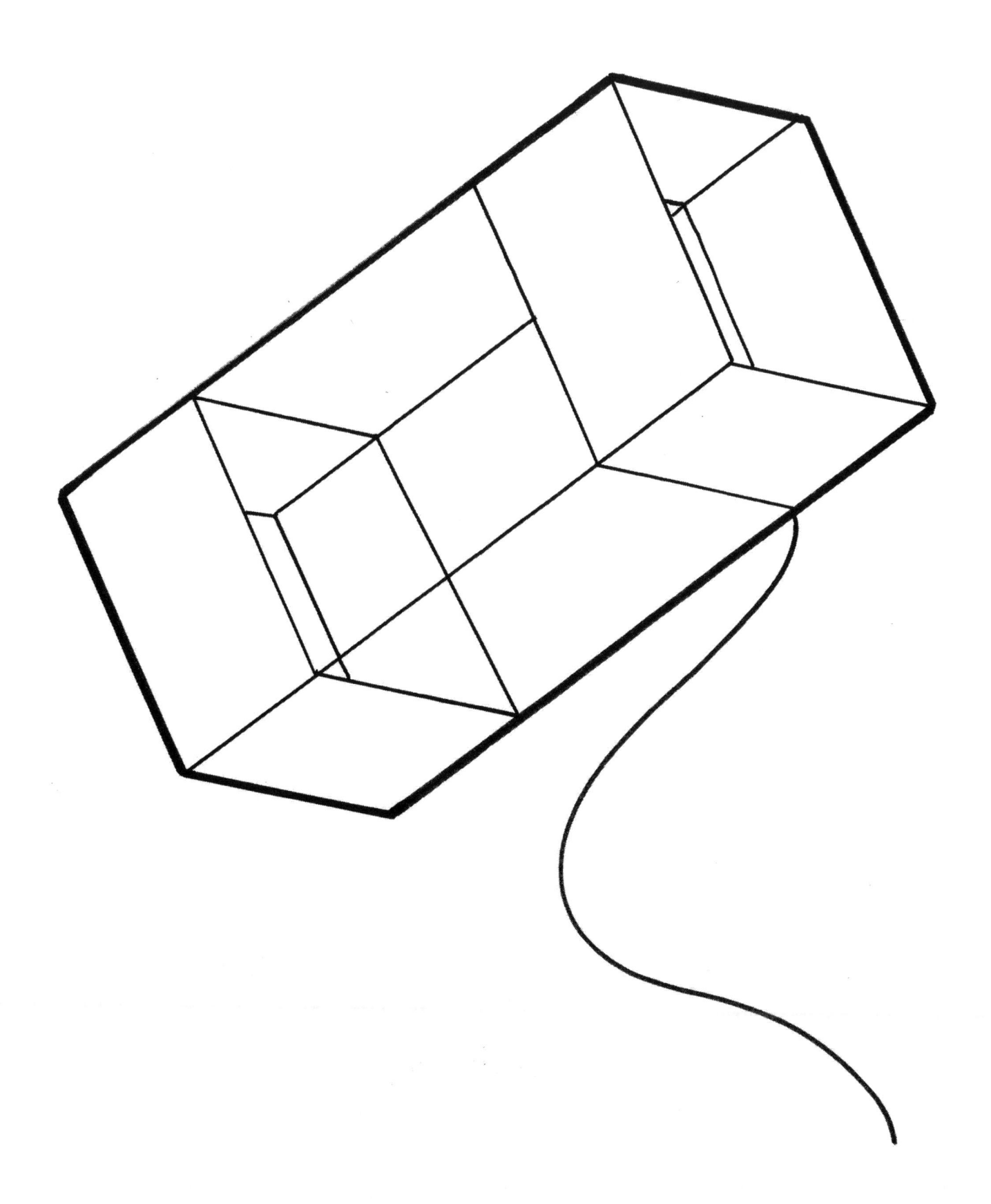

kite (standard)

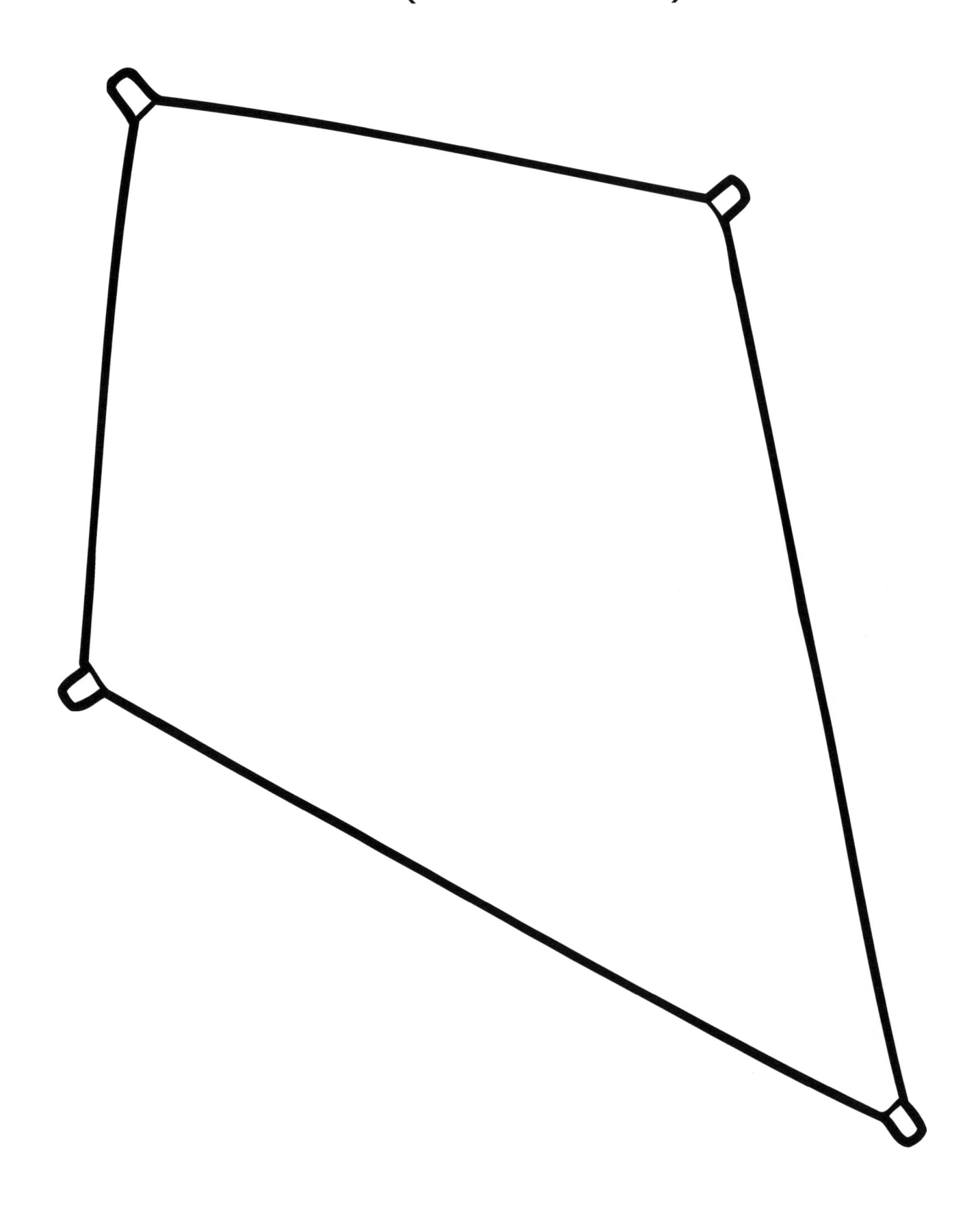

kitten

LAB201412P • THE PATTERN LIBRARY • VOLUME TWO • I-Z • 978-1-937257-63-7 • © 2014 Little Acorn Books™

51

knives (butter and steak)

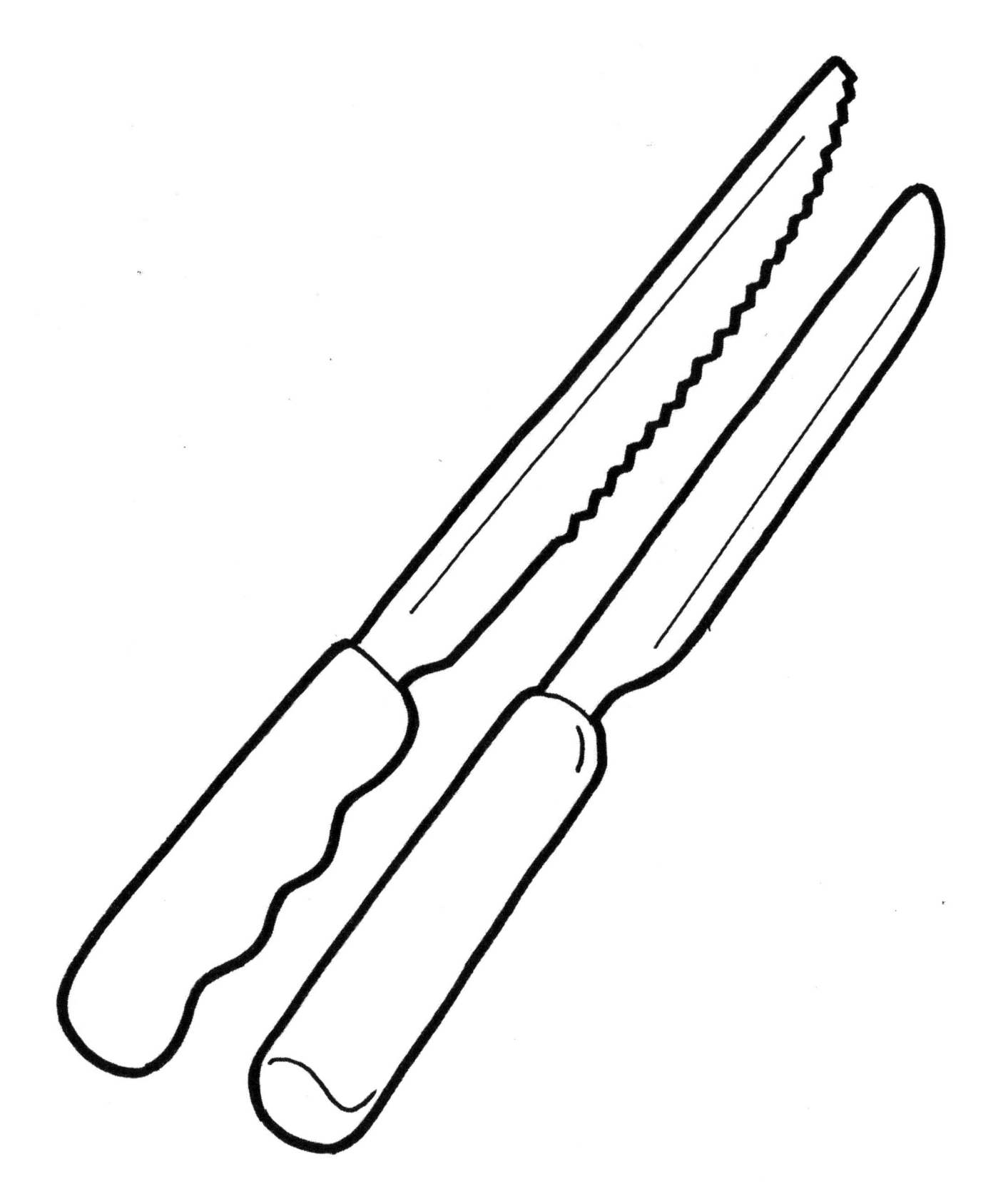

koala

ladle (gravy)

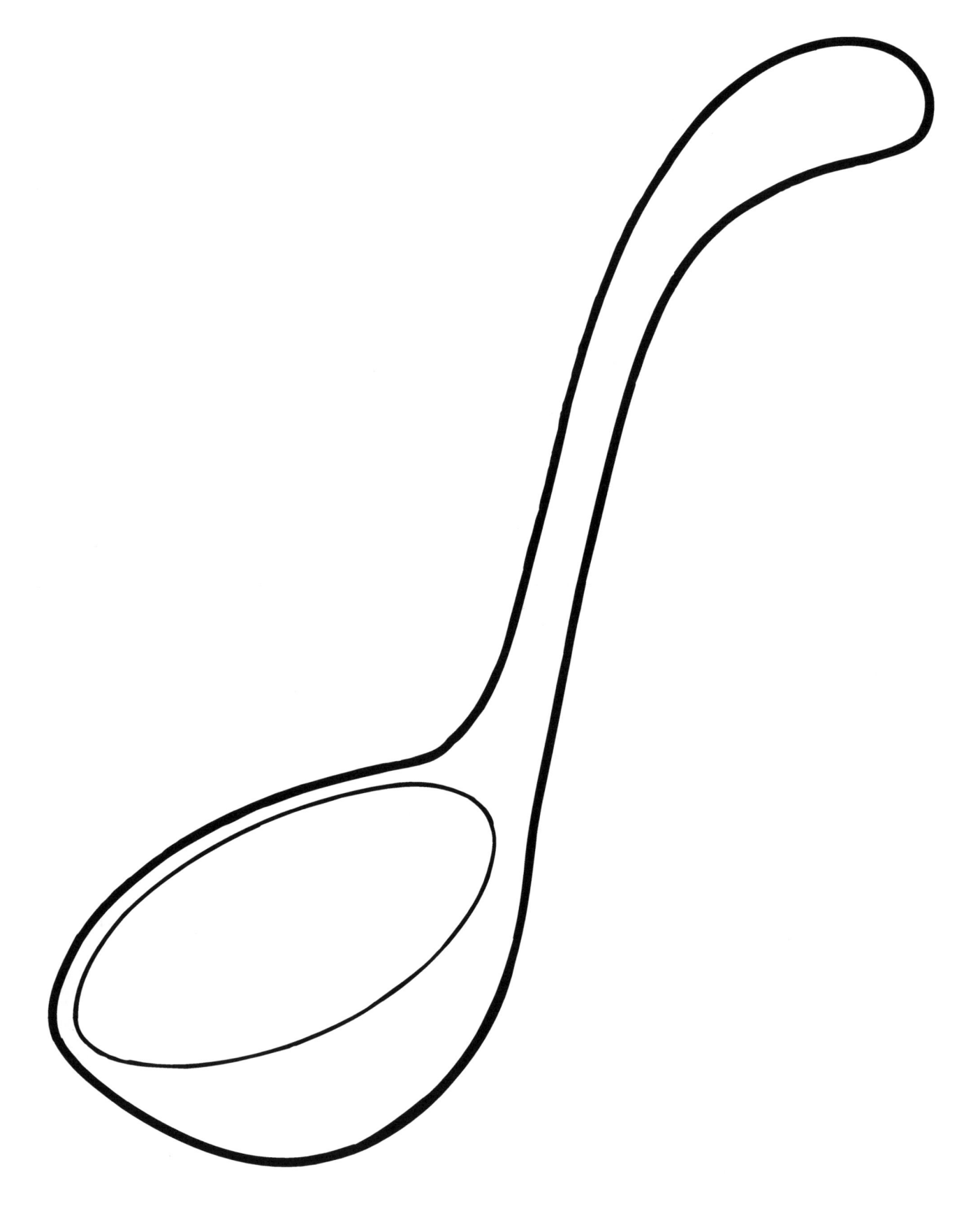

ladle (soup)

ladybug

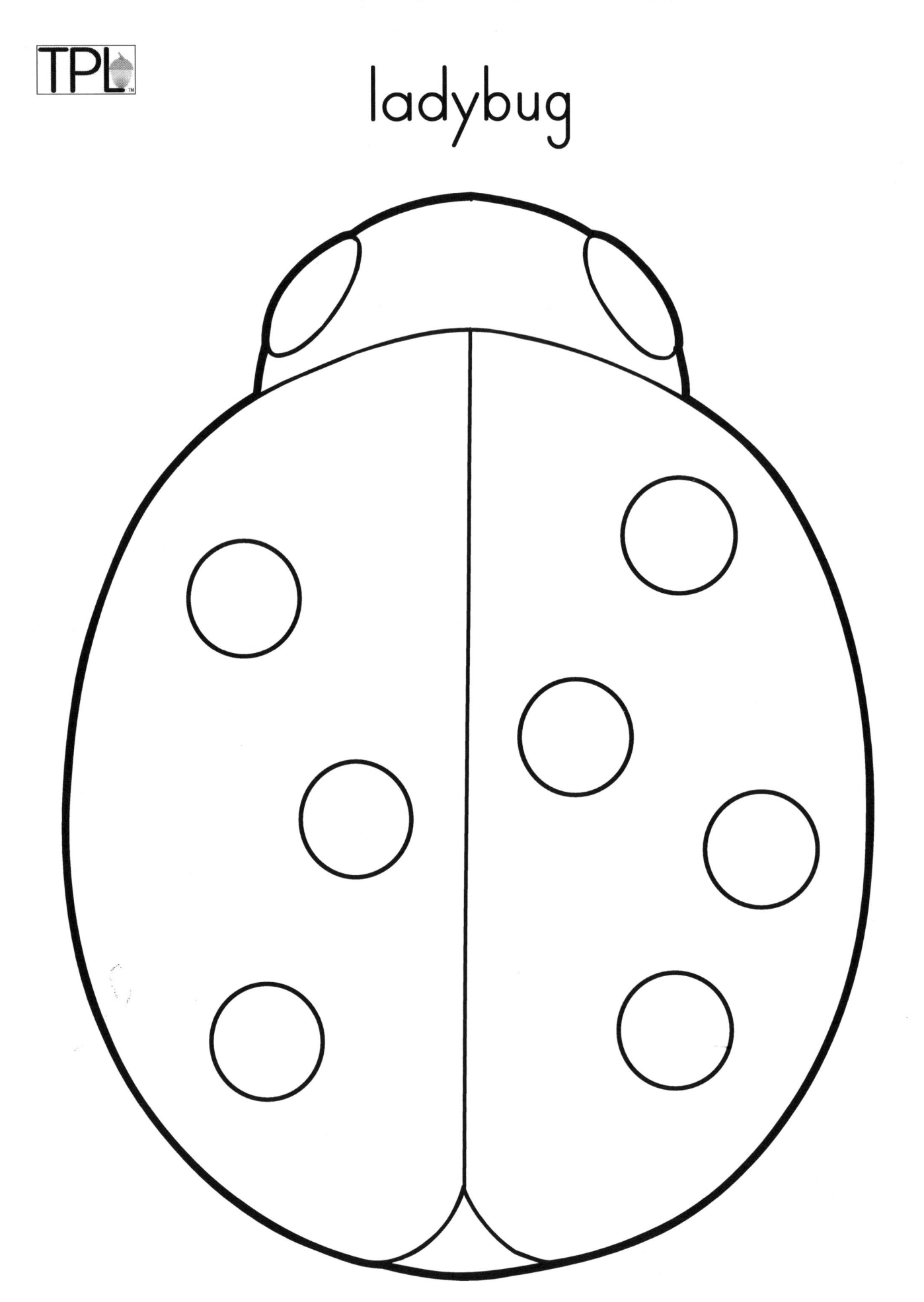

lamb

leaf (dogwood)

leaf (ginkgo)

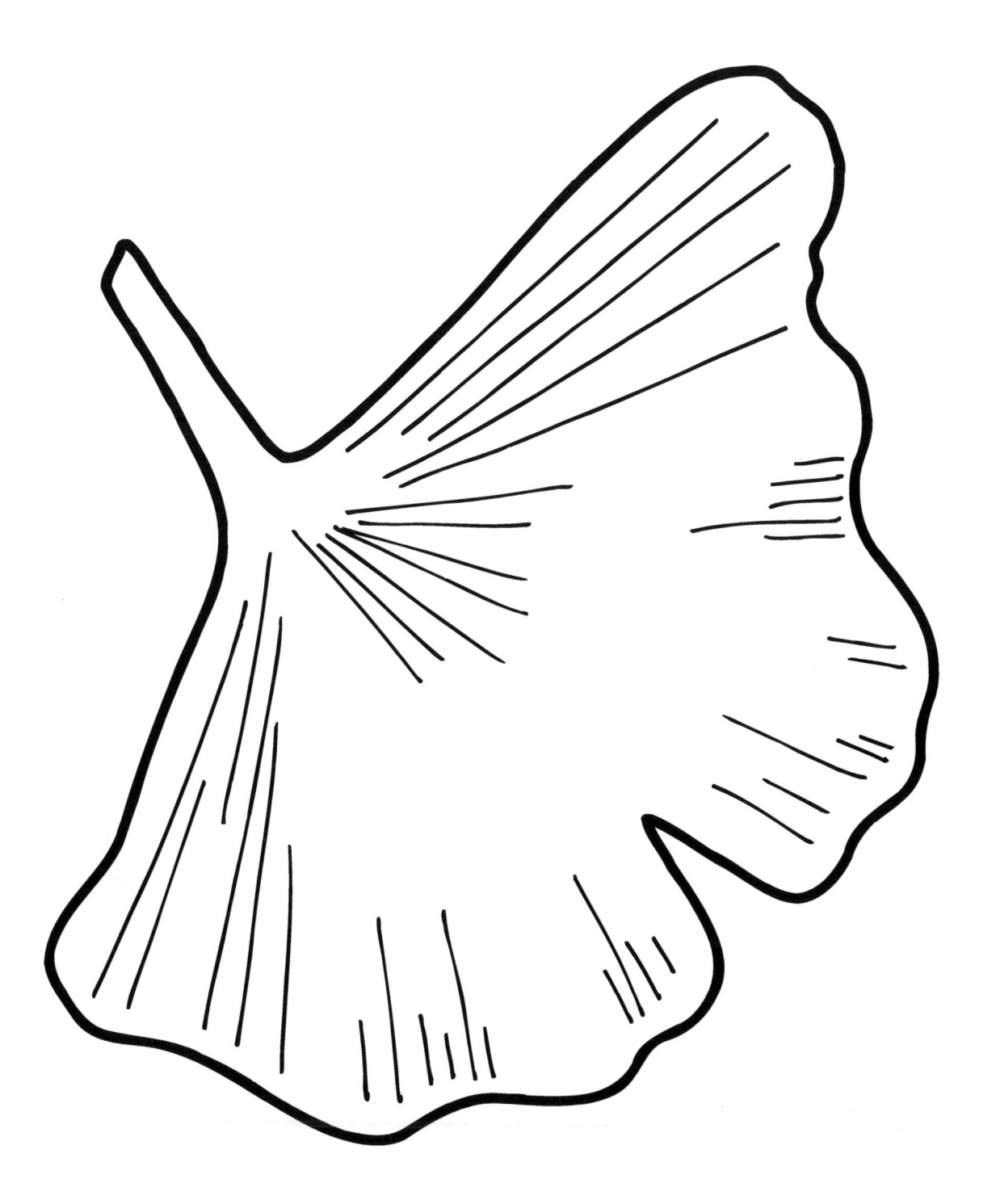

leaf (hickory)

leaf (maple)

leaf (maple, outline)

leaf (oak)

leopard

leprechaun

leprechaun (torso)

light bulb

lion (head)

lion (laying)

lizard

llama

lobster

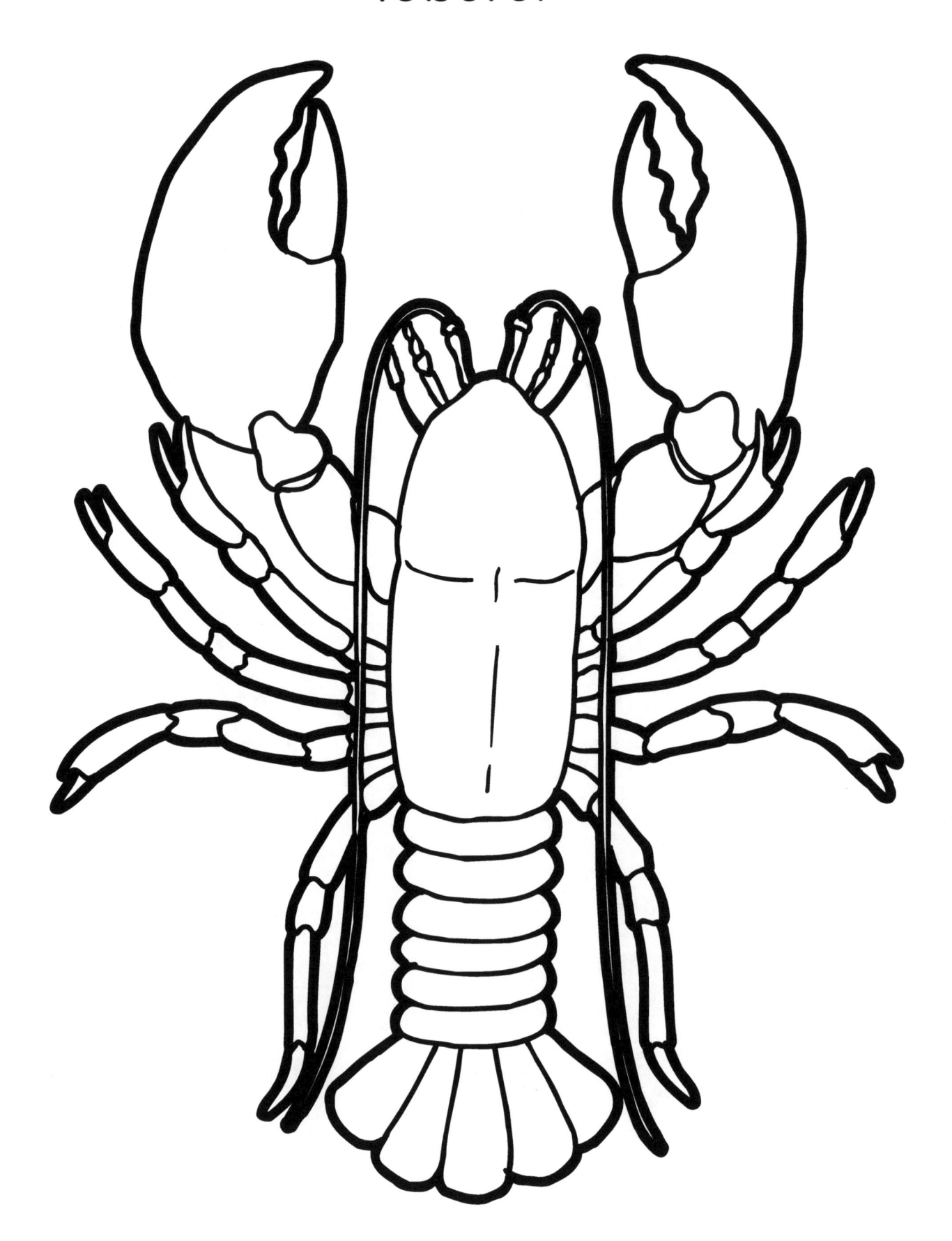

lock

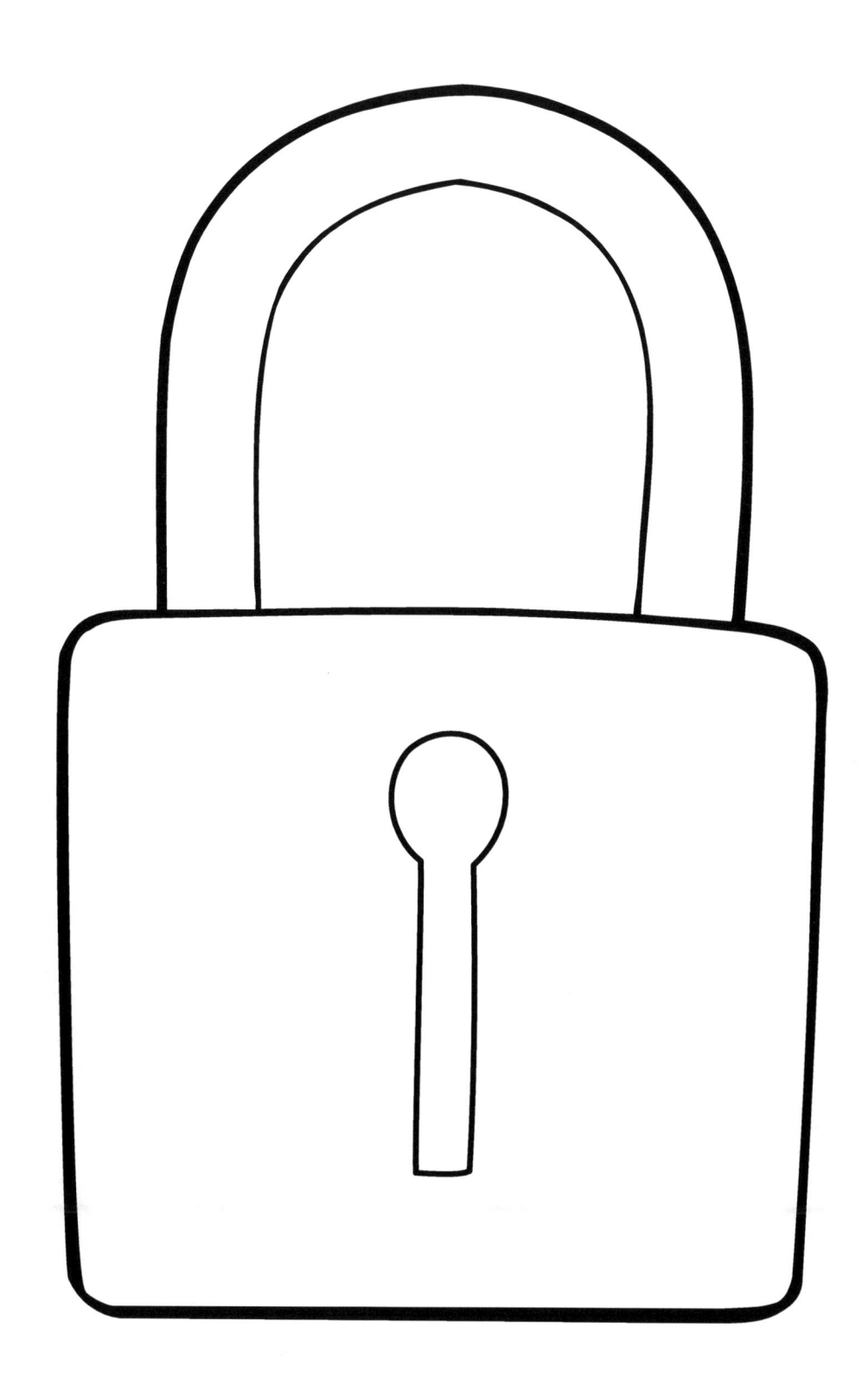

lollipop (flat)

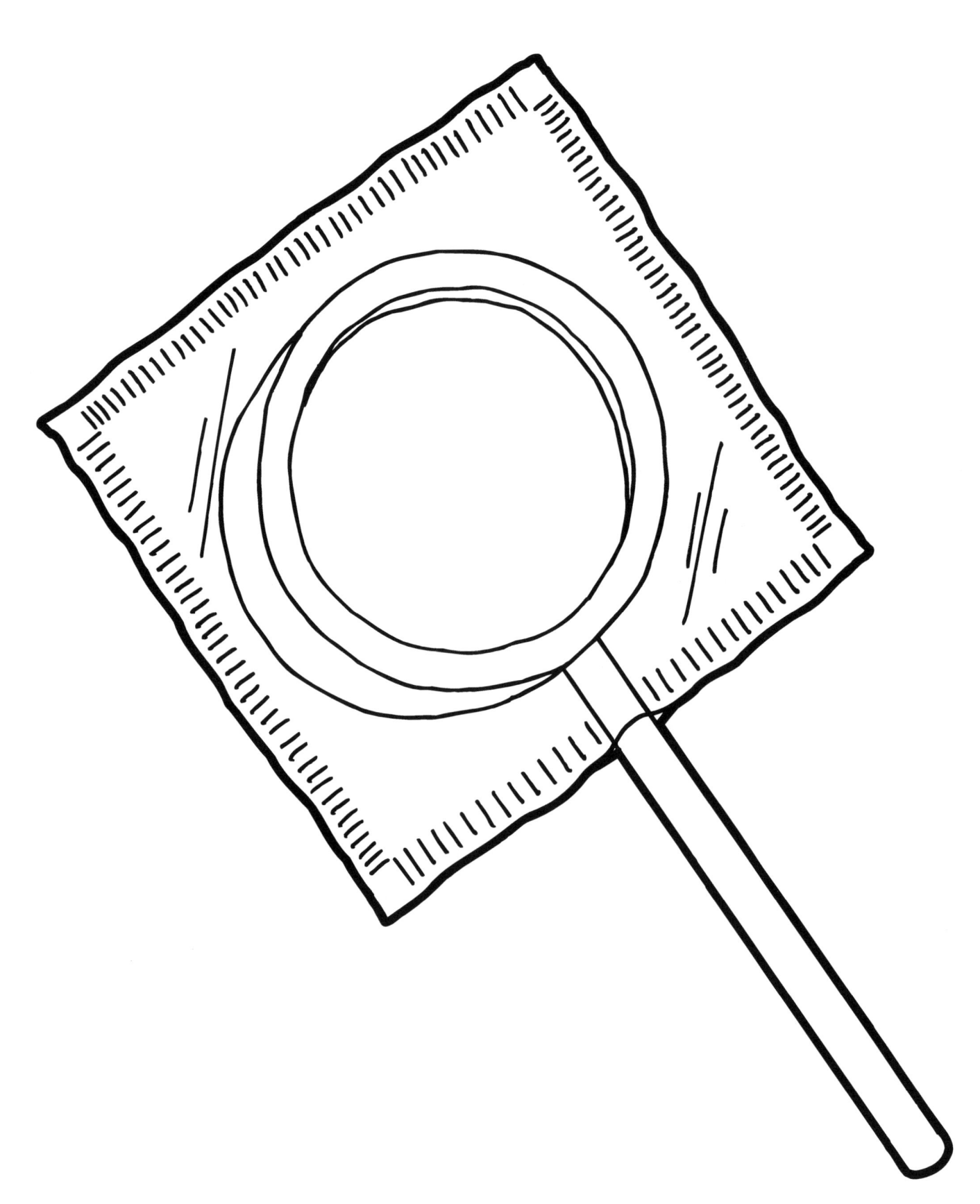

lollipop (round)

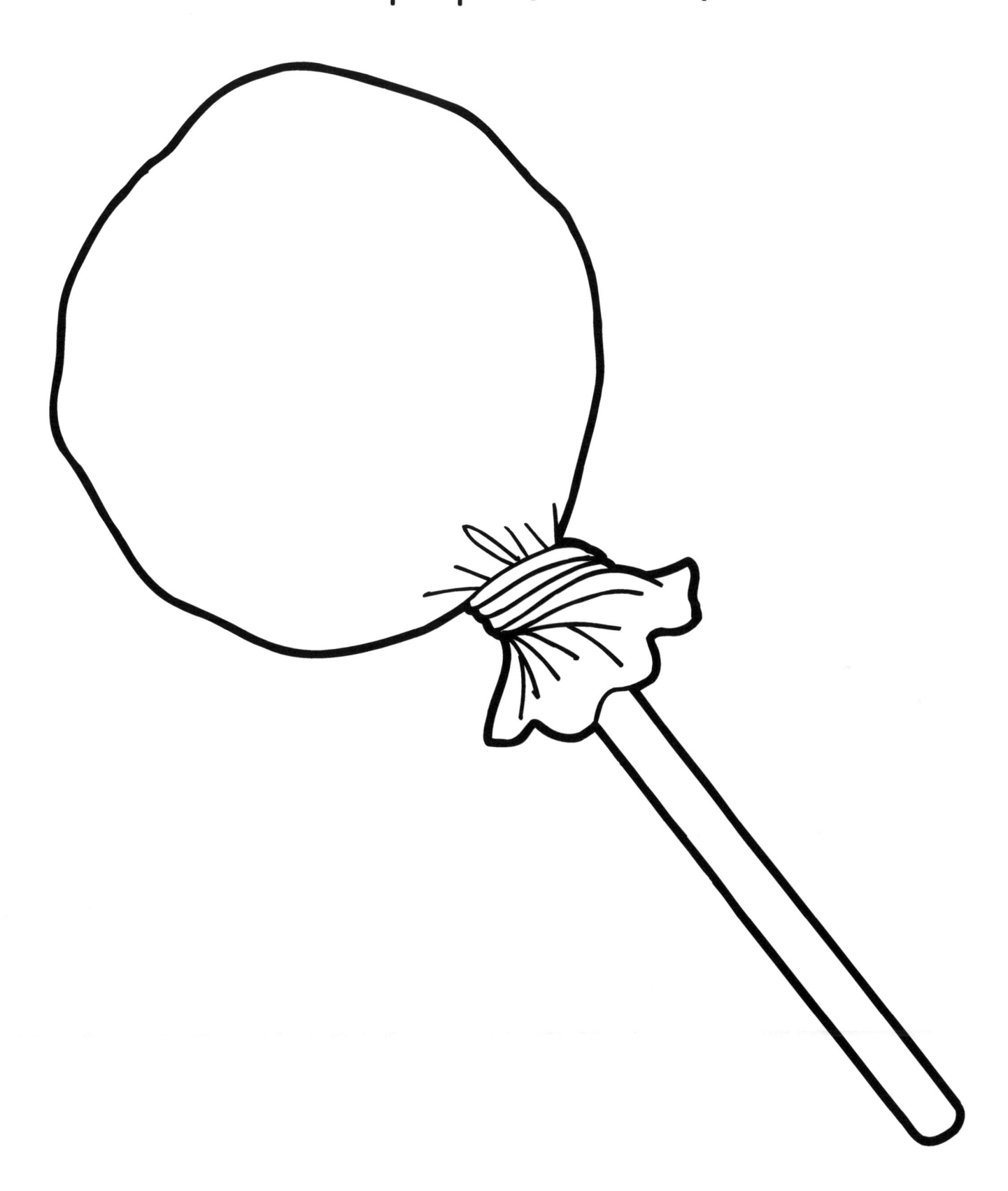

Louisiana, USA

North
West　East
South

Maps are representations and boundaries are not exact.

Louisiana Purchase

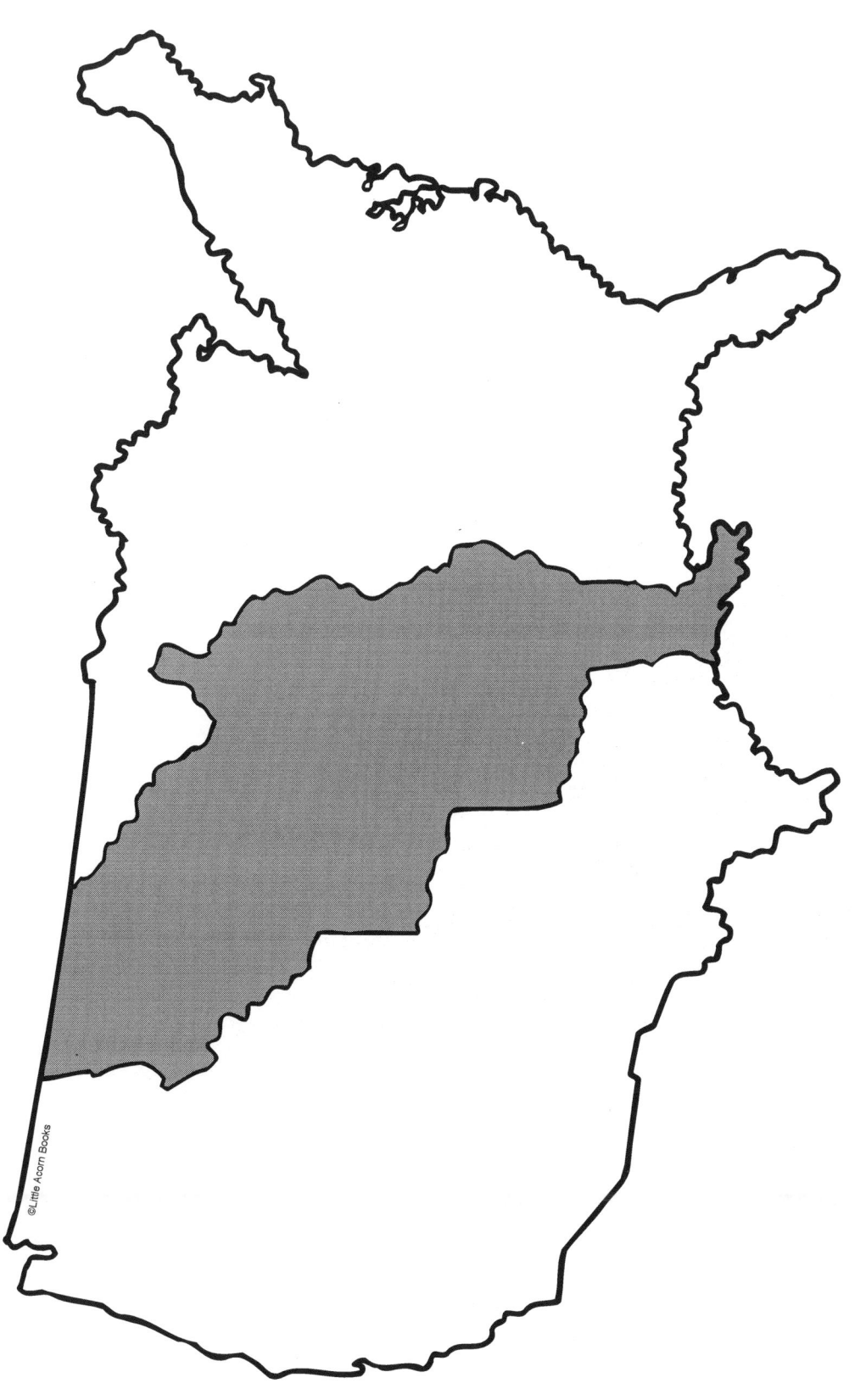

Maps are representations and boundaries are not exact.

lunch box

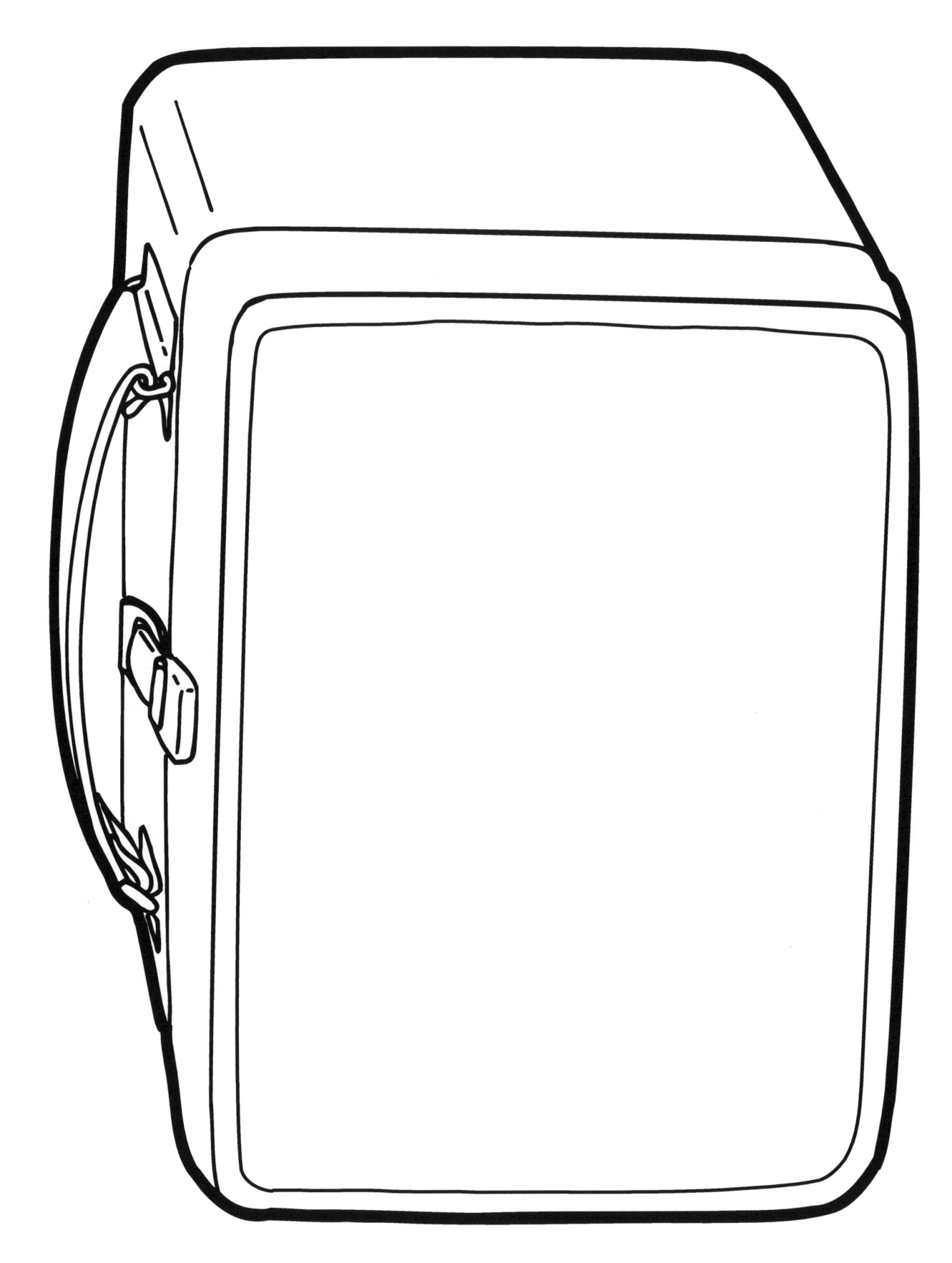

lyre

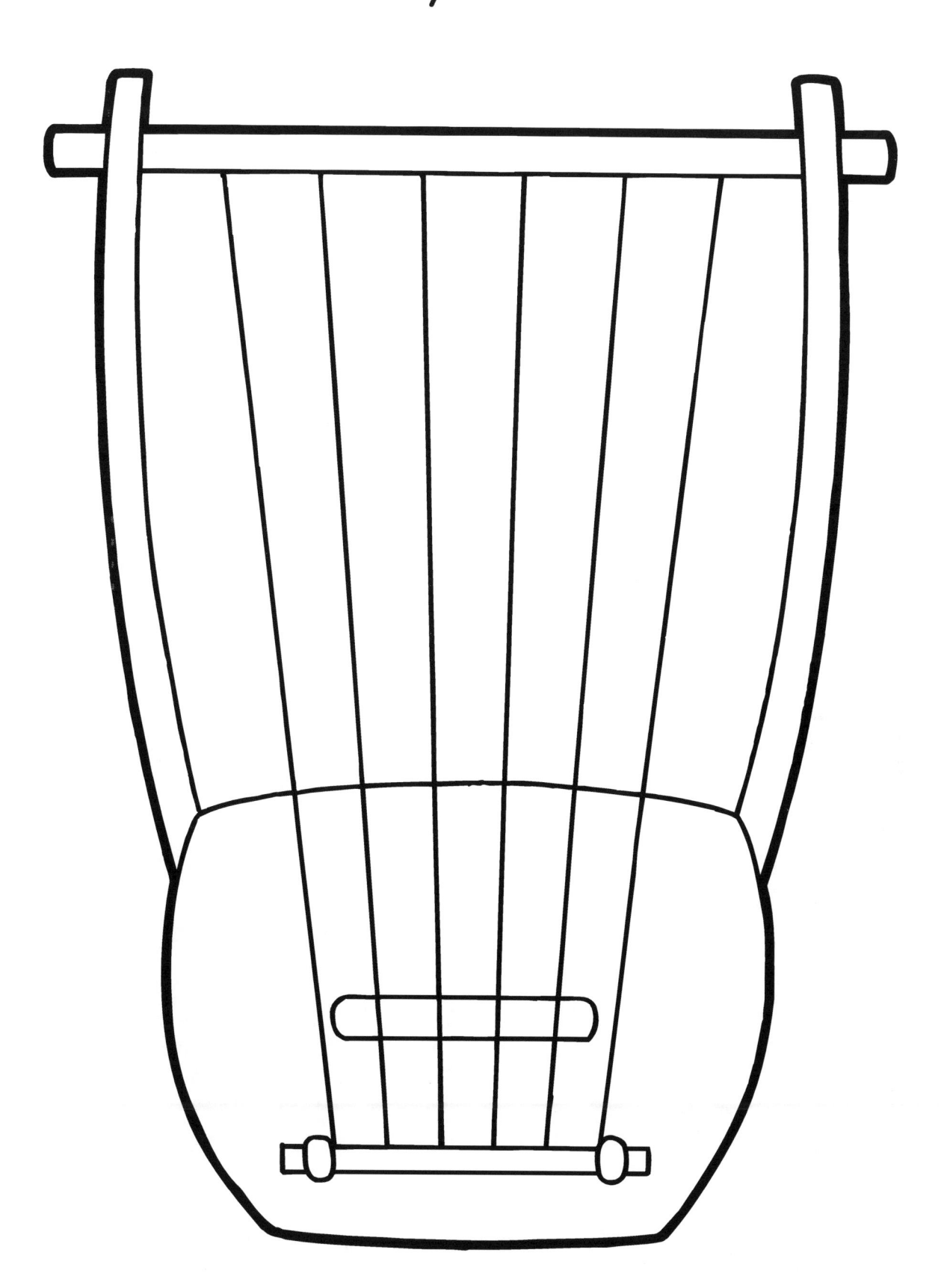

Maine, USA

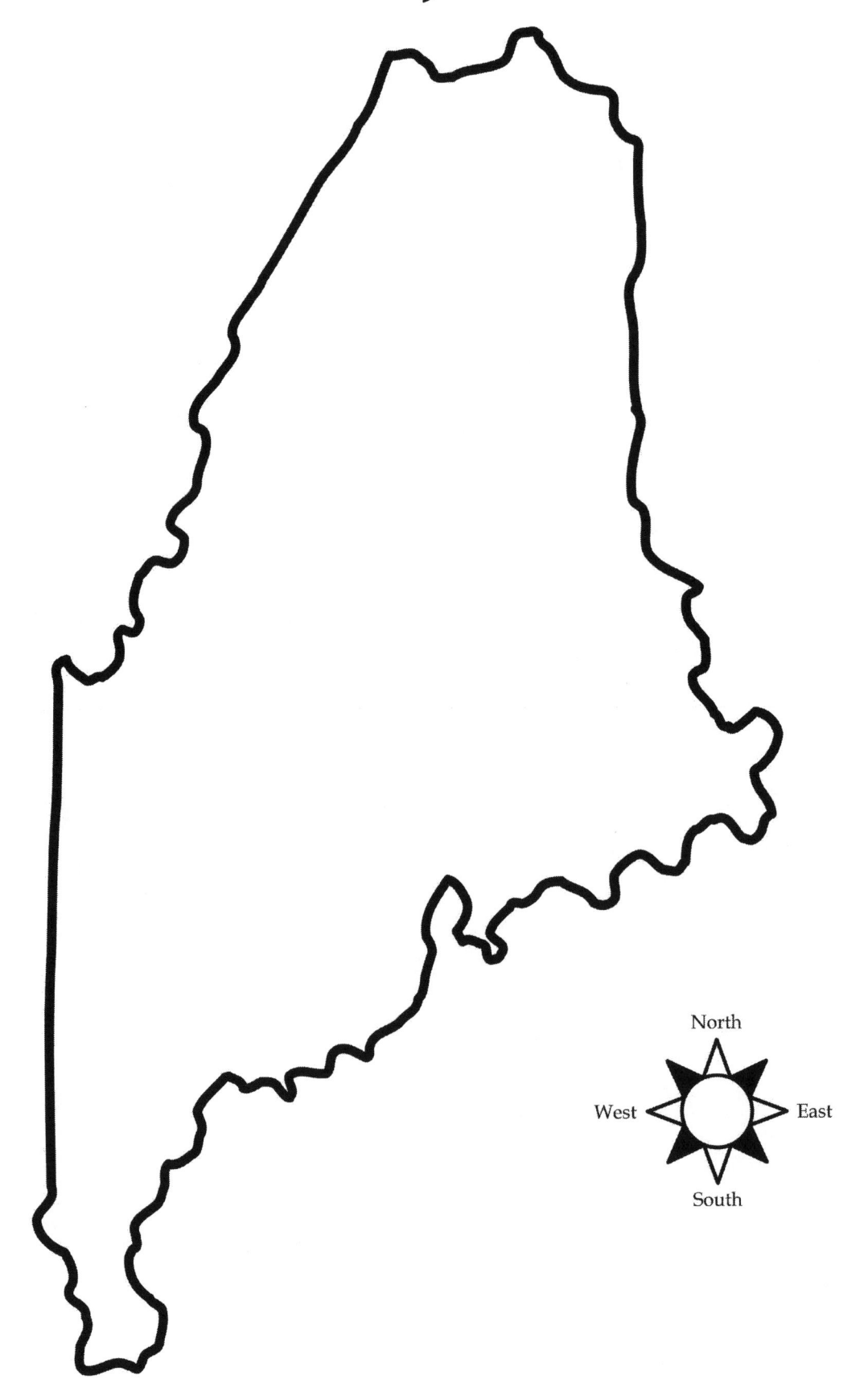

Maps are representations and boundaries are not exact.

manatee

mandolin

madril

Manitoba, Canada

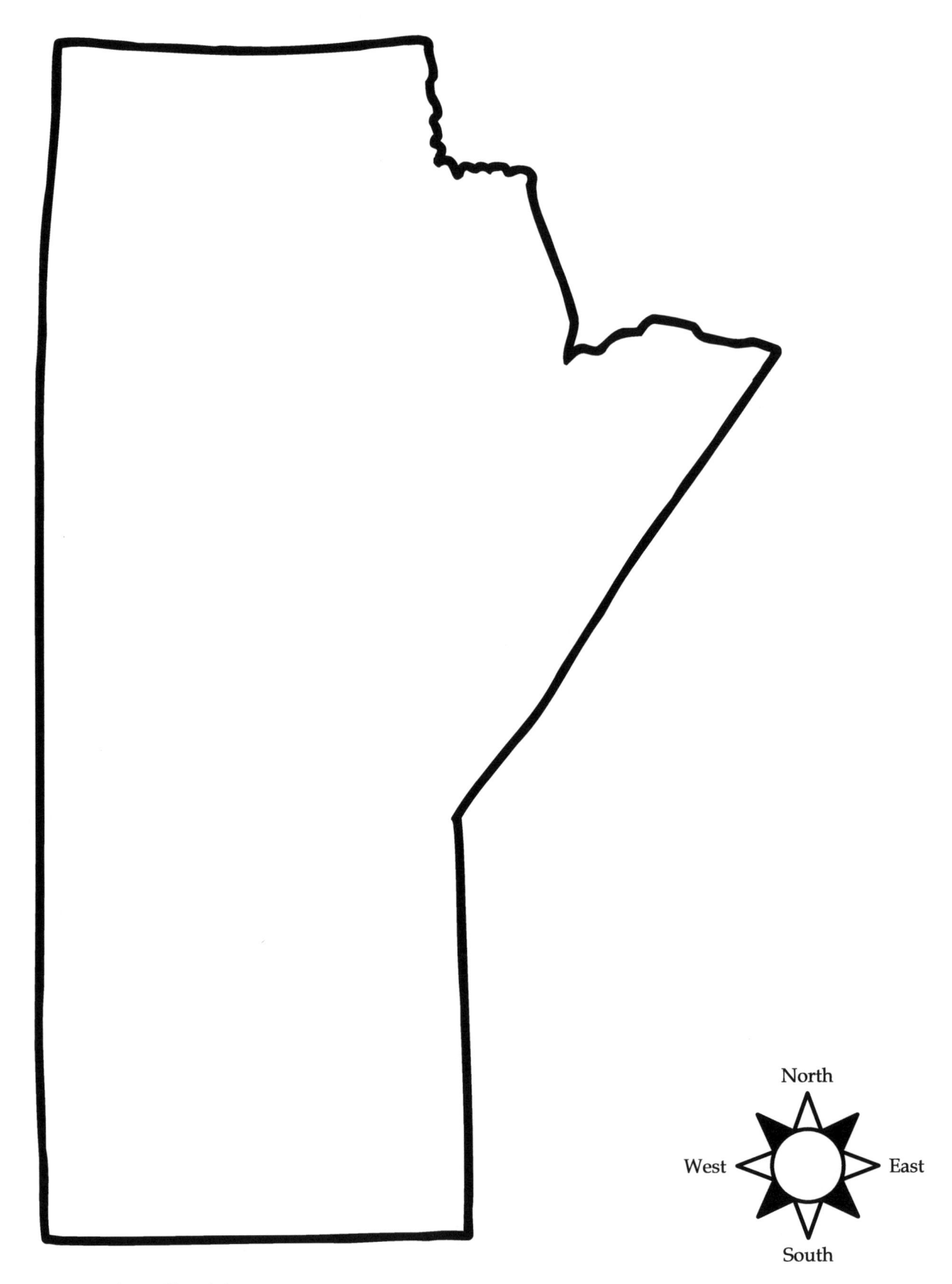

North
West — East
South

Maps are representations and boundaries are not exact.

maracas

Maryland, USA

Maps are representations and boundaries are not exact.

mask (tiger)

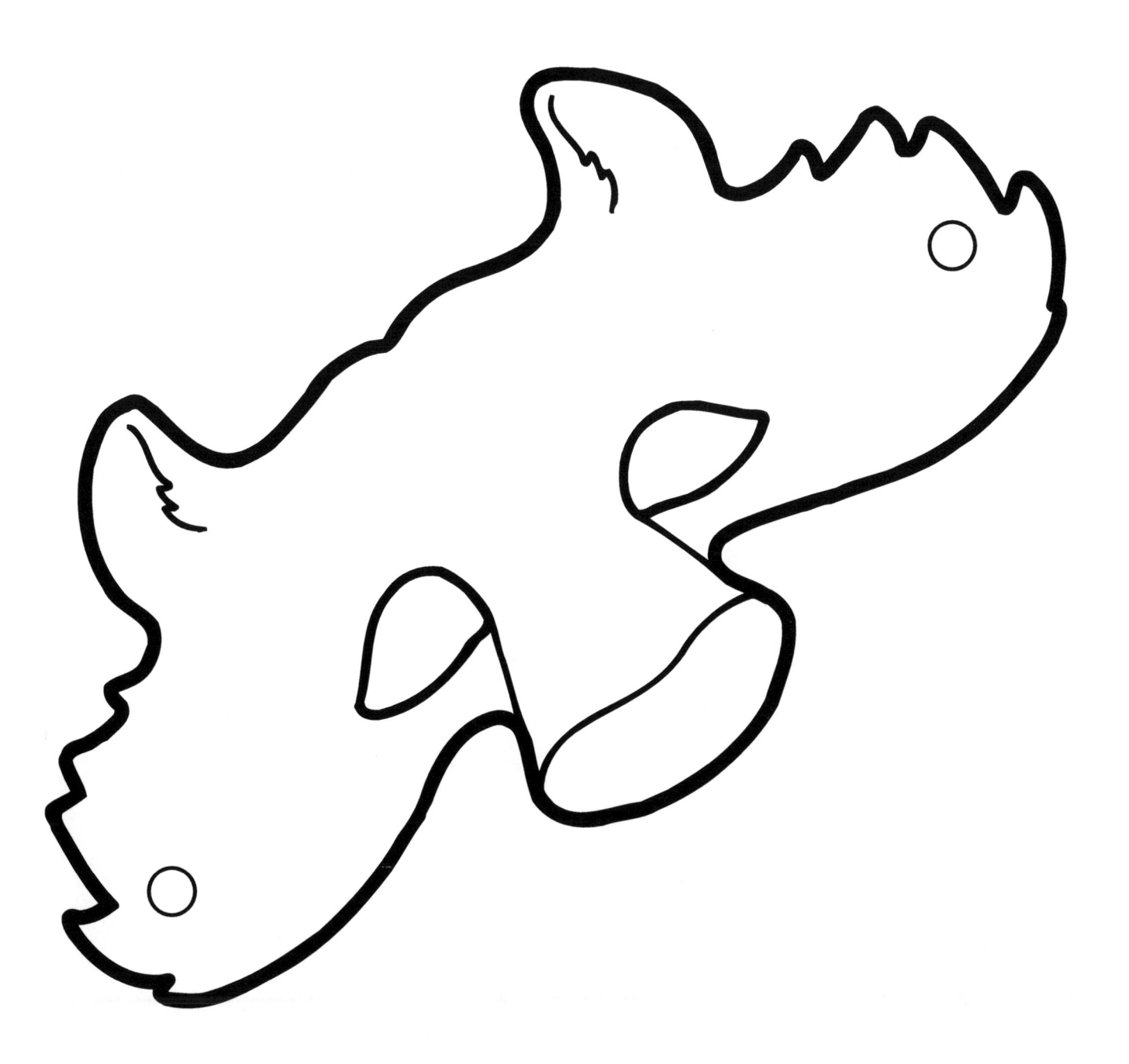

masks

Massachusetts, USA

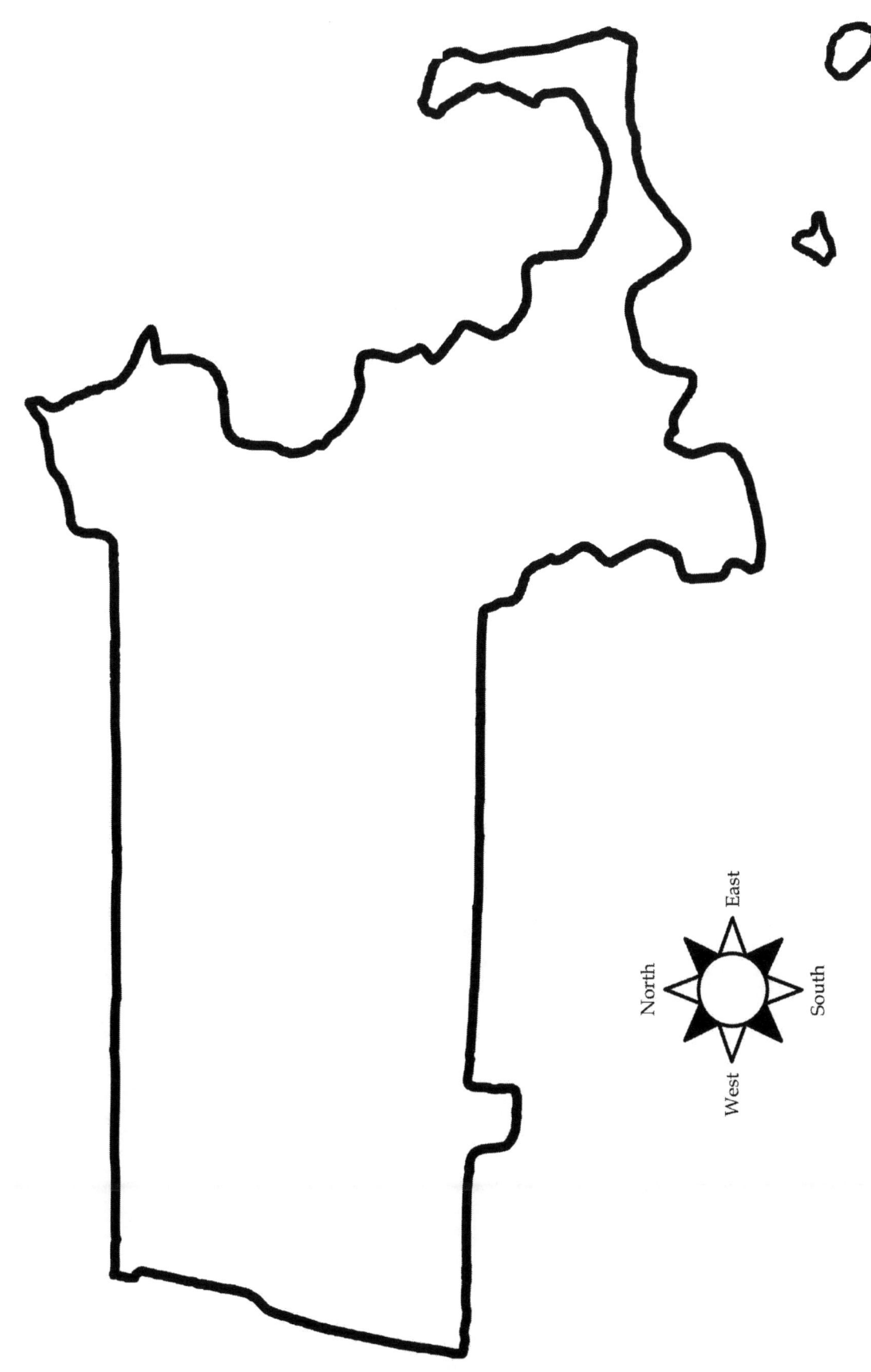

Maps are representations and boundaries are not exact.

matches (closed book)

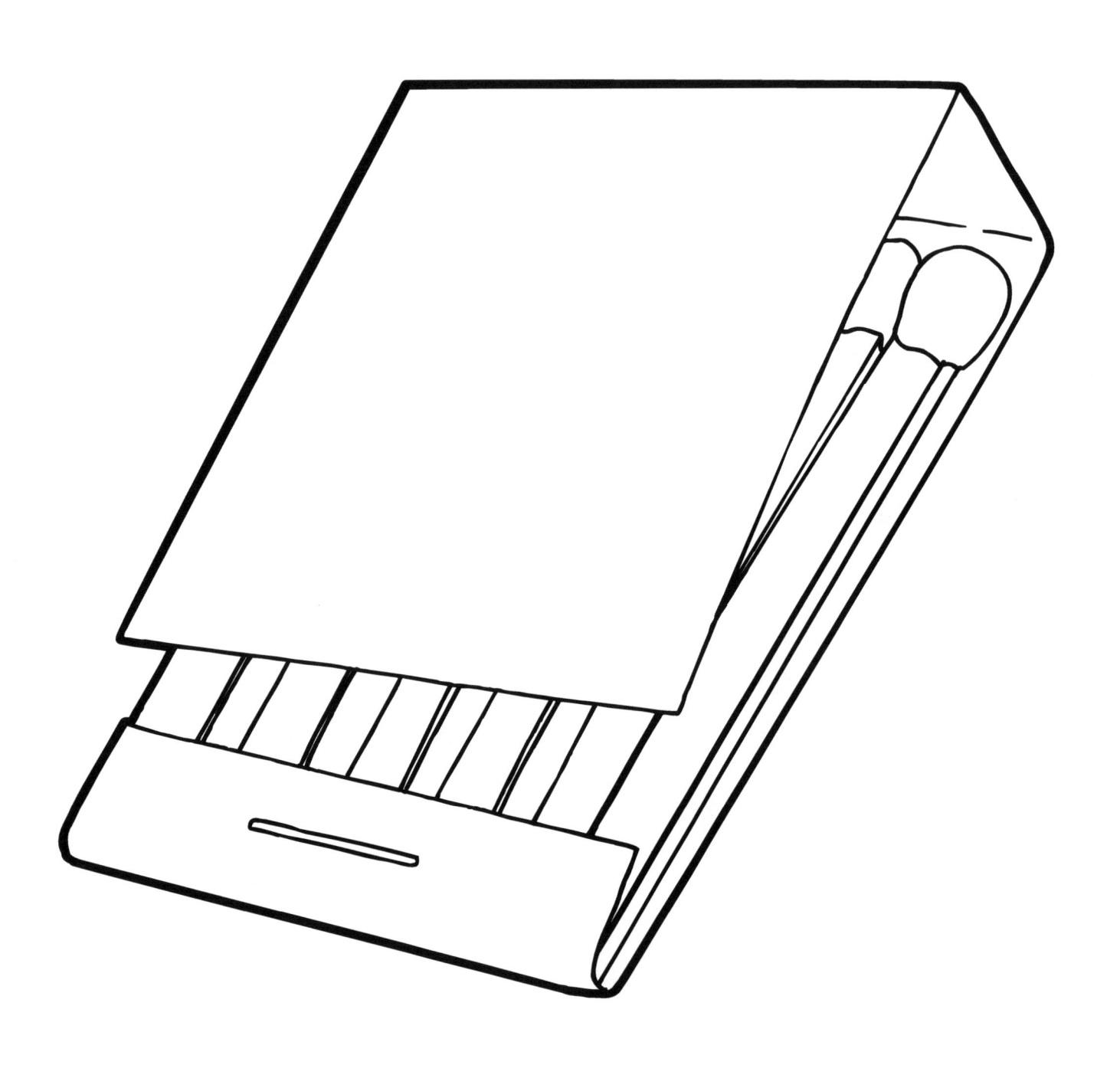

matches (open book)

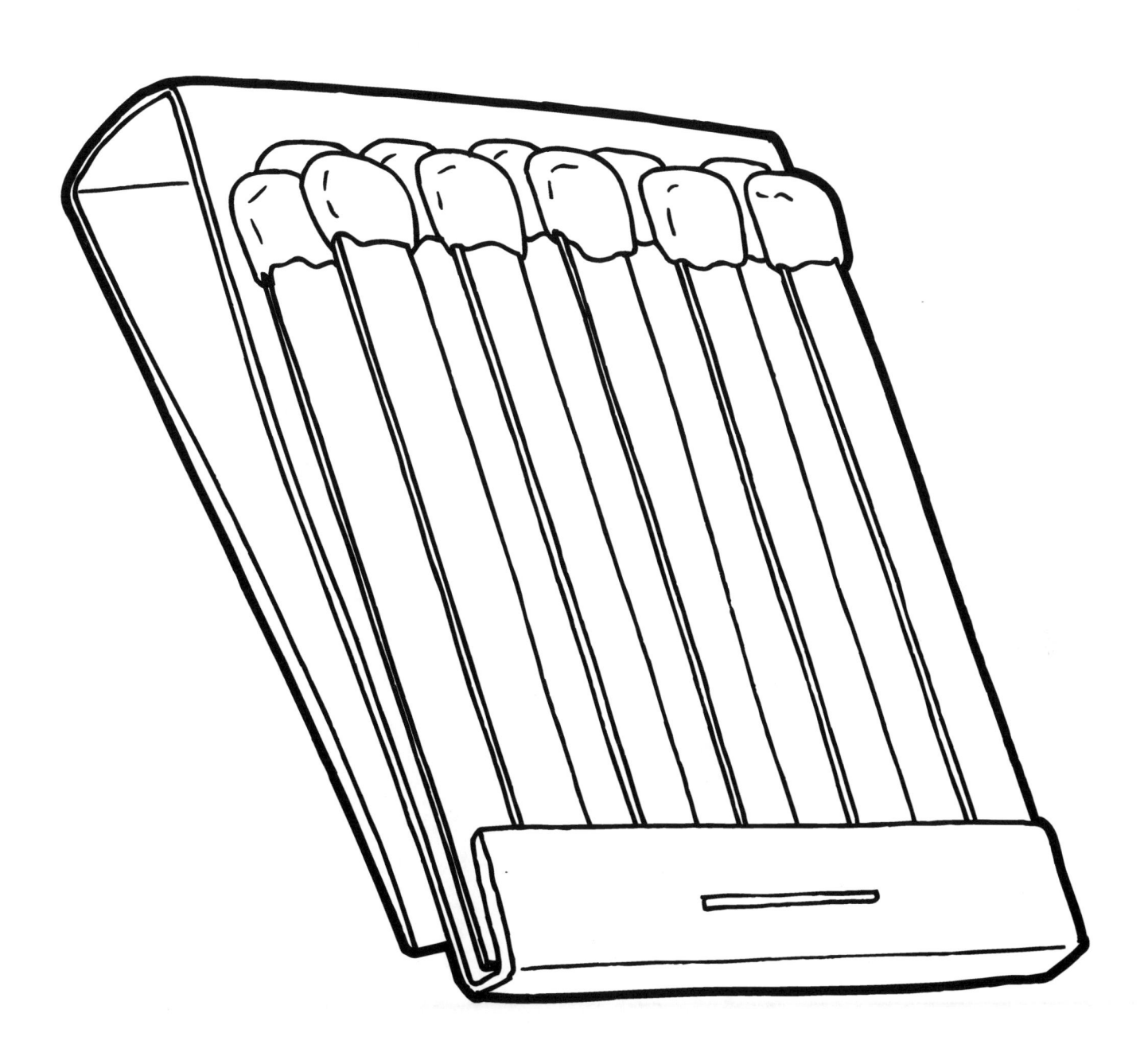

menorah

menorah (outline)

Mexico

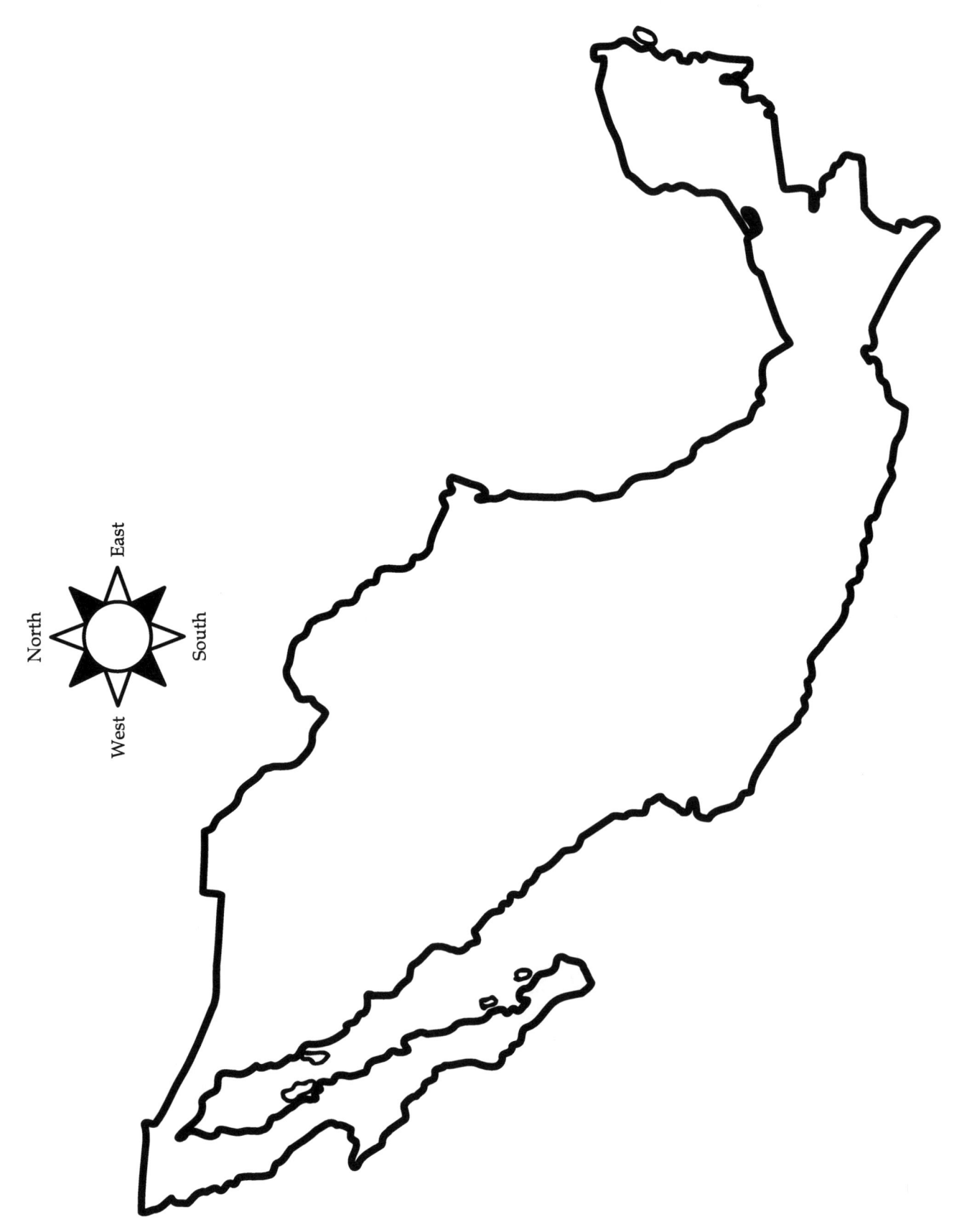

North East South West

Maps are representations and boundaries are not exact.

Michigan, USA

Maps are representations and boundaries are not exact.

microscope

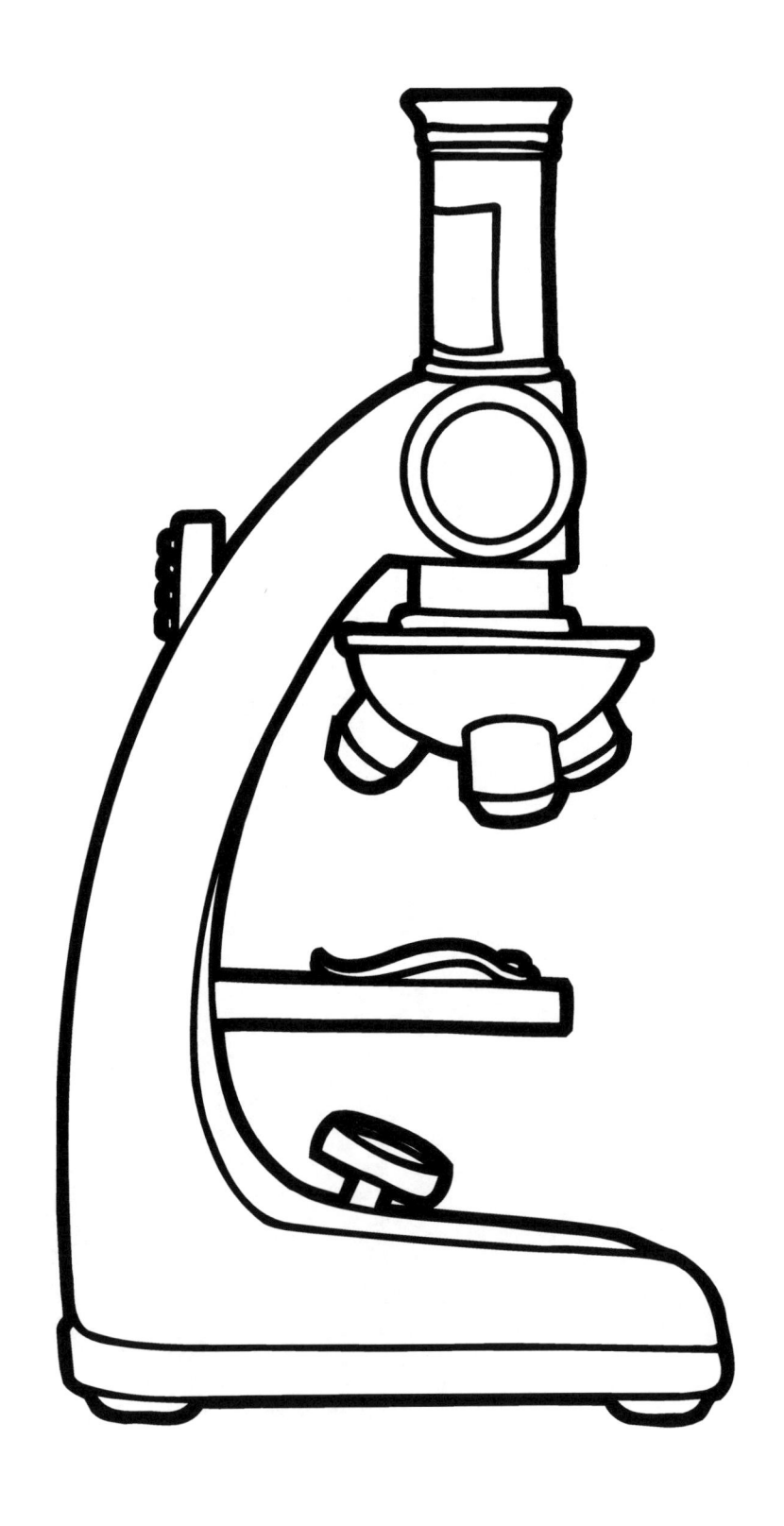

Minnesota, USA

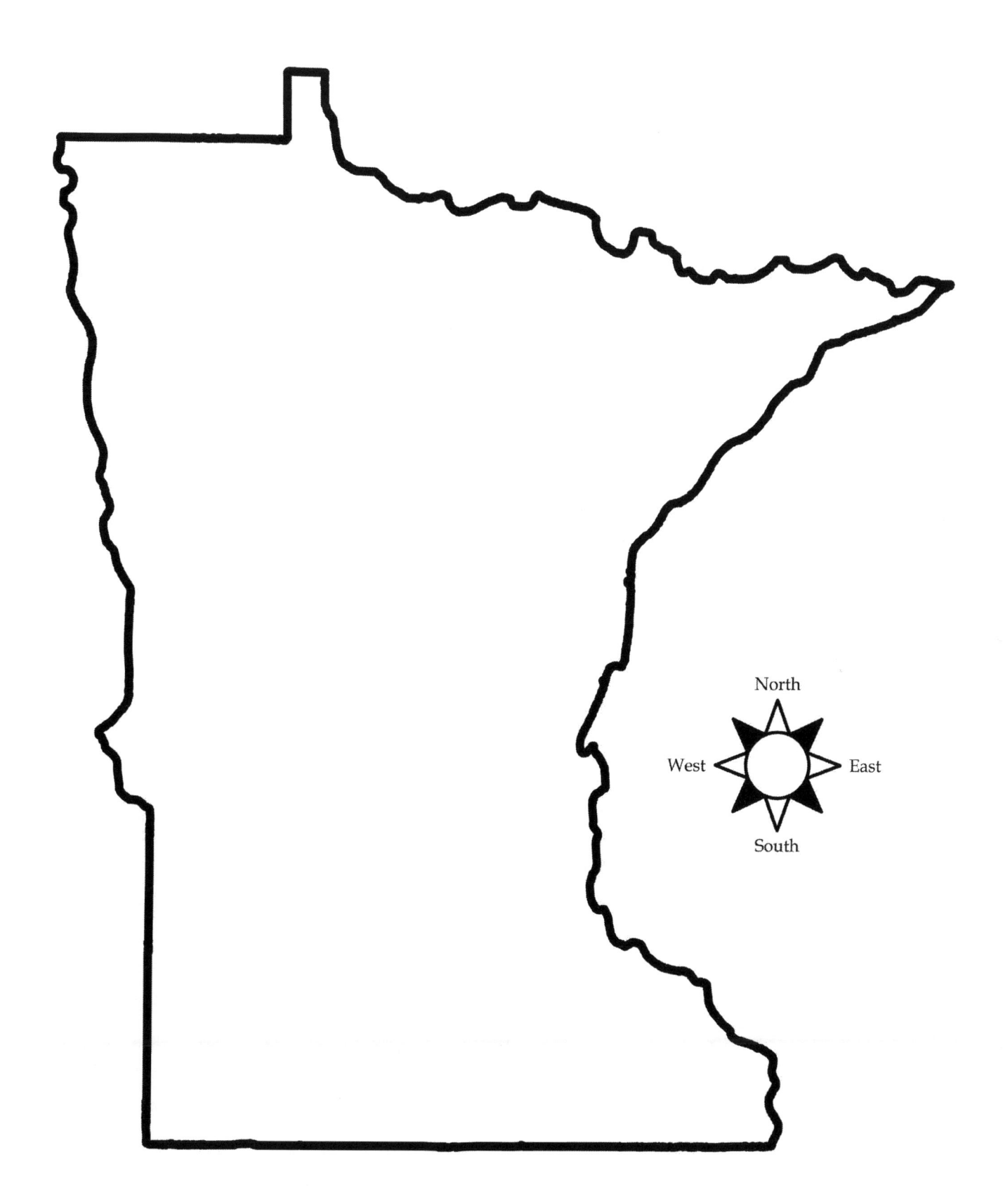

Maps are representations and boundaries are not exact.

Mississippi, USA

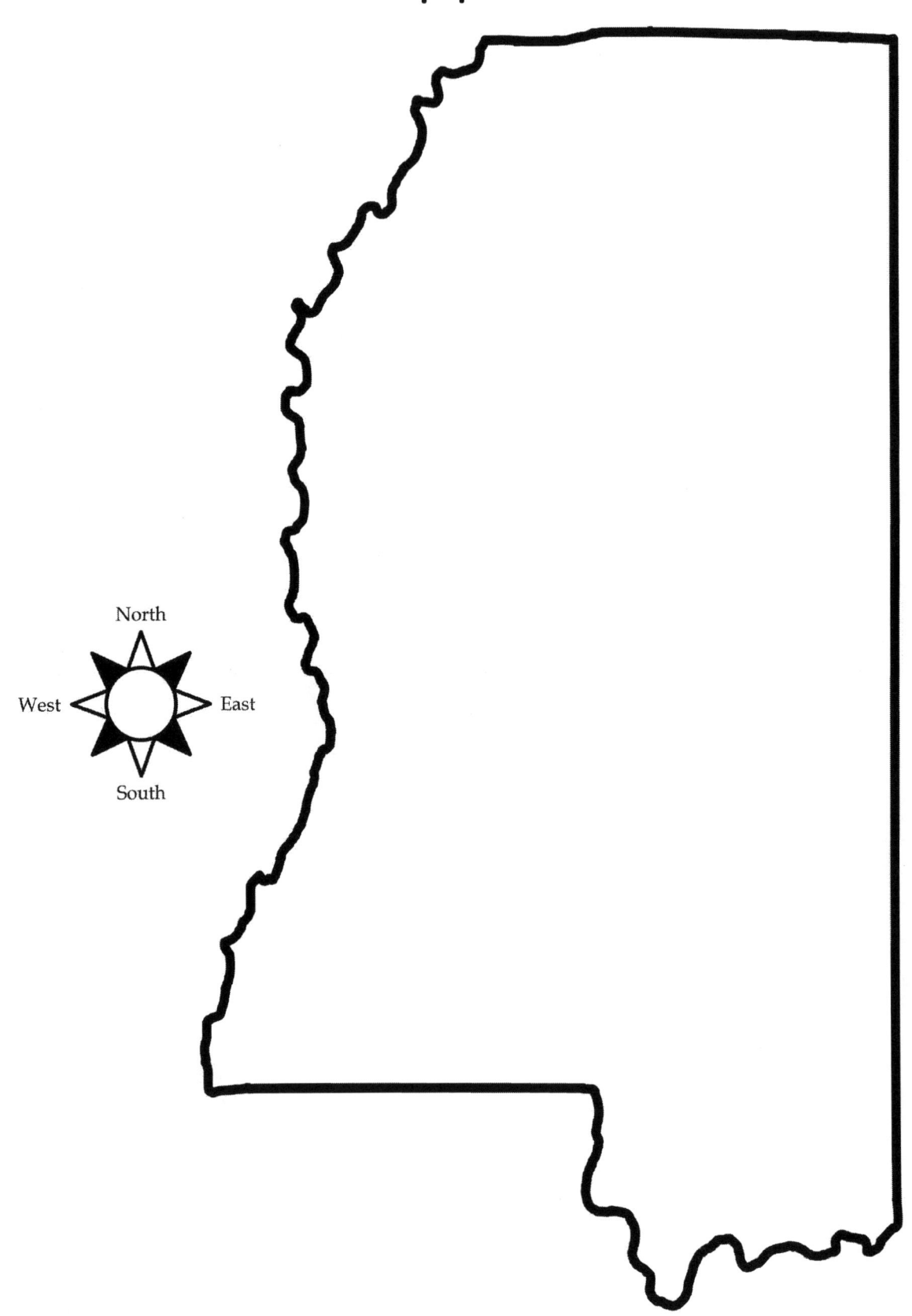

North
West   East
South

Maps are representations and boundaries are not exact.

Missouri, USA

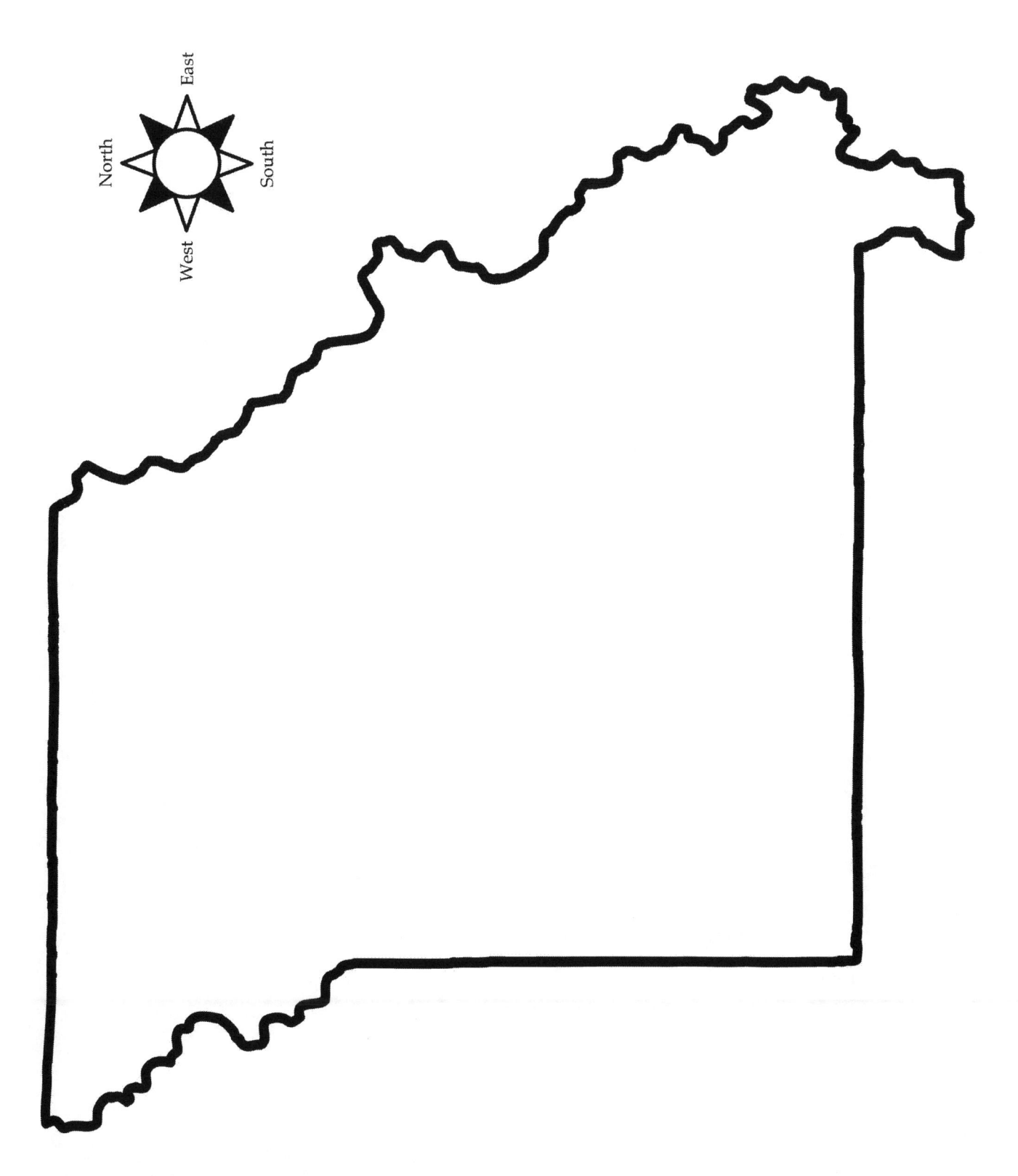

North East South West

Maps are representations and boundaries are not exact.

mitt (3D)

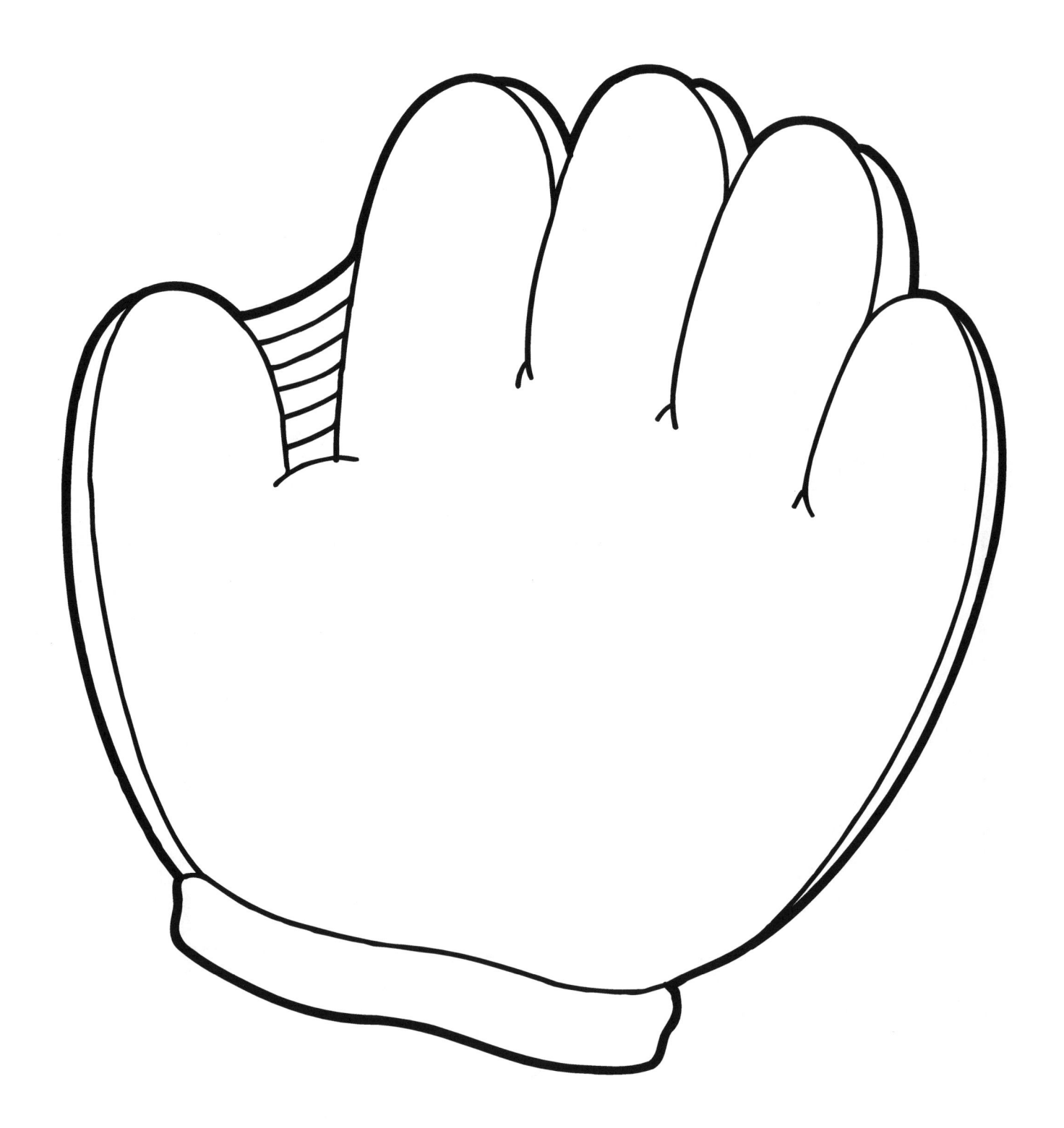

mitt (plain)

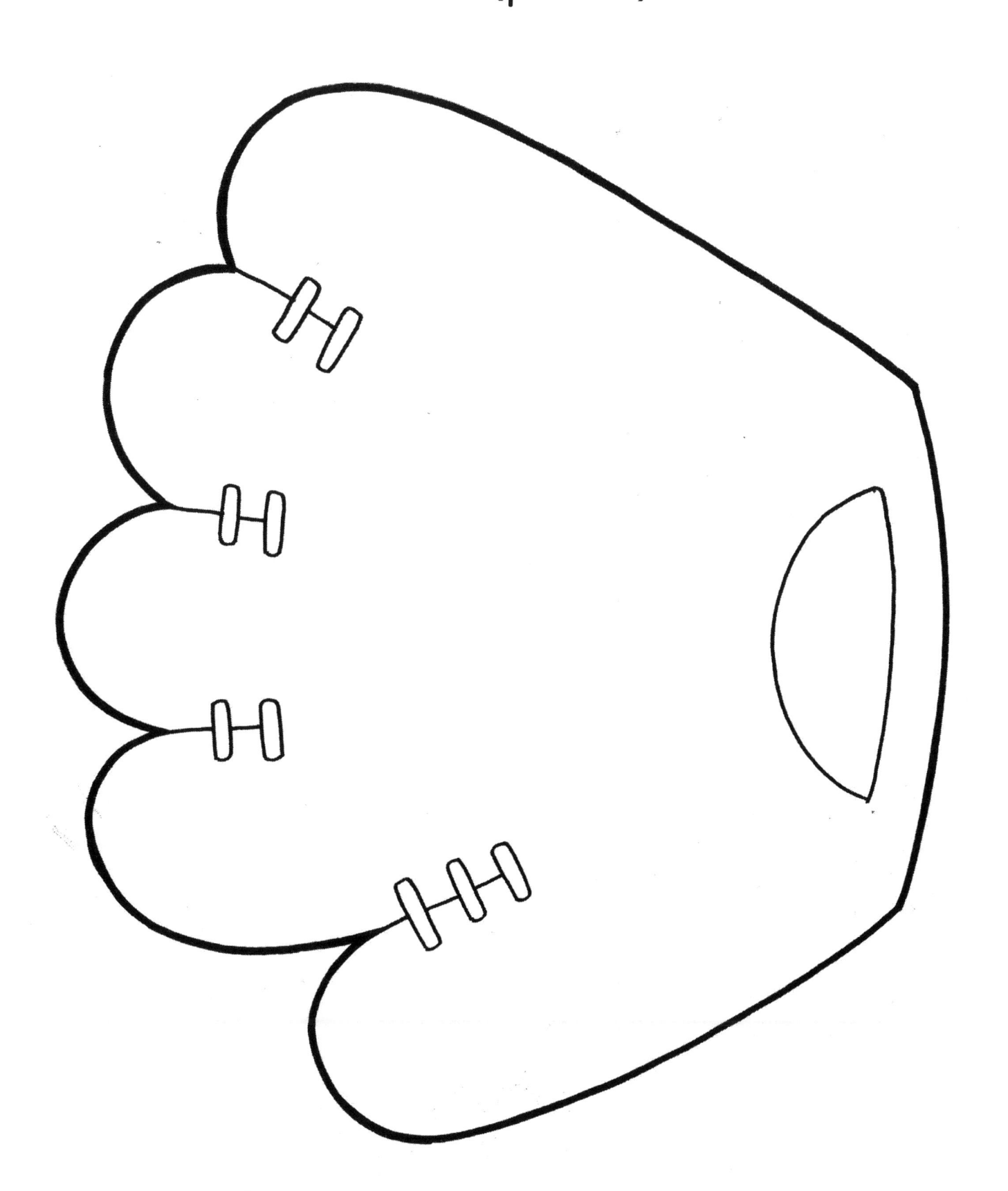

mitten (left)

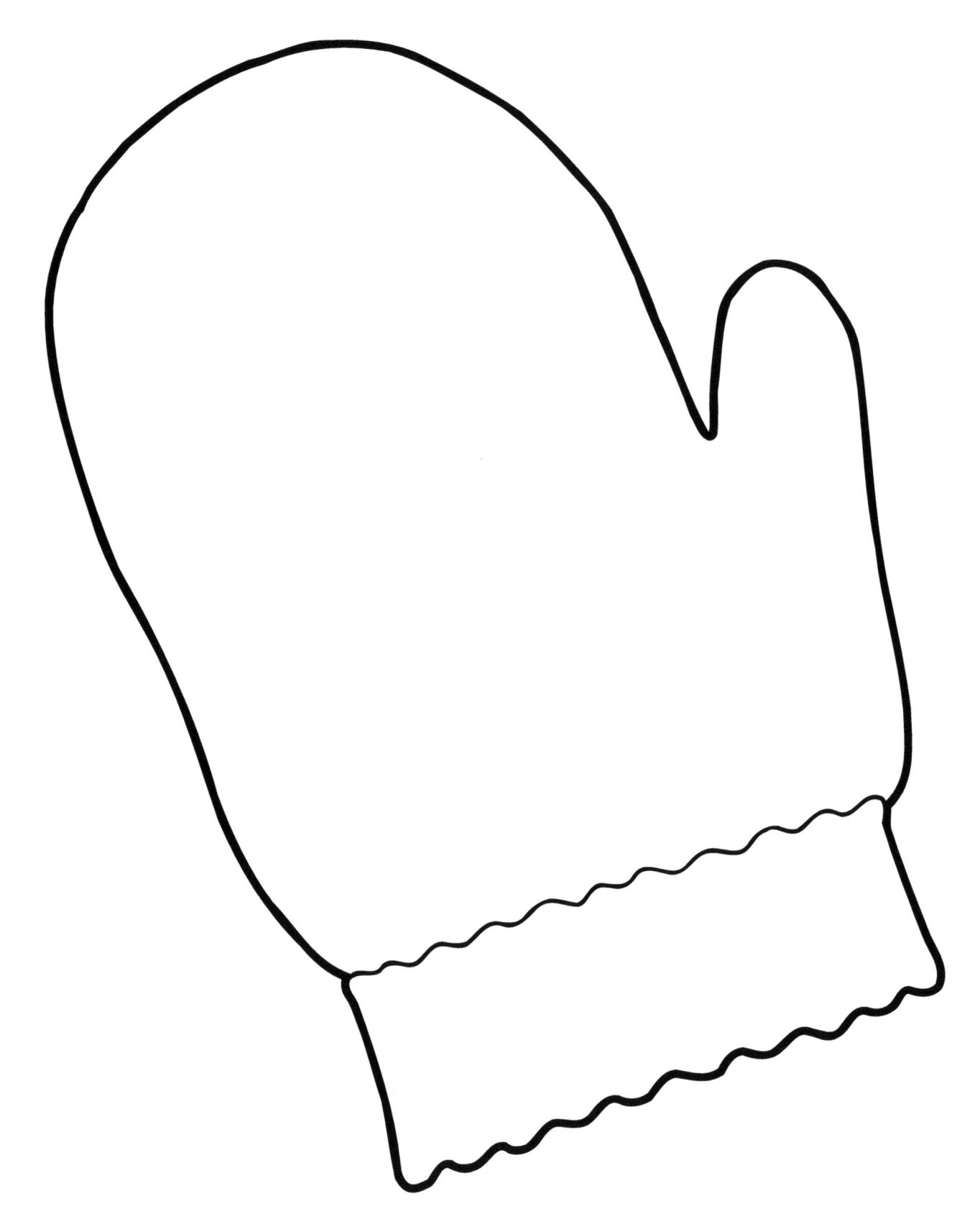

mitten (right)

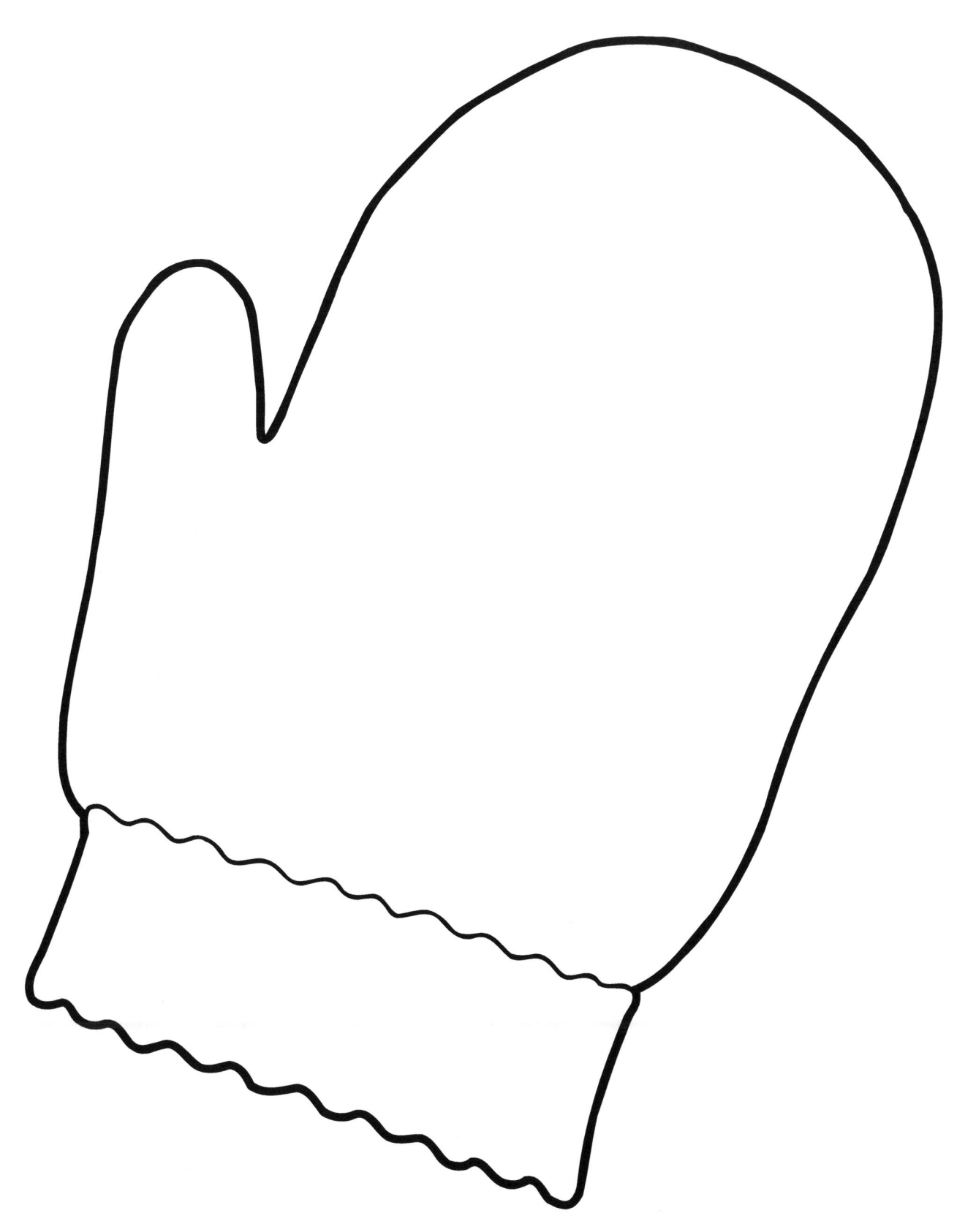

mittens

monkey

monster (head)

Montana, USA

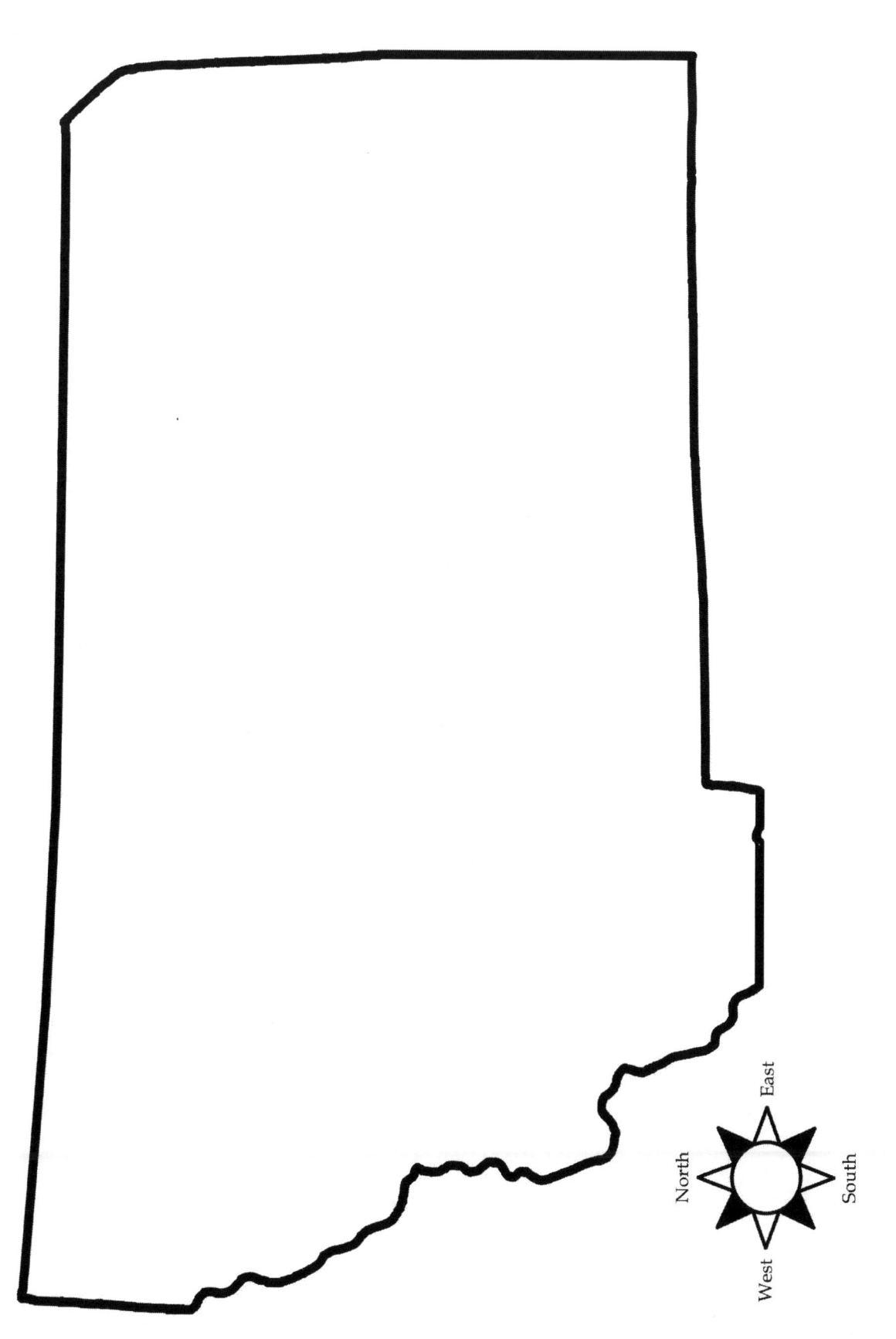

Maps are representations and boundaries are not exact.

LAB201412P • THE PATTERN LIBRARY • VOLUME TWO • I-Z • 978-1-937257-63-7 • © 2014 Little Acorn Books™   107

moon

moon (with night cap)

moose

mouse (animated)

mouse (animated, waving)

mouse (animated, winter)

mushroom (bell-shaped)

mushroom (conical)

mushroom (convex)

mushroom
(convex with skirt)

narwhal

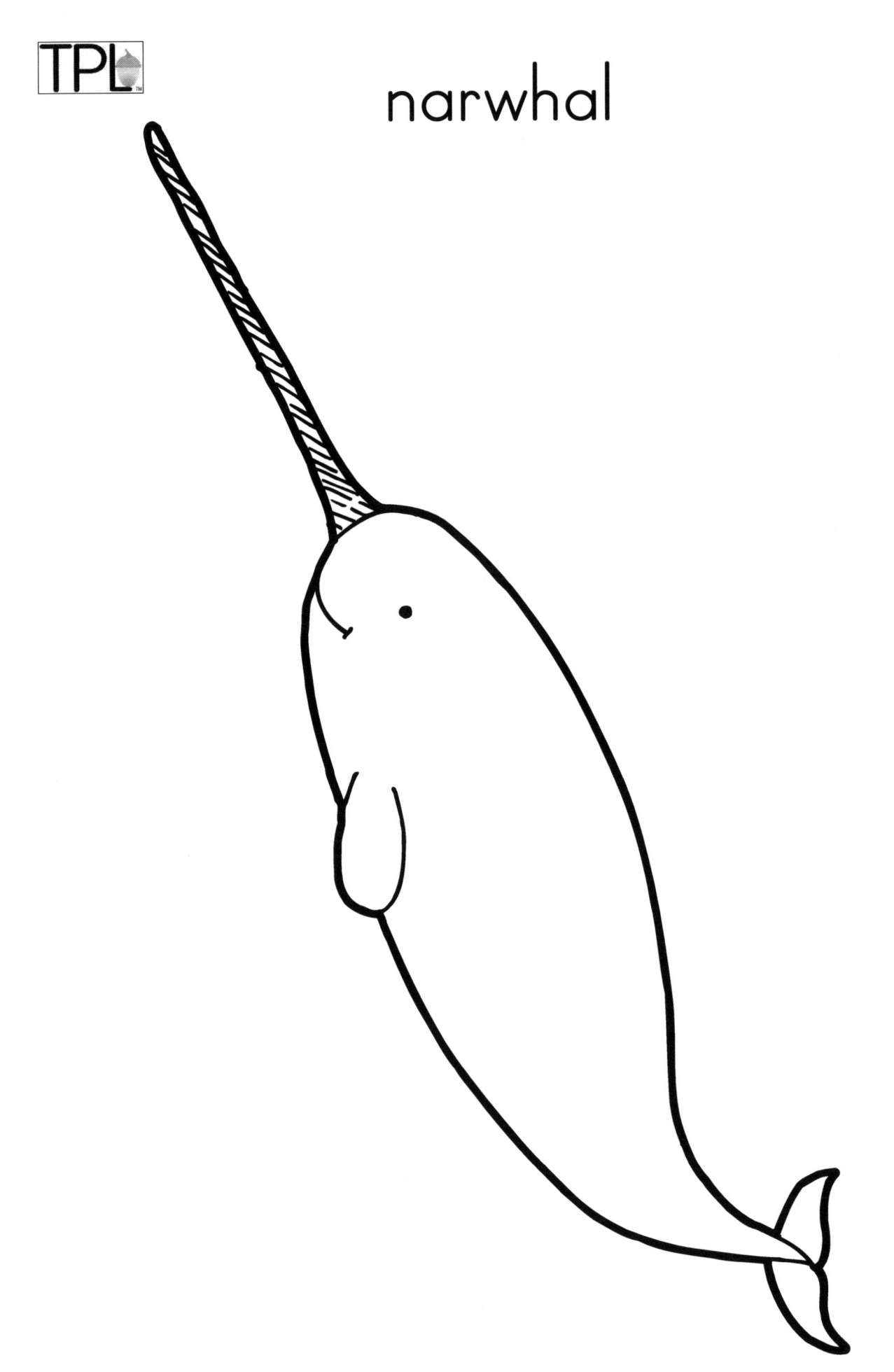

nautilus

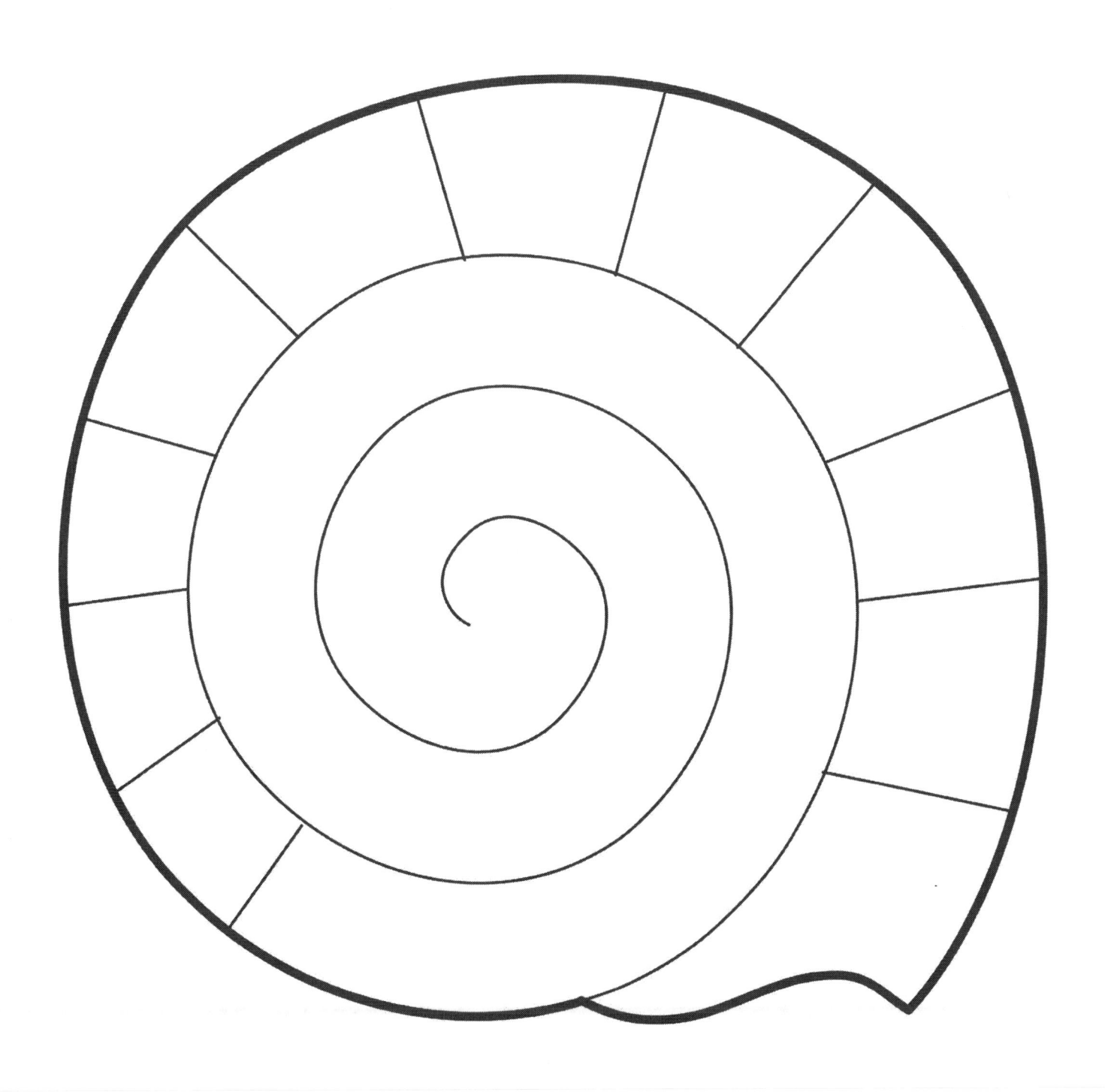

Nebraska, USA

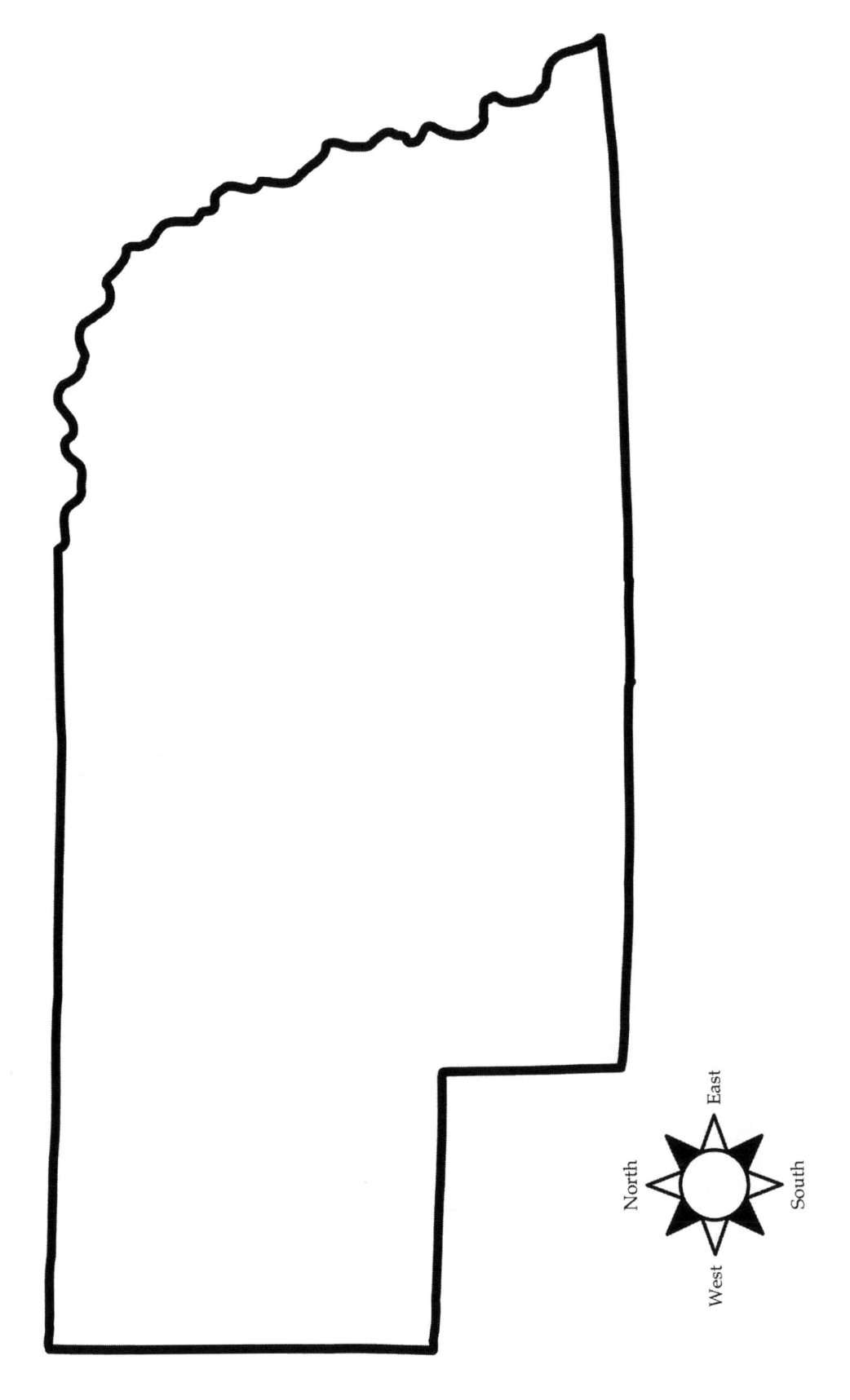

Maps are representations and boundaries are not exact.

120 LAB201412P • THE PATTERN LIBRARY • VOLUME TWO • I-Z • 978-1-937257-63-7 • © 2014 Little Acorn Books™

necklace

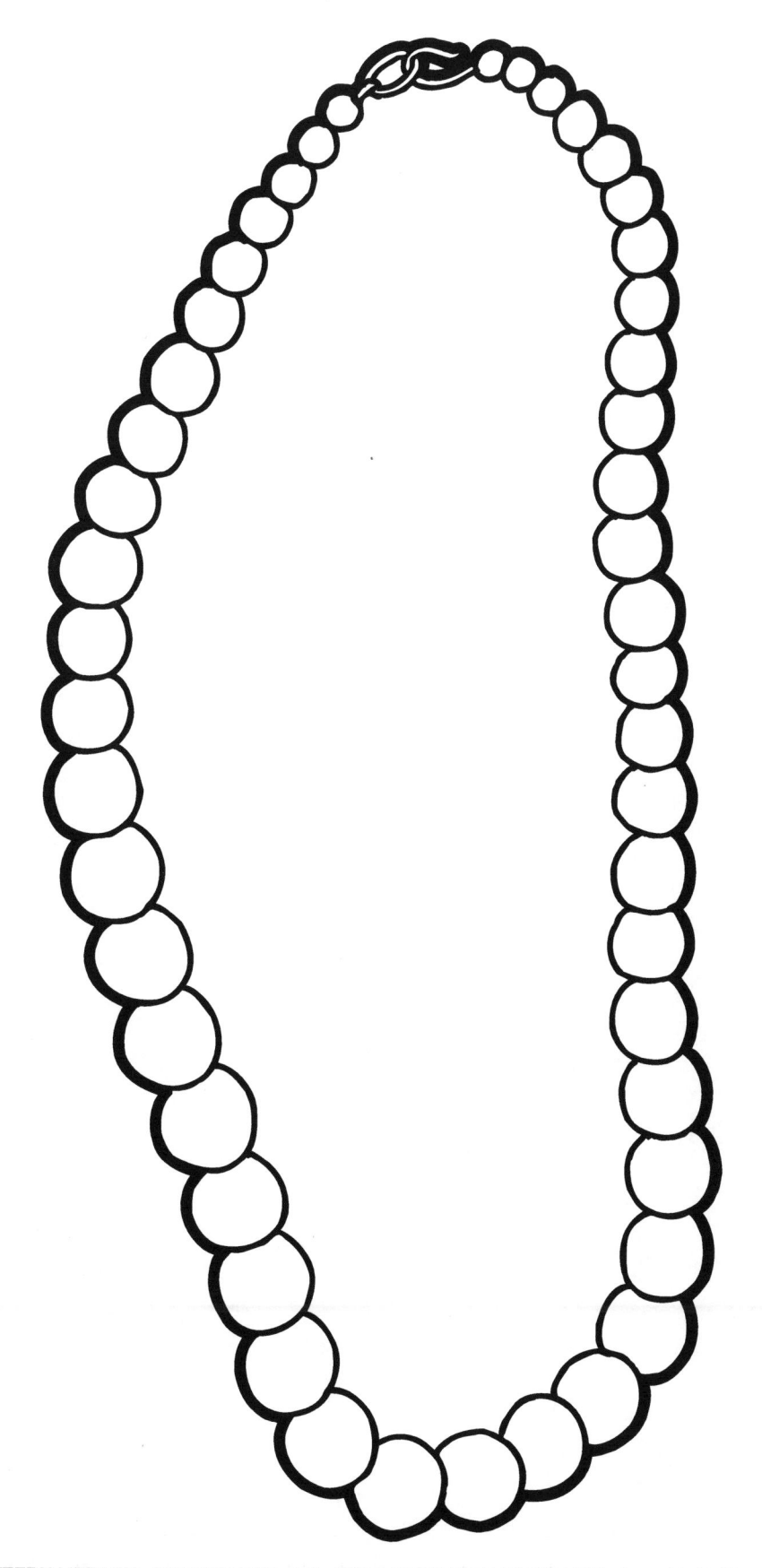

necktie

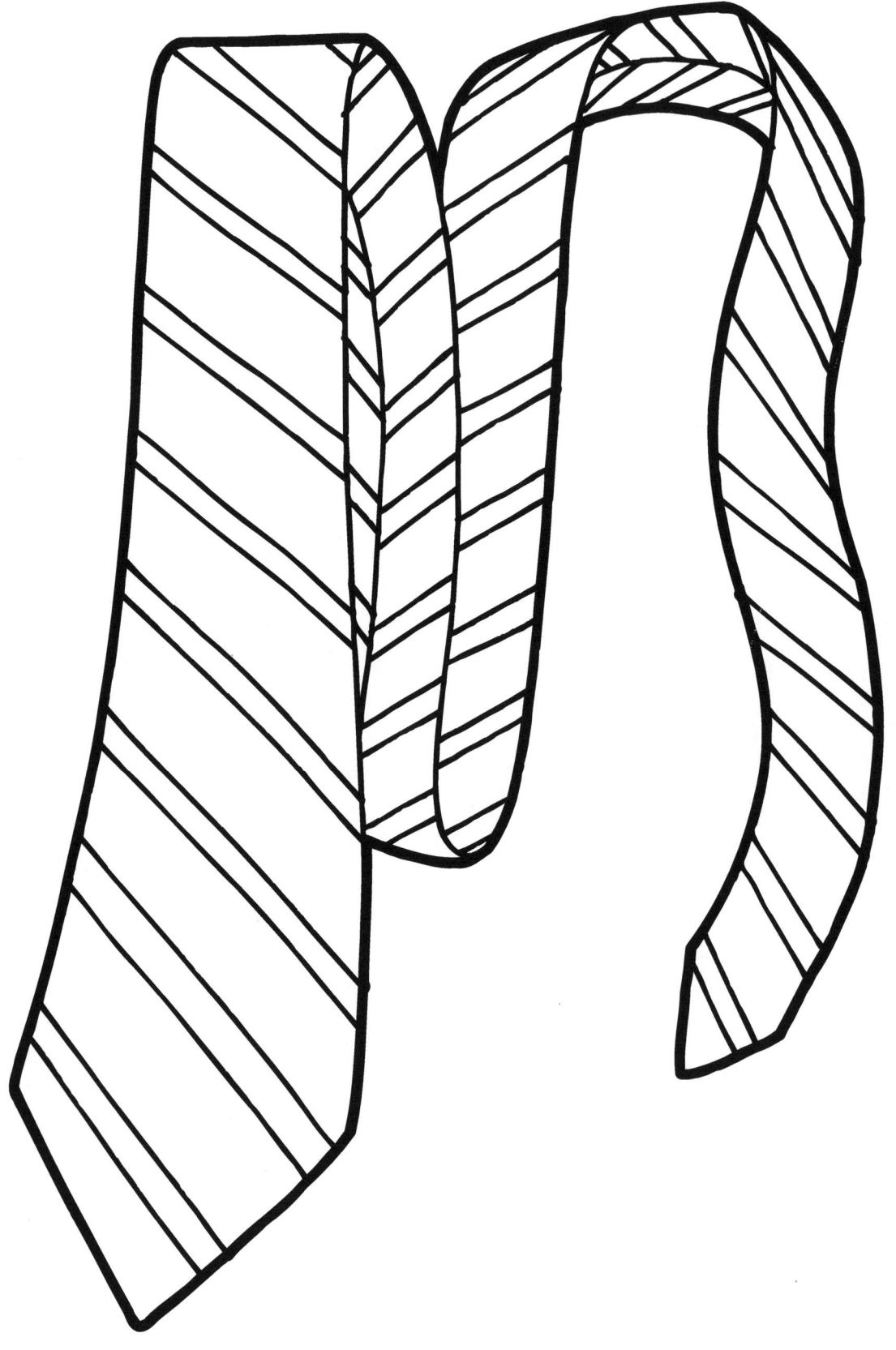

needle (sewing)

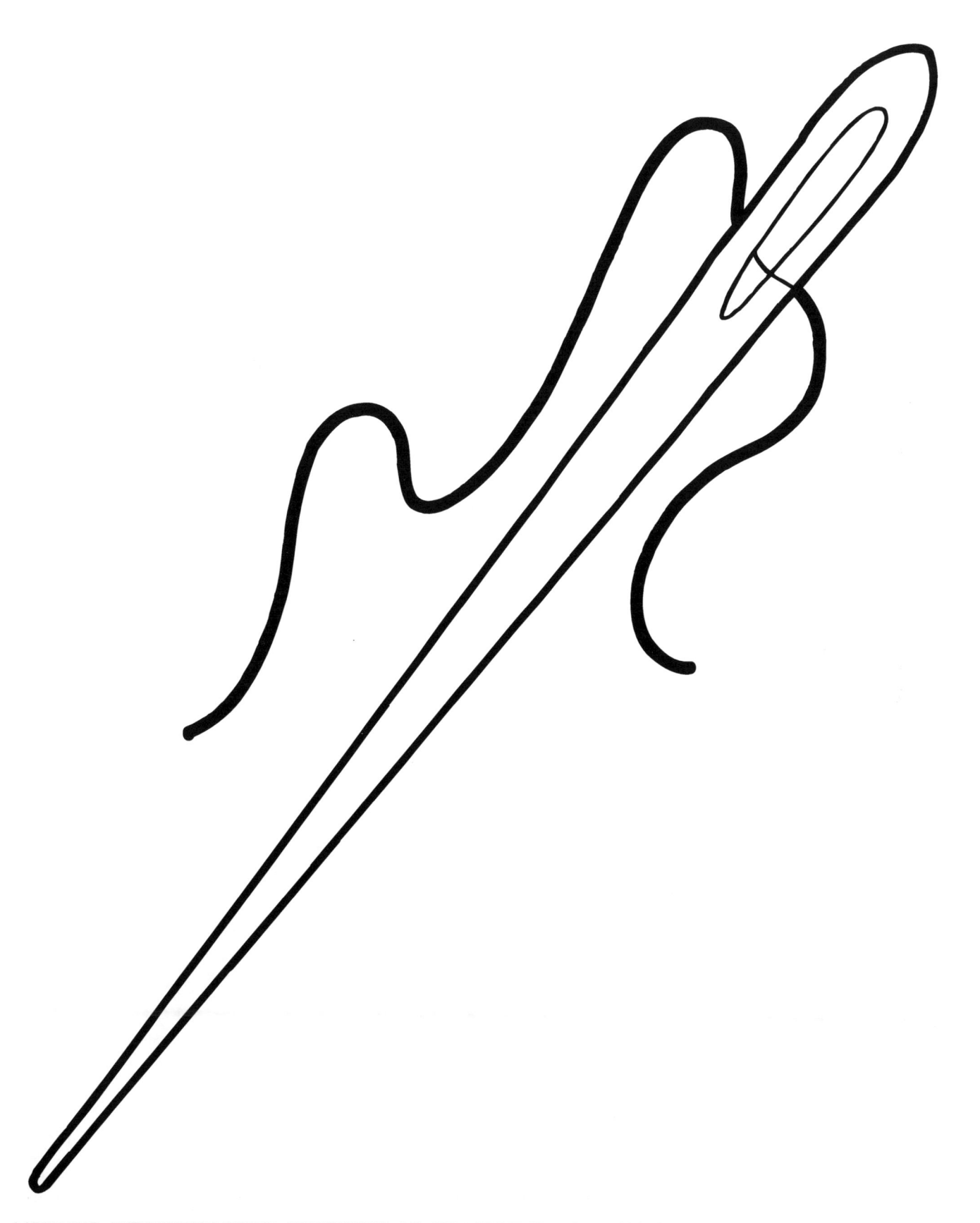

nest

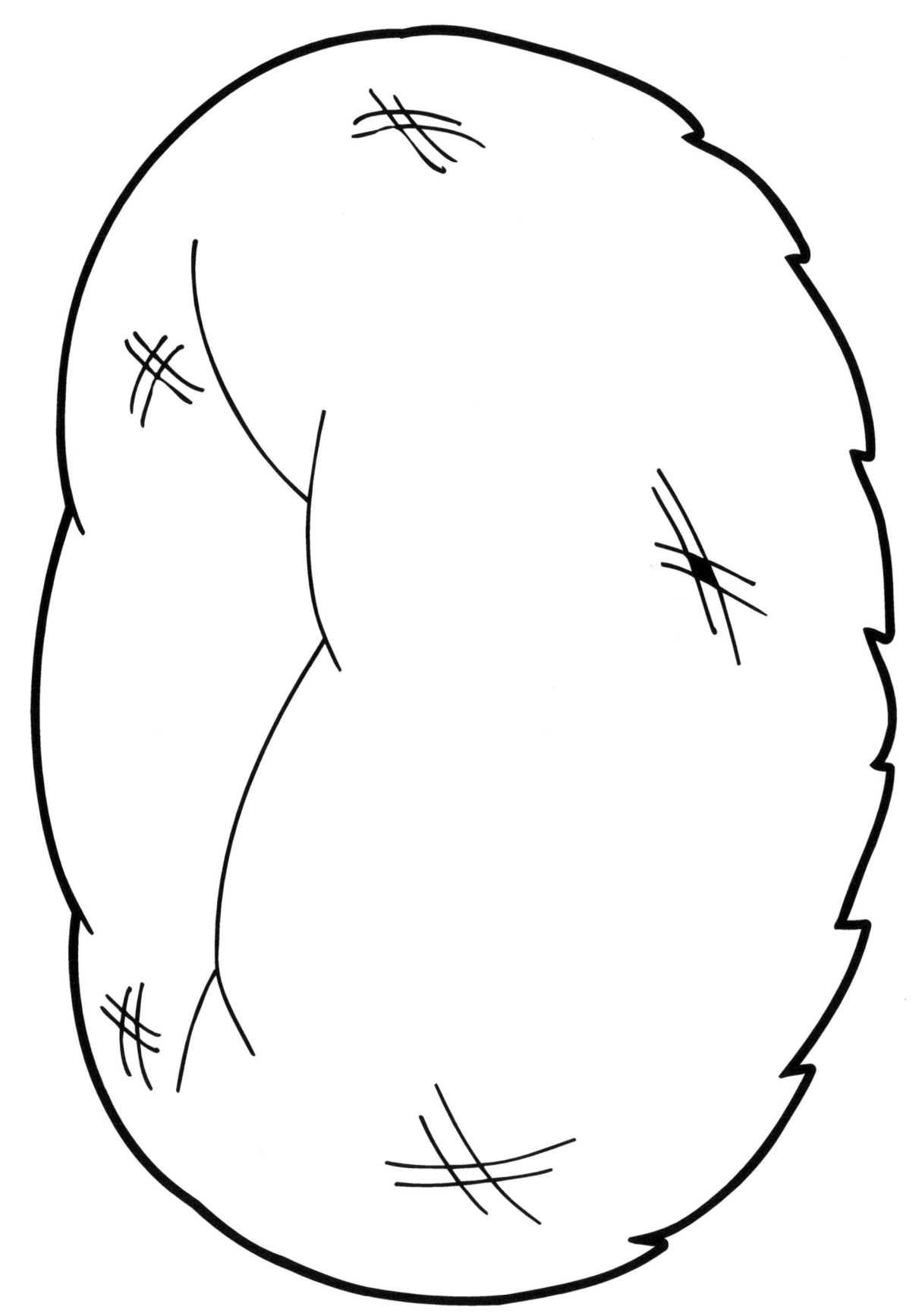

nest (outline)

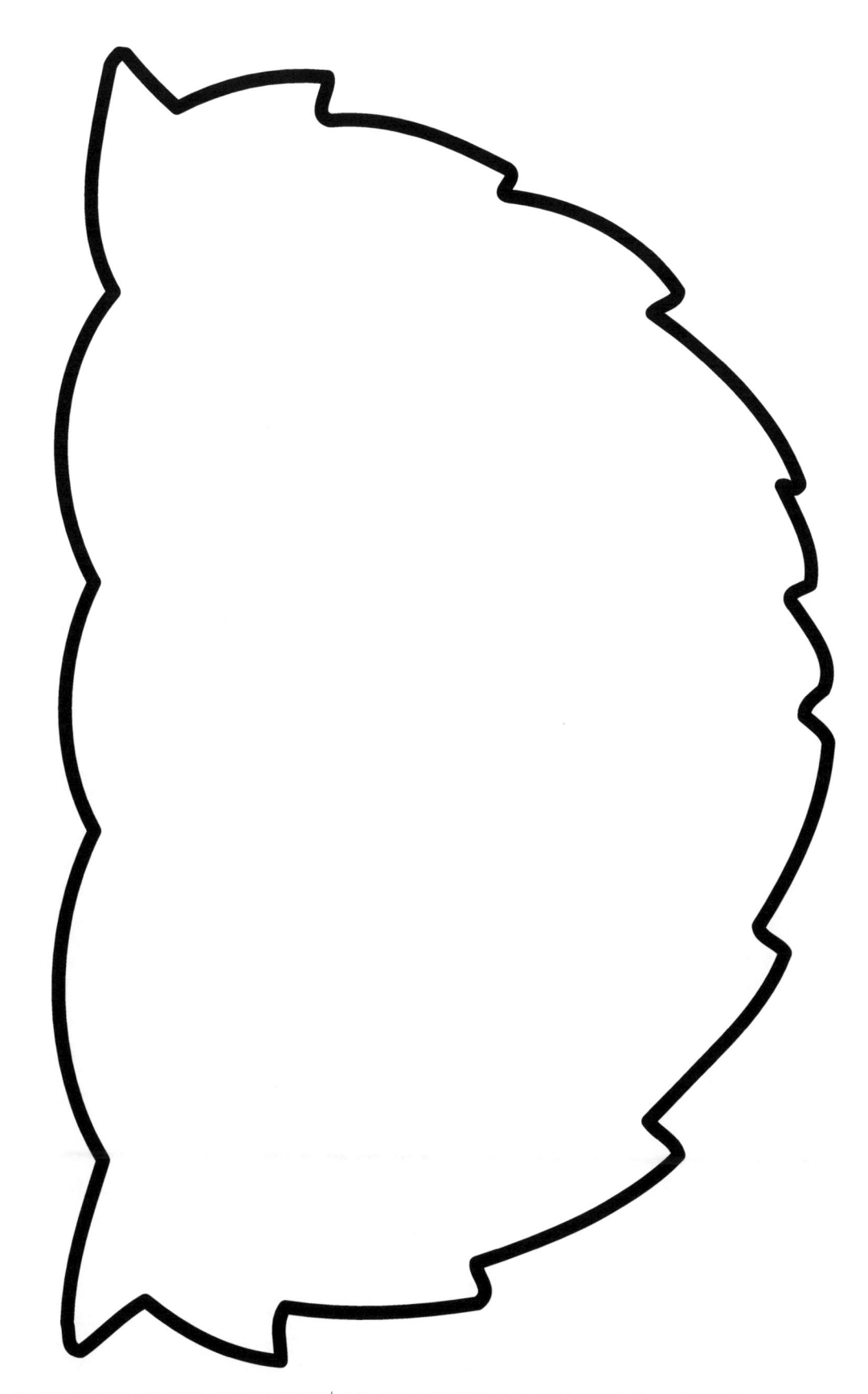

net (without handle)

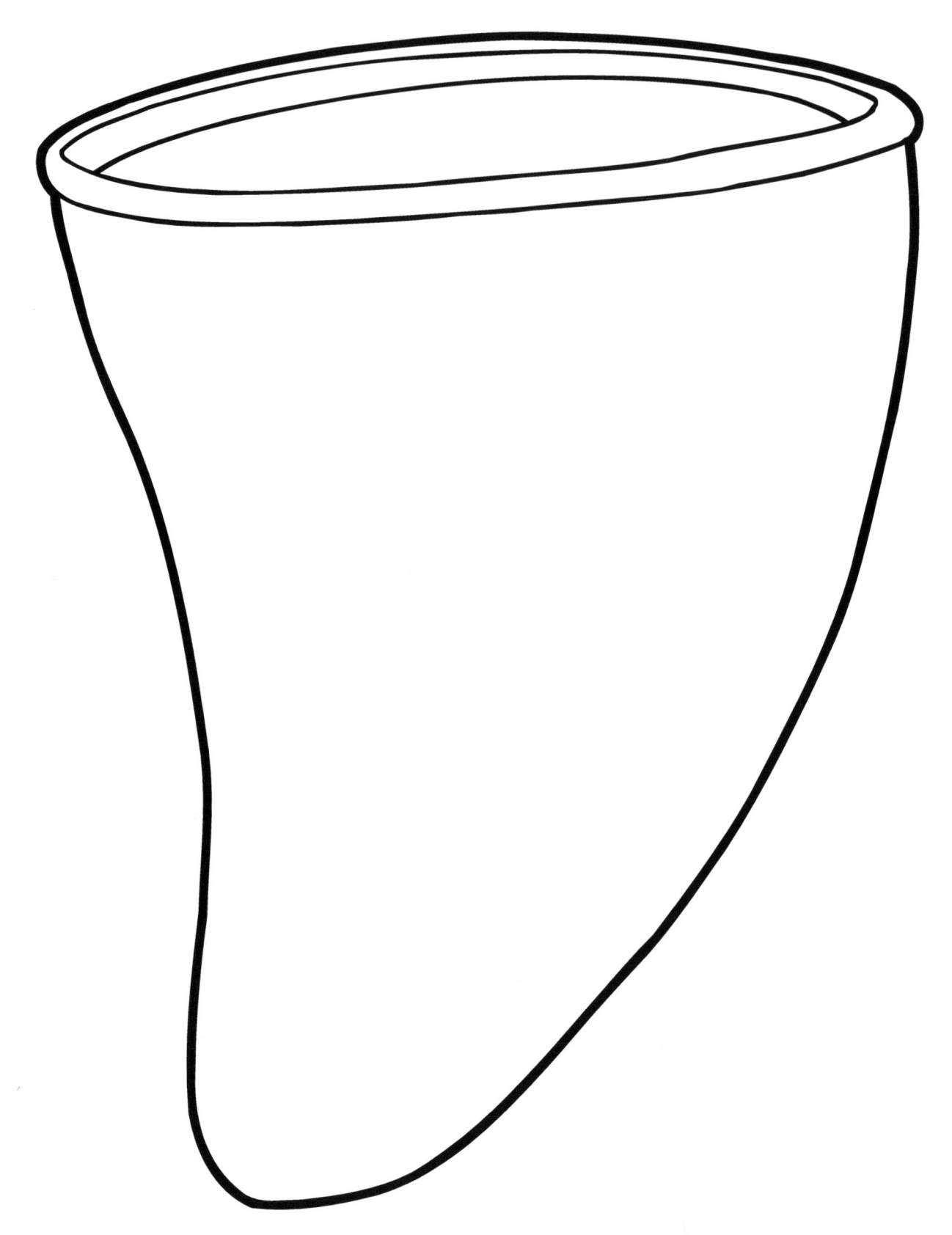

Nevada, USA

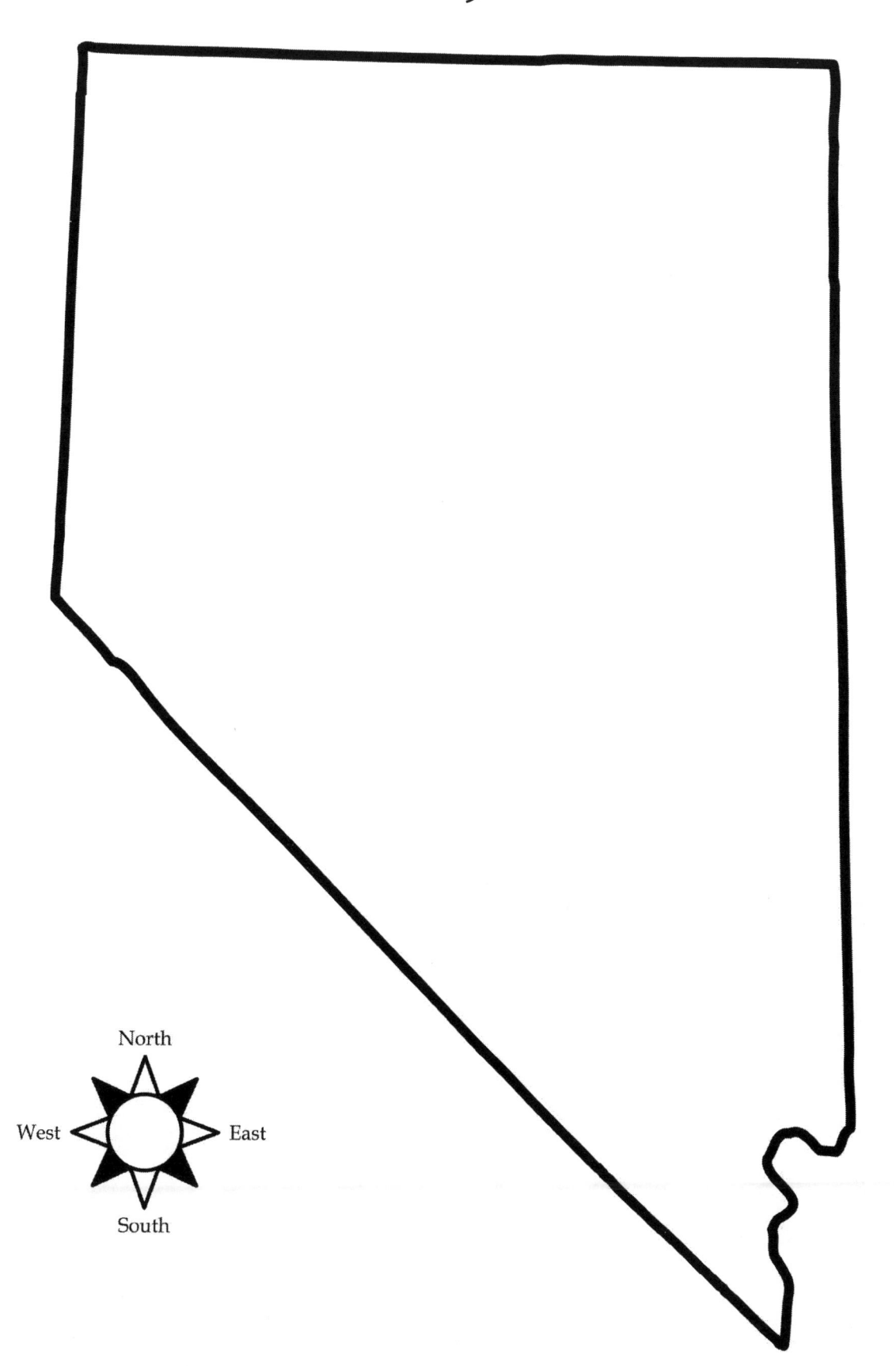

North
West East
South

Maps are representations and boundaries are not exact.

New Brunswick, Canada

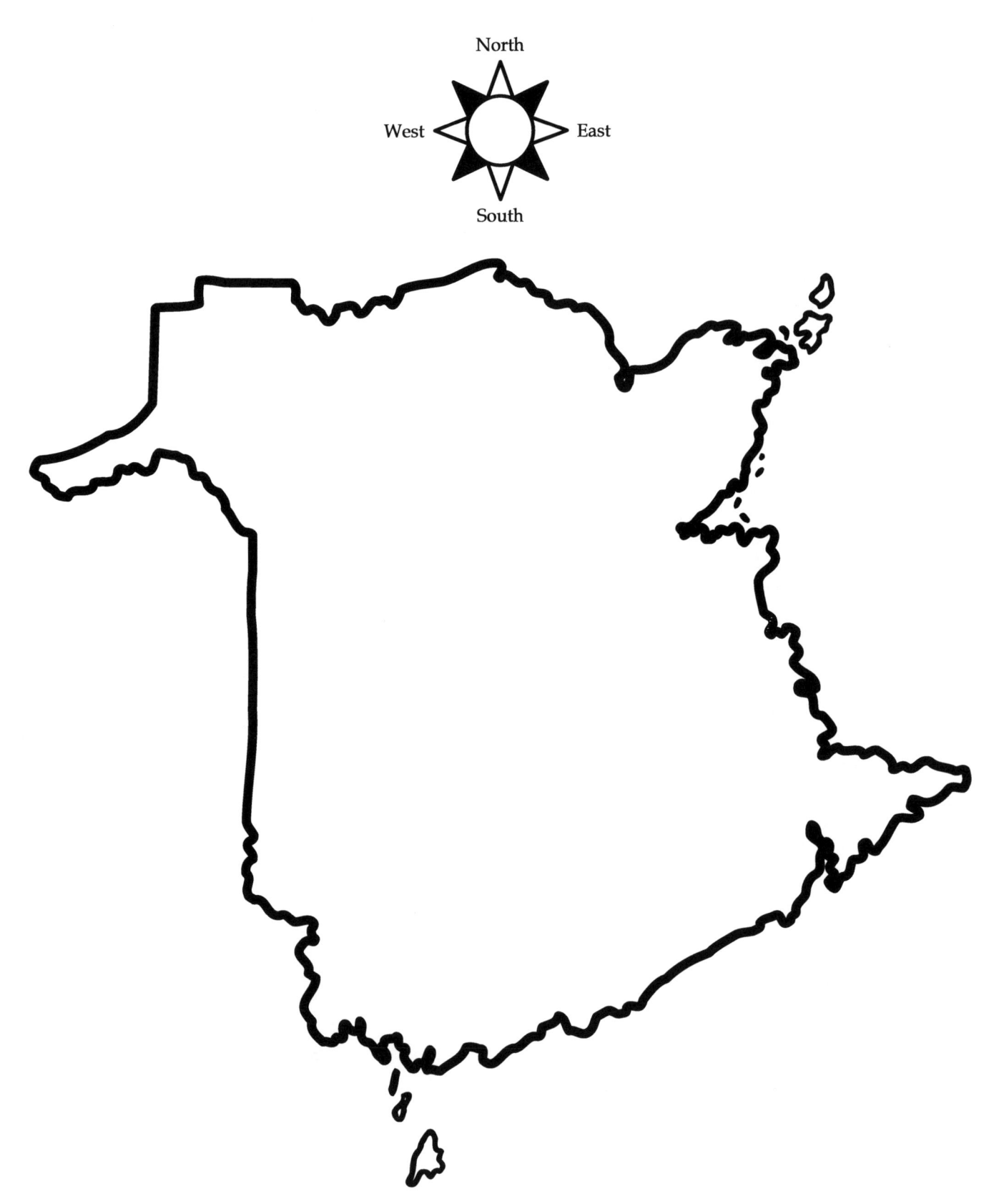

North
West
East
South

Maps are representations and boundaries are not exact.

Newfoundland & Labrador, Canada

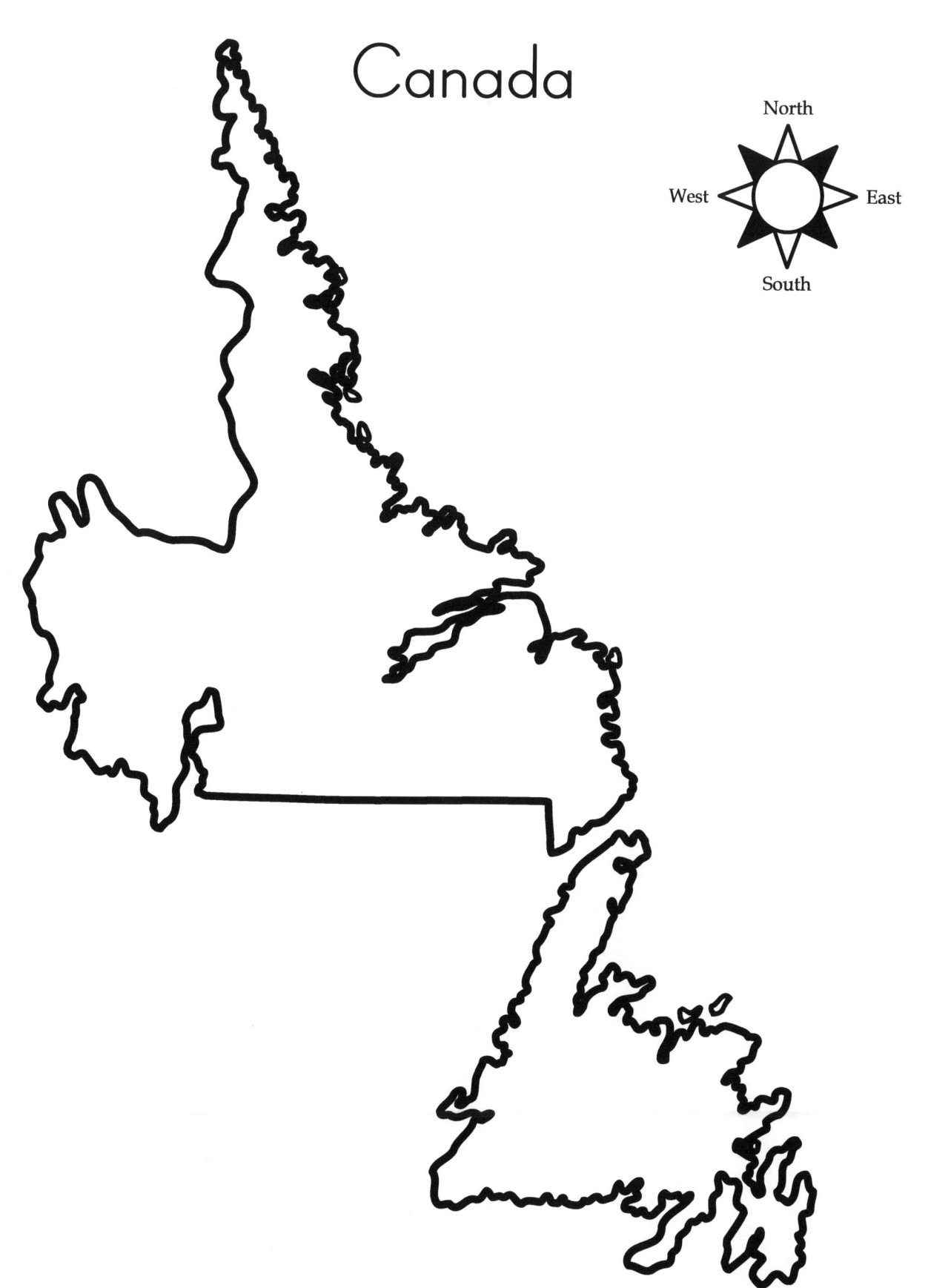

West — North — East — South

Maps are representations and boundaries are not exact.

New Hampshire, USA

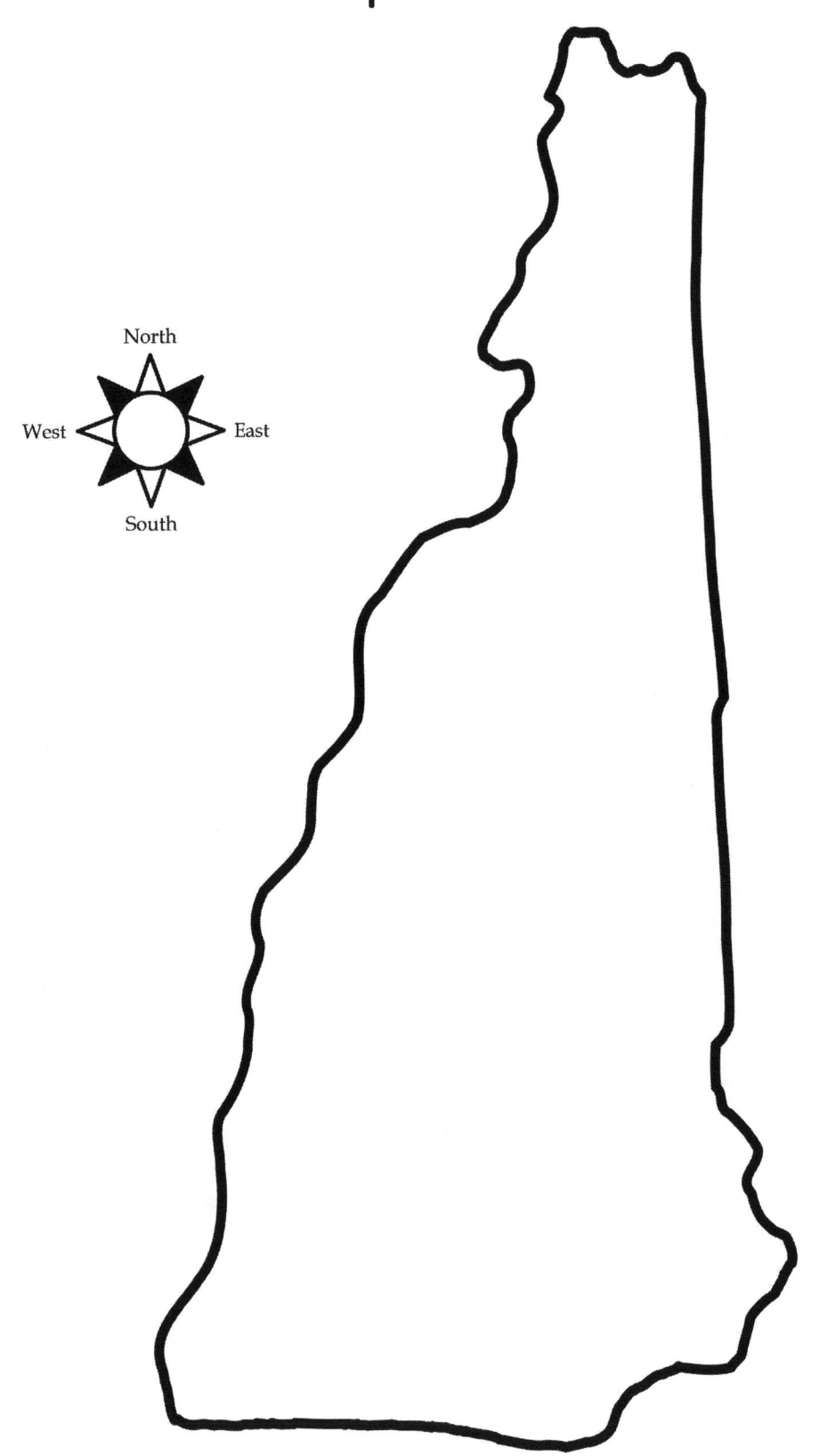

North
West East
South

Maps are representations and boundaries are not exact.

New Jersey, USA

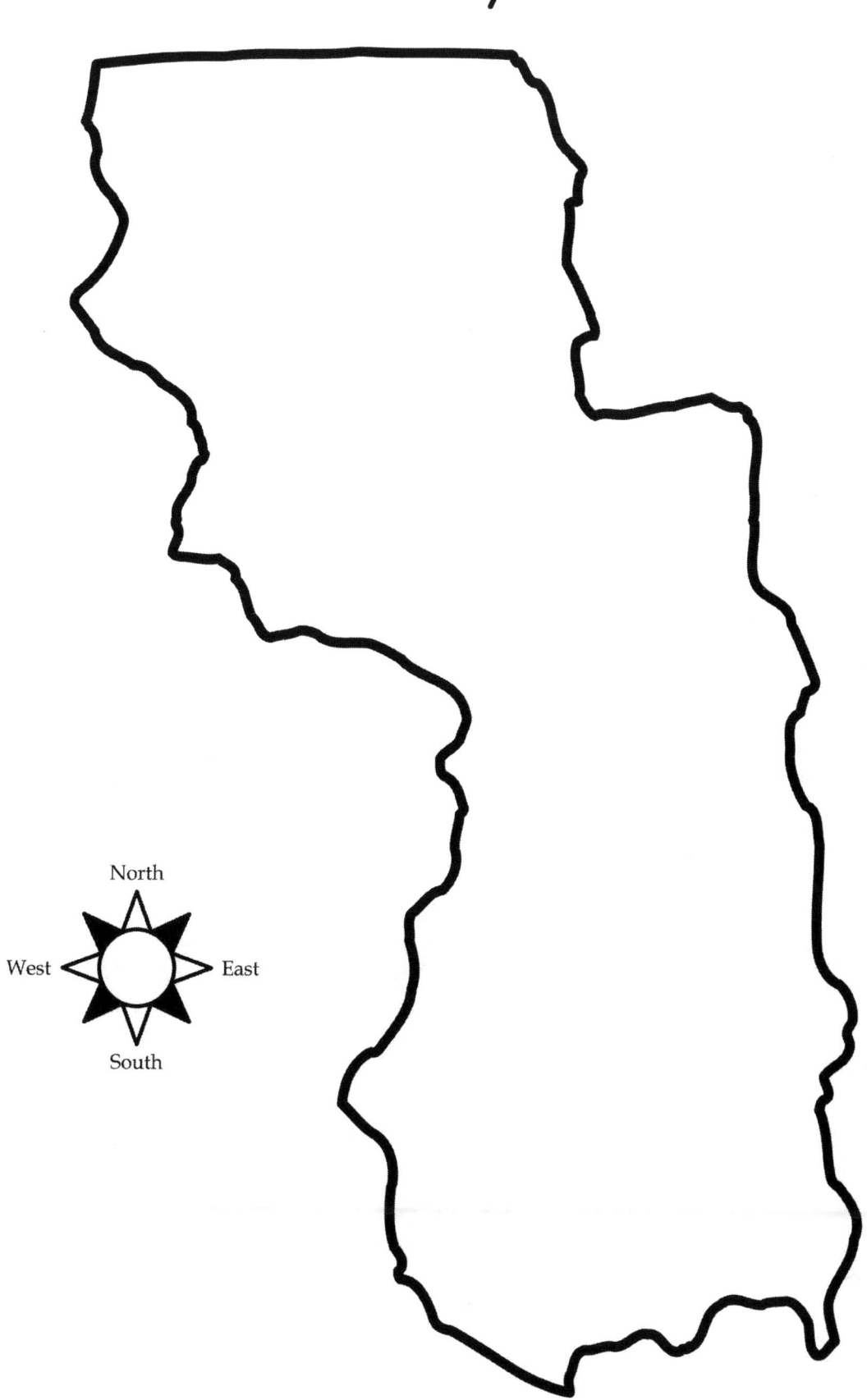

Maps are representations and boundaries are not exact.

New Mexico, USA

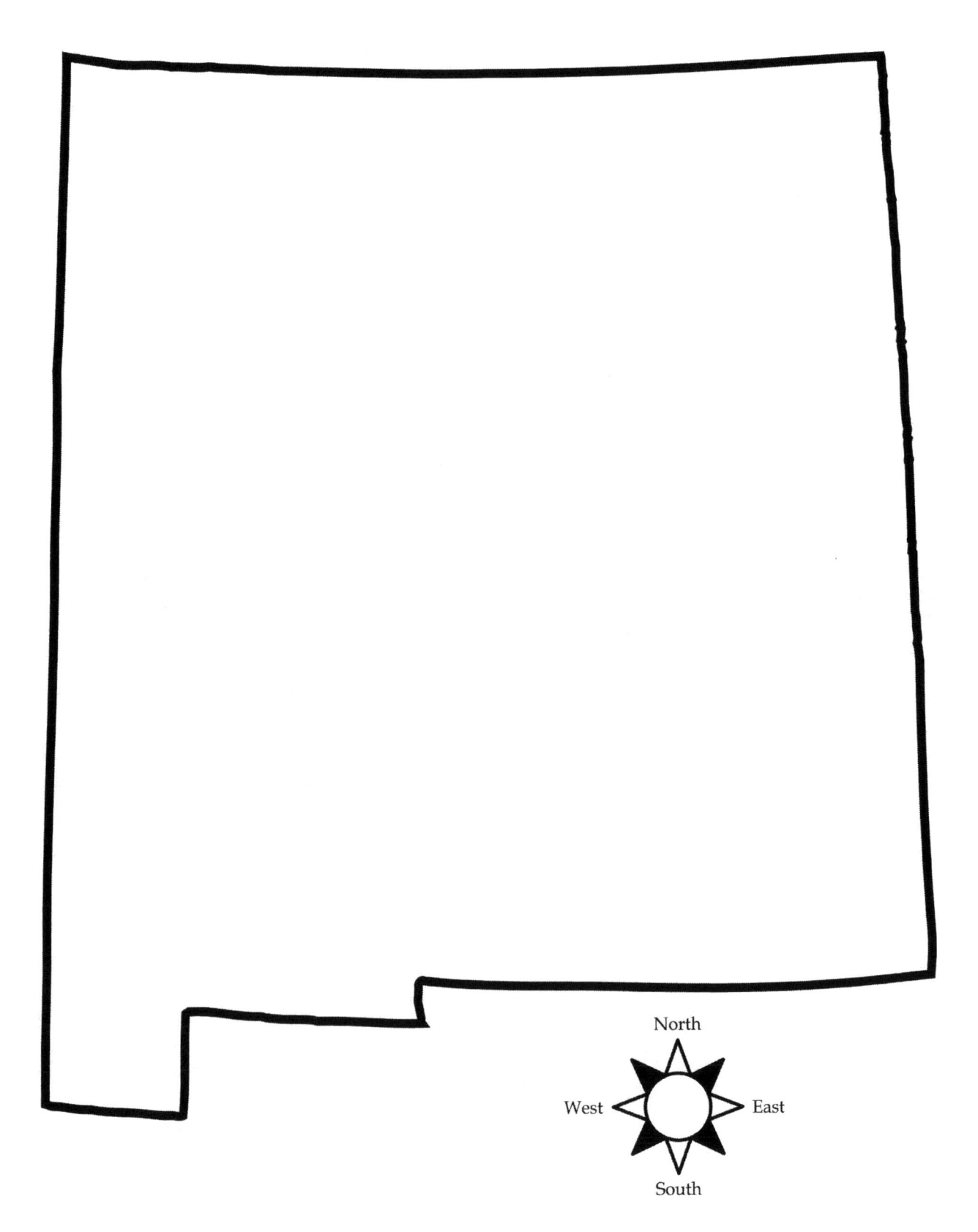

West — North — East — South

Maps are representations and boundaries are not exact.

newspaper (folded)

New York, USA

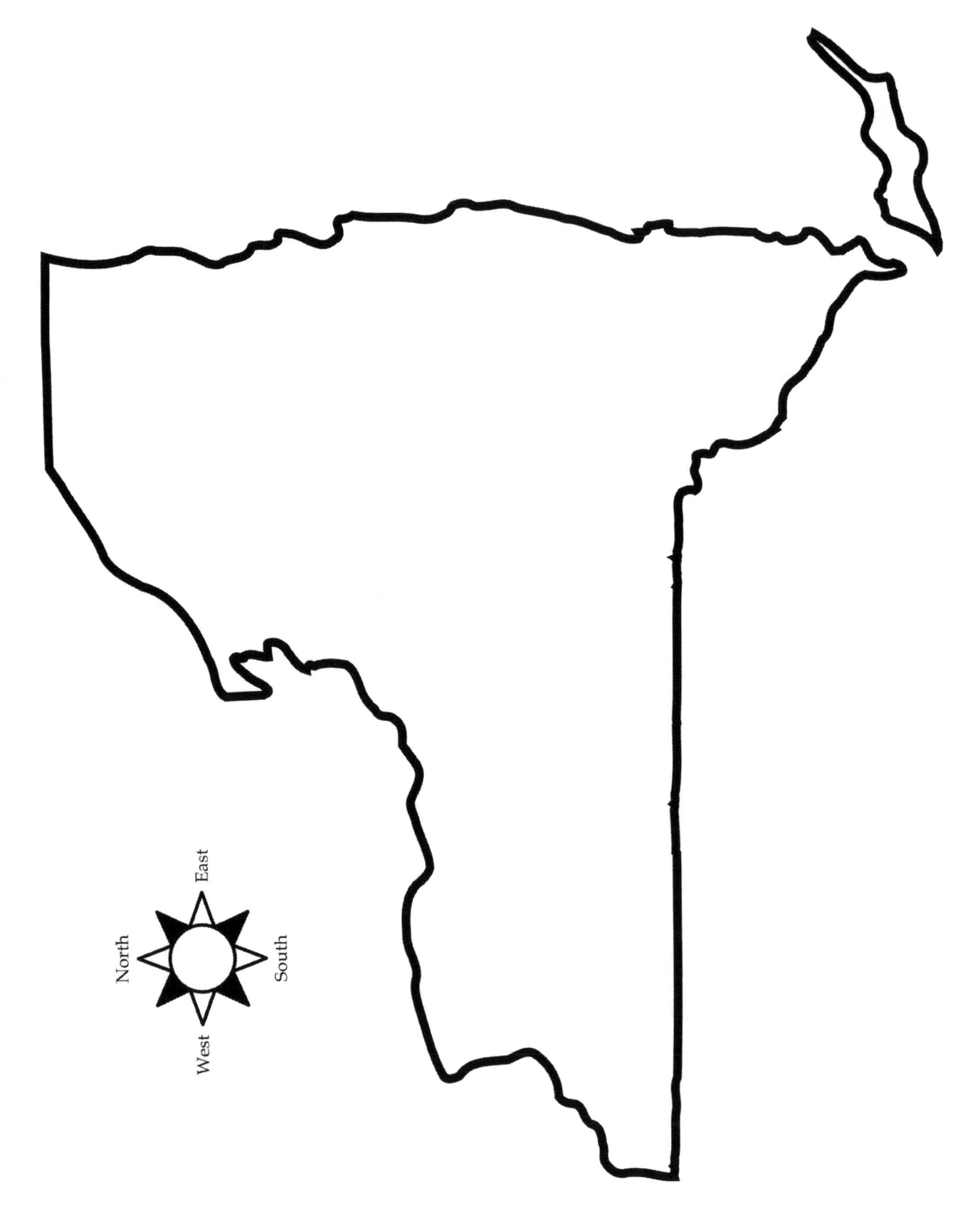

Maps are representations and boundaries are not exact.

newt

nickels

North America

North
West East
South

Maps are representations and boundaries are not exact.

North Carolina, USA

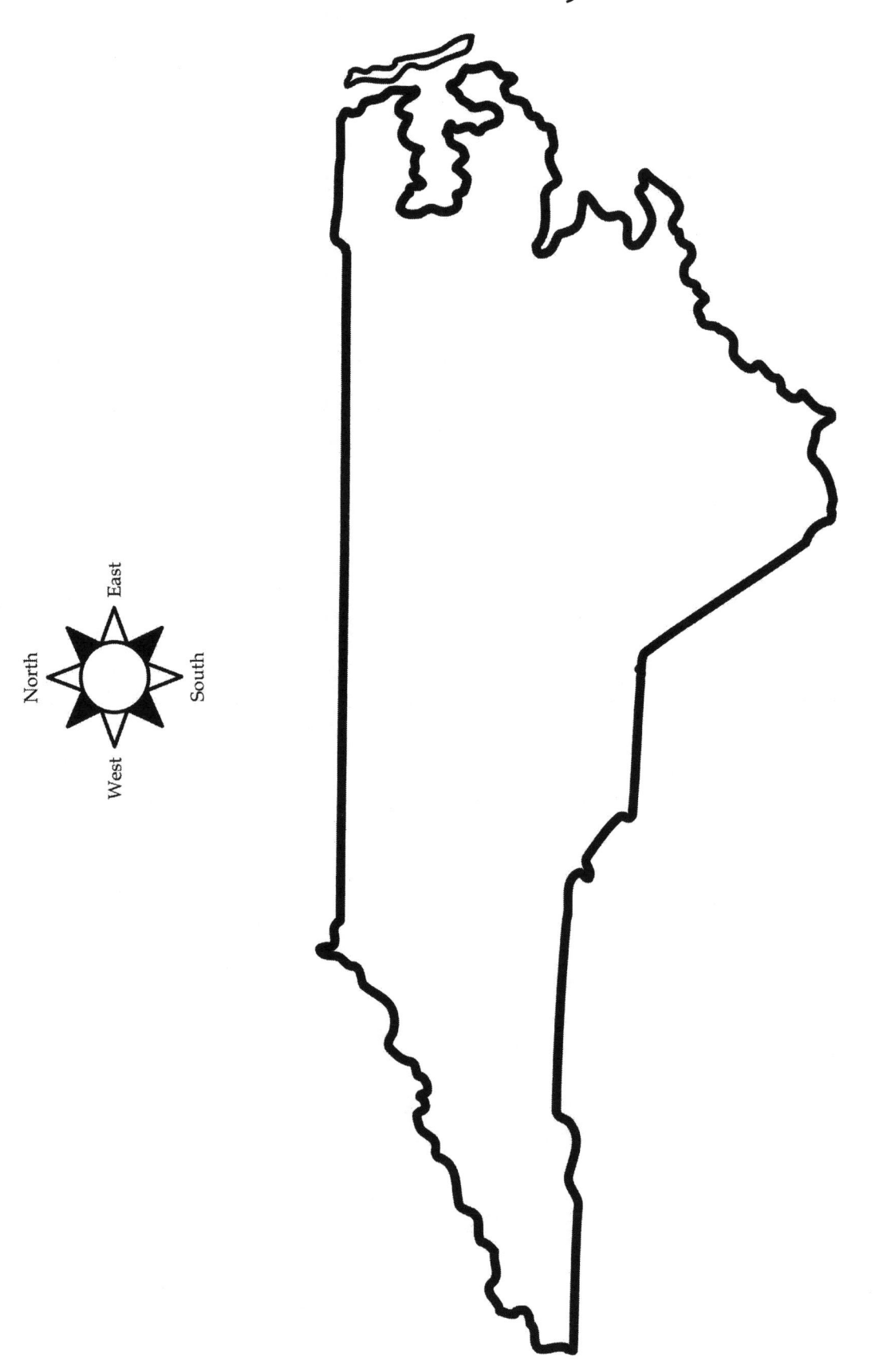

Maps are representations and boundaries are not exact.

North Dakota, USA

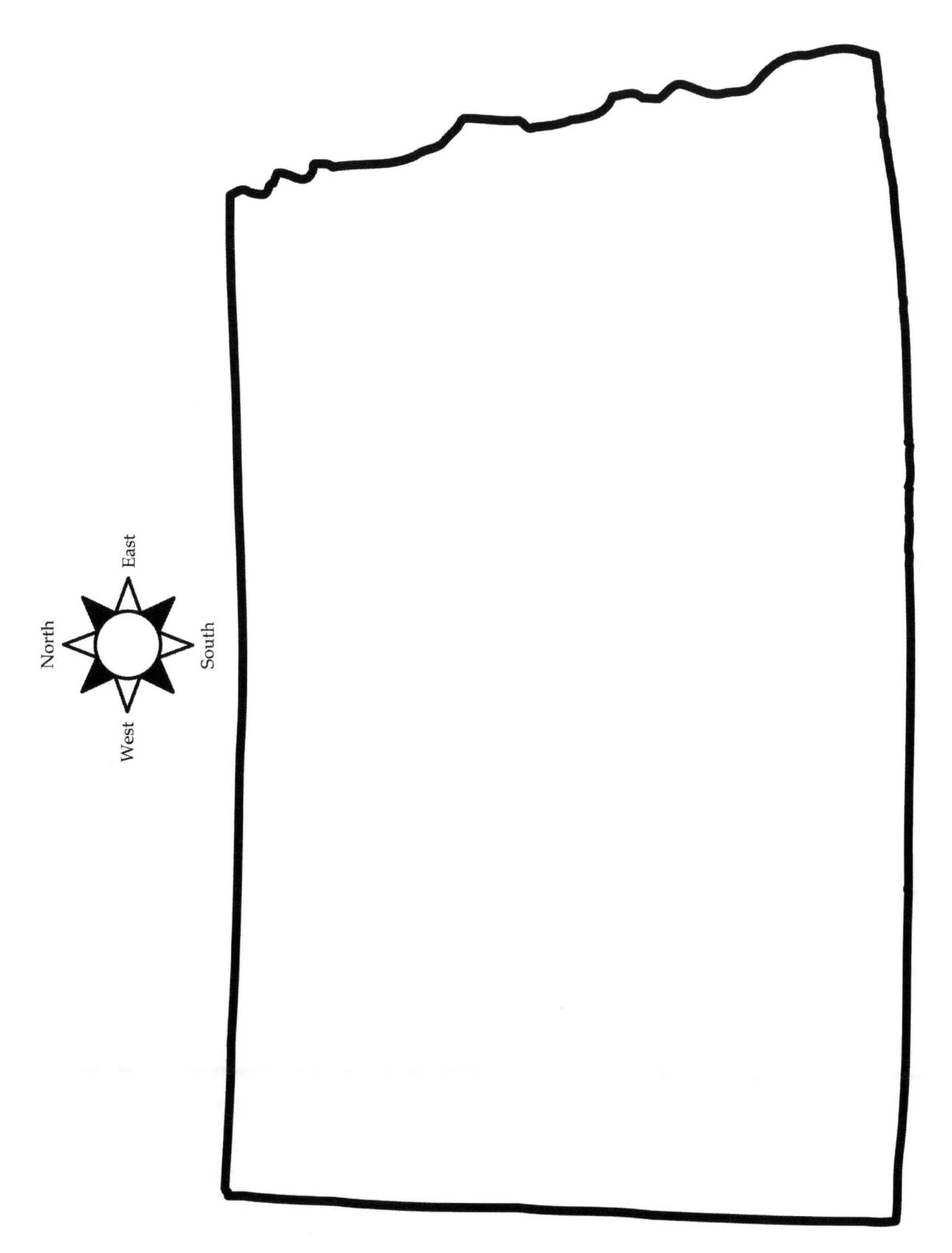

North
East
South
West

Maps are representations and boundaries are not exact.

LAB201412P • THE PATTERN LIBRARY • VOLUME TWO • I-Z • 978-1-937257-63-7 • © 2014 Little Acorn Books™

Northern Territory & Nunavut, Canada

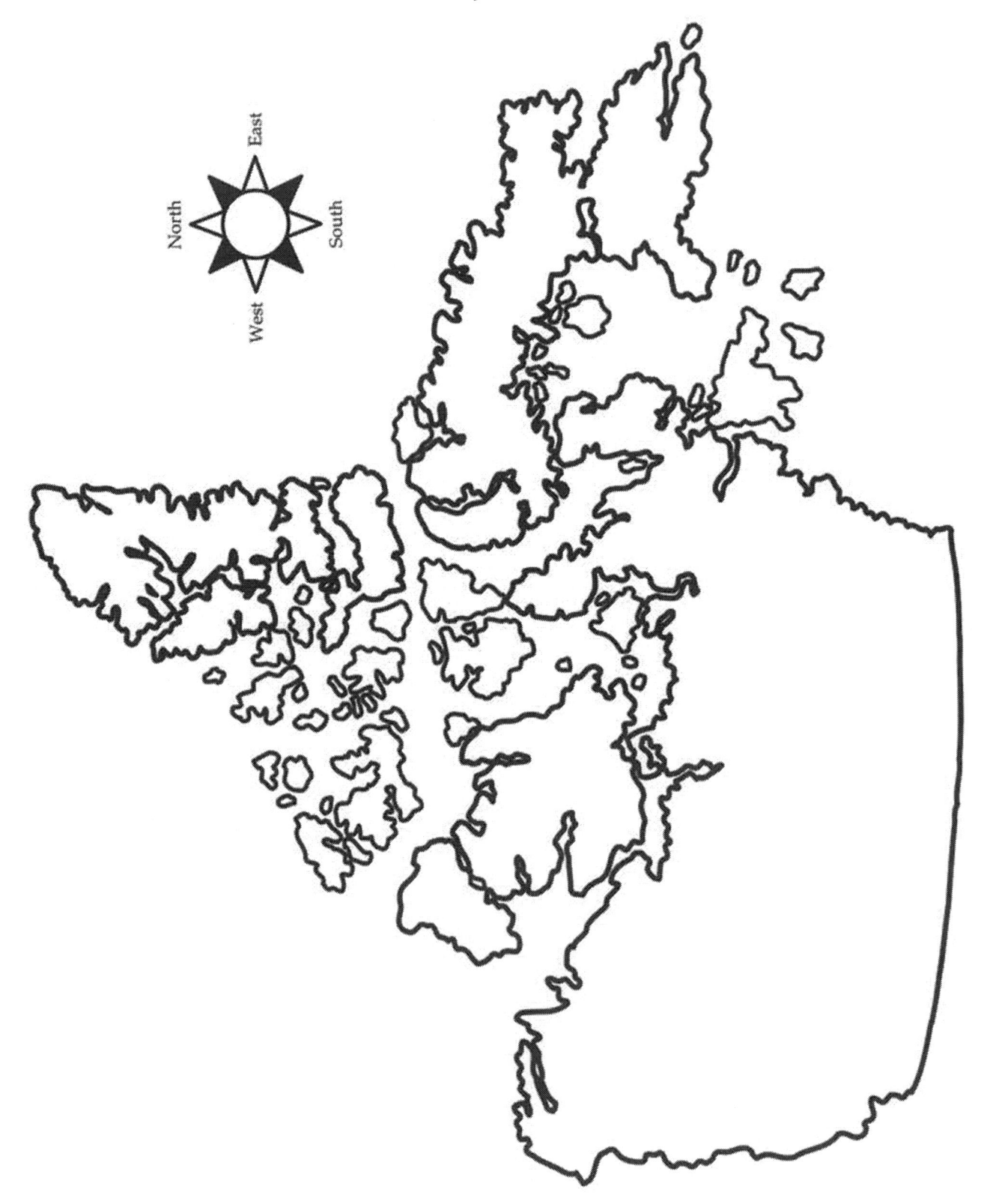

Maps are representations and boundaries are not exact.

Nova Scotia, Canada

Maps are representations and boundaries are not exact.

octopus (floating)

octopus (poster)

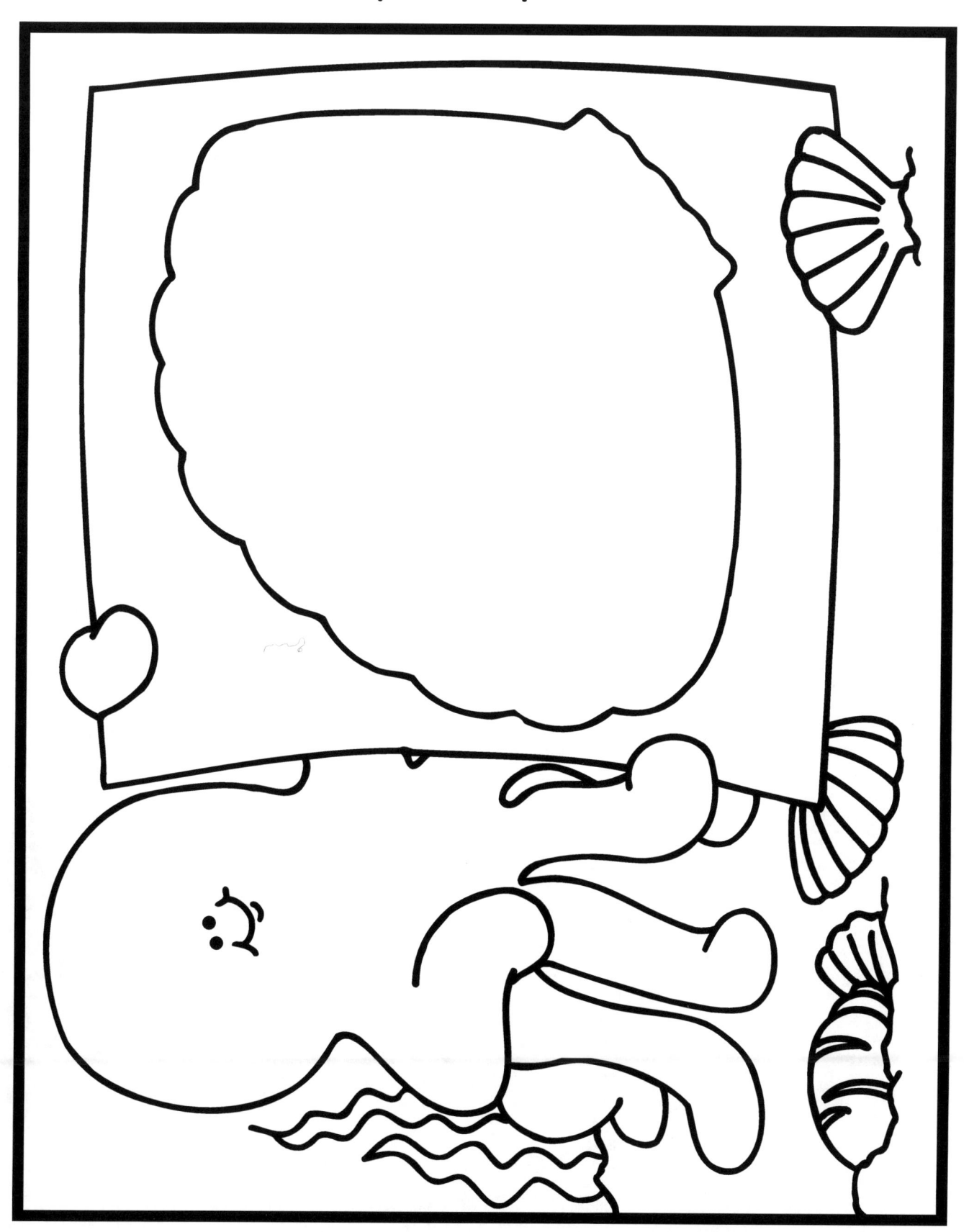

octopus (sitting)

Ohio, USA

North
West   East
South

Maps are representations and boundaries are not exact.

LAB201412P • THE PATTERN LIBRARY • VOLUME TWO • I-Z • 978-1-937257-63-7 • © 2014 Little Acorn Books™

okapi

Oklahoma, USA

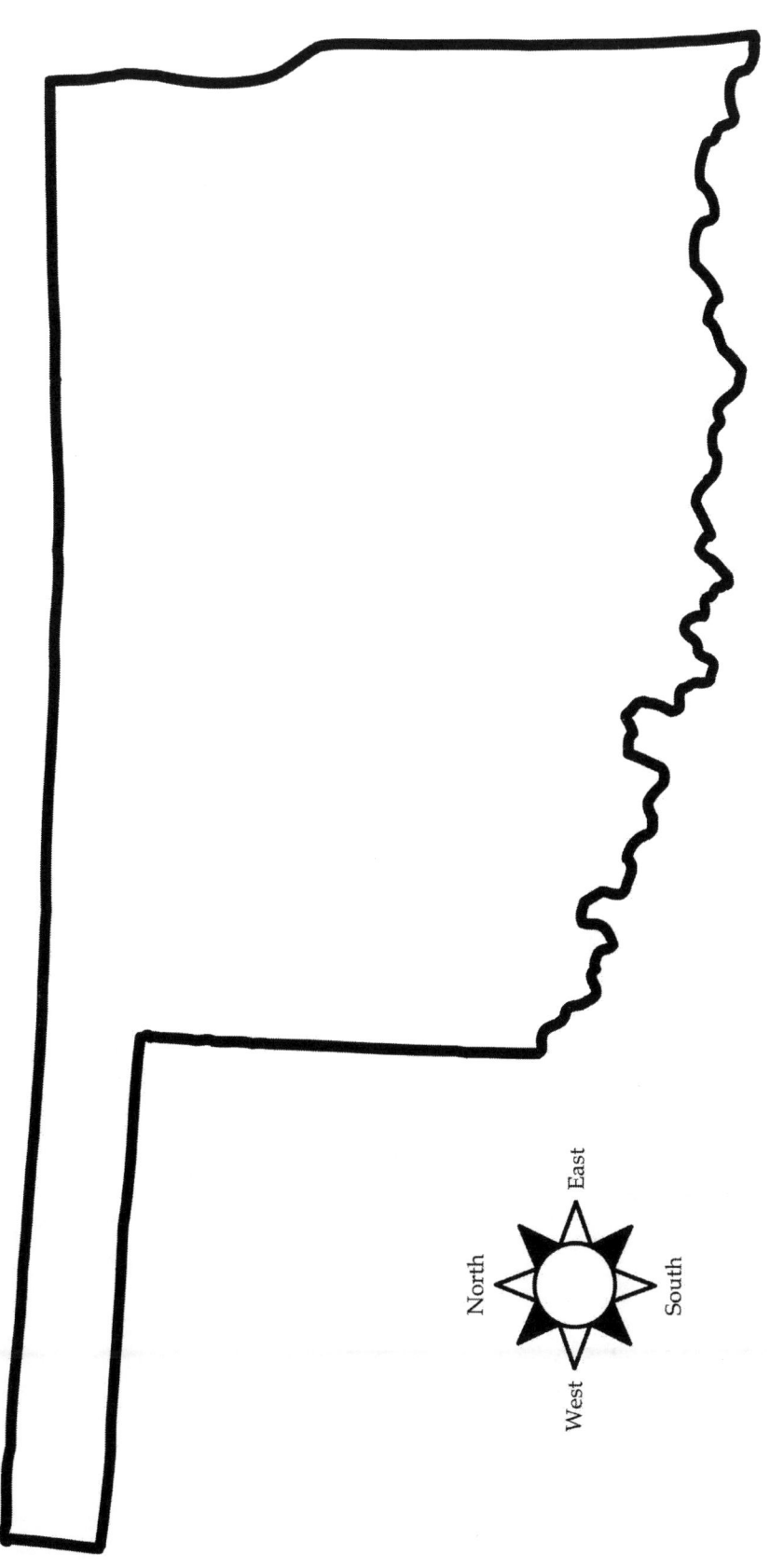

Maps are representations and boundaries are not exact.

onion (spring)

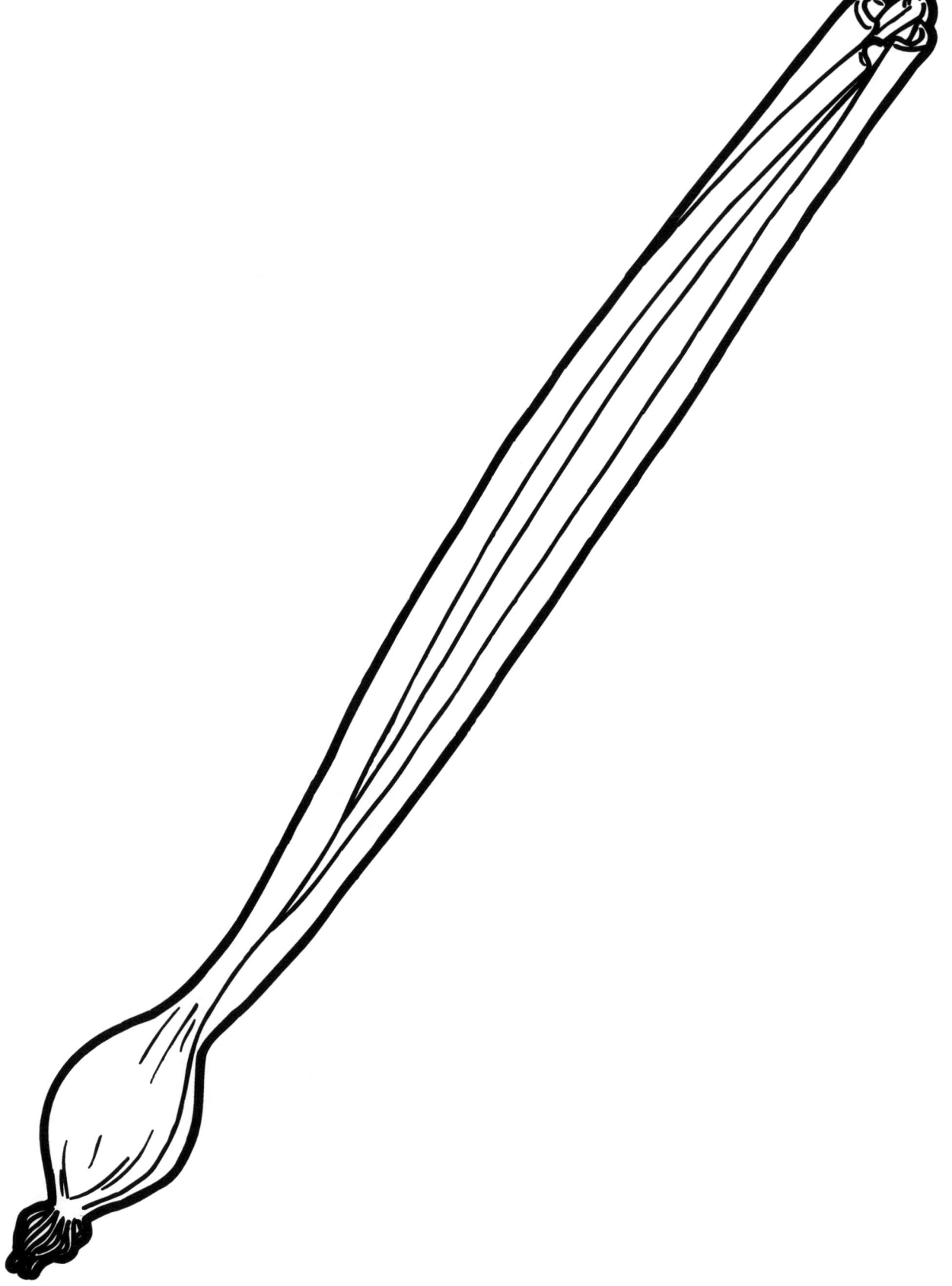

Ontario, Canada

Maps are representations and boundaries are not exact.

orangutan

Oregon, USA

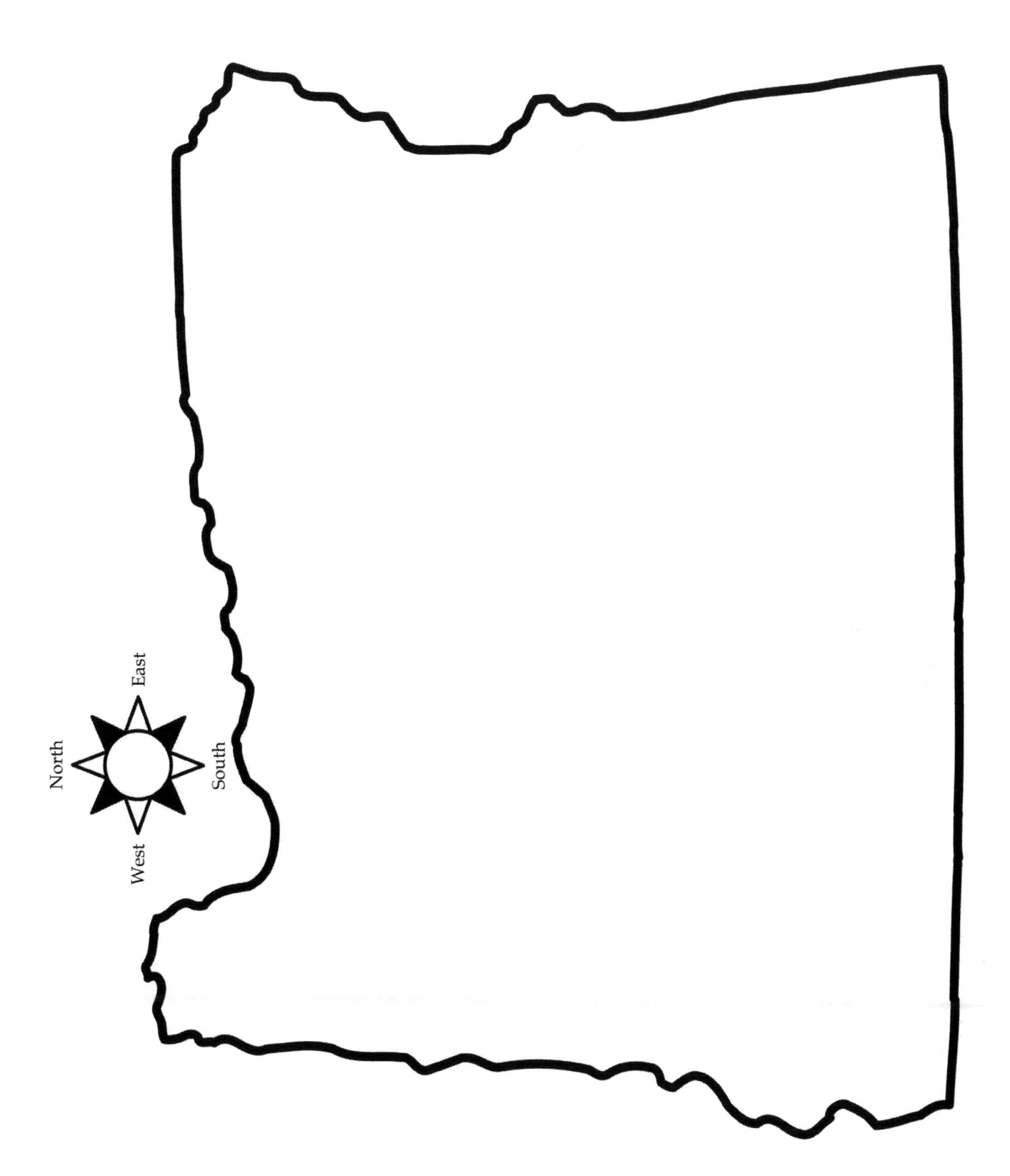

Maps are representations and boundaries are not exact.

ornament (pear-shape)

ornament (round)

ostrich

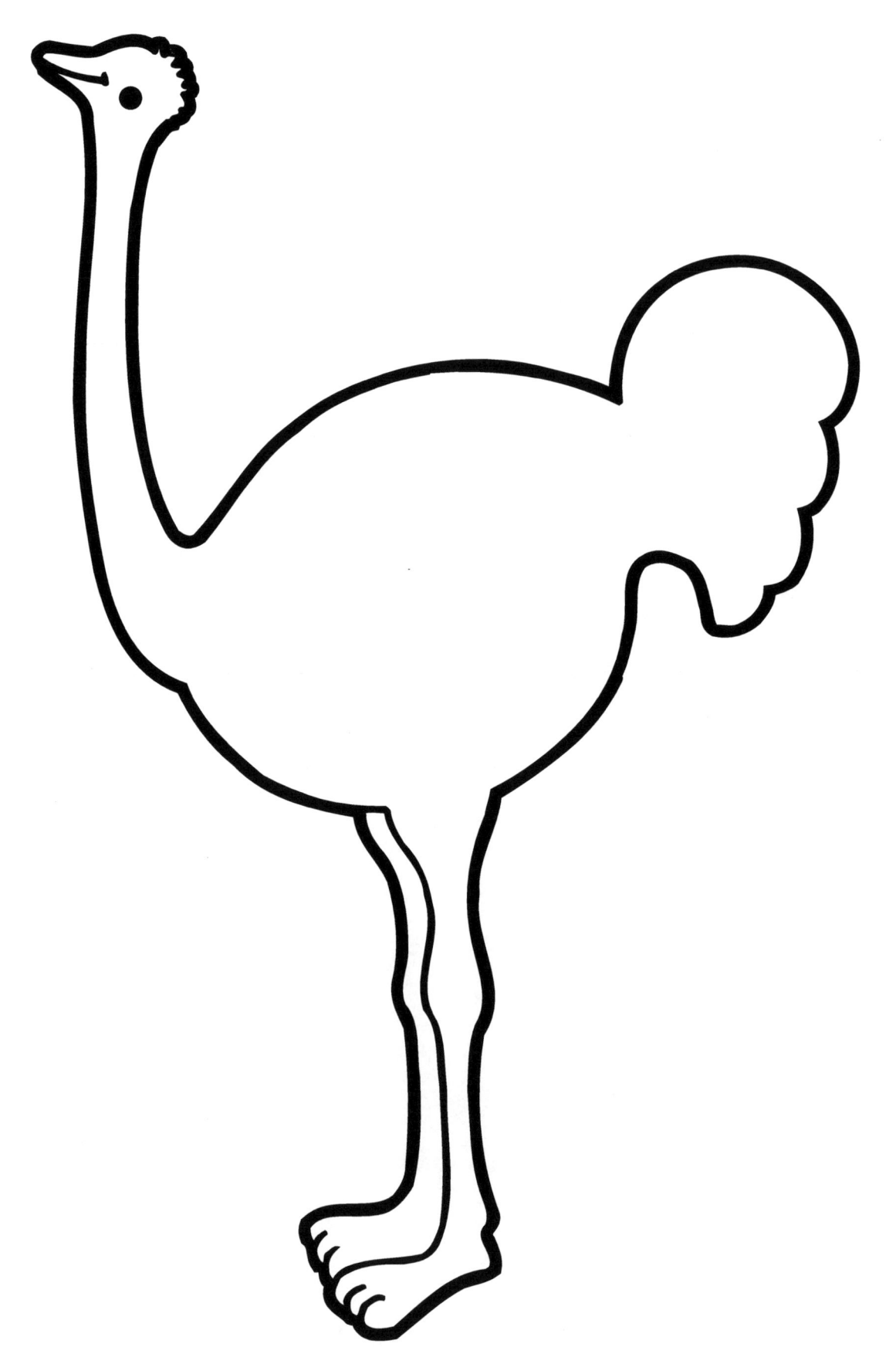

otter

overalls

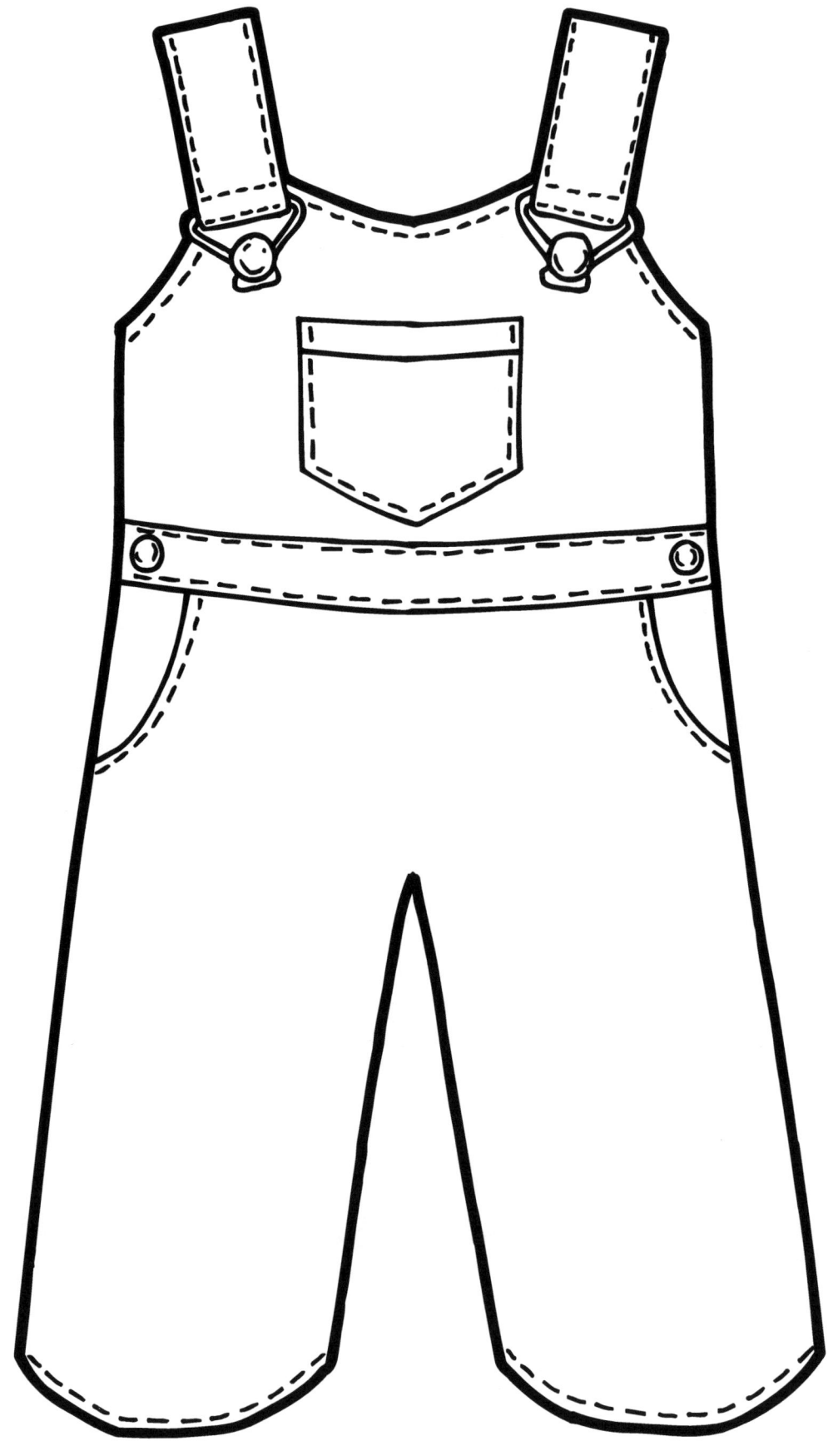

owl

ox (musk)

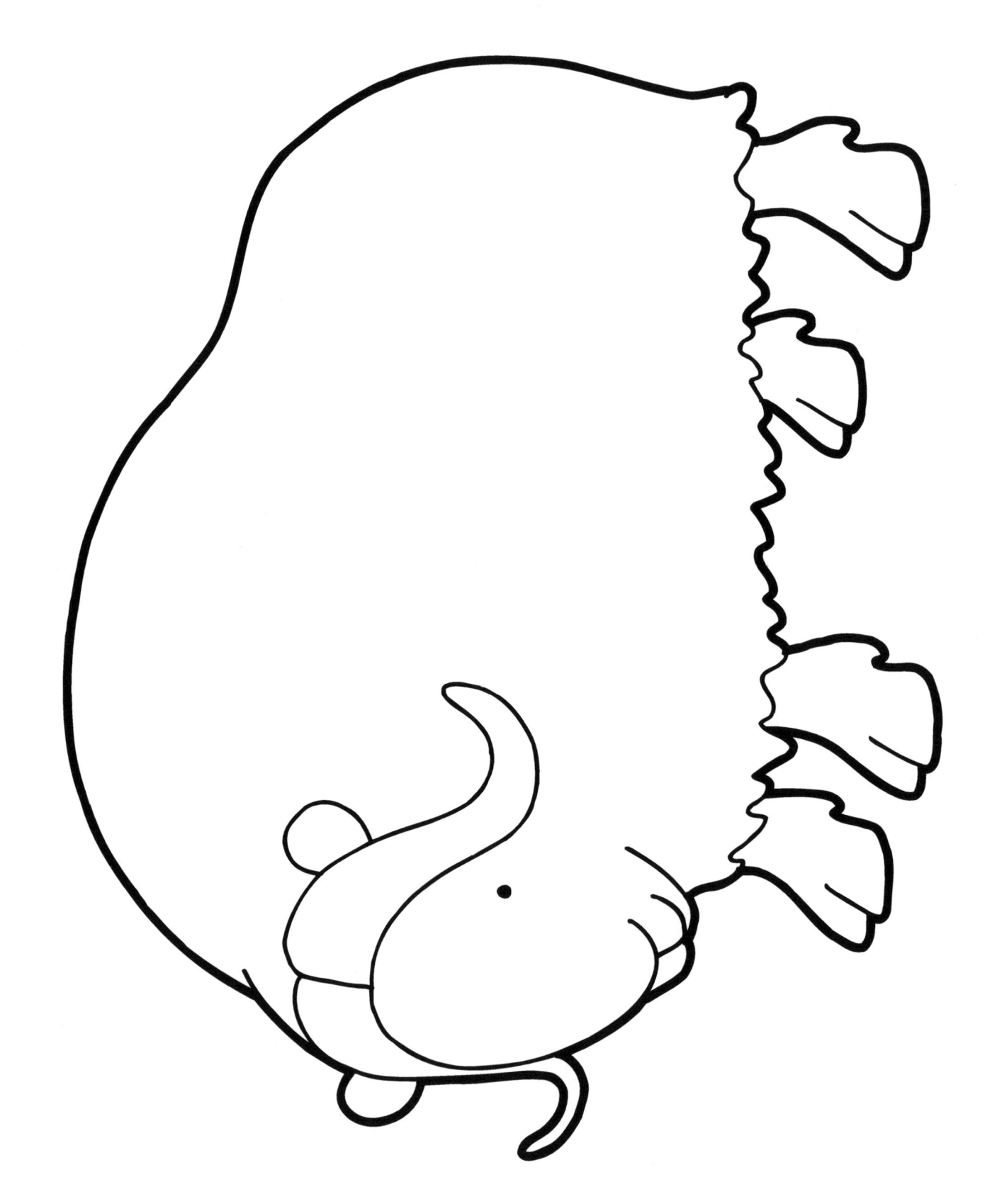

pail (handle down)

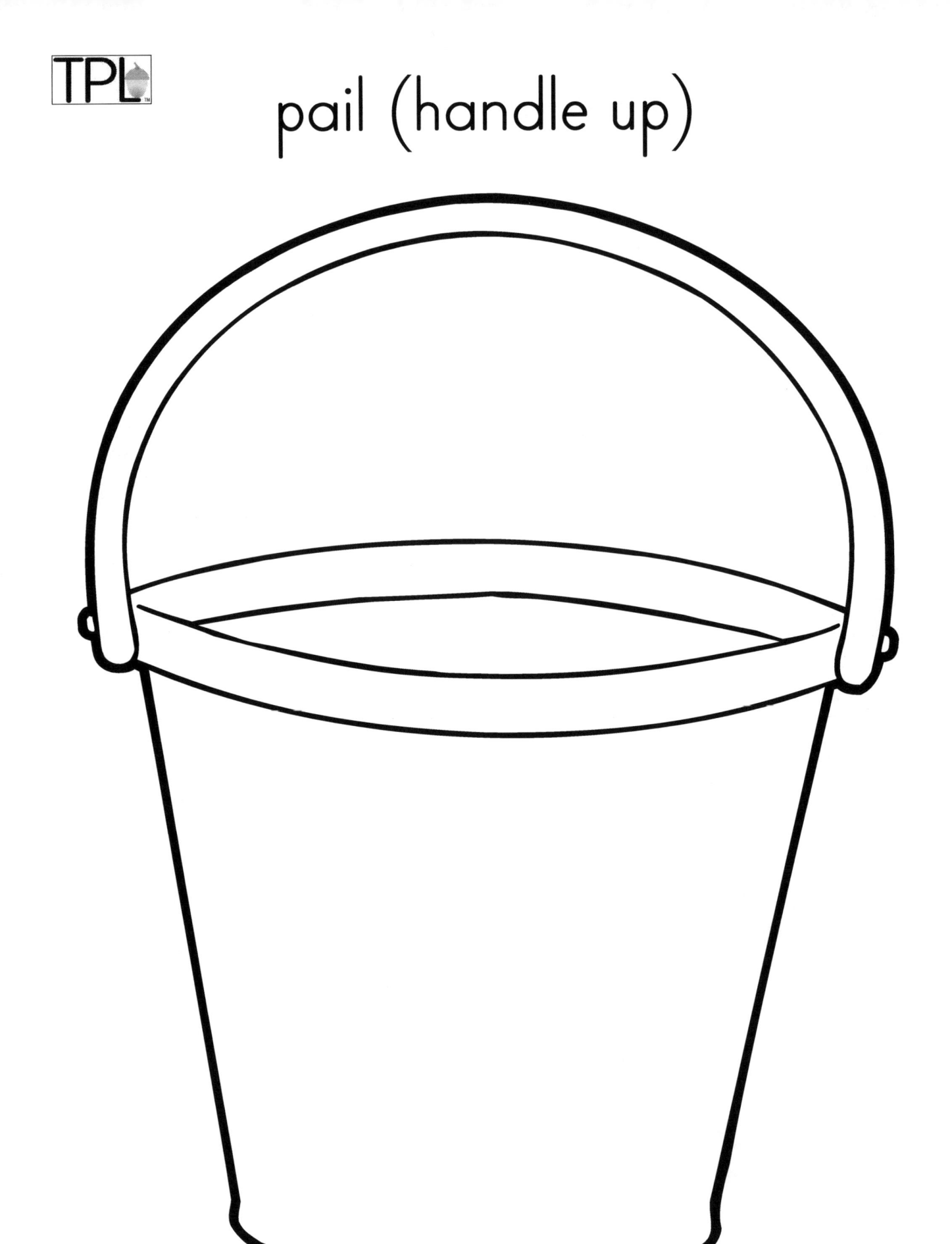

pail (handle up)

paintbrush (plain)

paintbrush (wide)

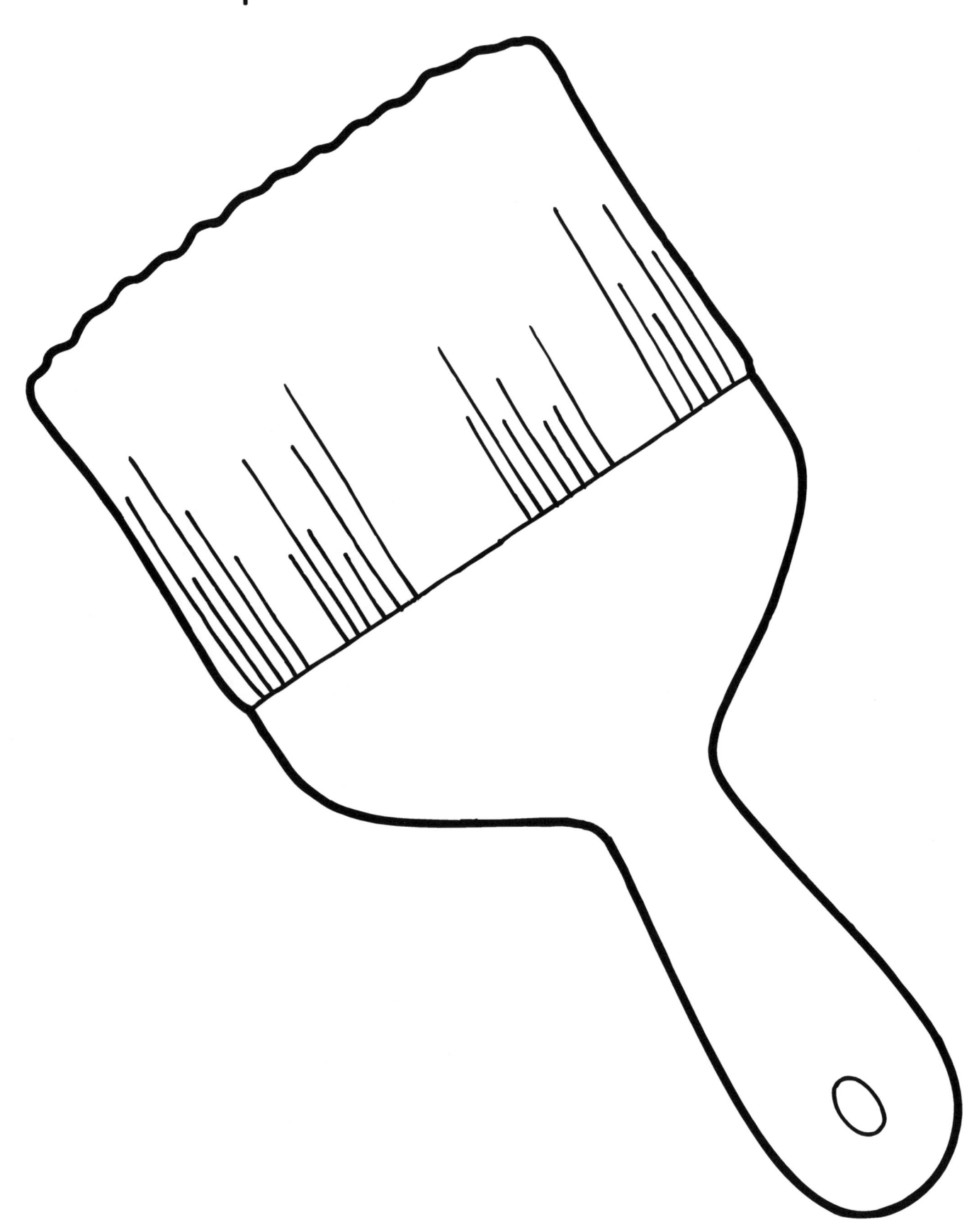

paintbrushes (art)

palette (outline)

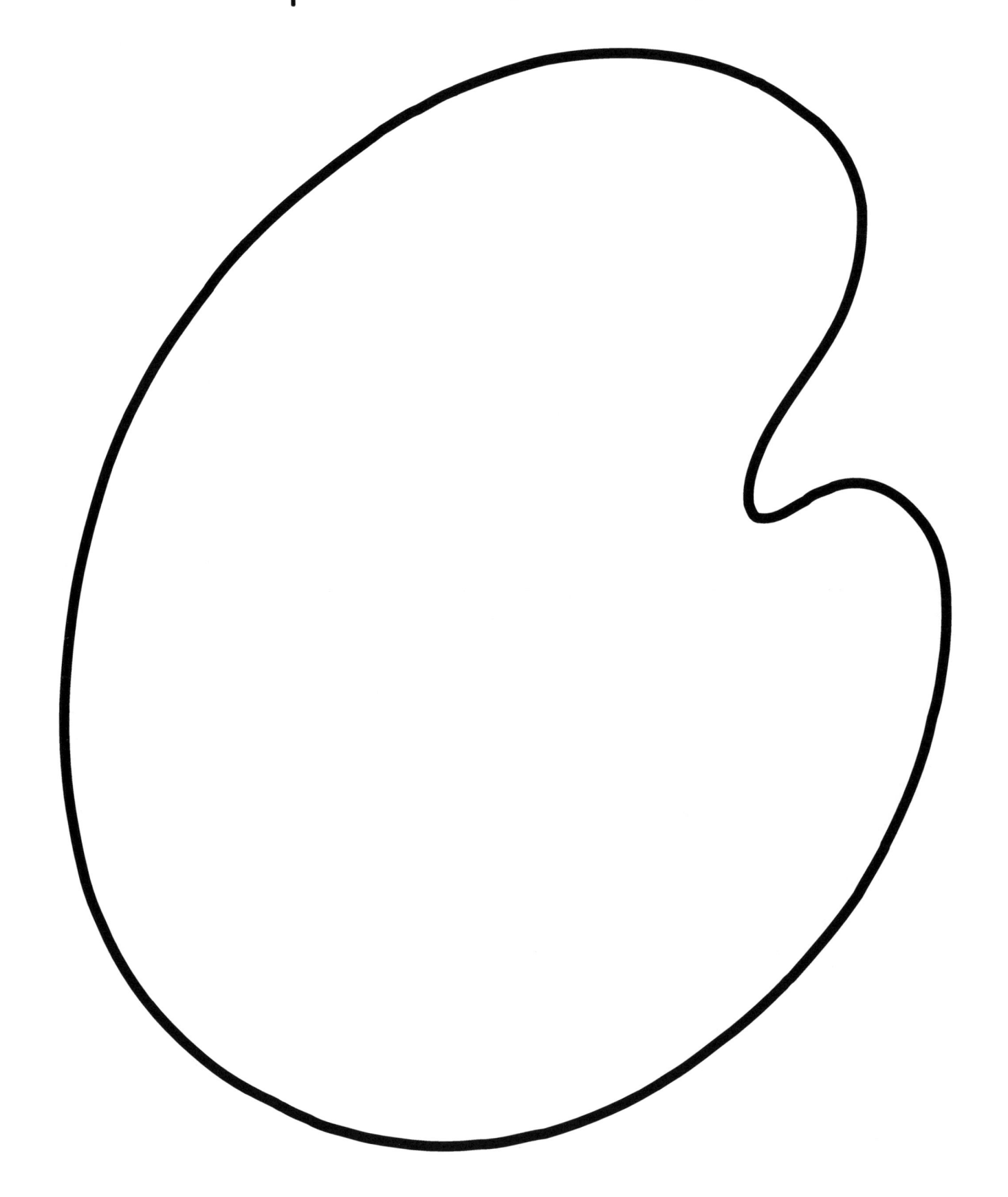

palette (with paint daubs)

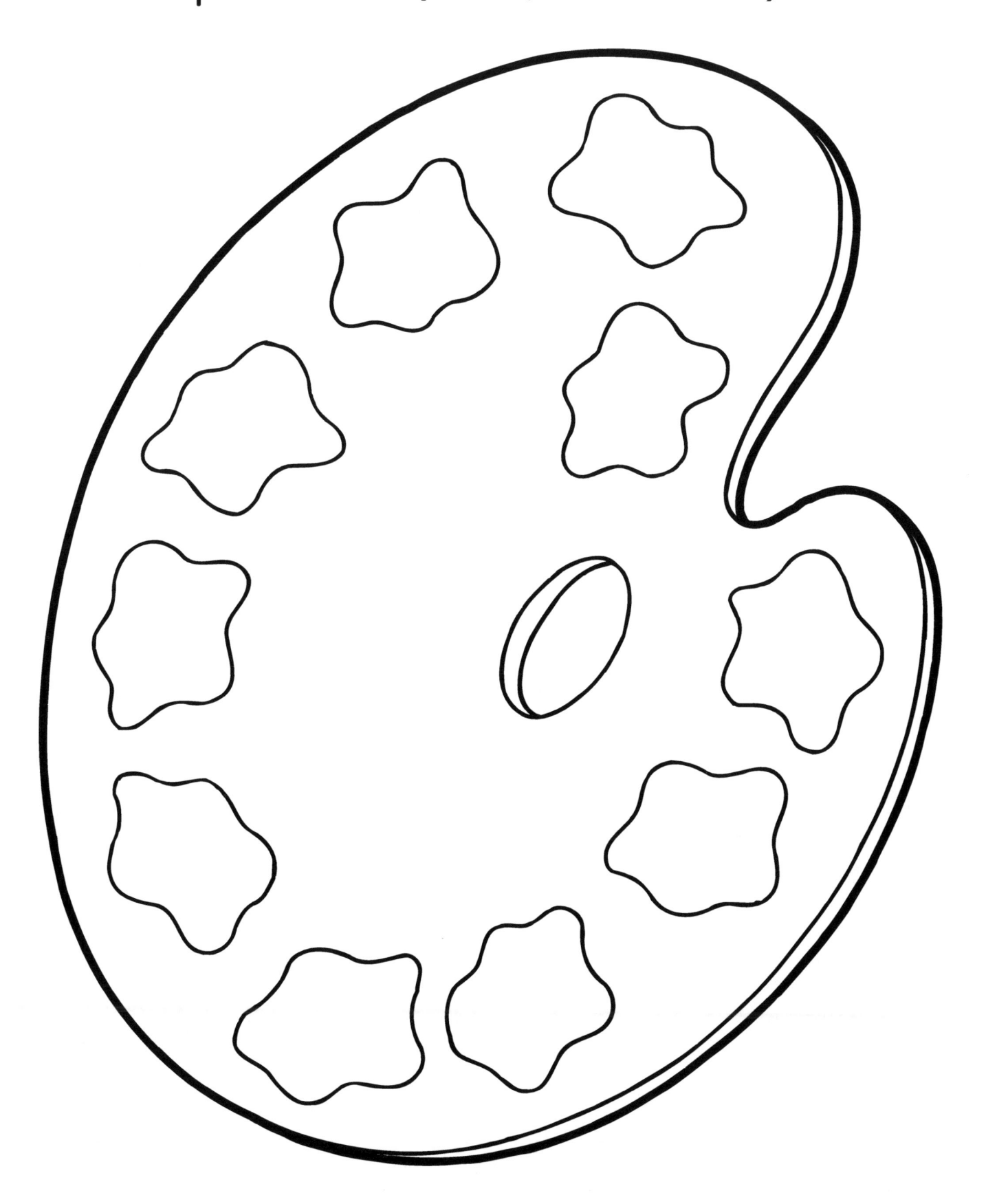

pan (frying)

papaya

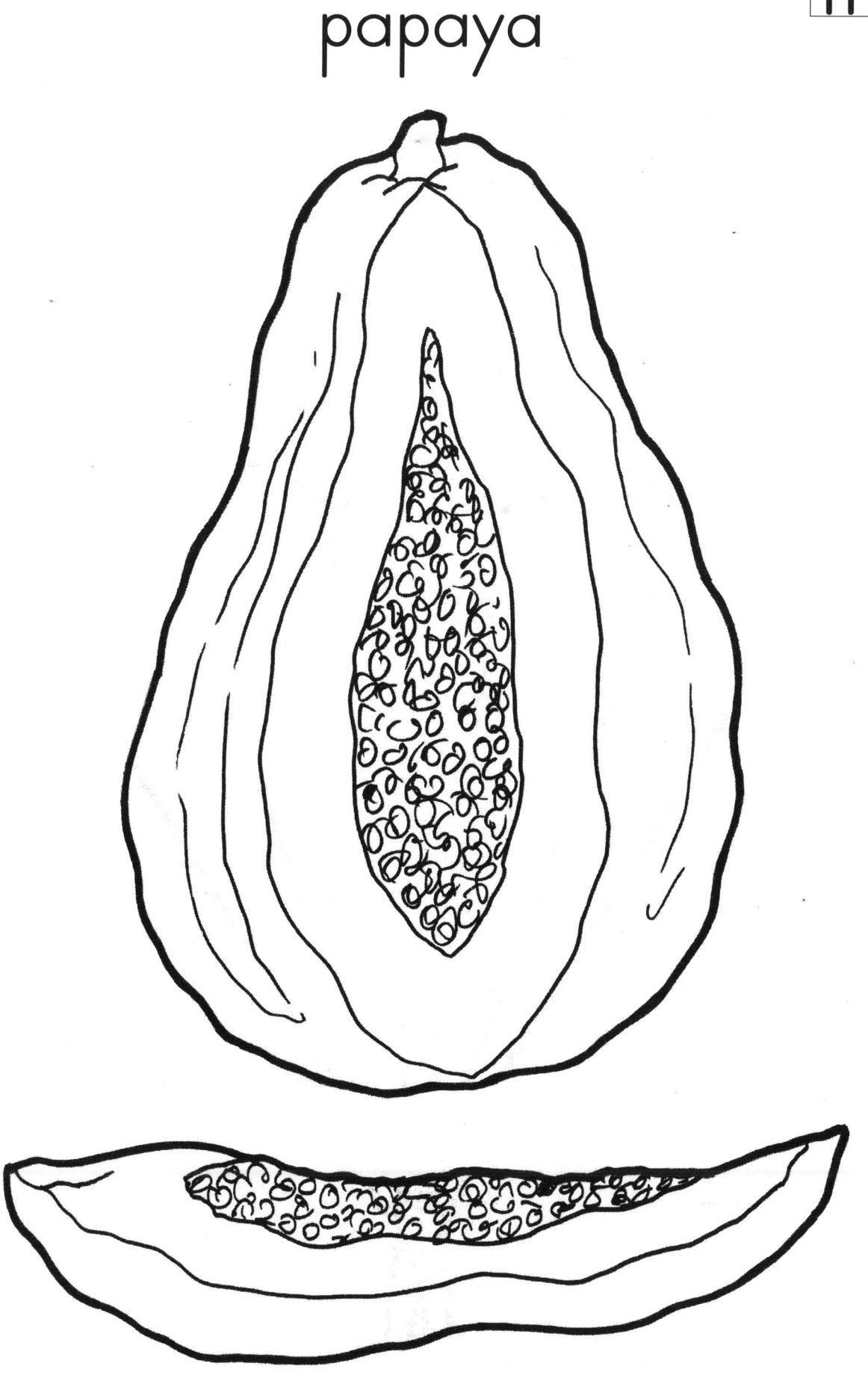

paper plate

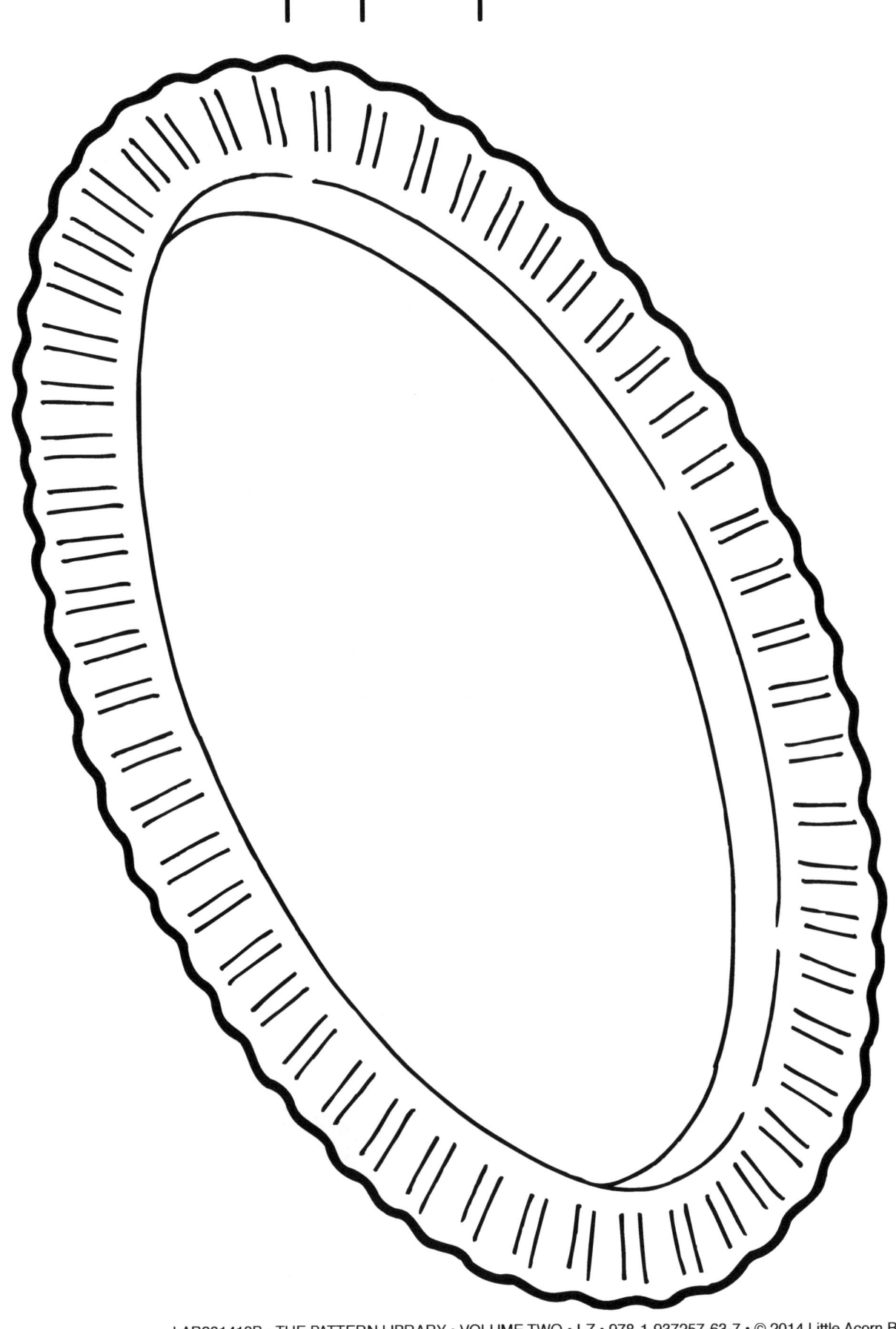

parchment (scroll)

parachute

parrot

paste (jar)

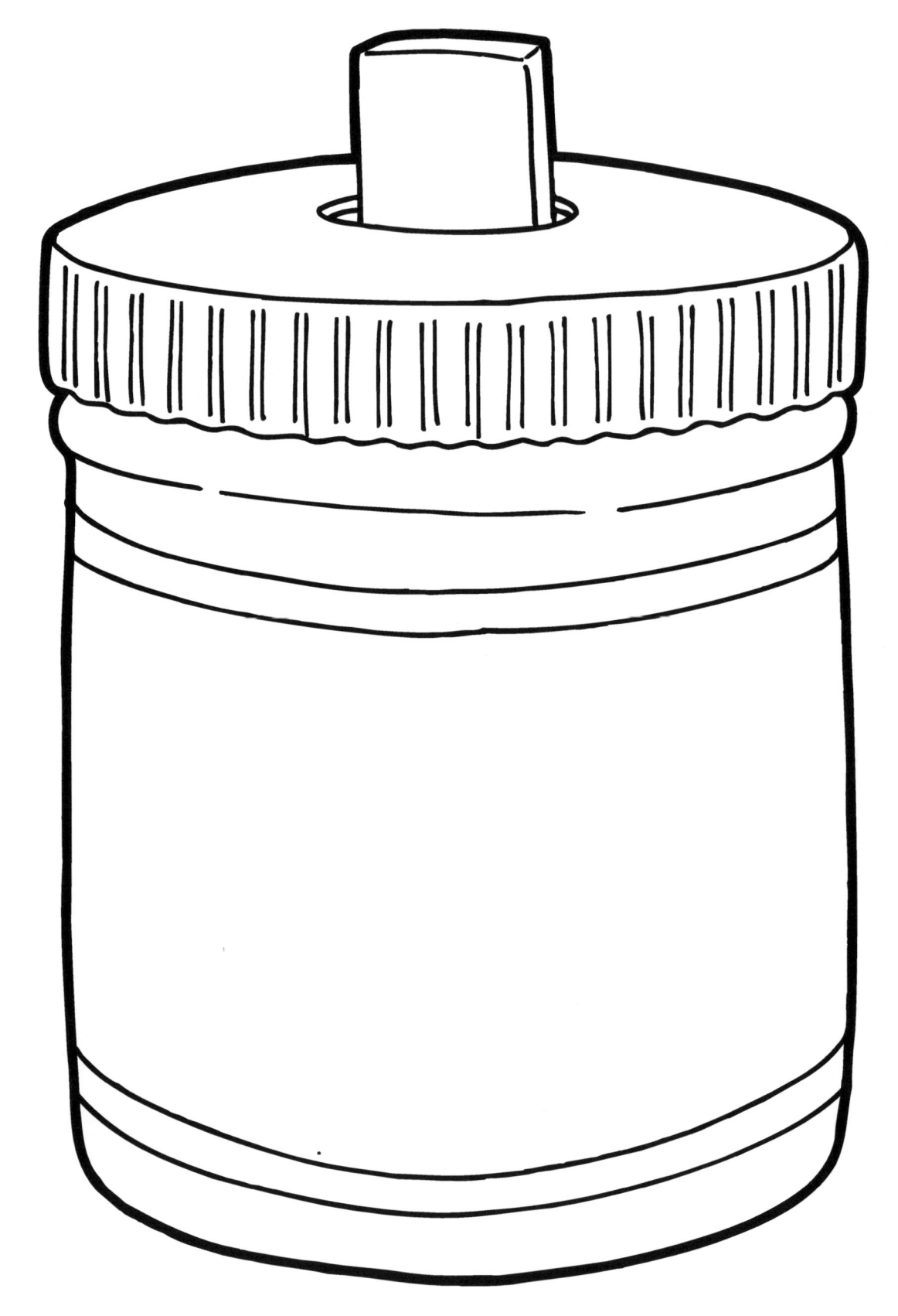

peanut

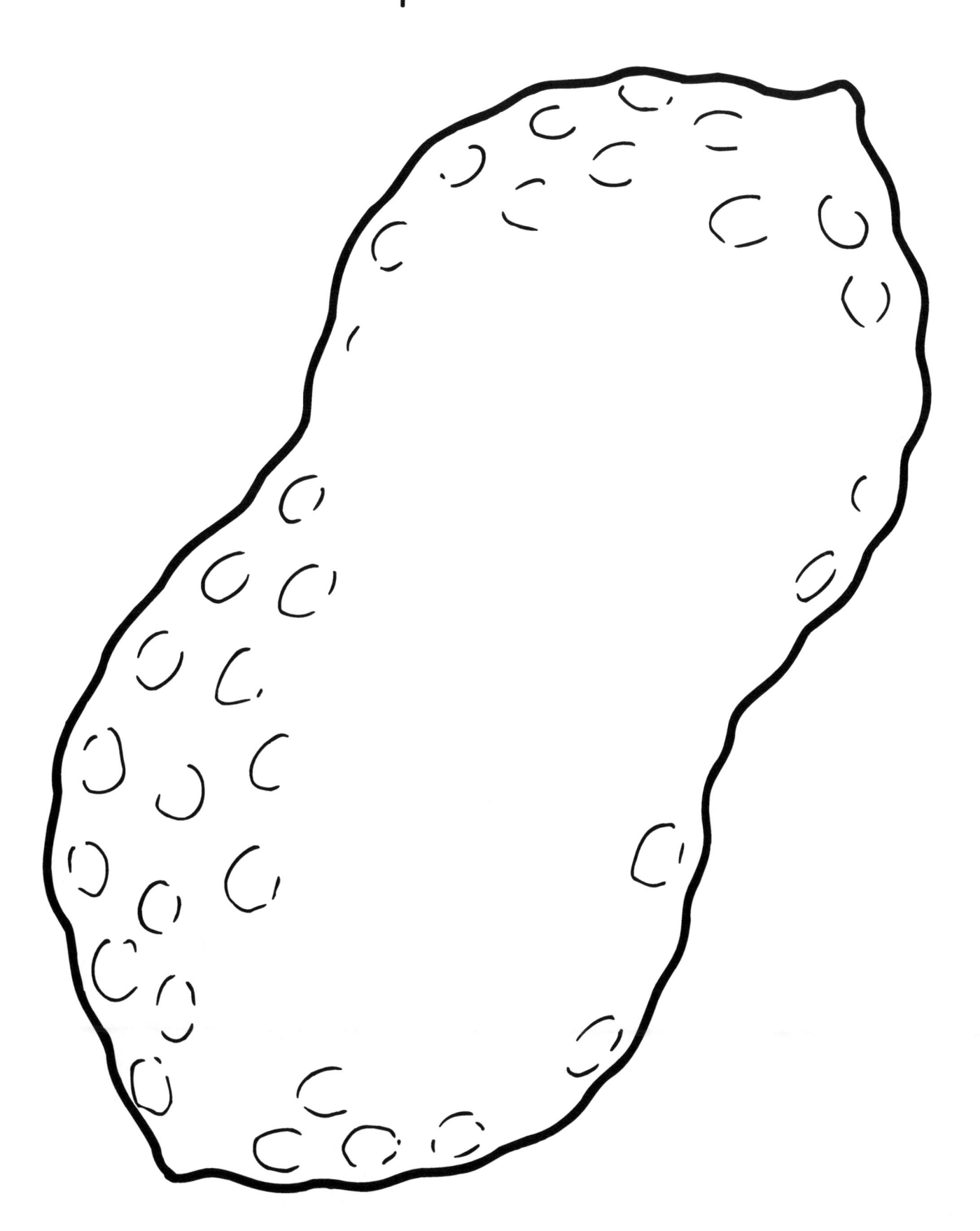

pear

peas

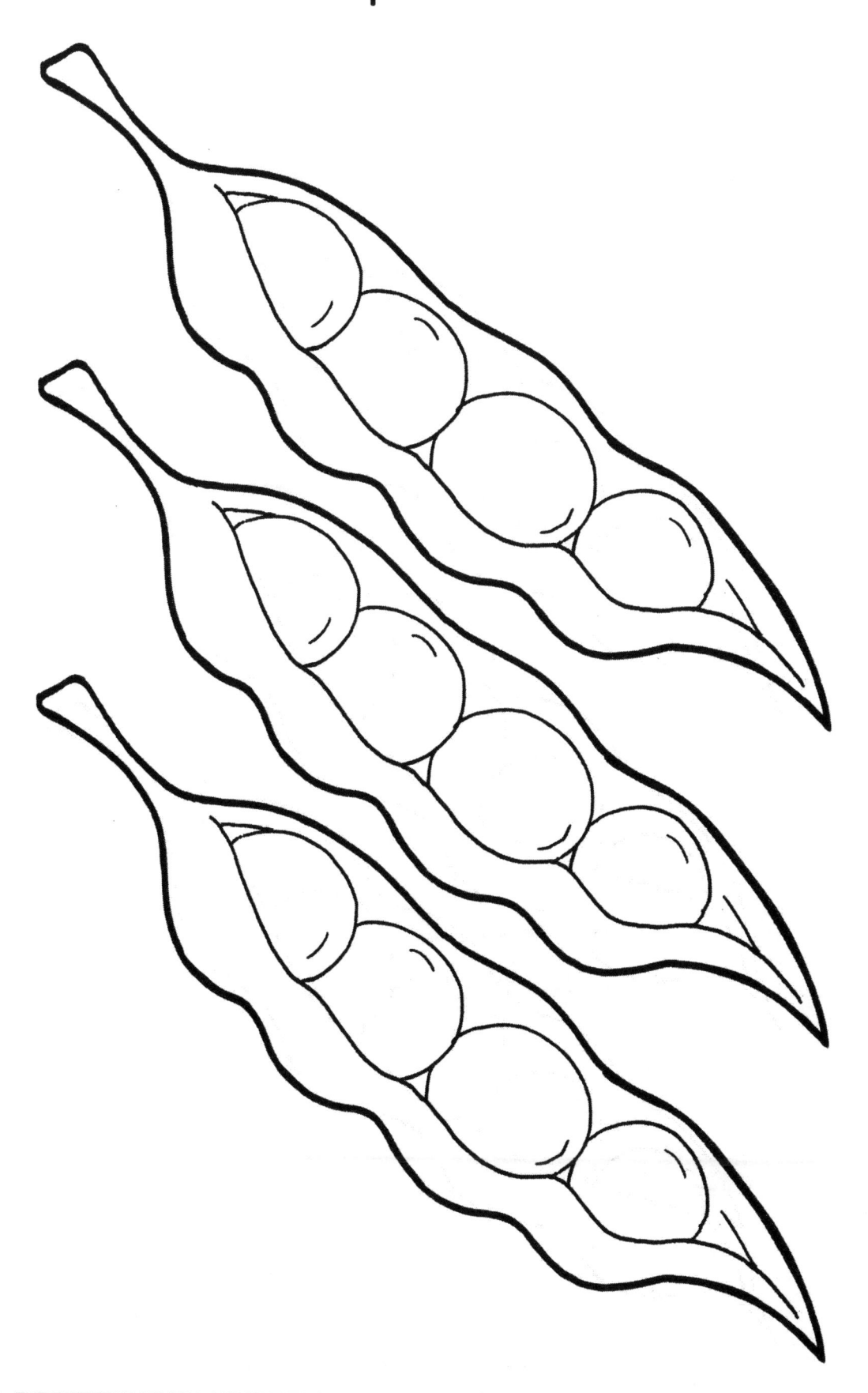

pens

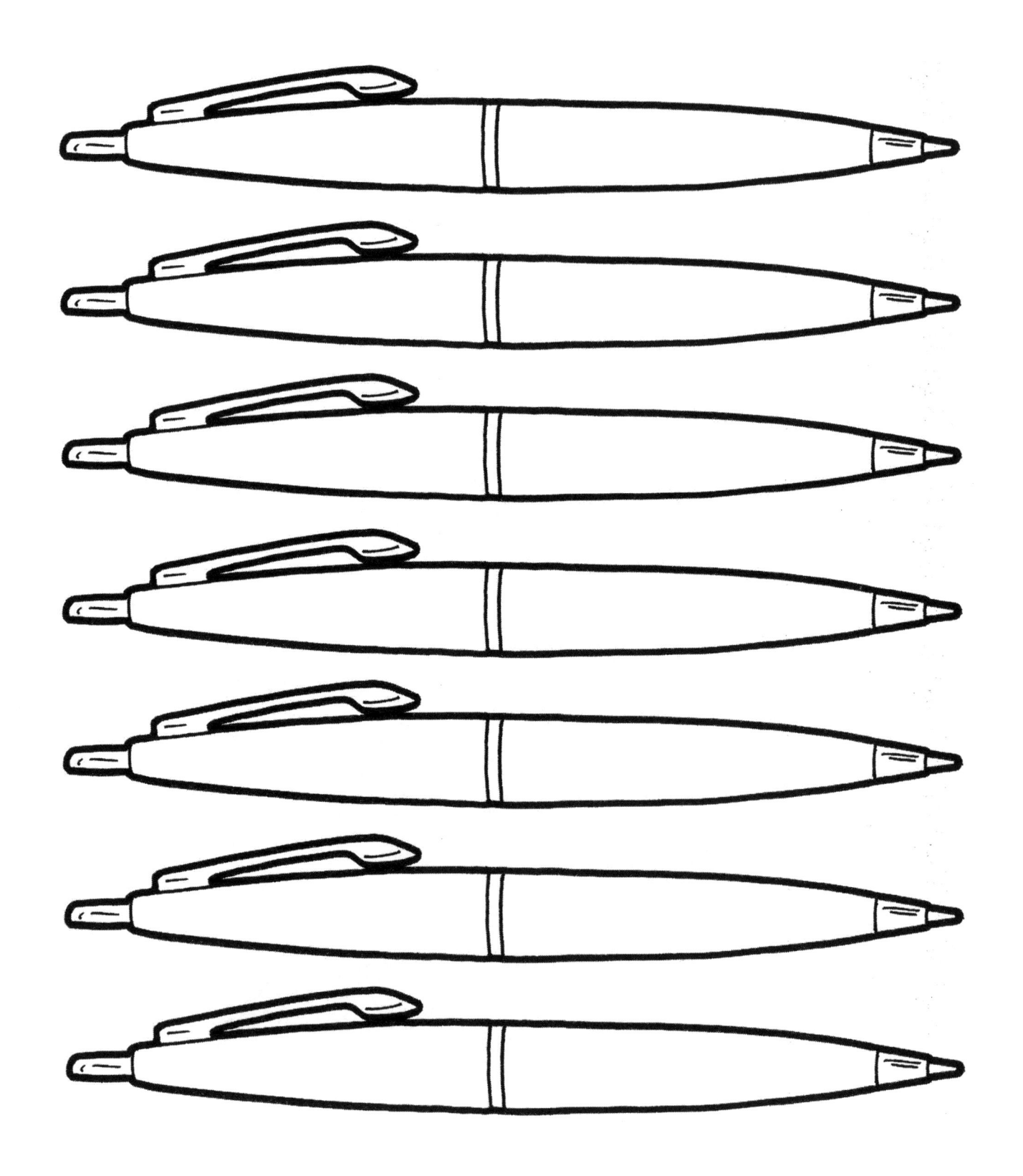

pencil (short and stout)

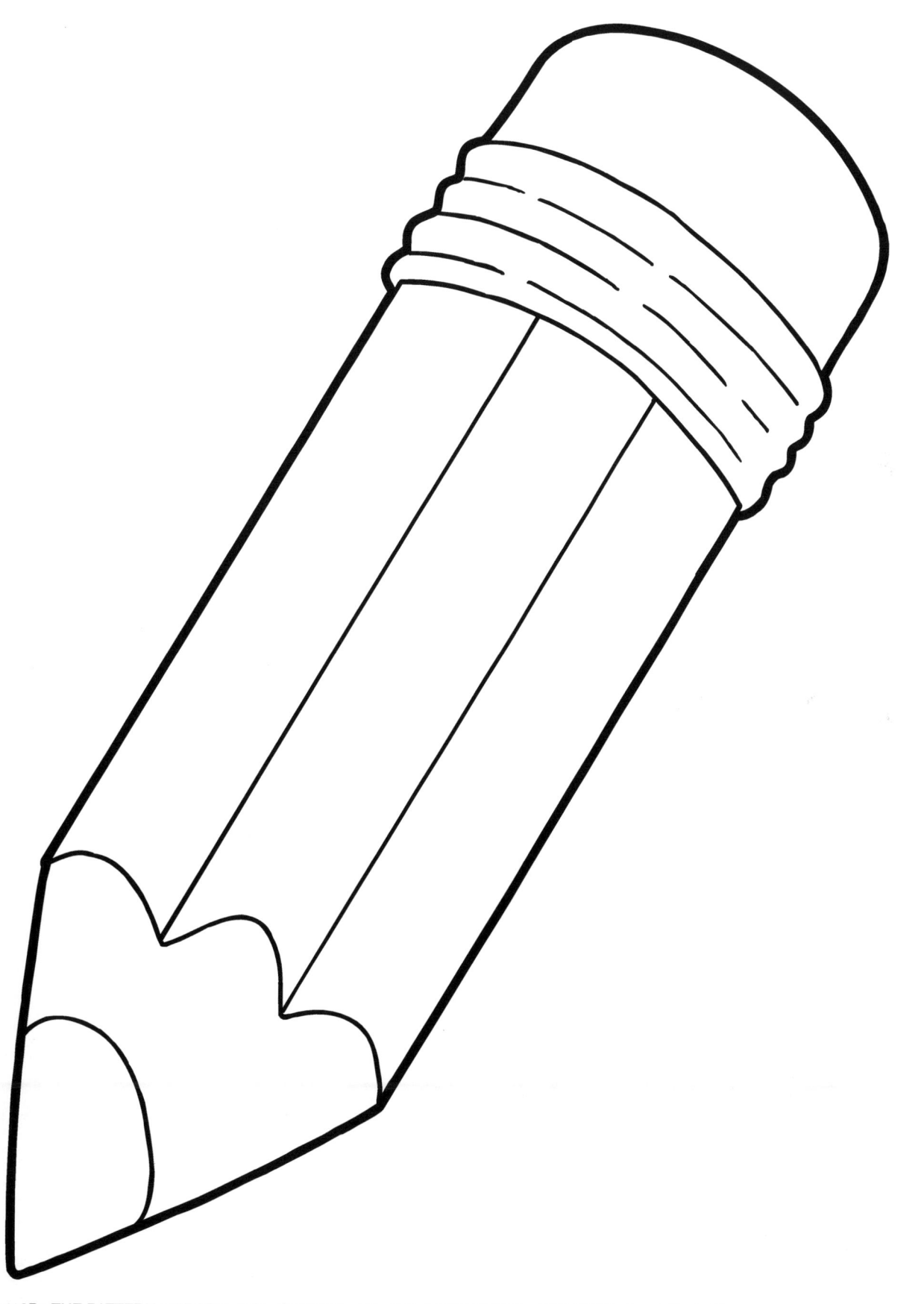

pencil (standard)

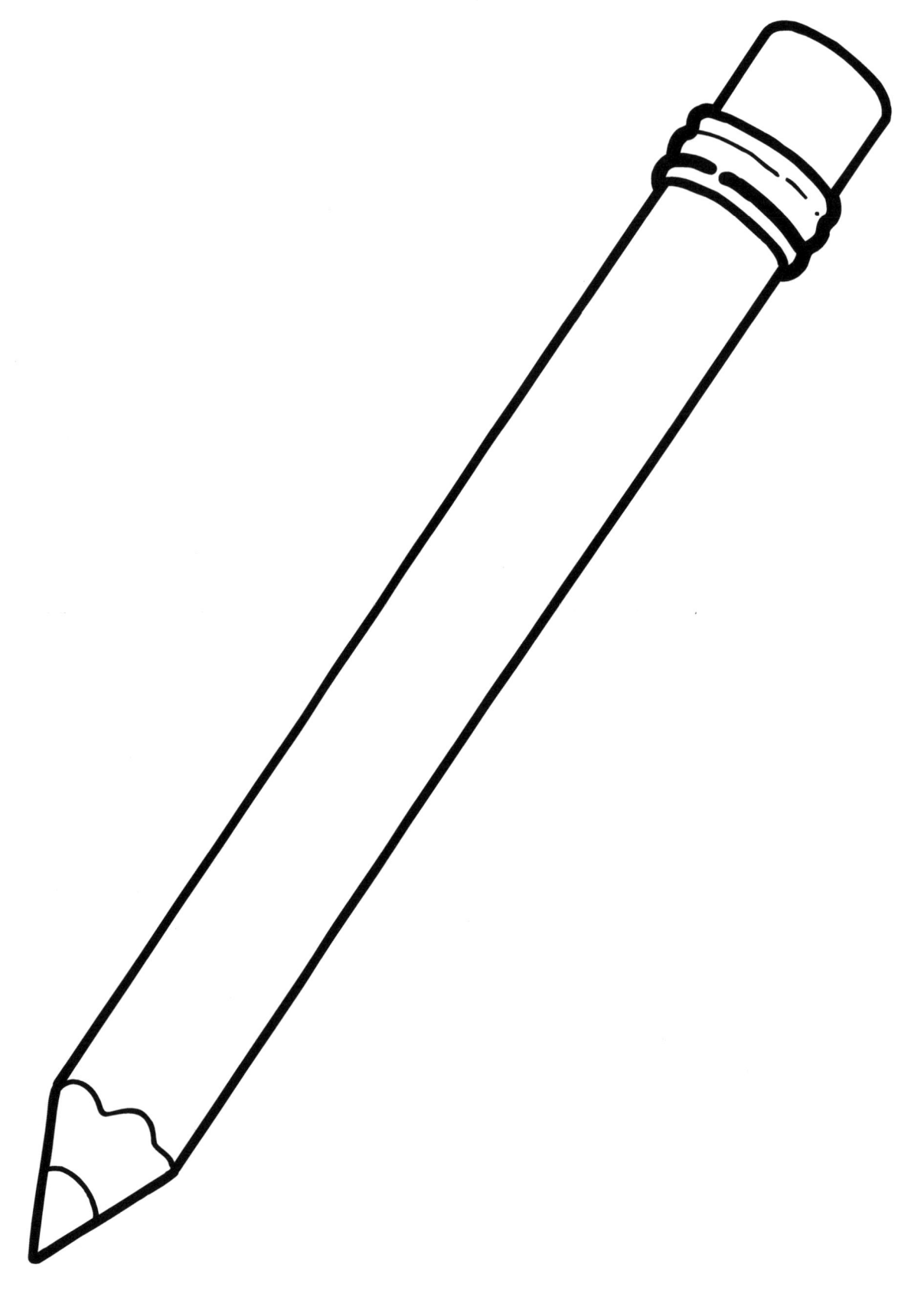

penguin

penguin (animated with hat)

pennies

Pennsylvania, USA

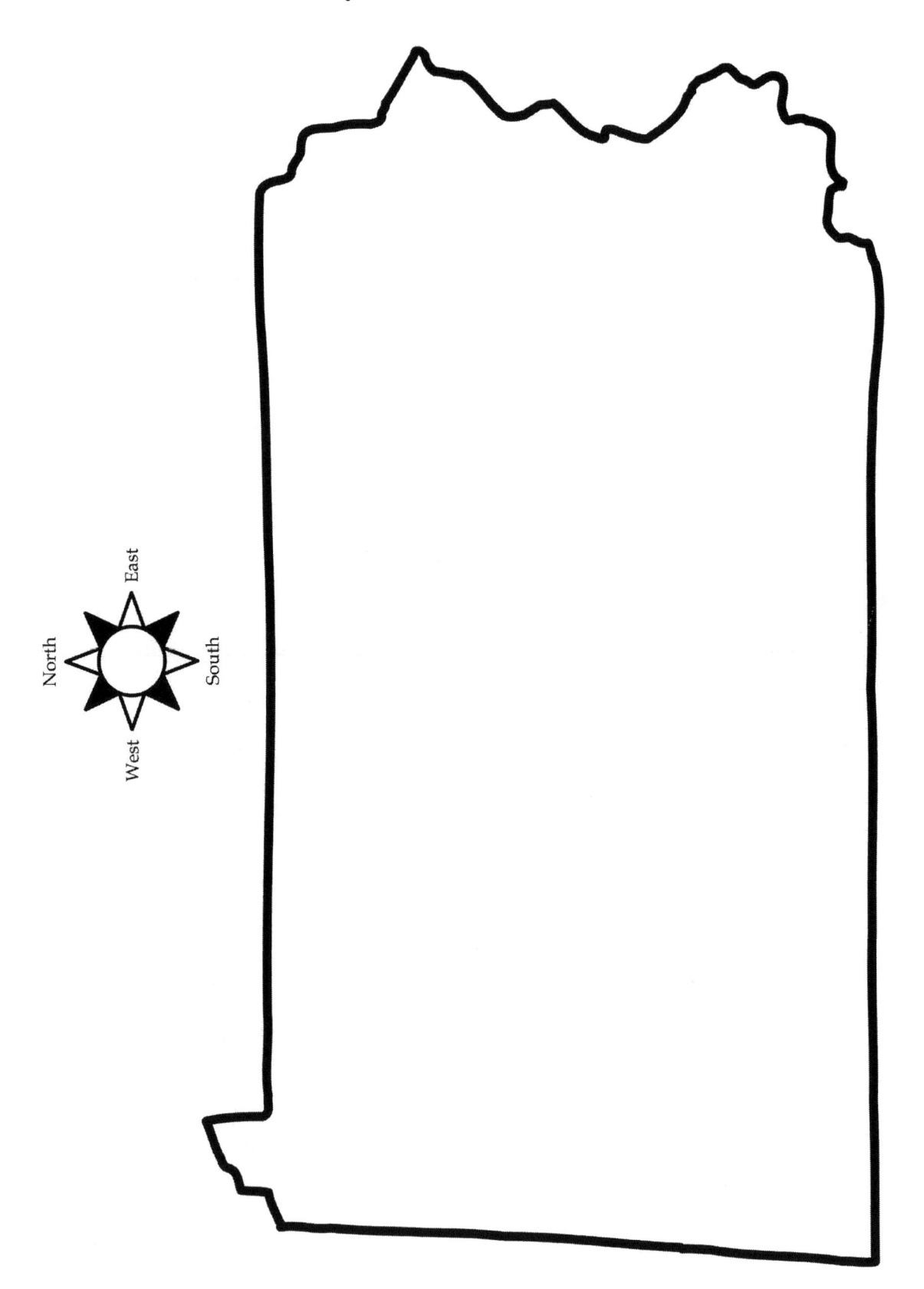

Maps are representations and boundaries are not exact.

pentagon (shape)

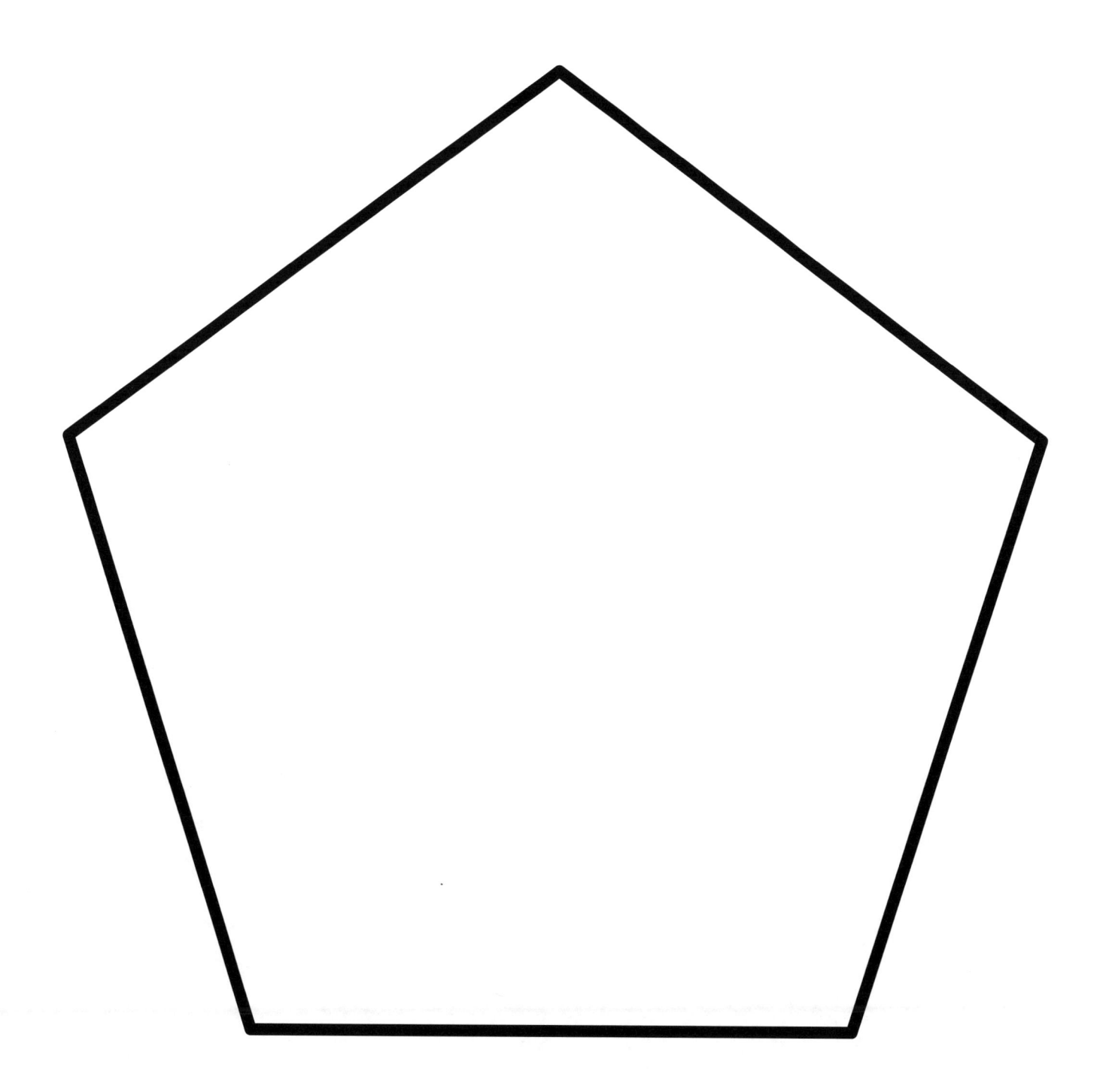

perch

pie

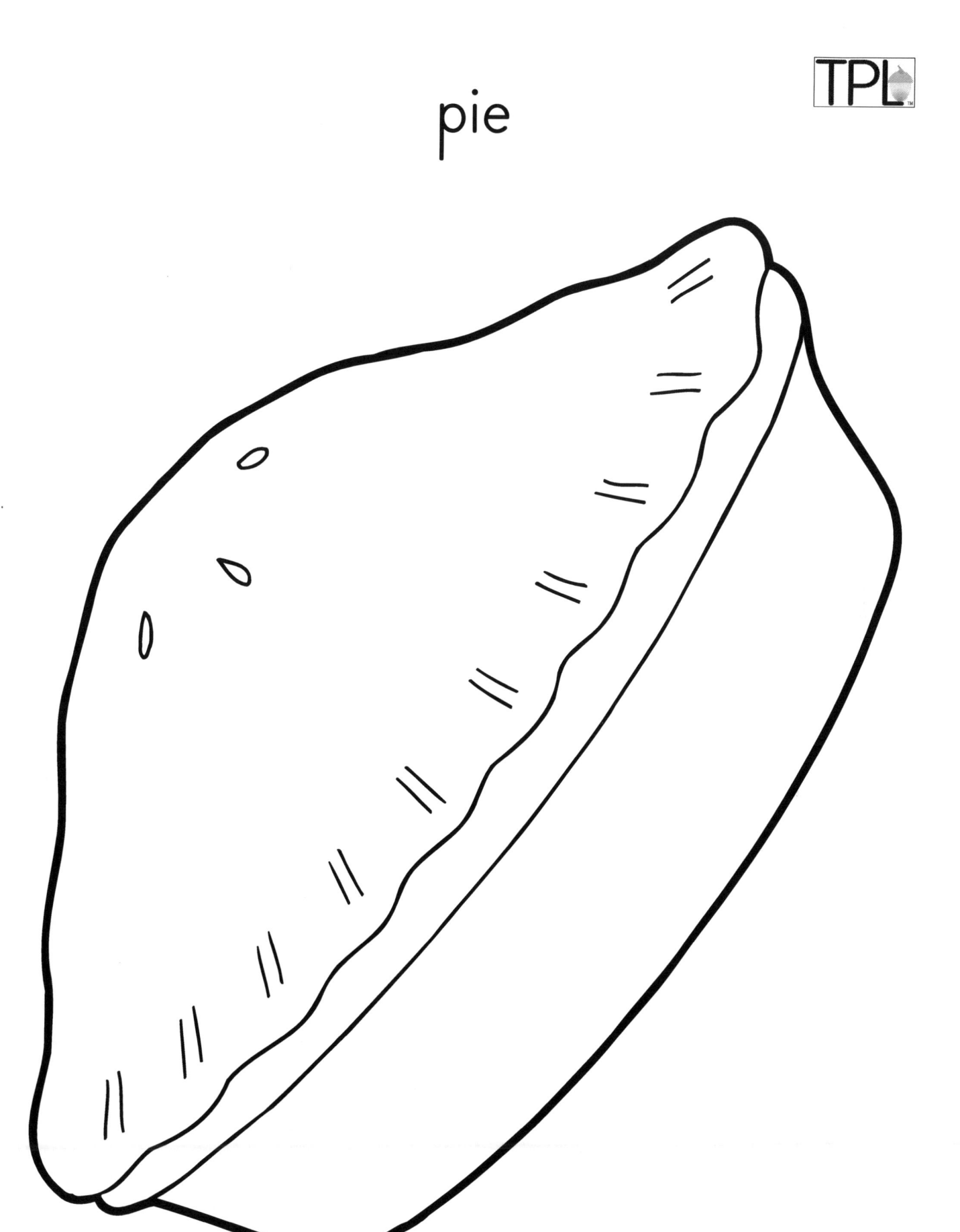

pig

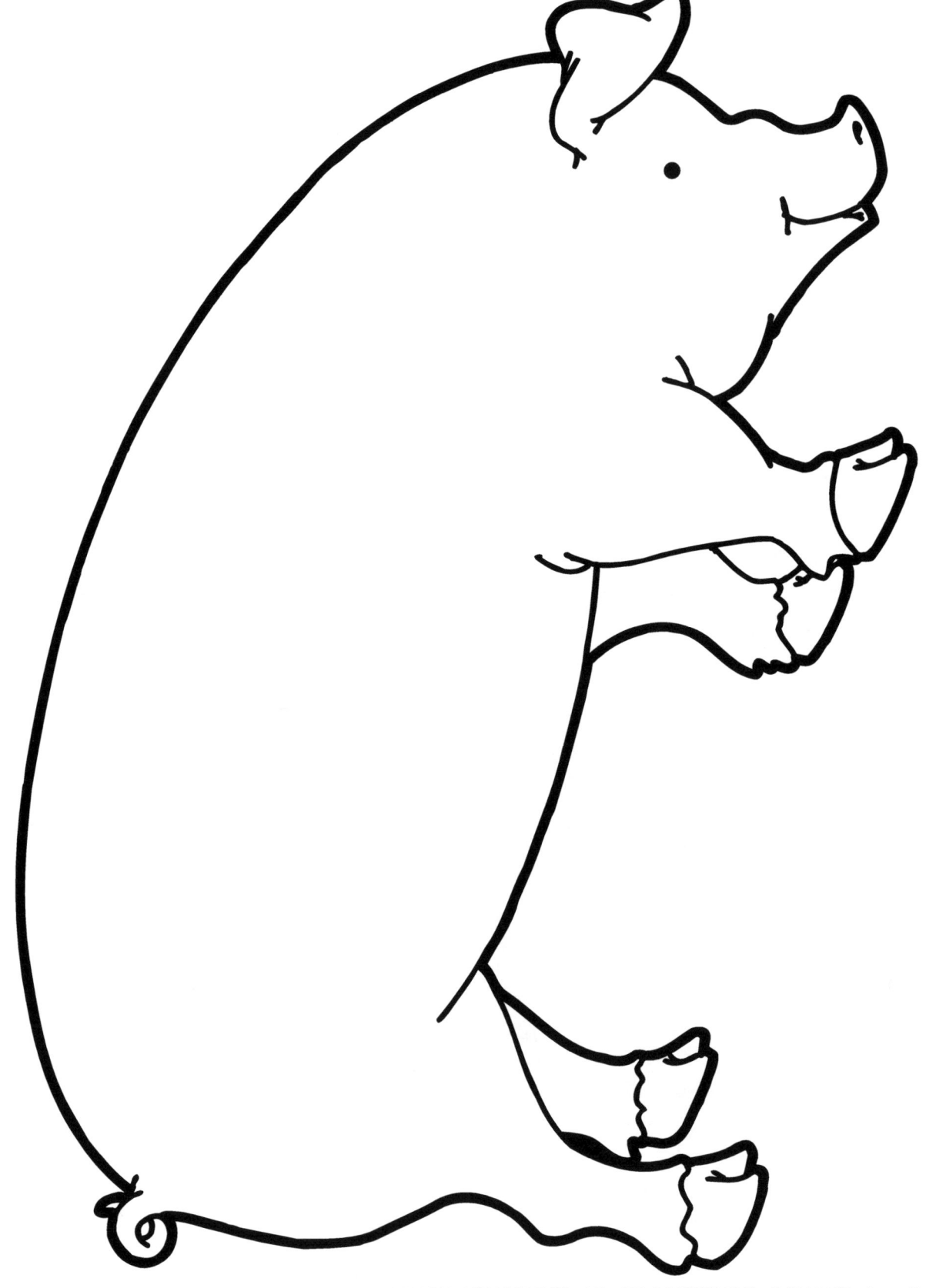

pig (animated)

pig (outline)

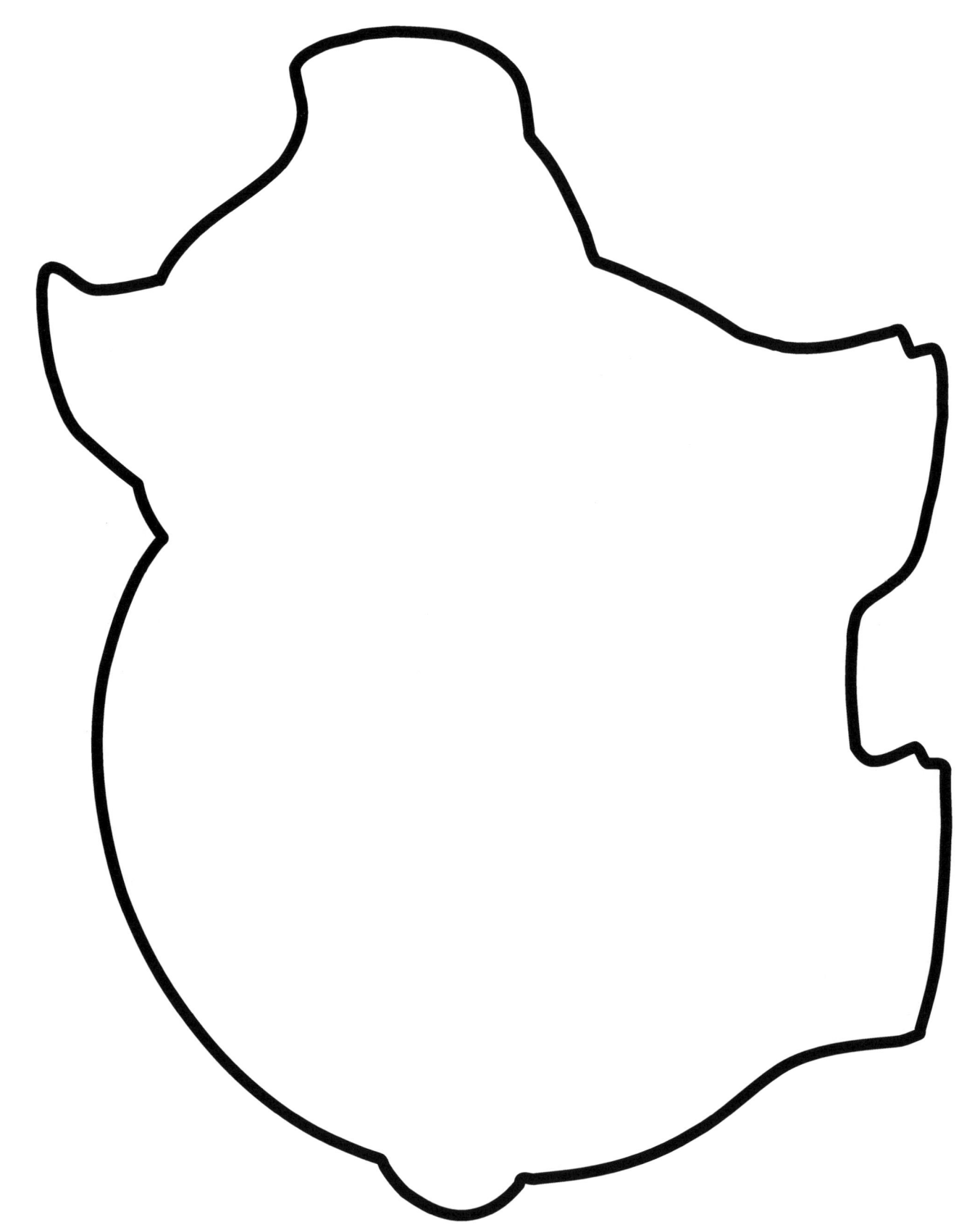

piggy bank

pinecone

pink (crayon)

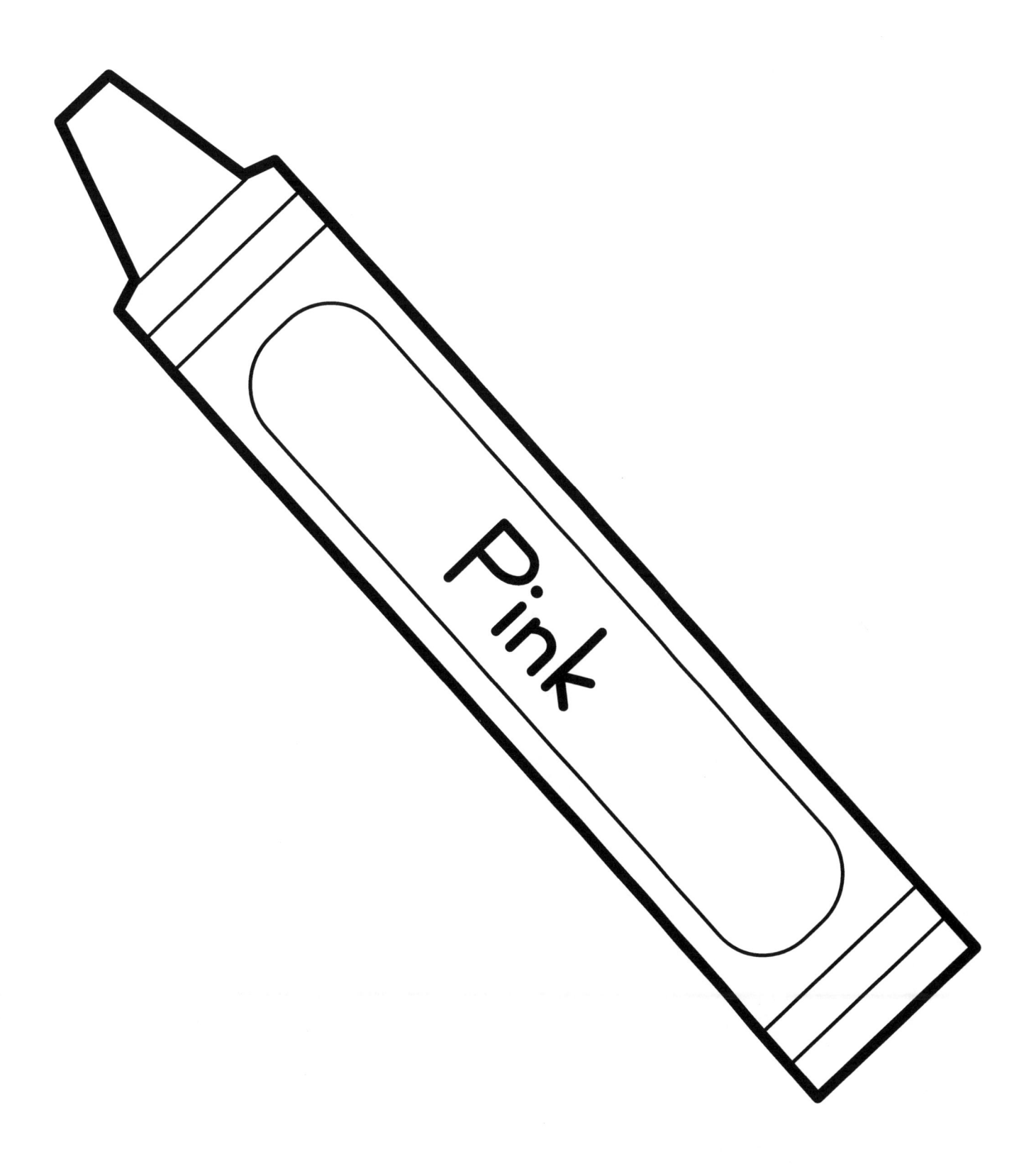

pitcher

planet (with ring)

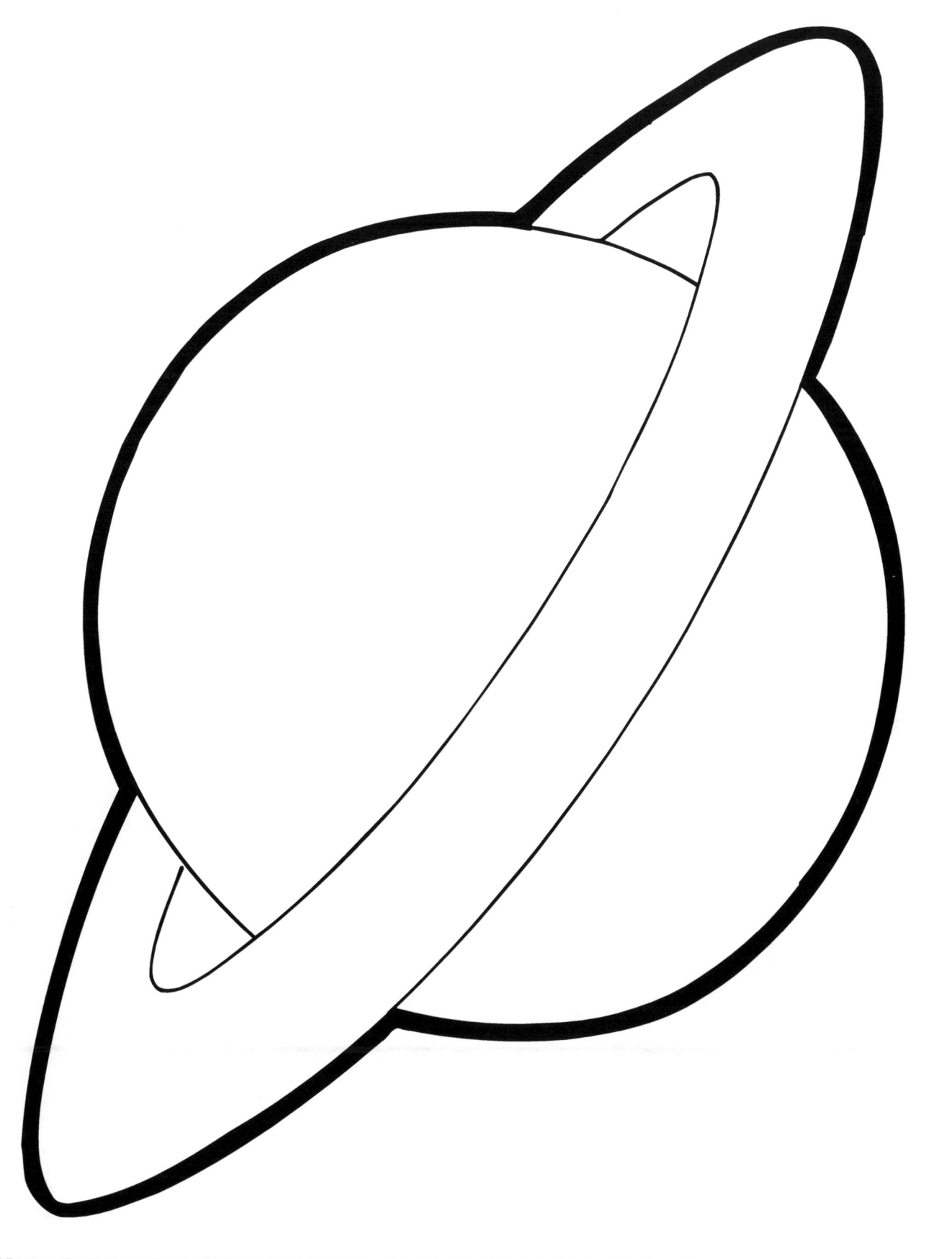

platypus

pocket (with stitches)

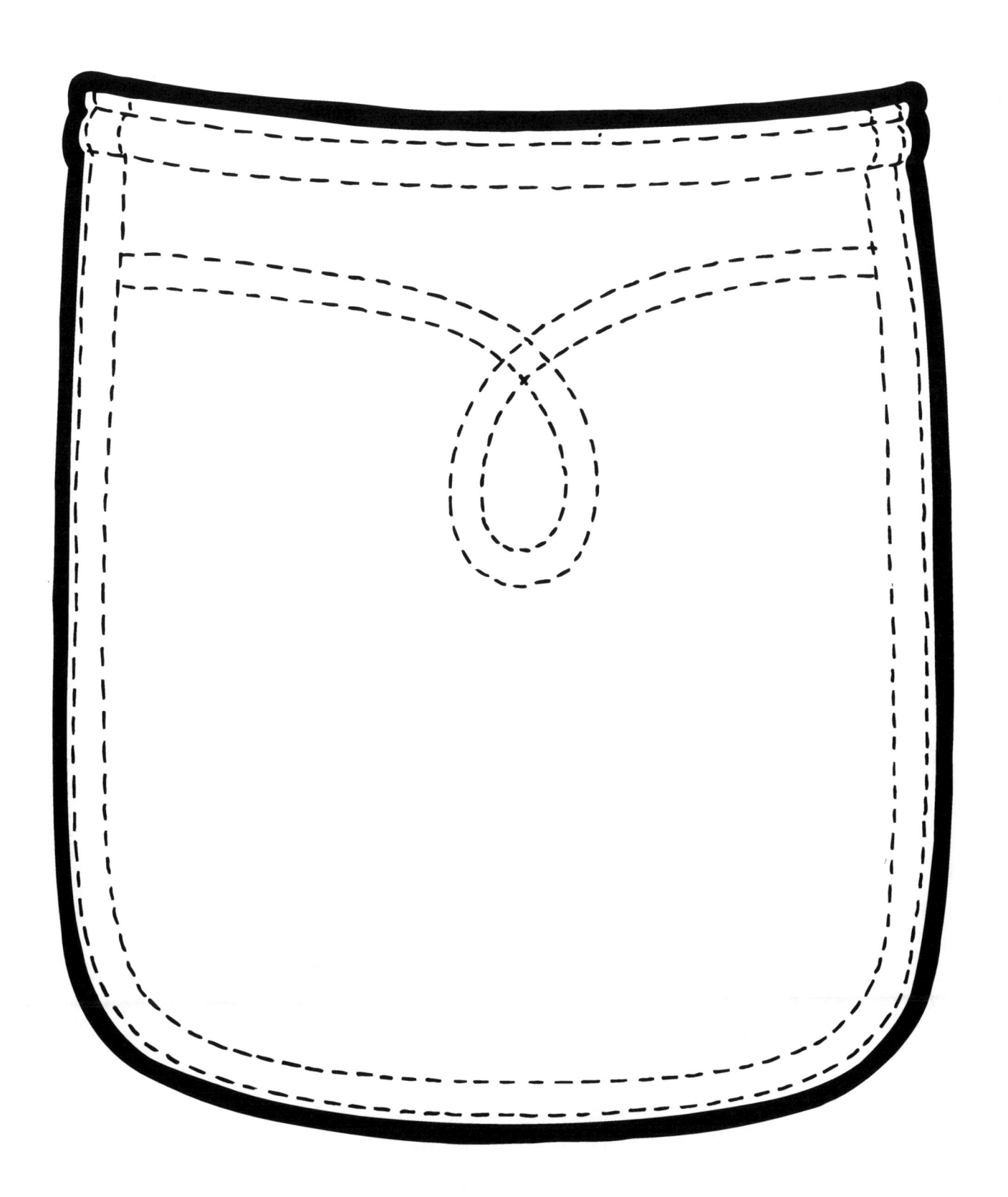

pocket watch

poinsettia (with veins)

poinsettia (without veins)

pony

popsicle

pot (cooking)

potato

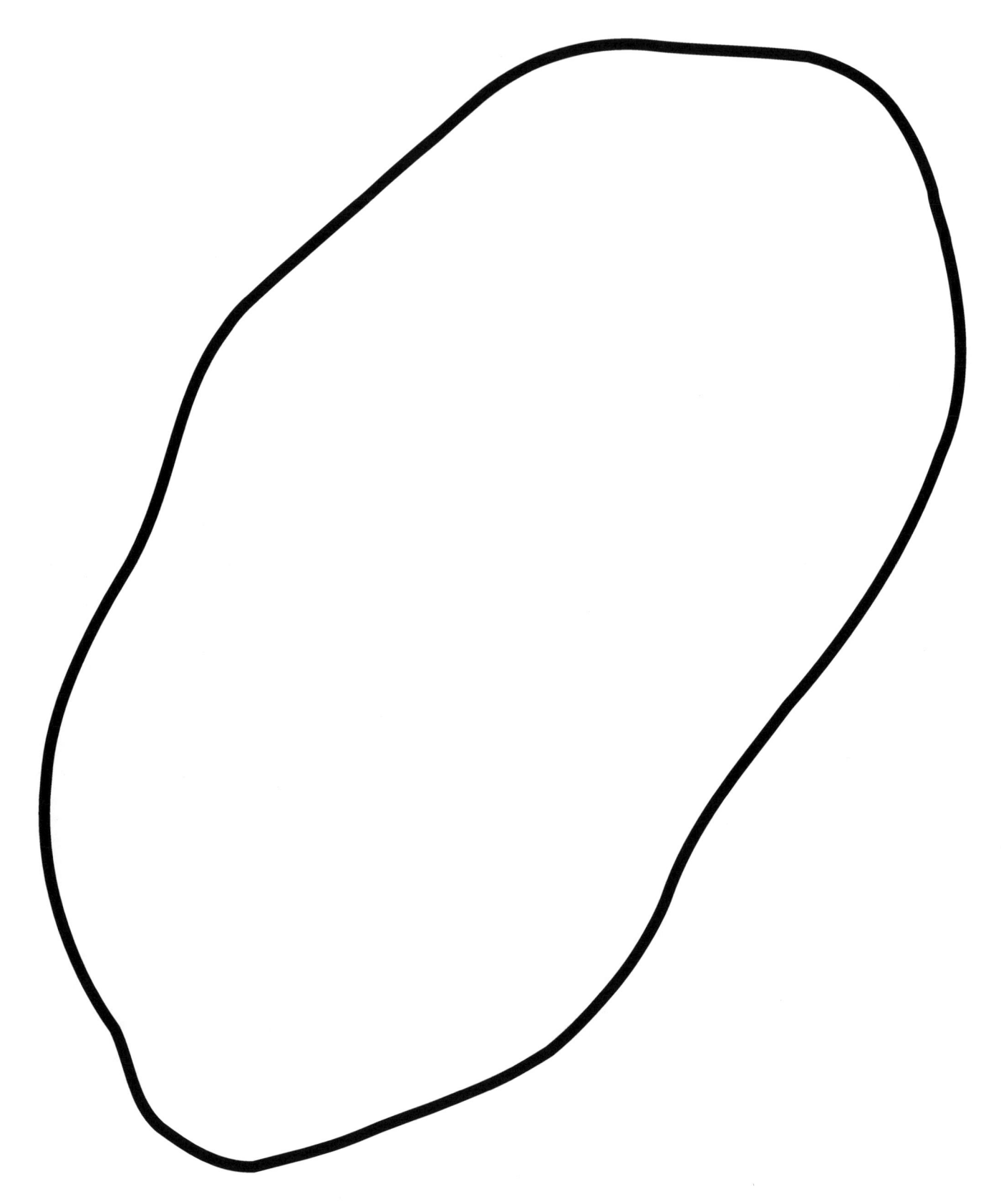

pretzel (twist)

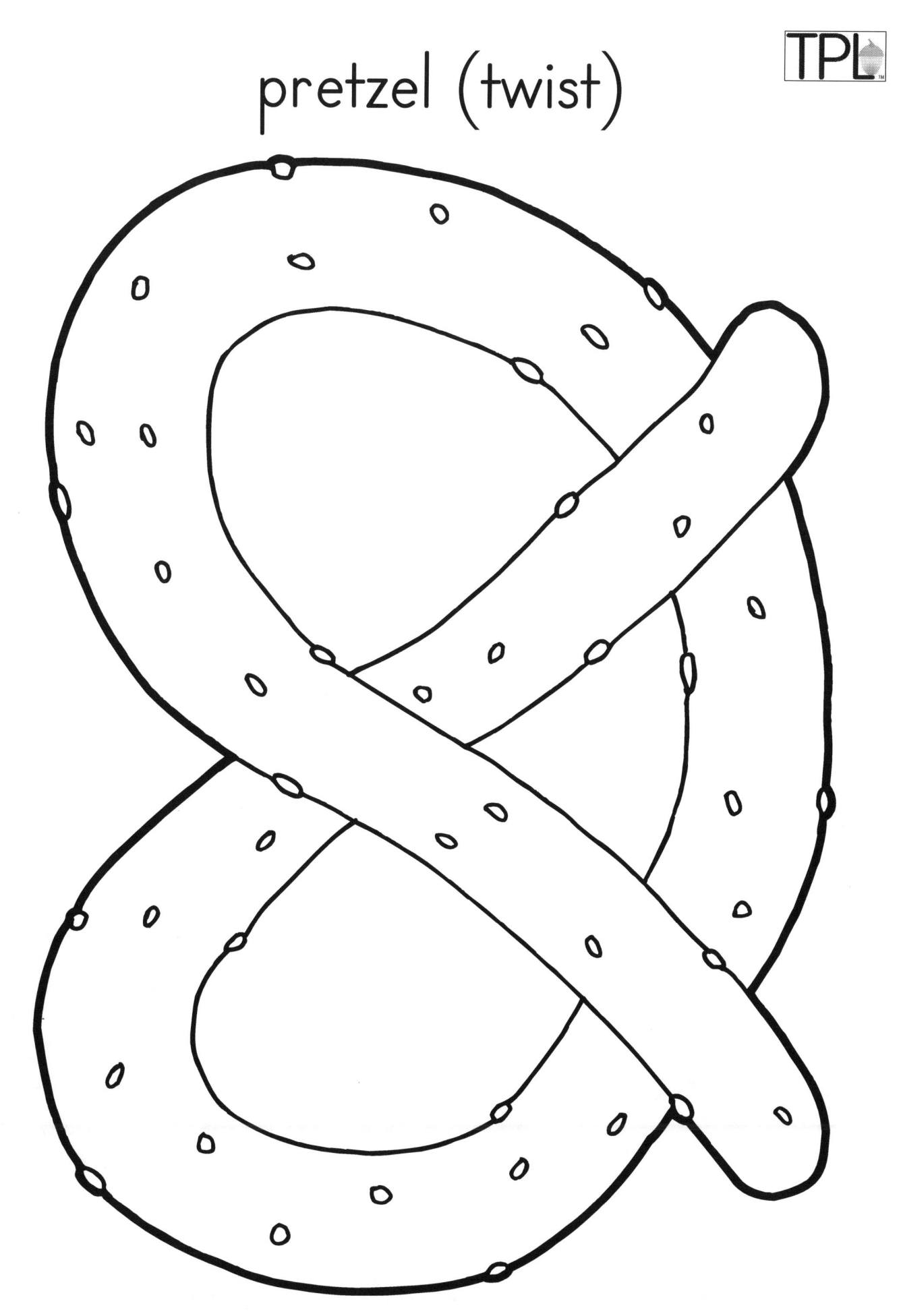

Prince Edward Island, Canada

Maps are representations and boundaries are not exact.

puffin

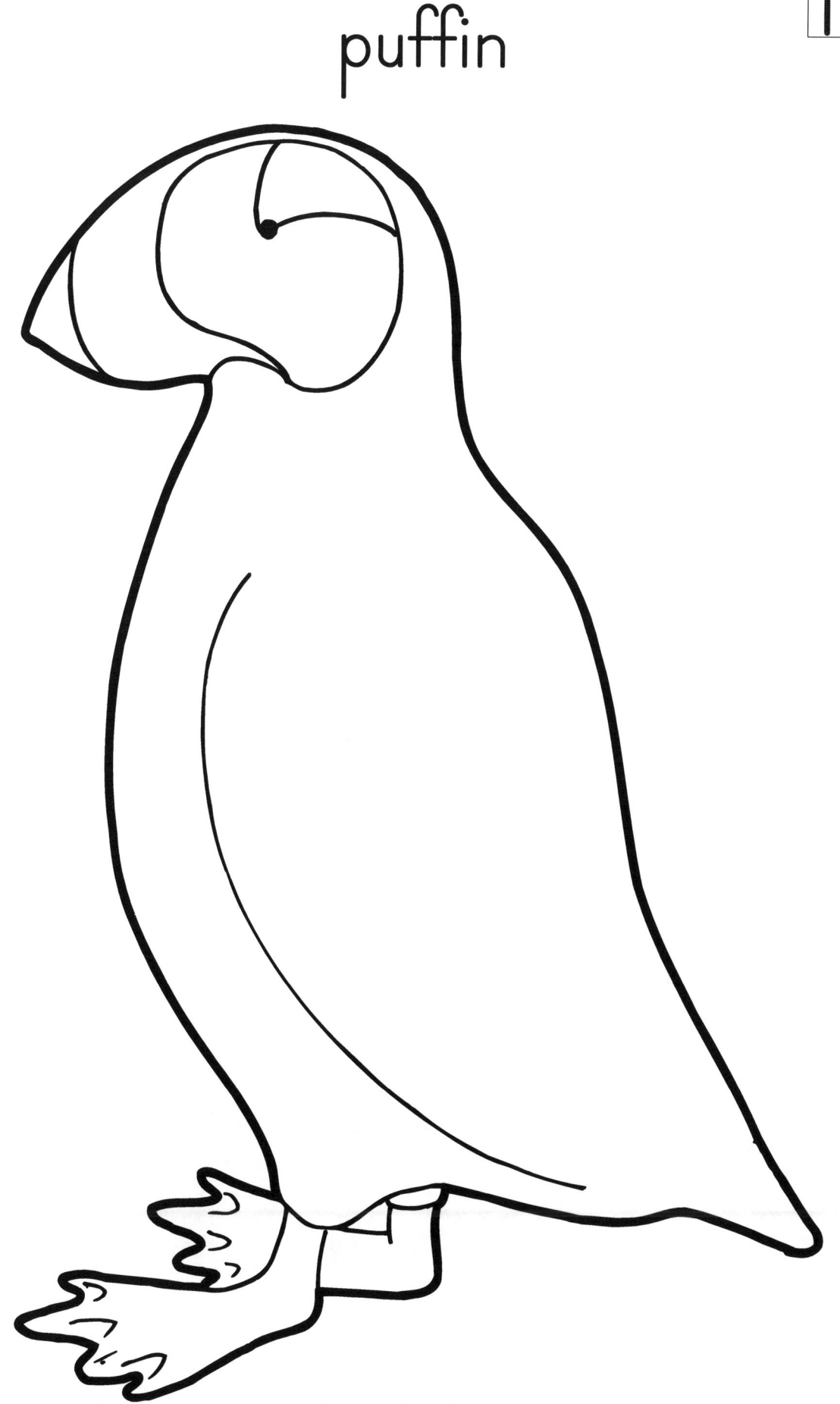

pumpkin

pumpkin

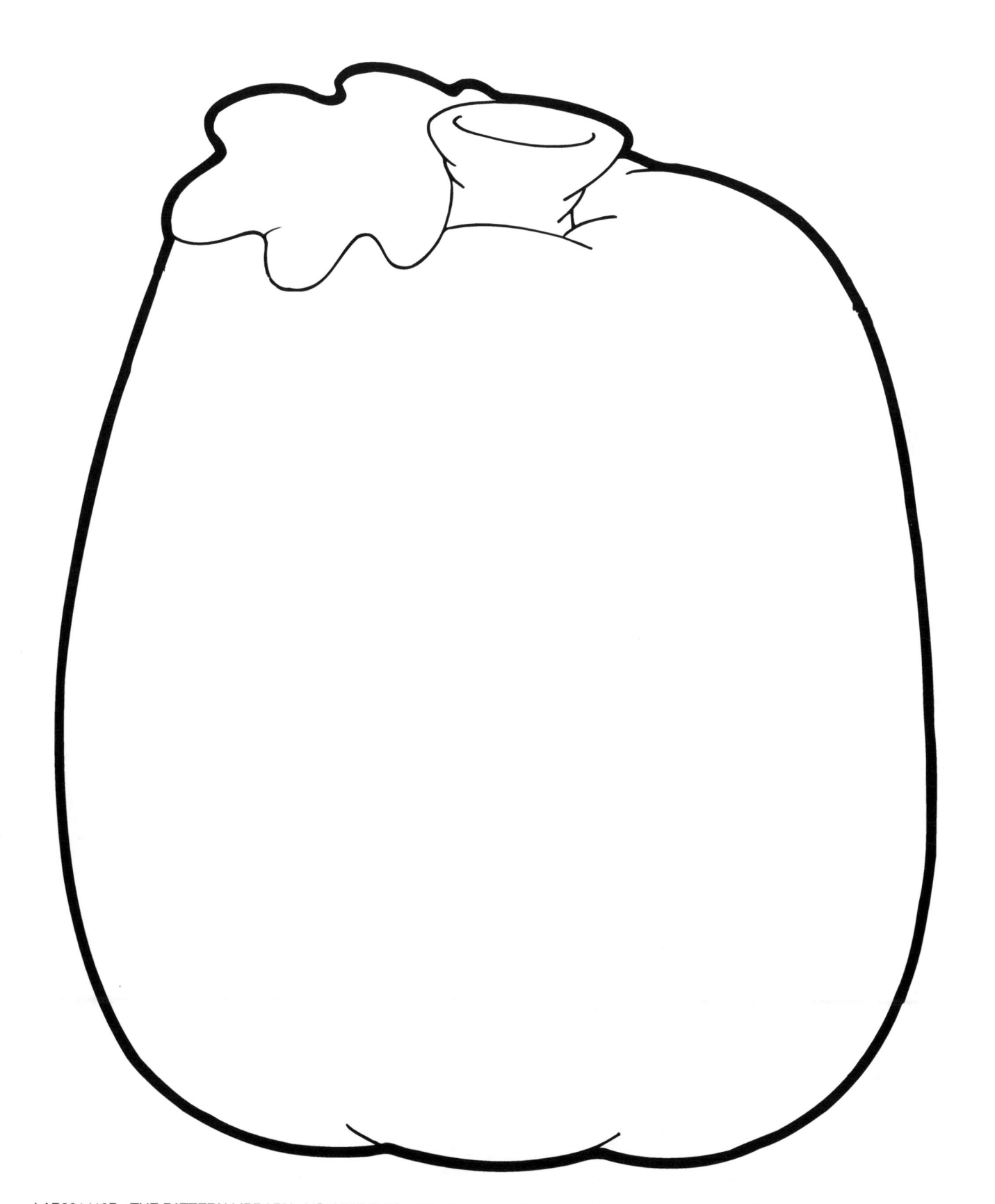

pumpkin

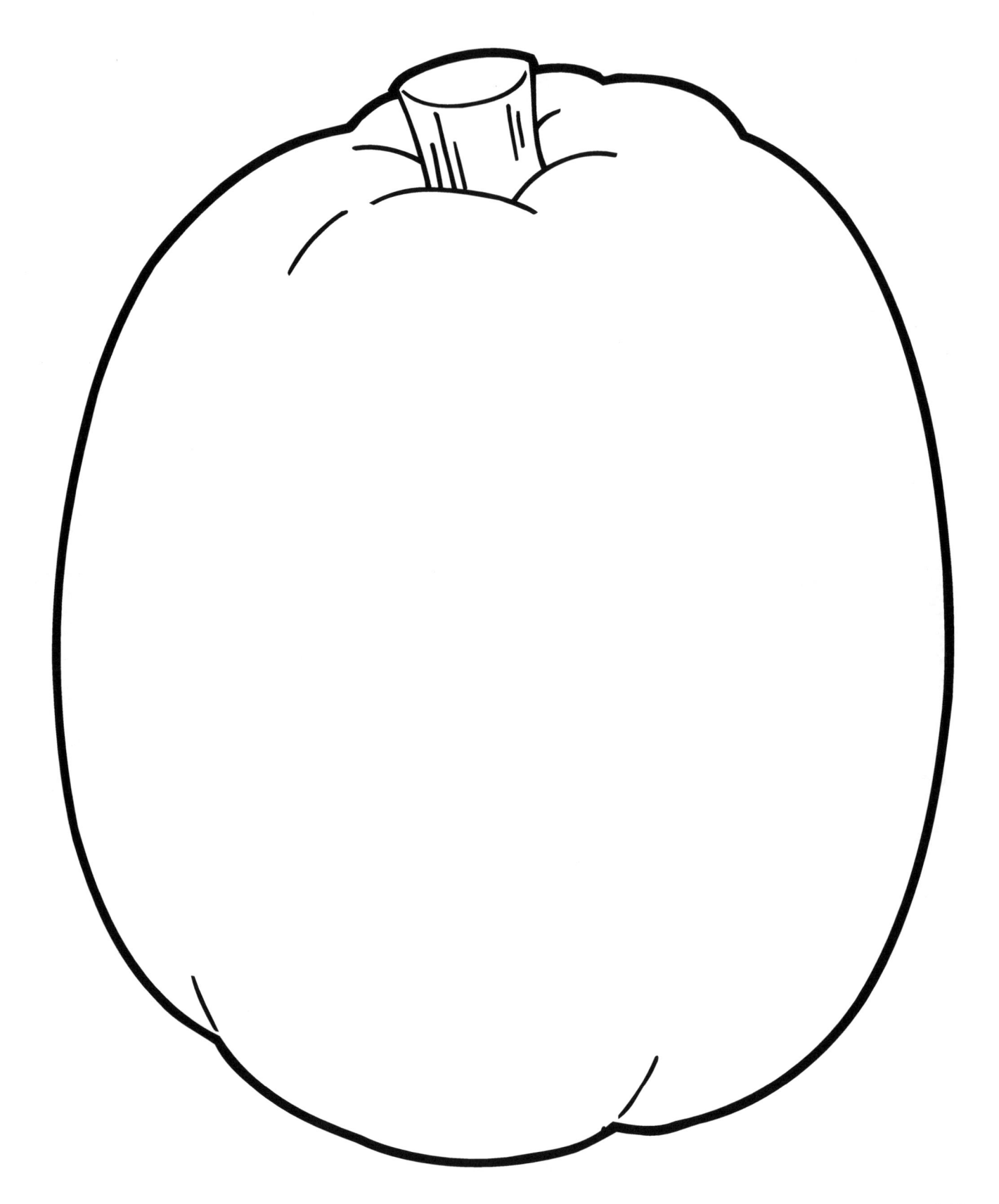

puppy

purple (crayon)

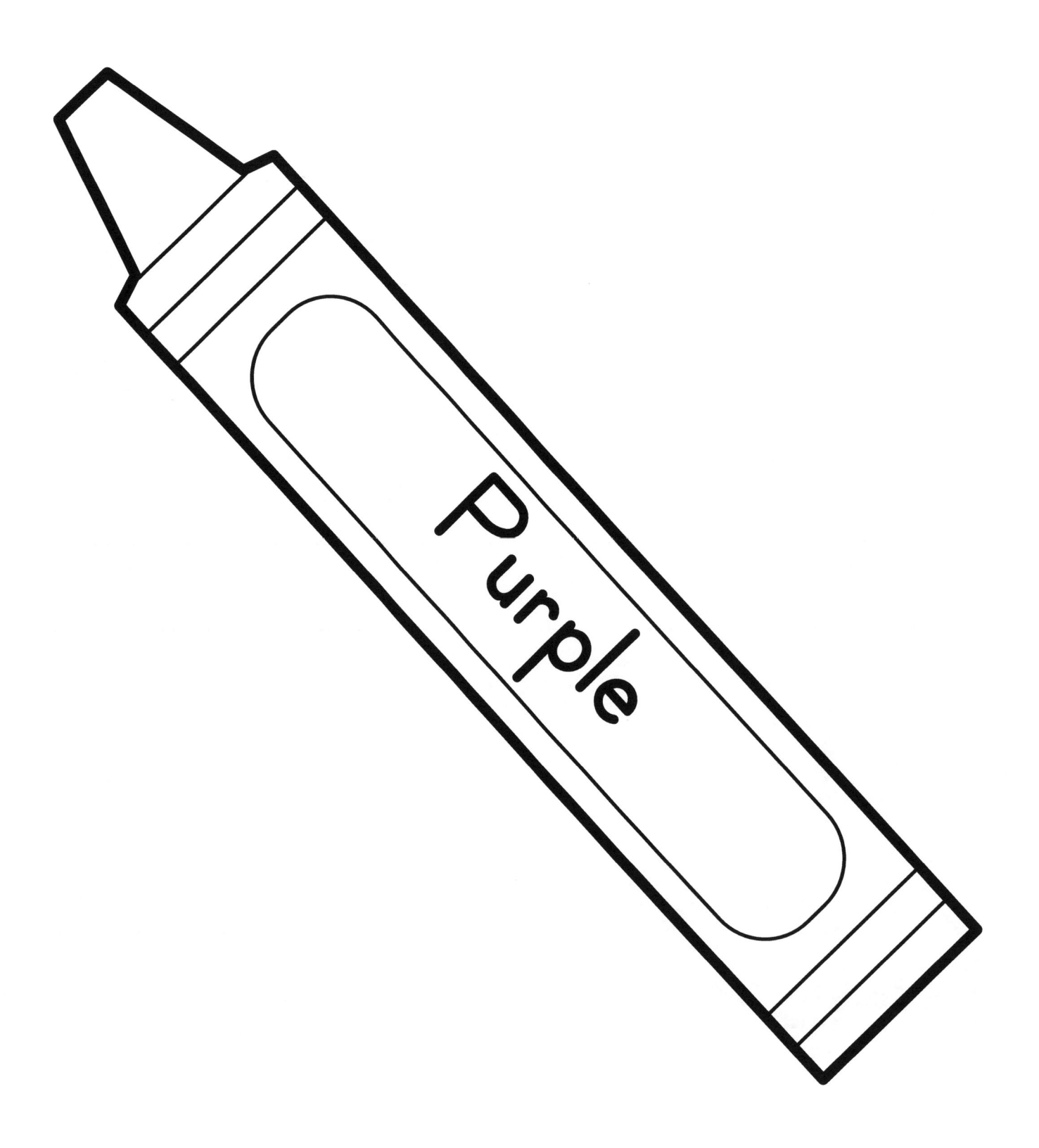

pushpin

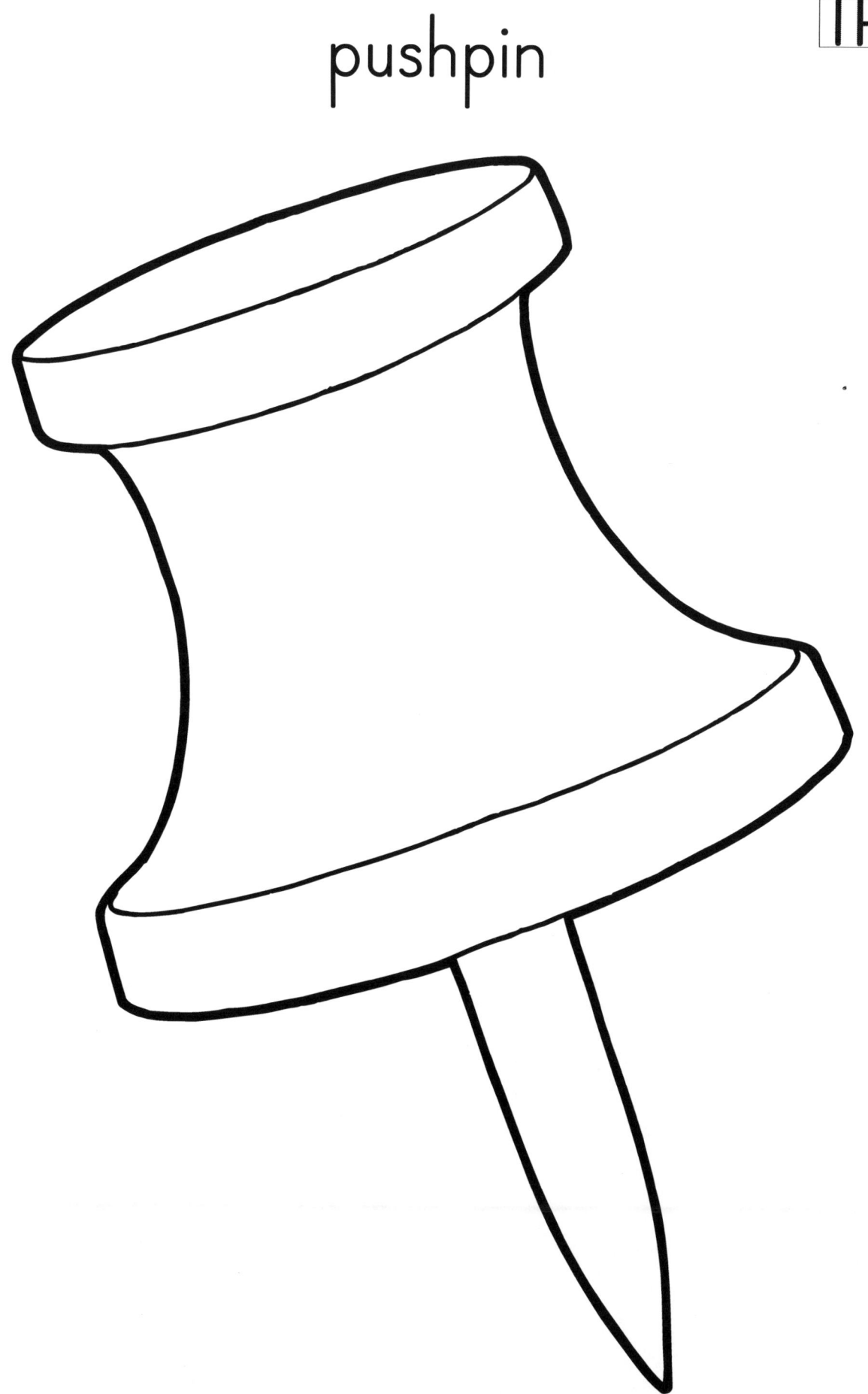

pyramid

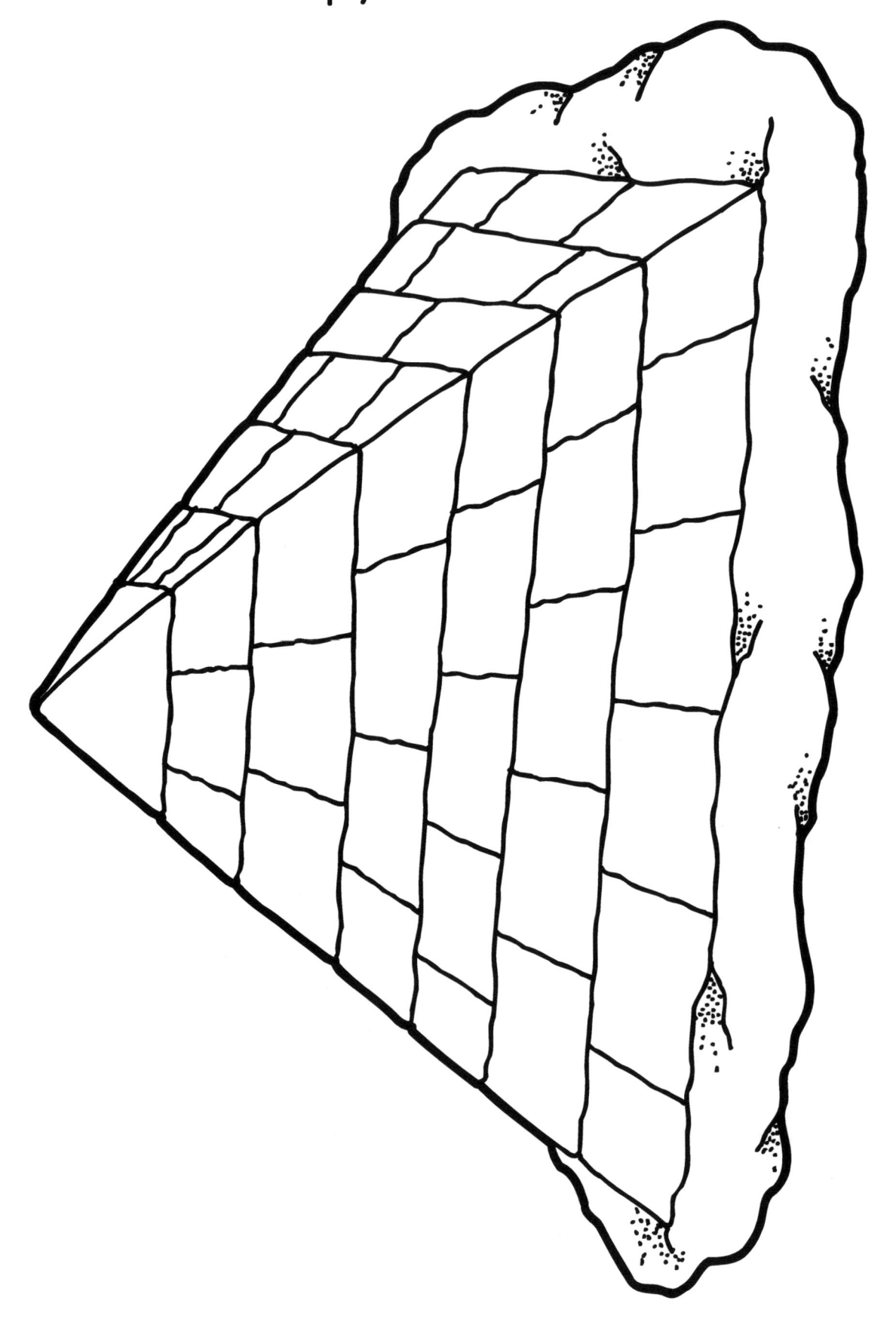

quail (animated)

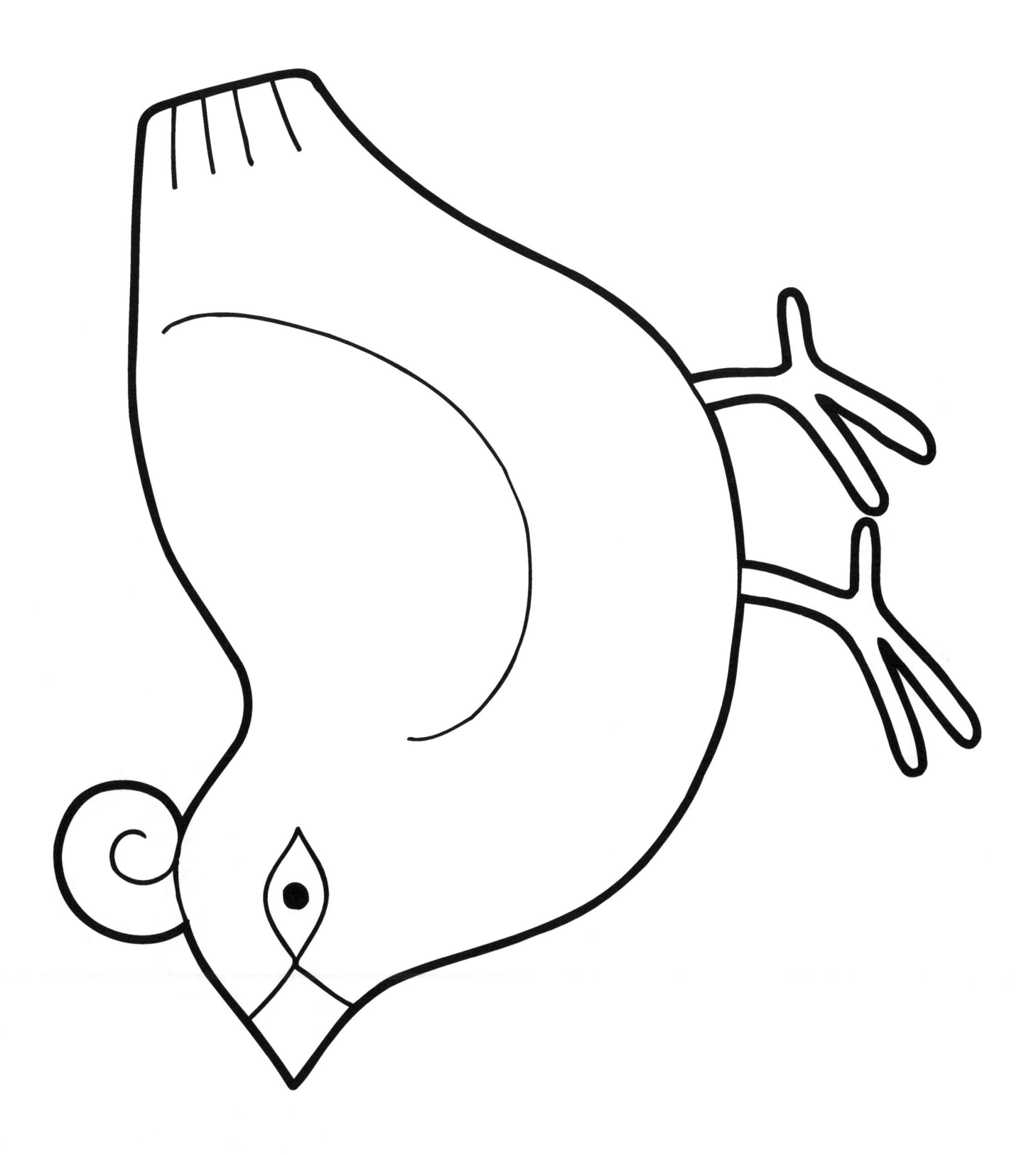

quail (stylized)

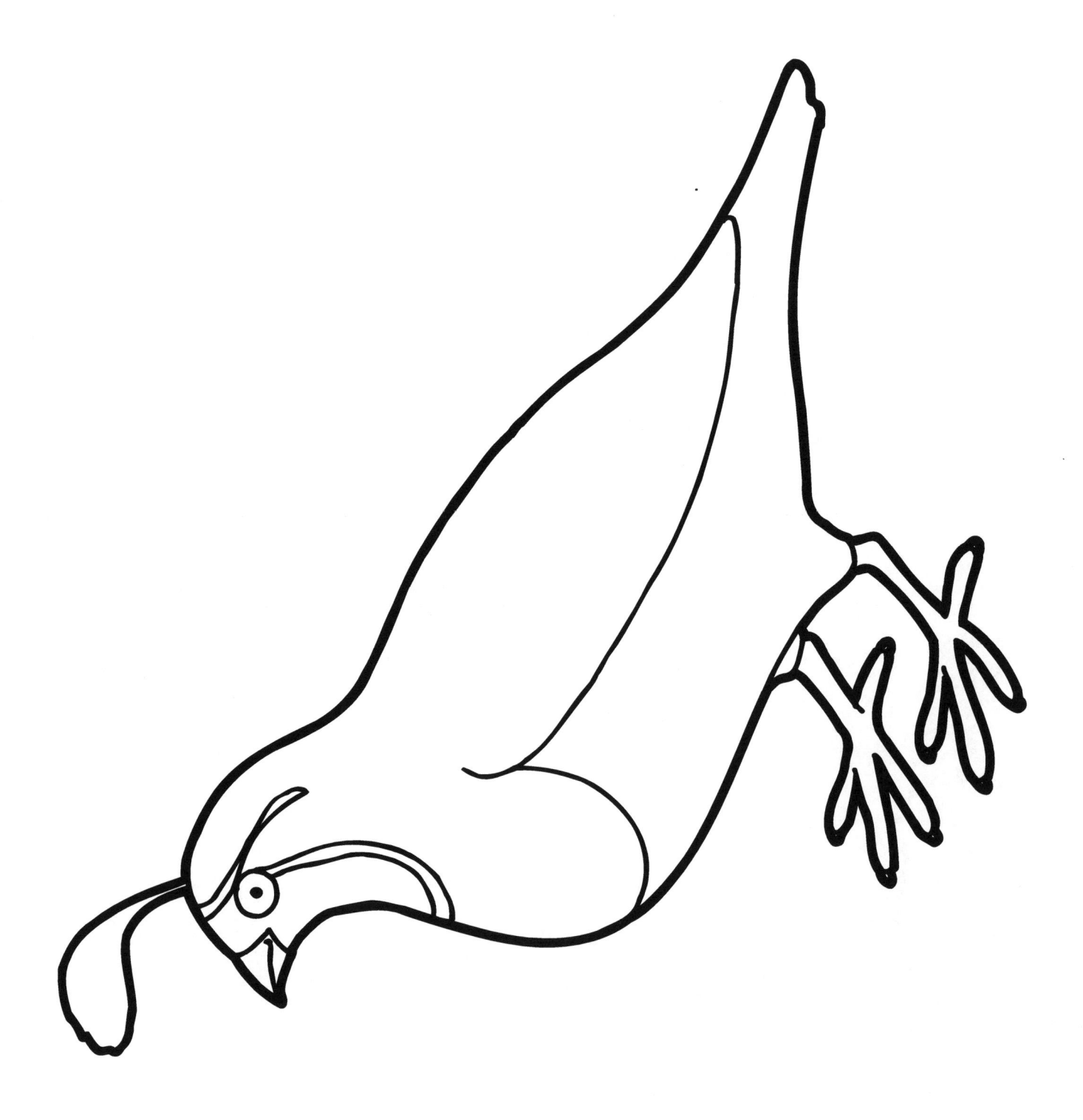

quarters

Quebec, Canada

North
West East
South

Maps are representations and boundaries are not exact.

queen

question mark

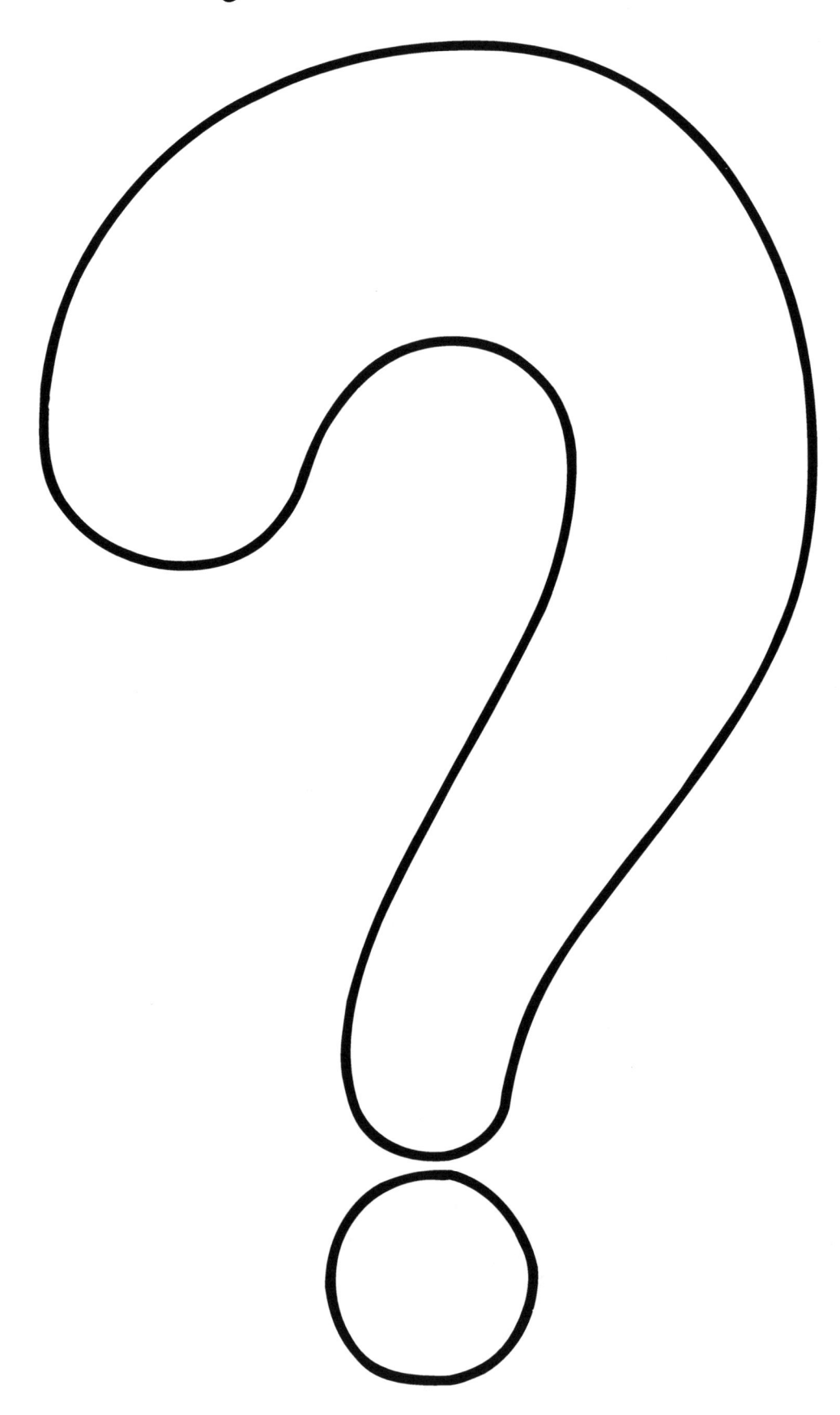

quetzal

quill (pen)

quilt

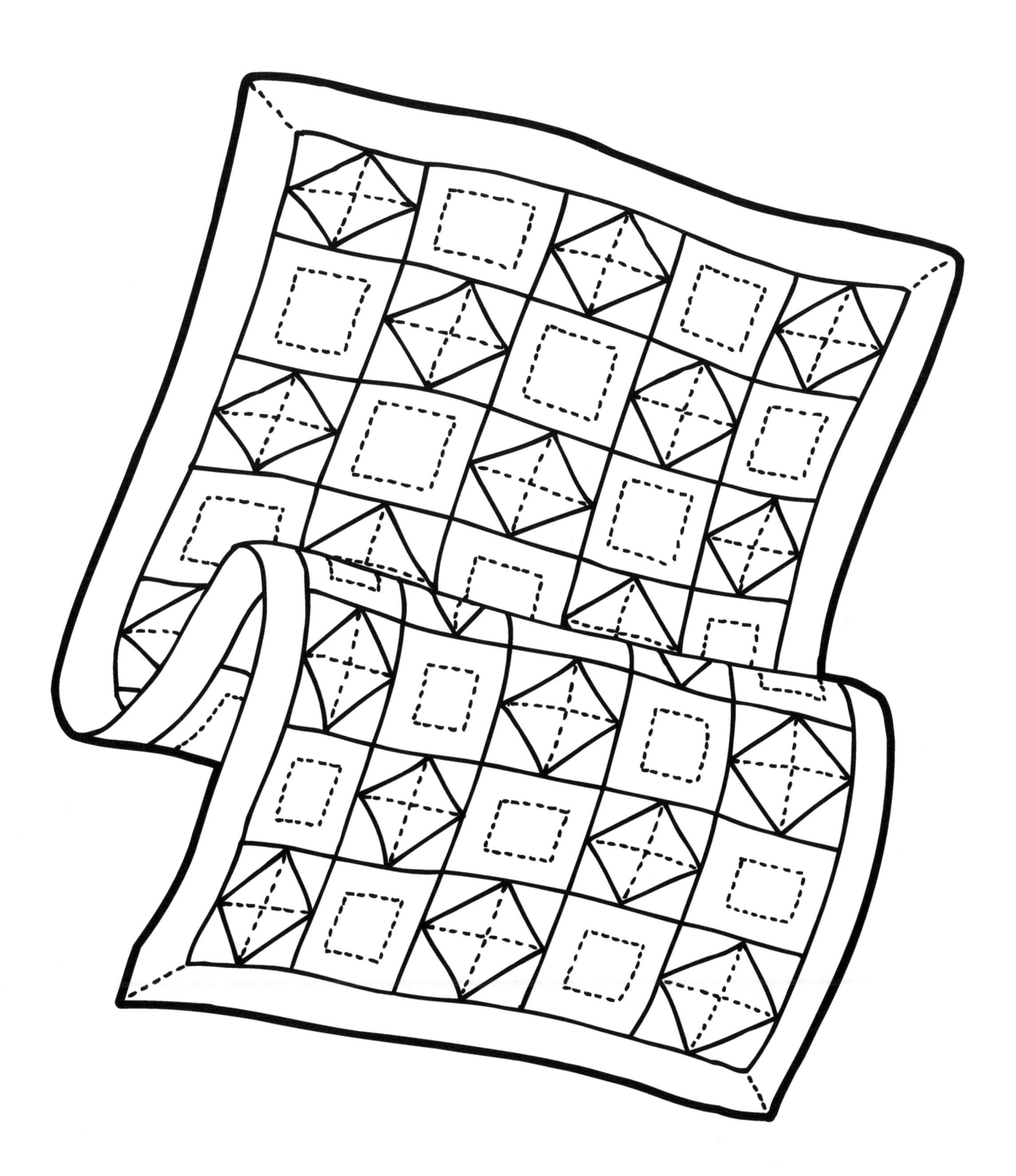

quiver

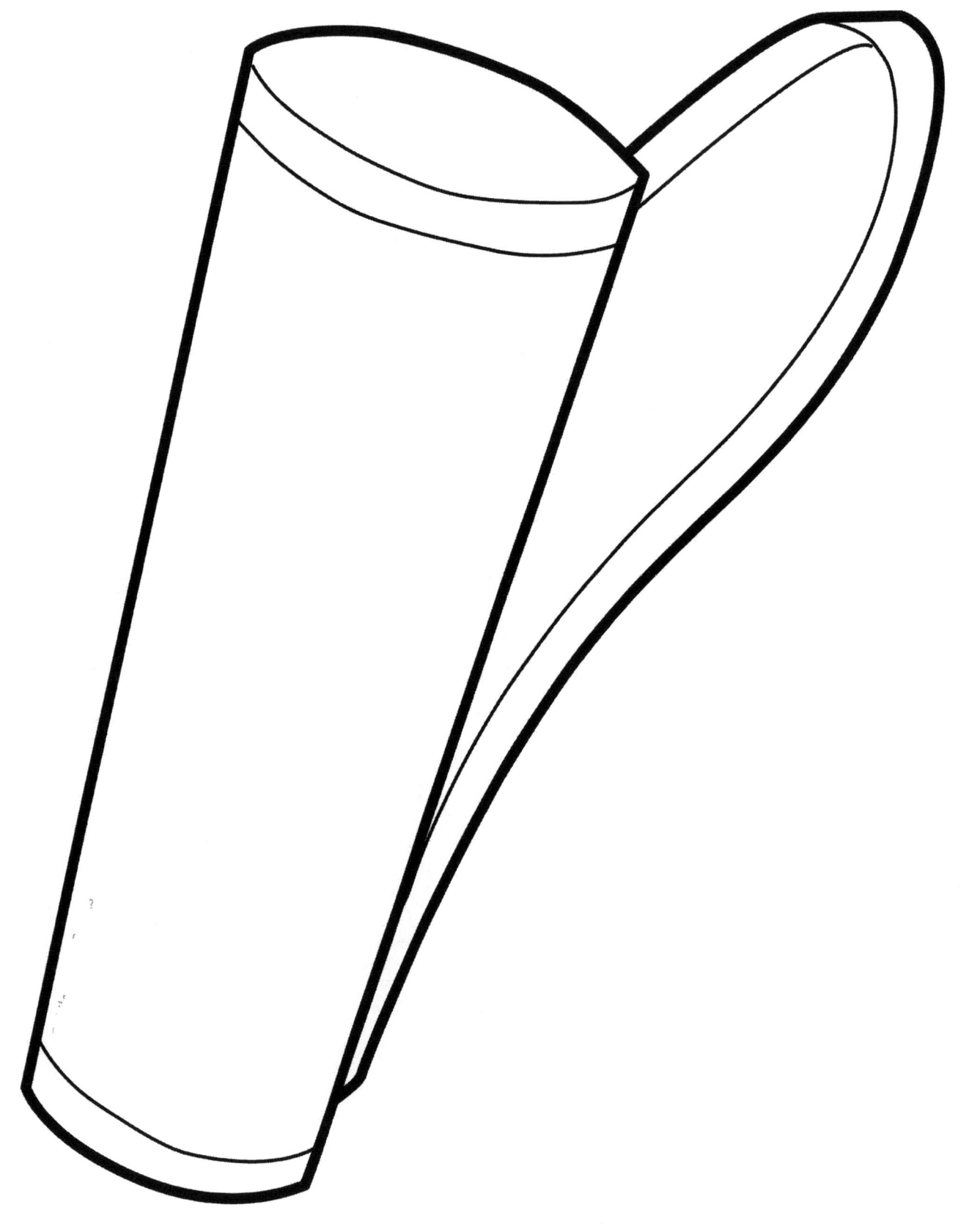

rabbit (animated, waving)

rabbit (animated, floppy ears)

rabbit (chocolate)

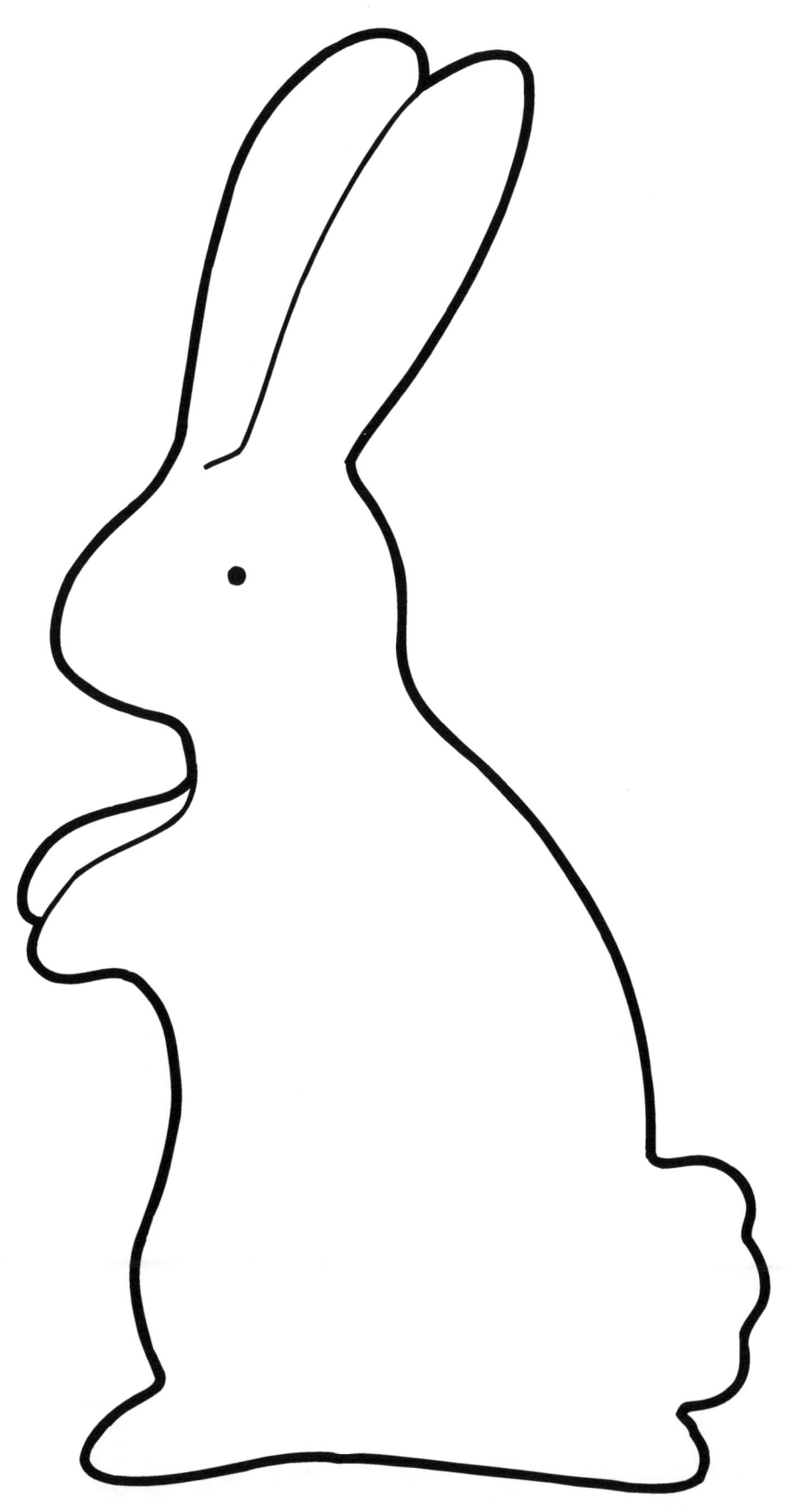

rabbit (outline)

rabbit (stylized)

raccoon

raccoon (waving)

raindrop

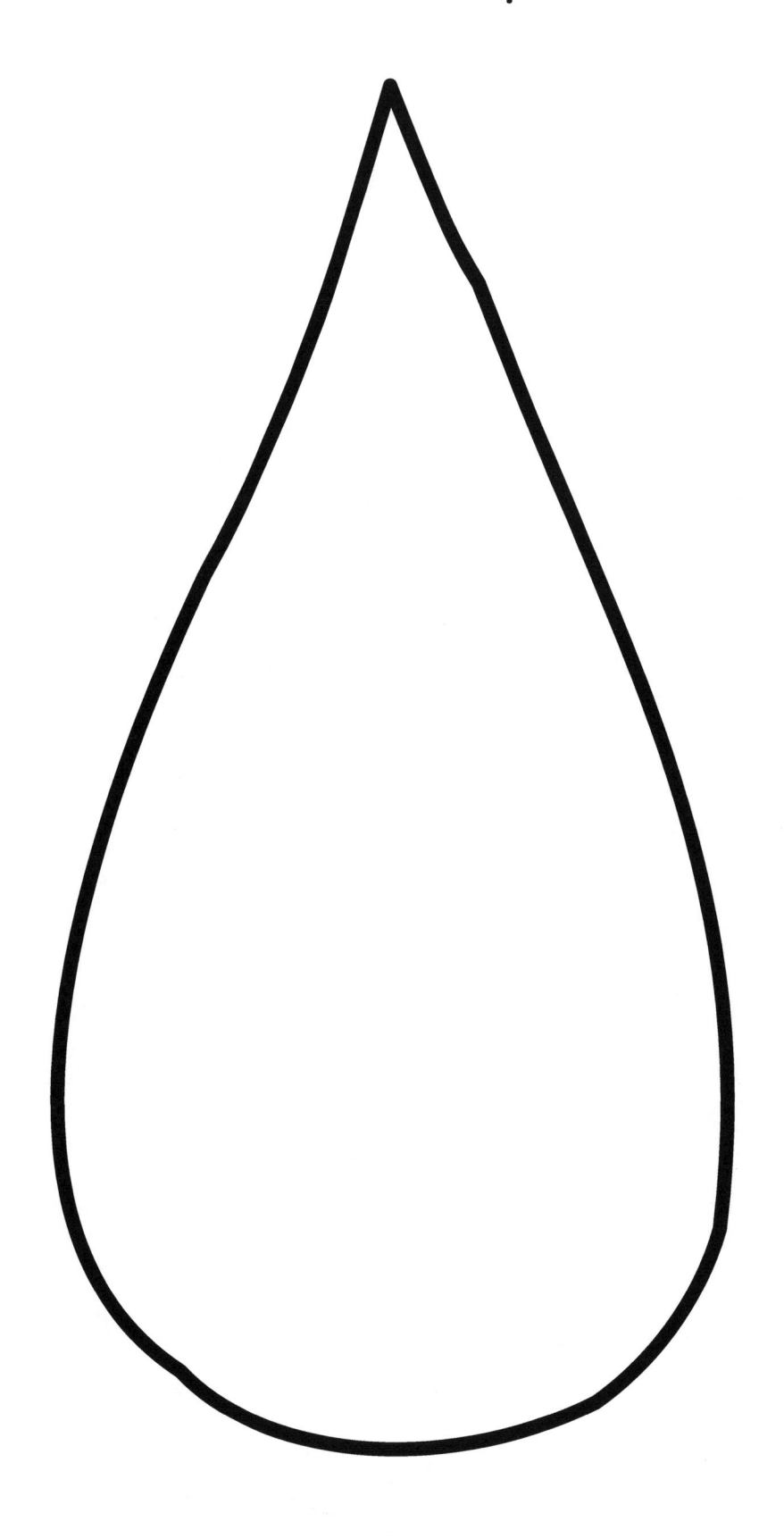

ram

red (crayon)

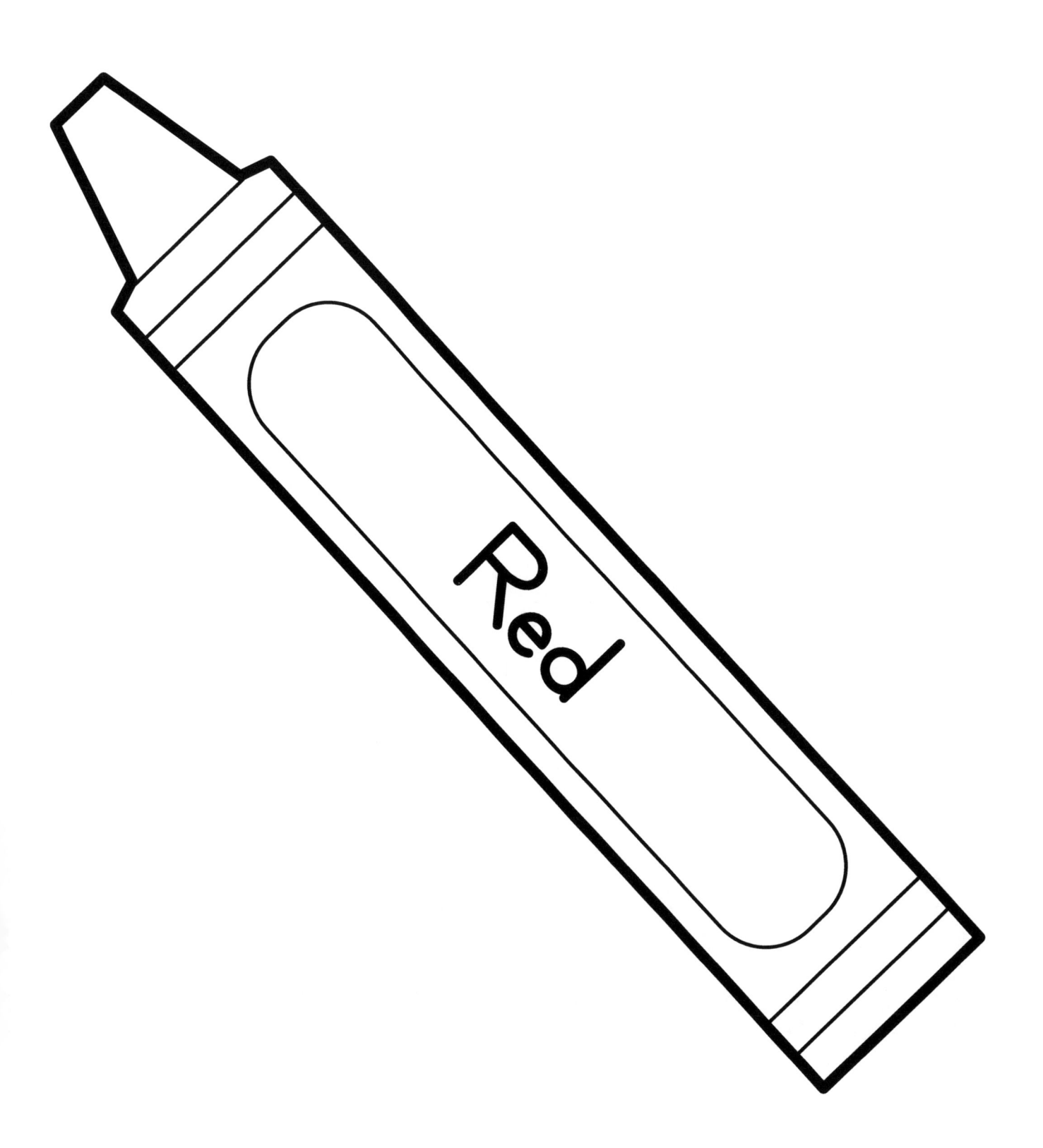

reindeer

rhinoceros

Rhode Island, USA

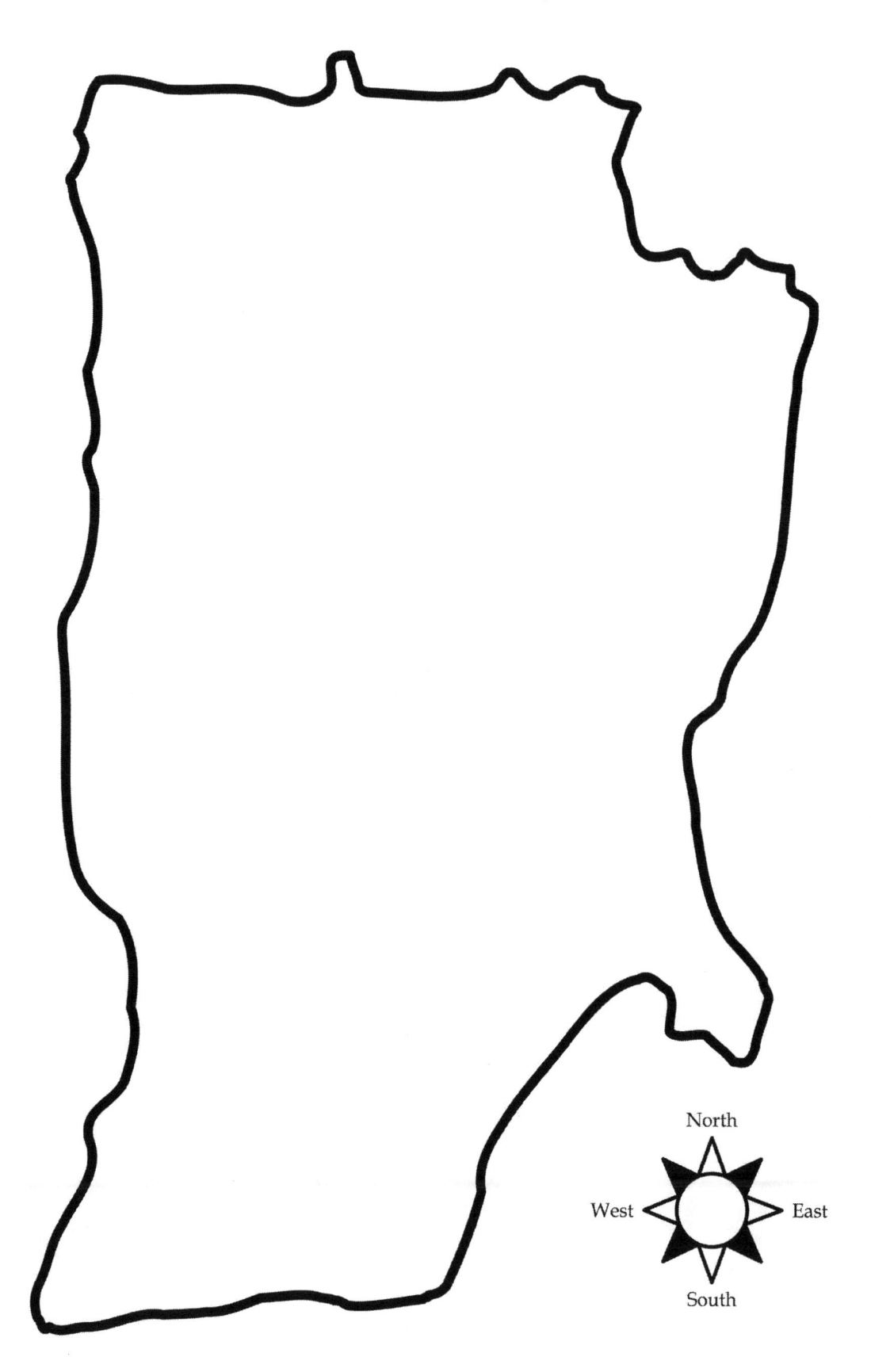

West — East
North
South

Maps are representations and boundaries are not exact.

rollerskate (left)

rollerskate (right)

rollerskate (child, left)

_# rollerskate (child, right)

rooster (animated)

rooster (stylized)

rose

safety pin (closed)

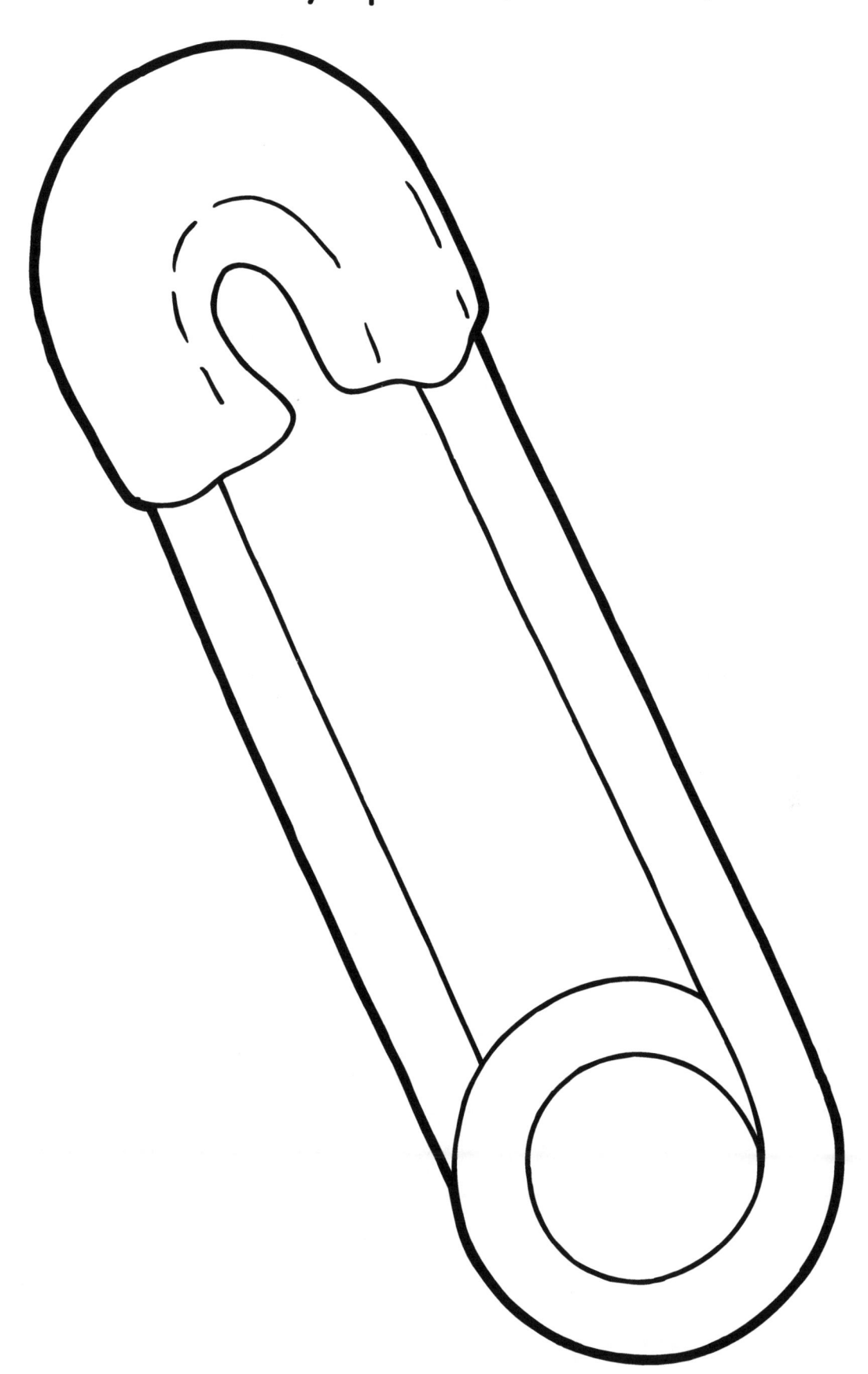

safety pin (open)

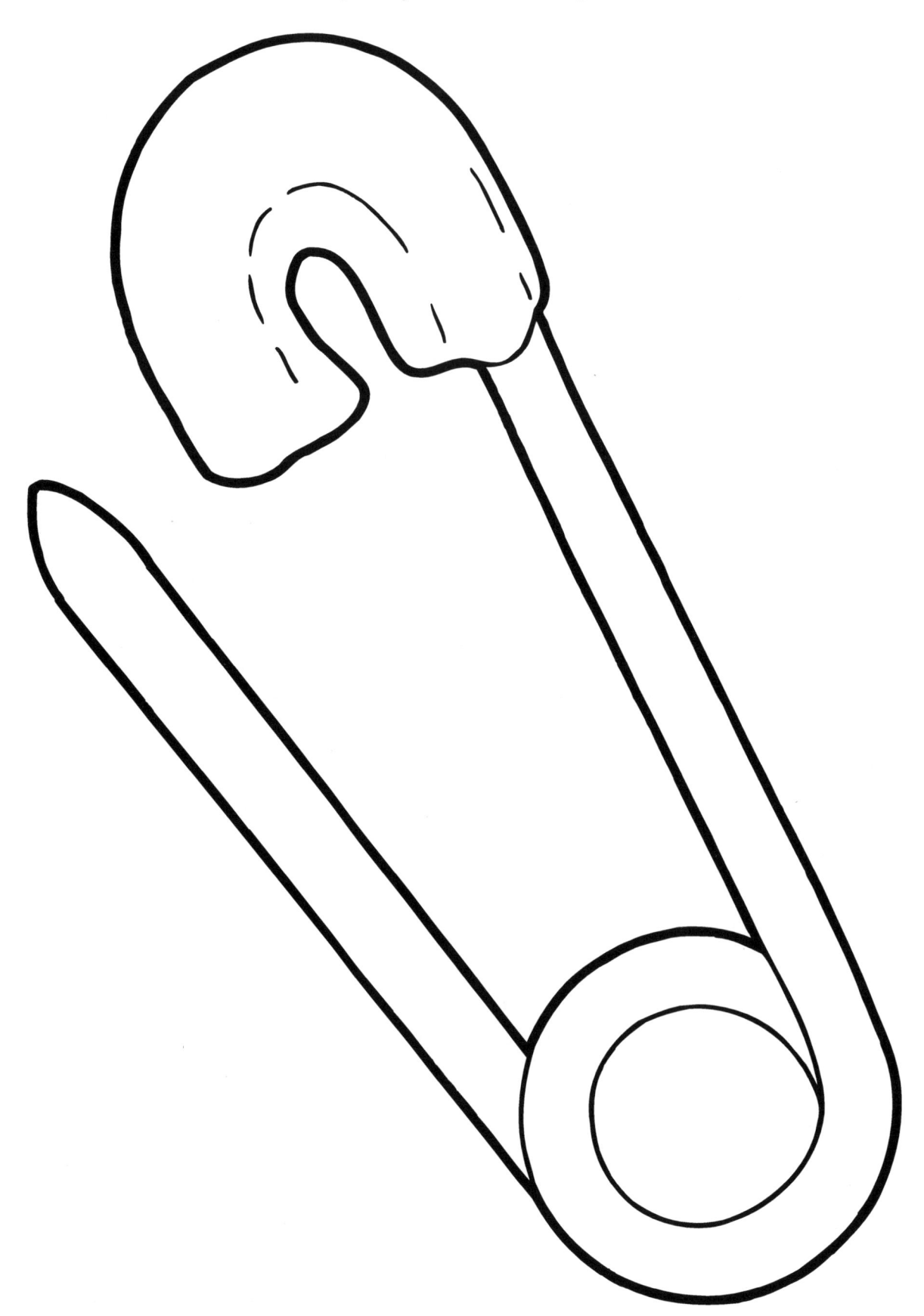

sailboat

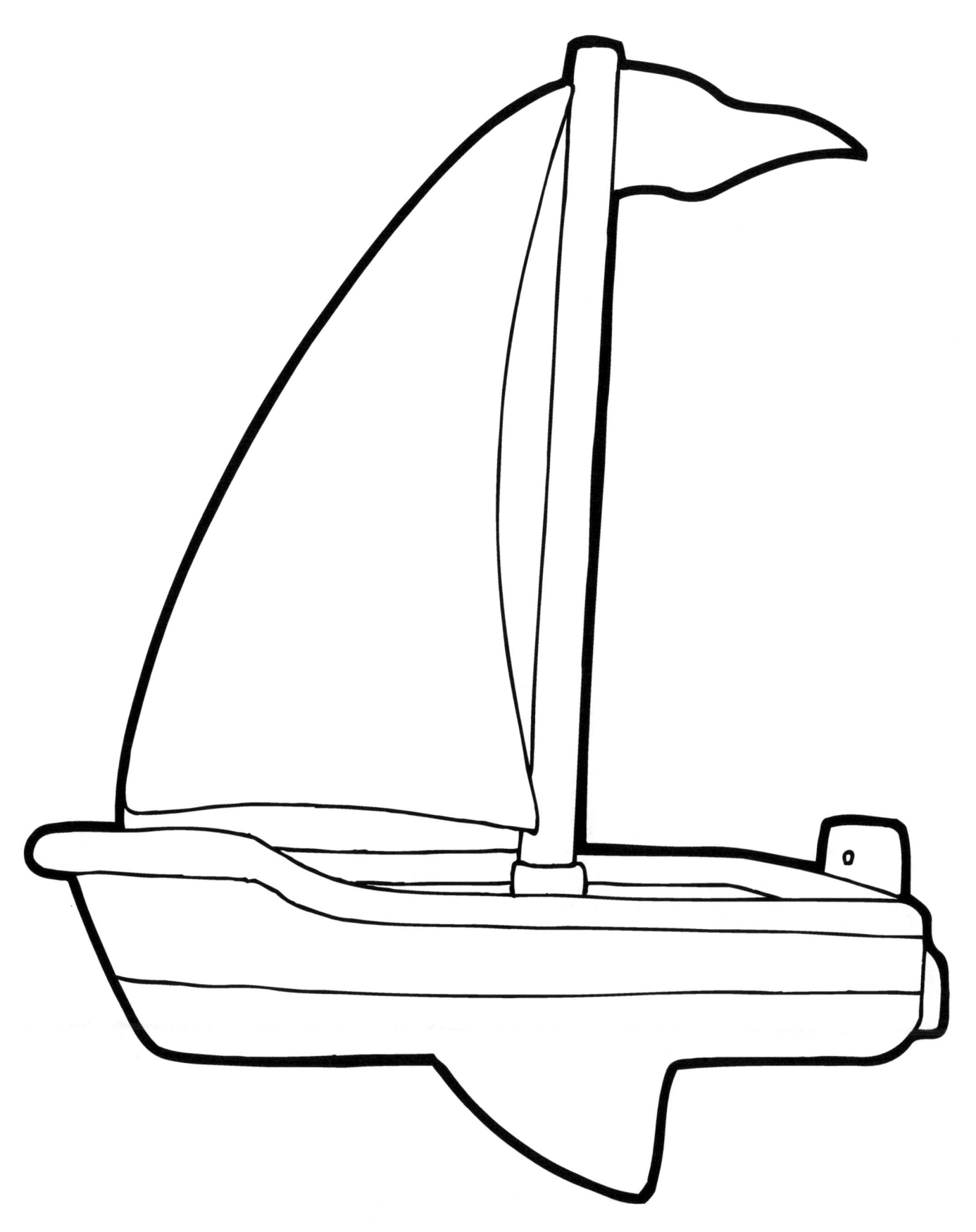

sailboat (outline)

salmon (Chinook)

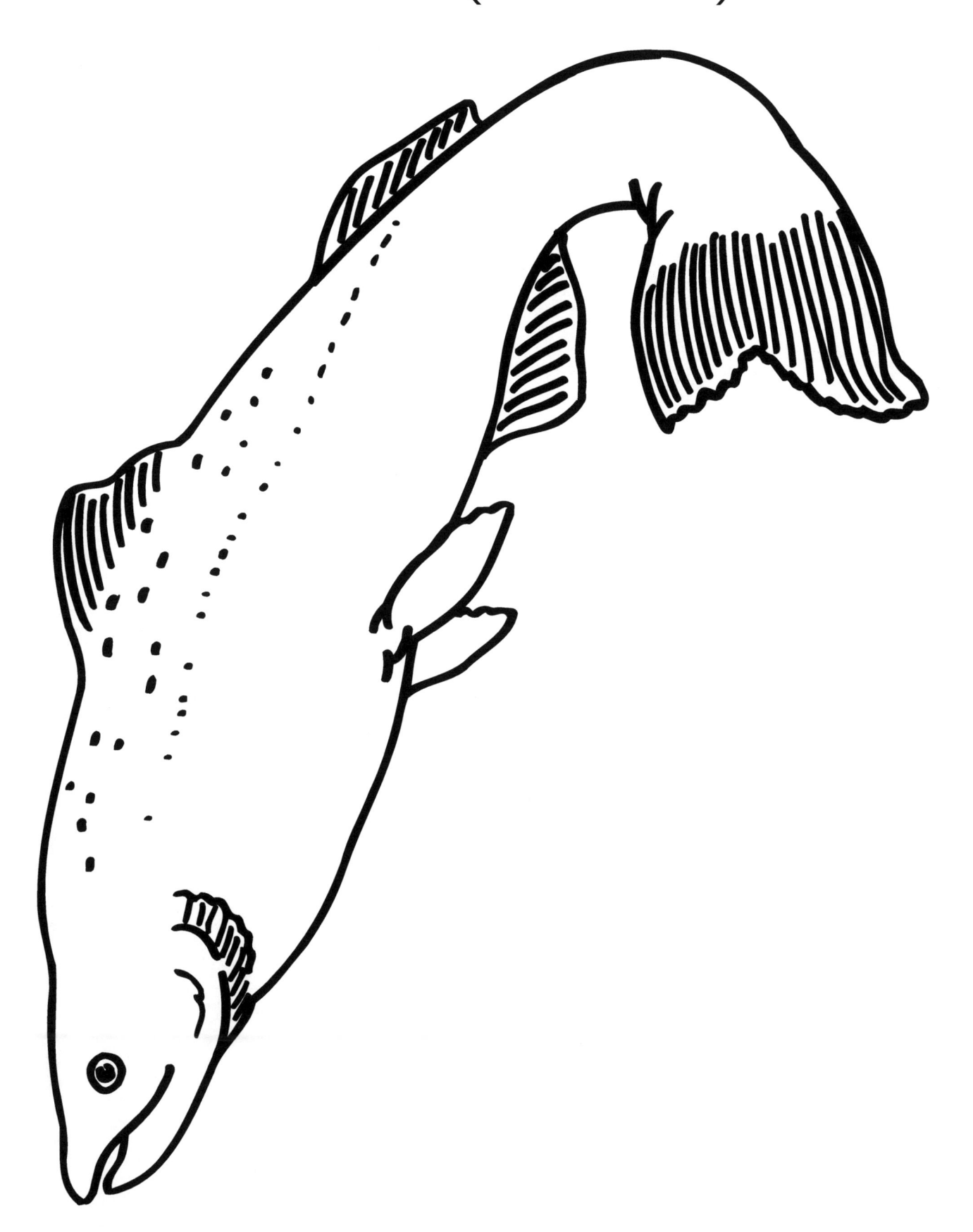

sand pail poster

Saskatchewan, Canada

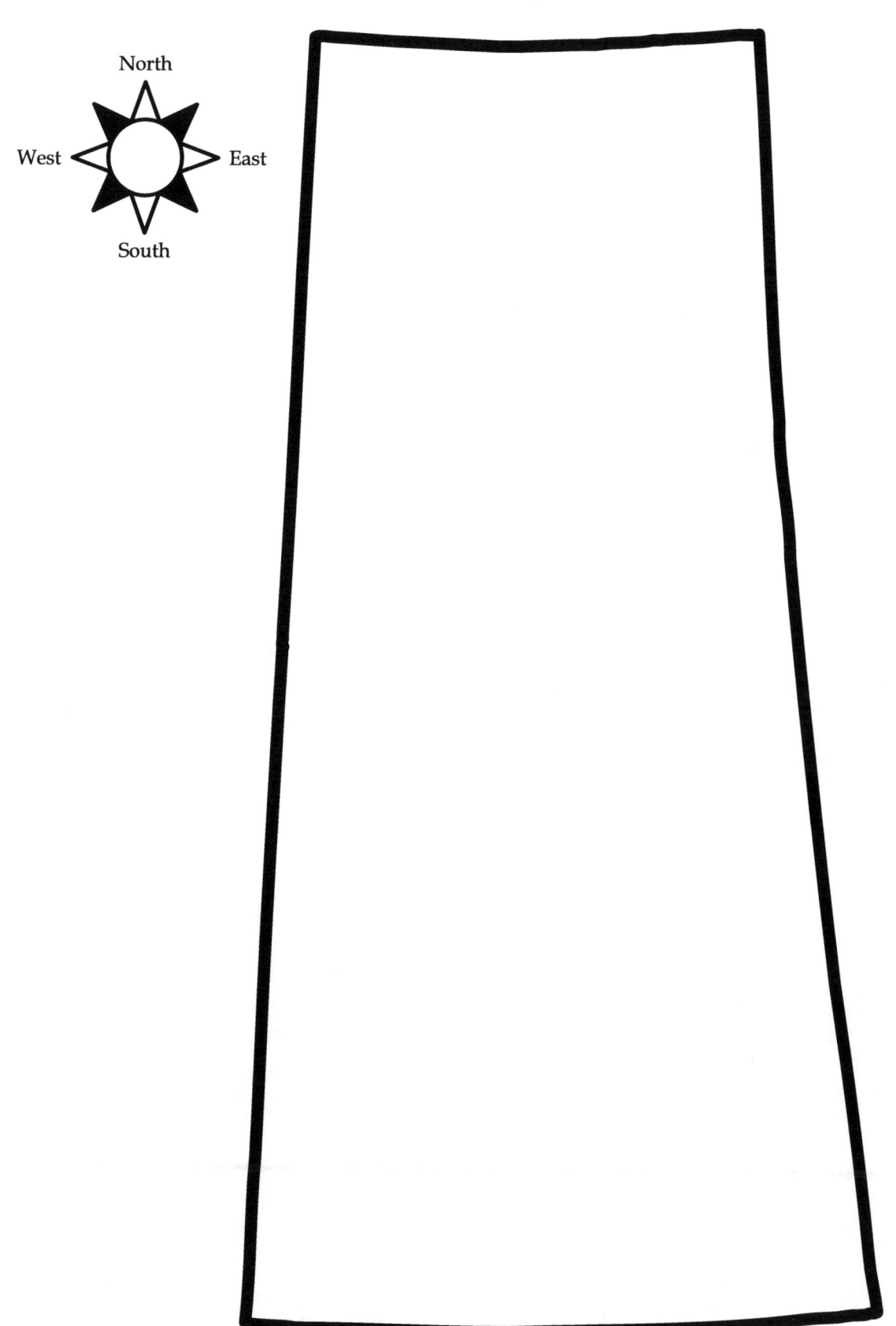

North
West East
South

Maps are representations and boundaries are not exact.

satellite

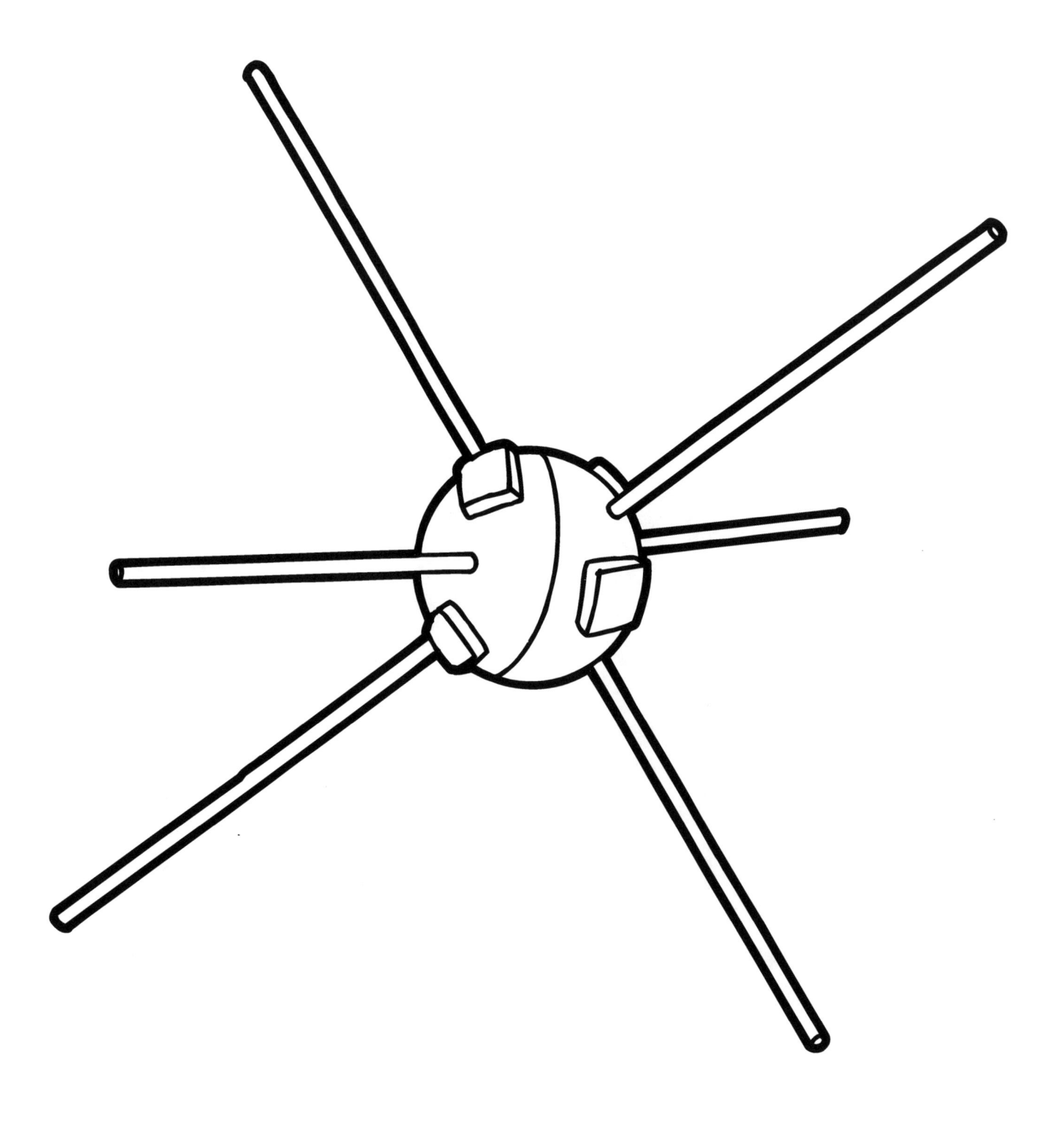

scissors (closed)

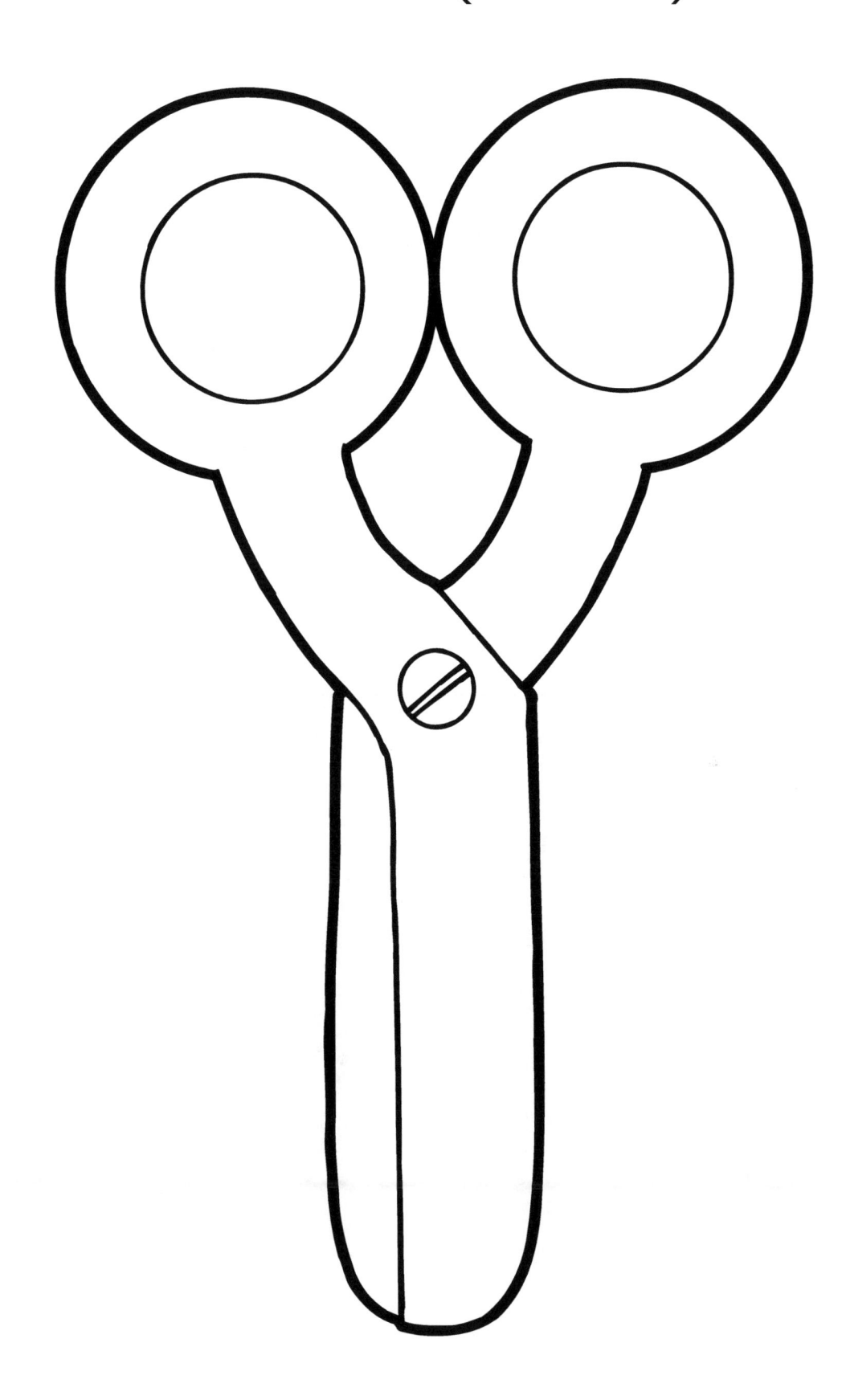

scissors (open)

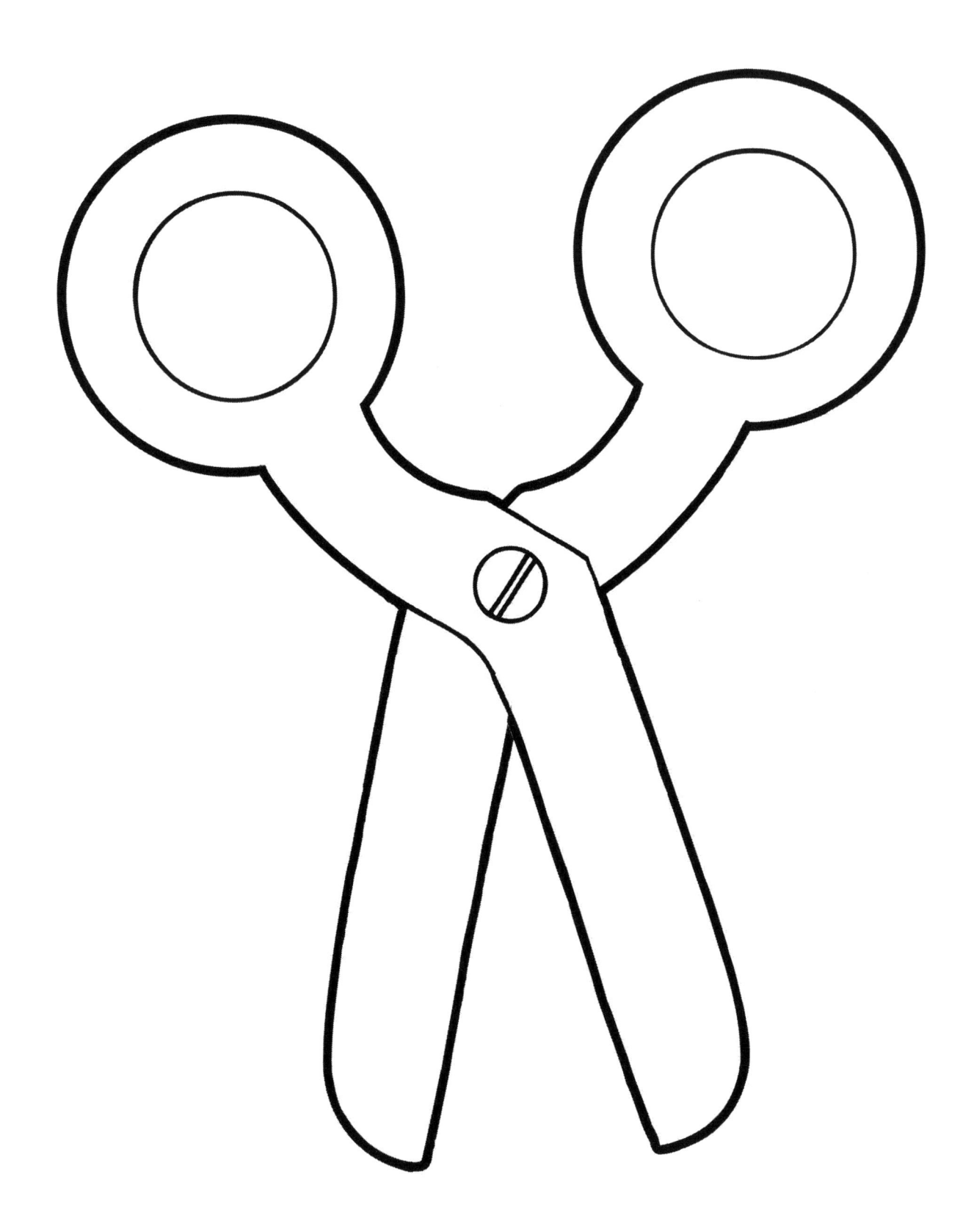

scissors (tailor's)

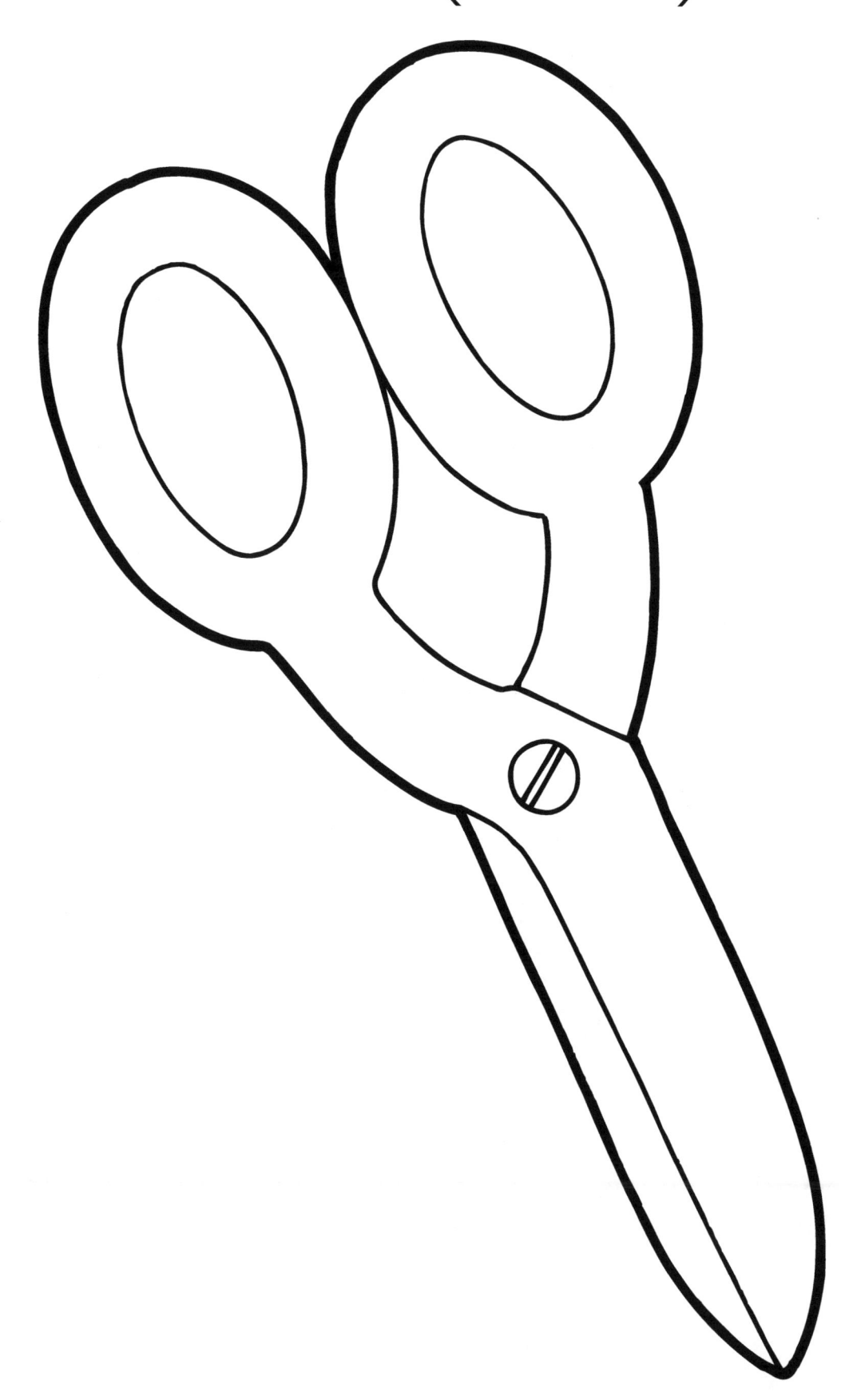

screw (flathead)

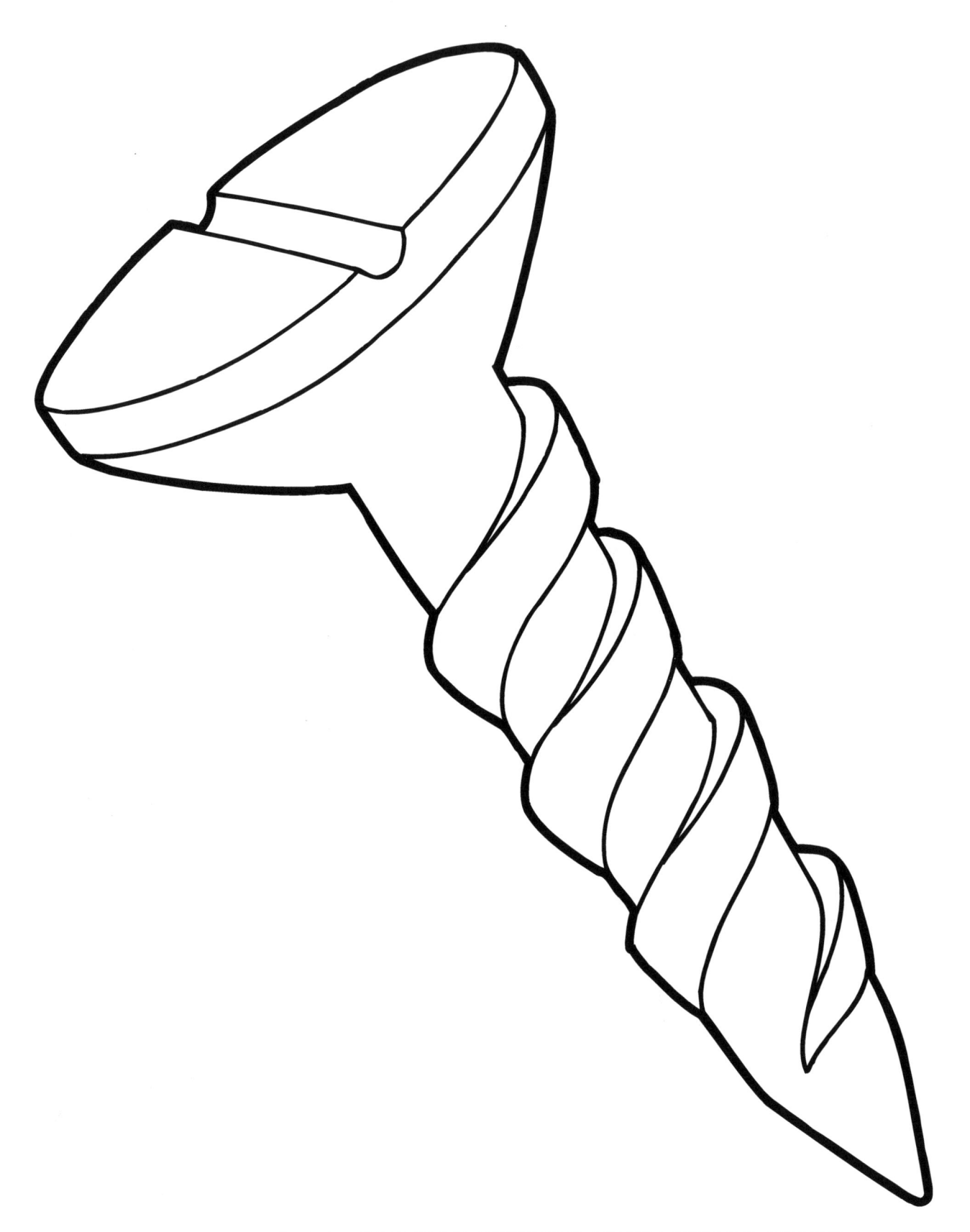

screw (Phillips)

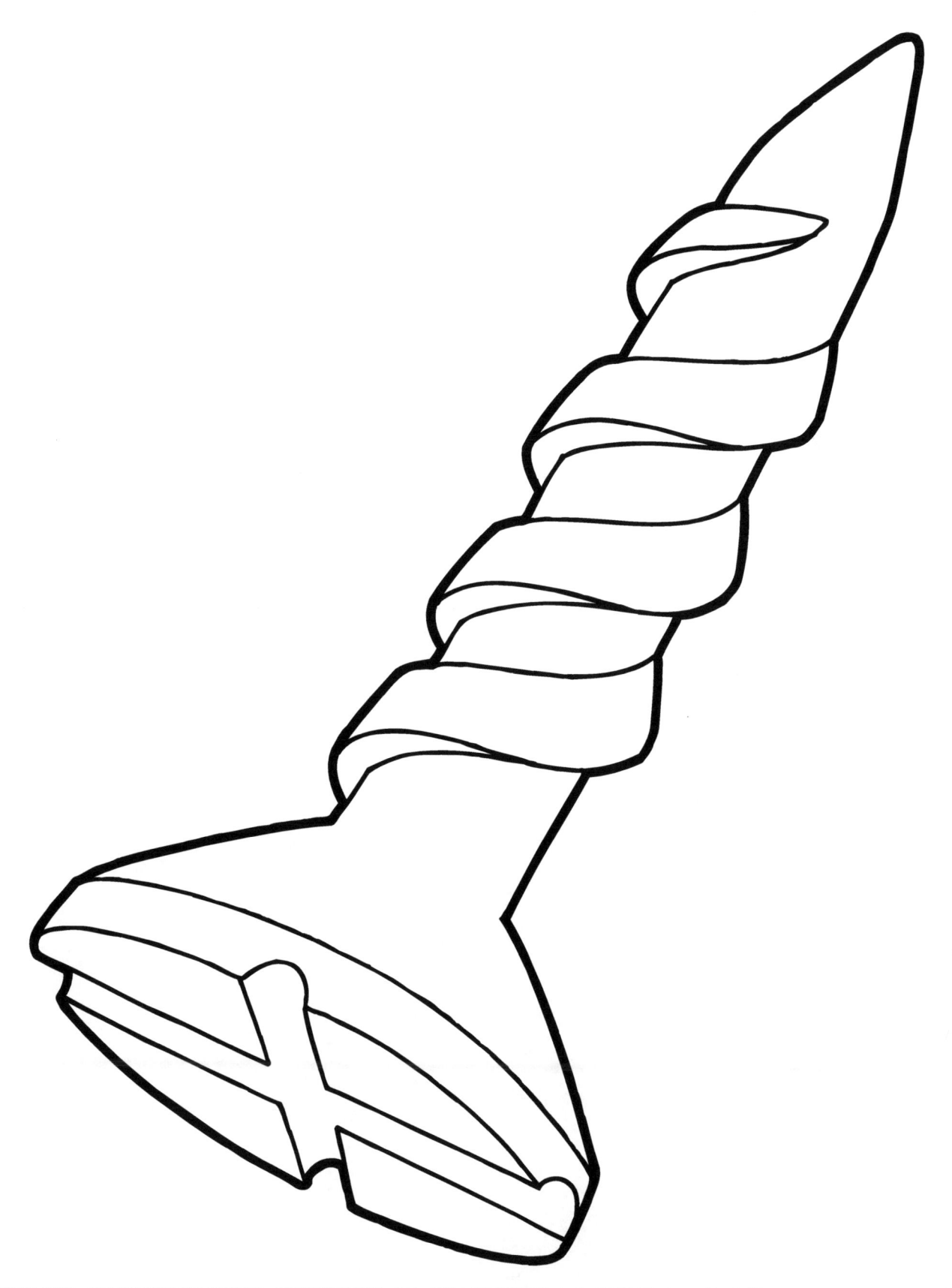

screwdriver (flathead)

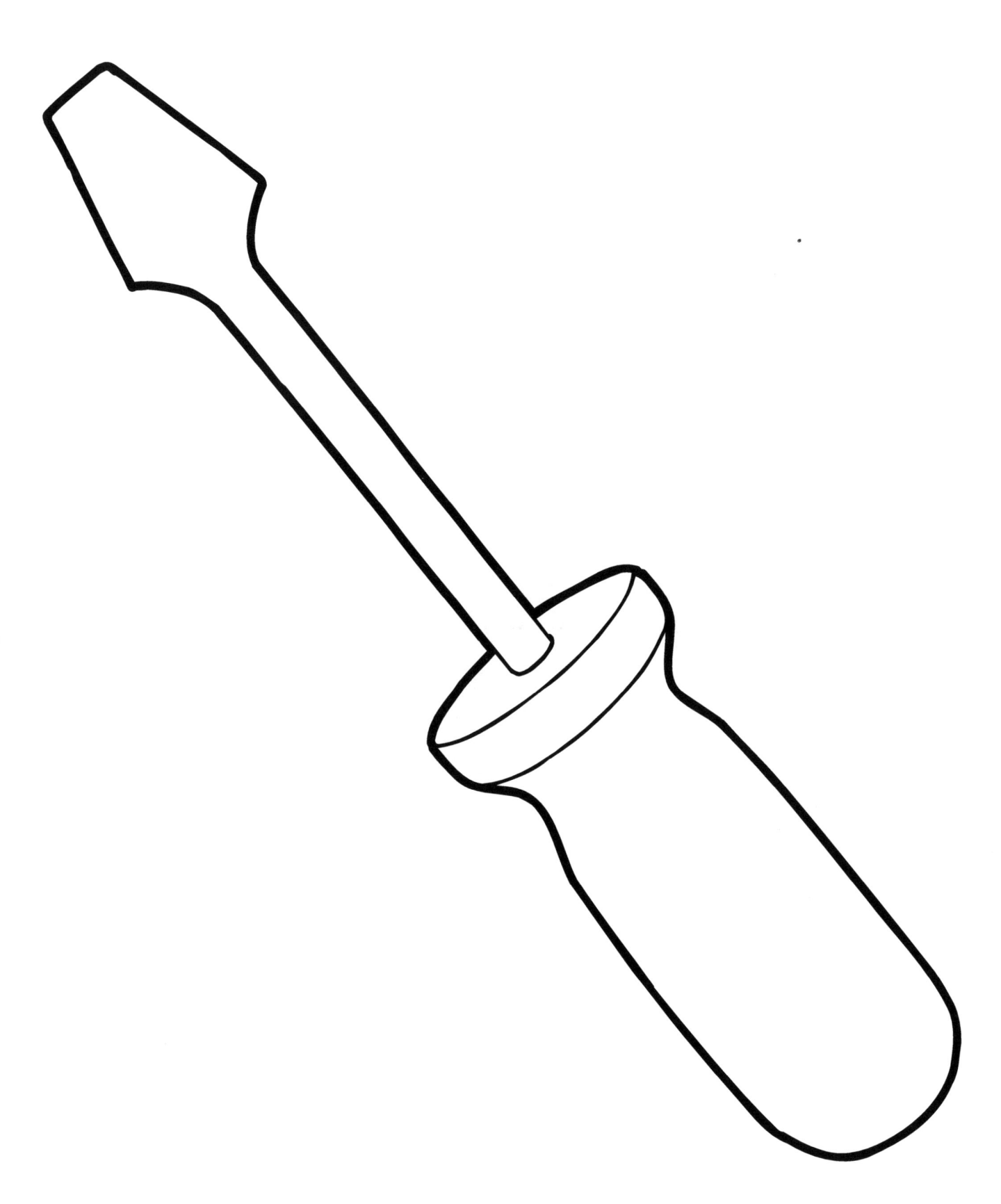

screwdriver (Phillips head)

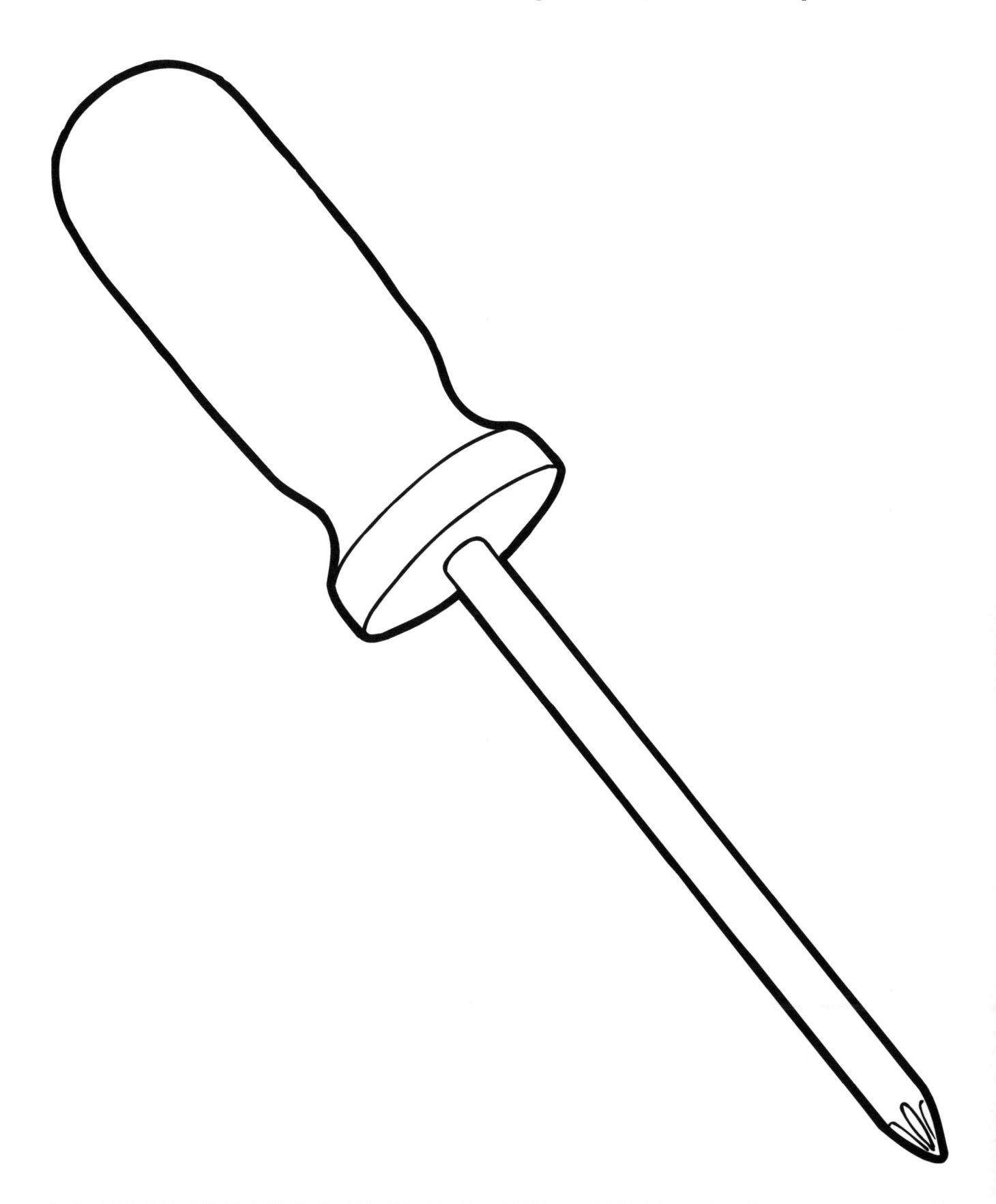

seal (animated)

seal (animated, wearing hat)

seashell

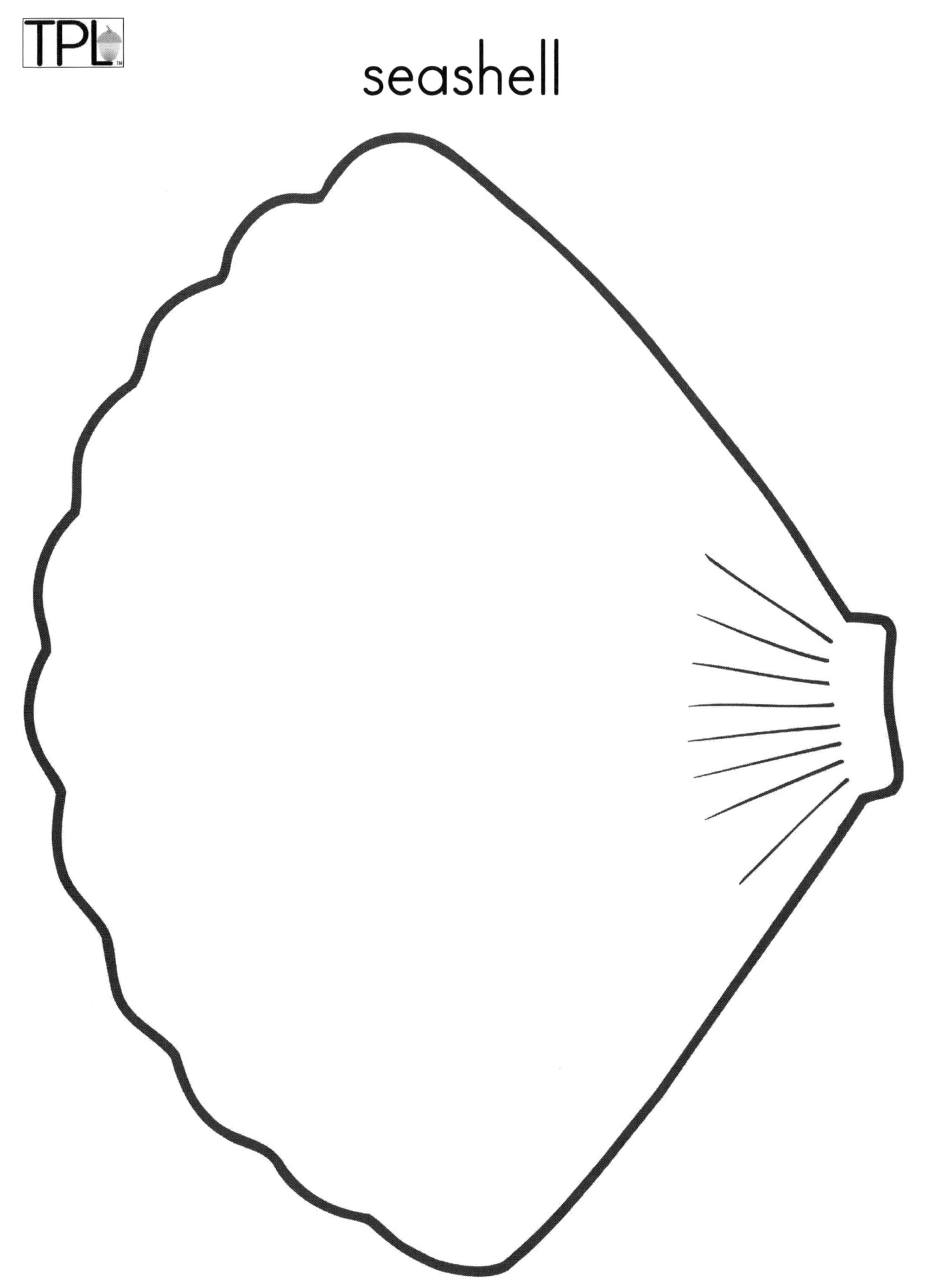

shaker (salt)

ship (toy)

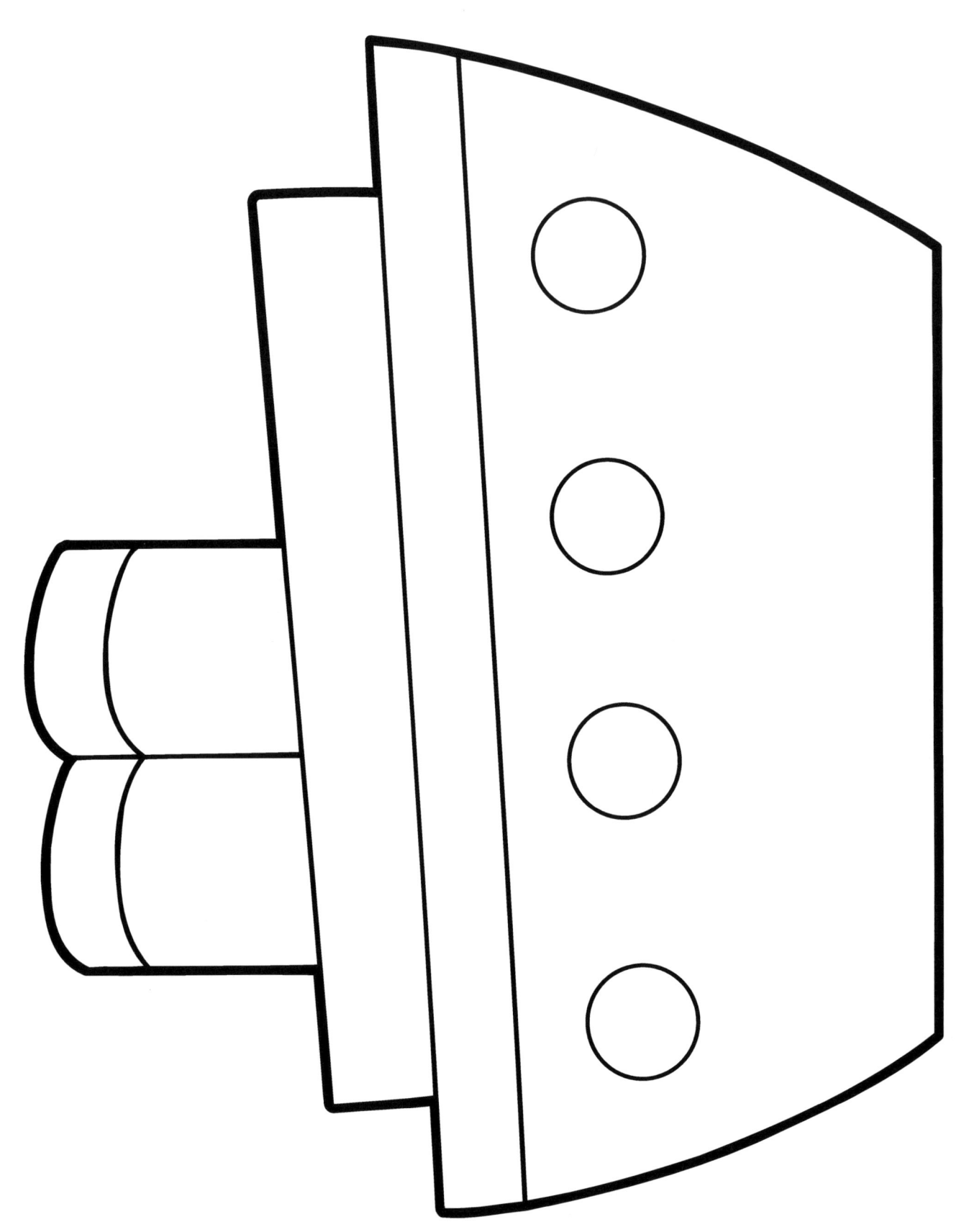

shoe (left-buckle)

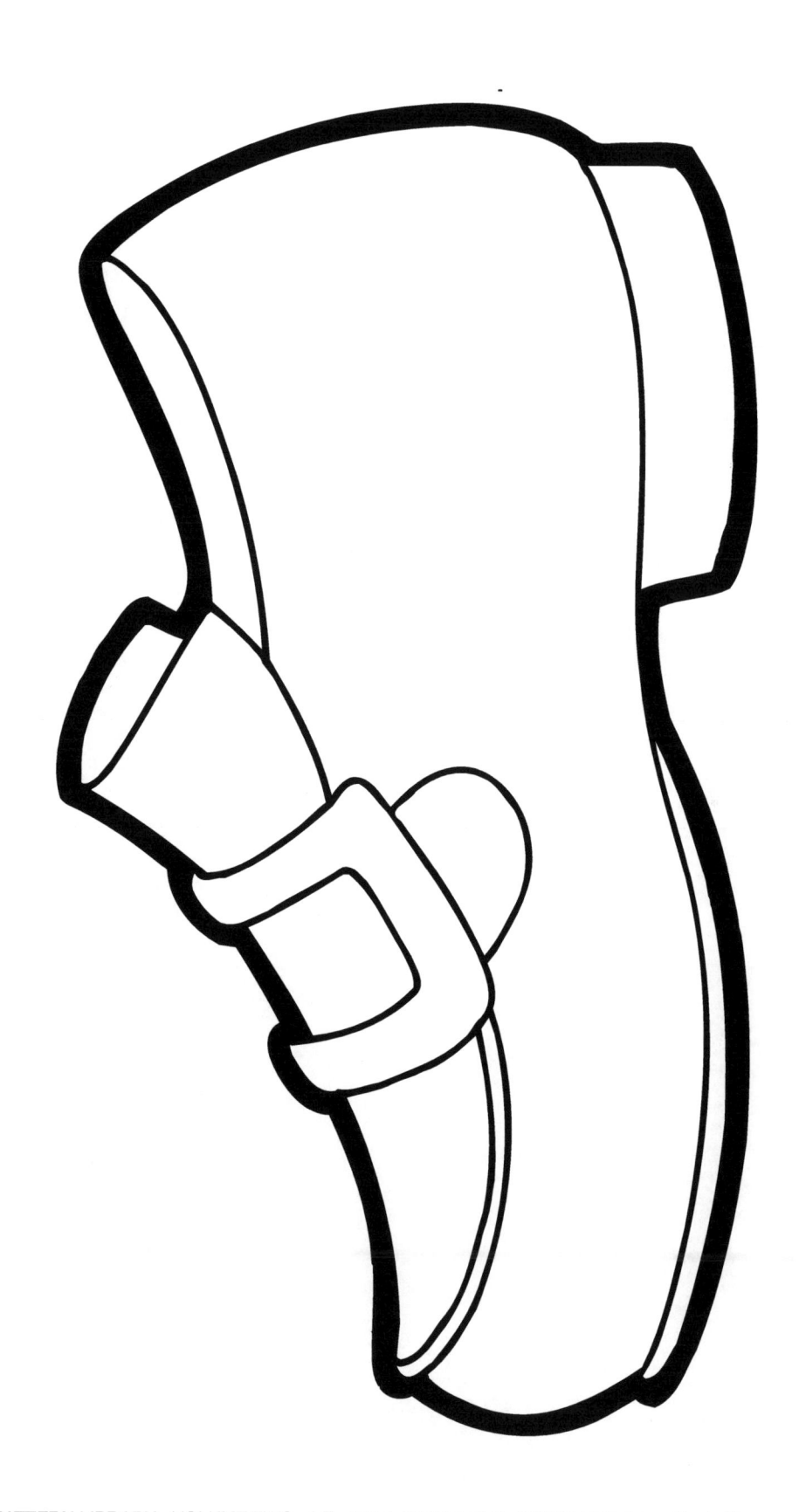

: # show (right-buckle)

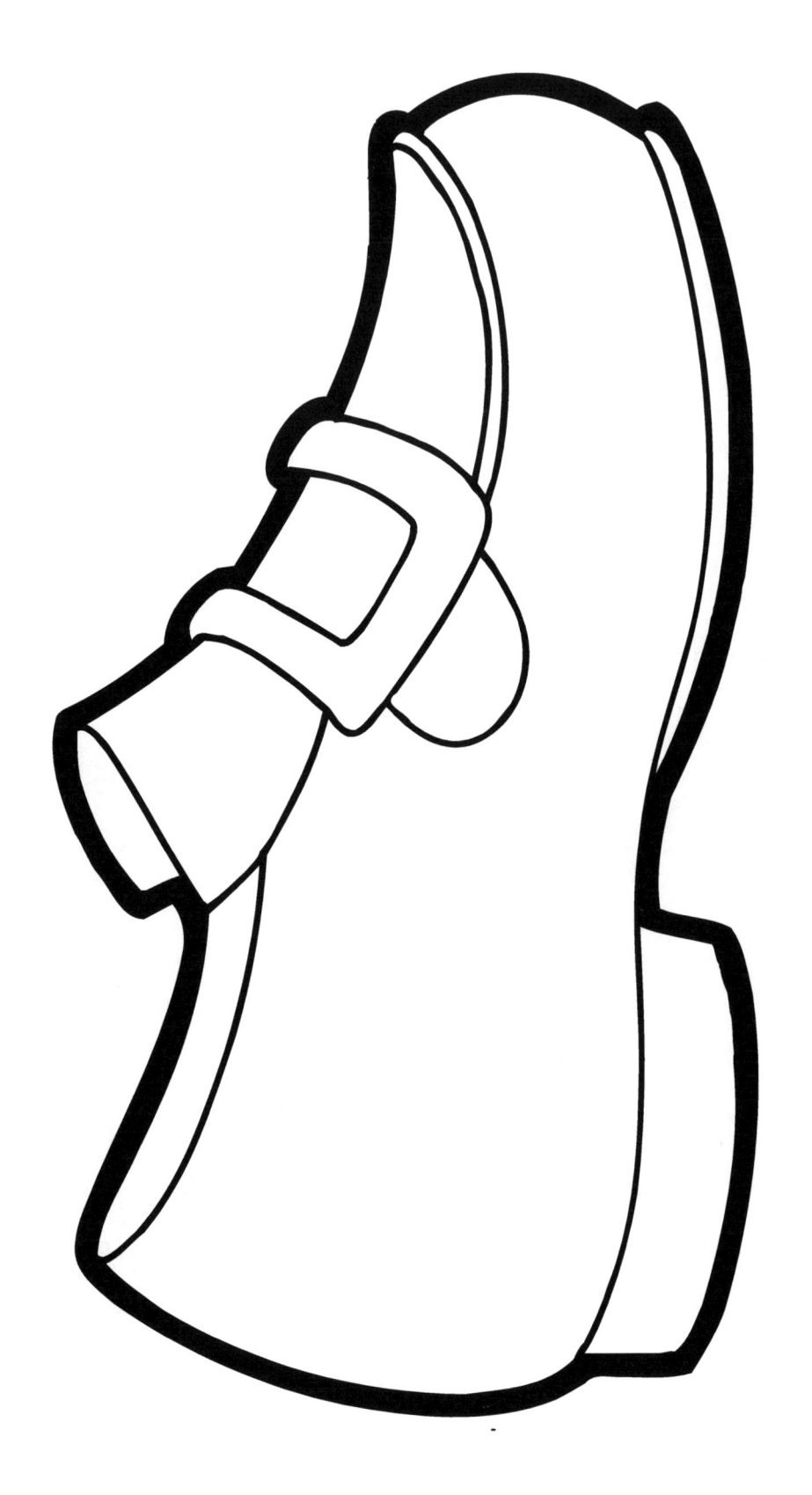

shoe (left-loafer)

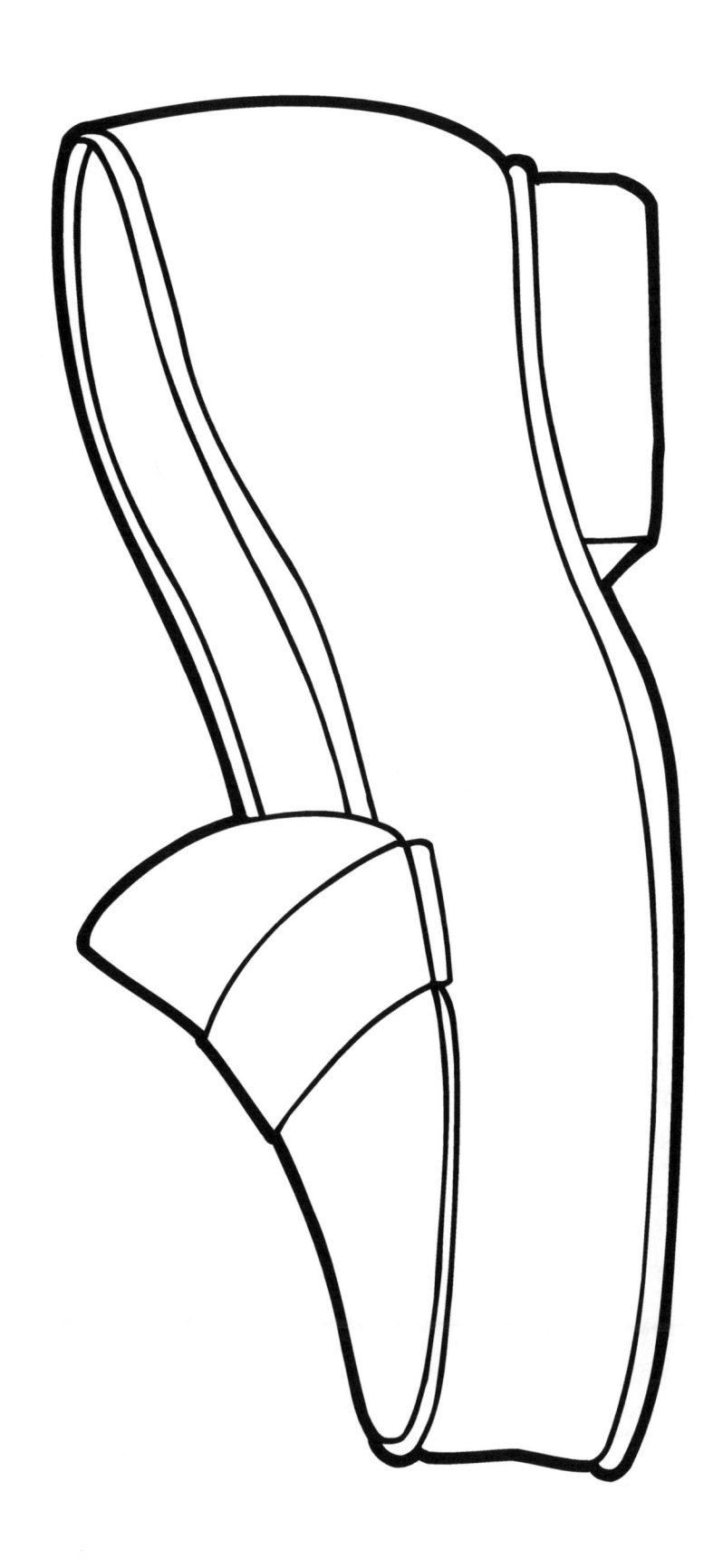

show (right-loafer)

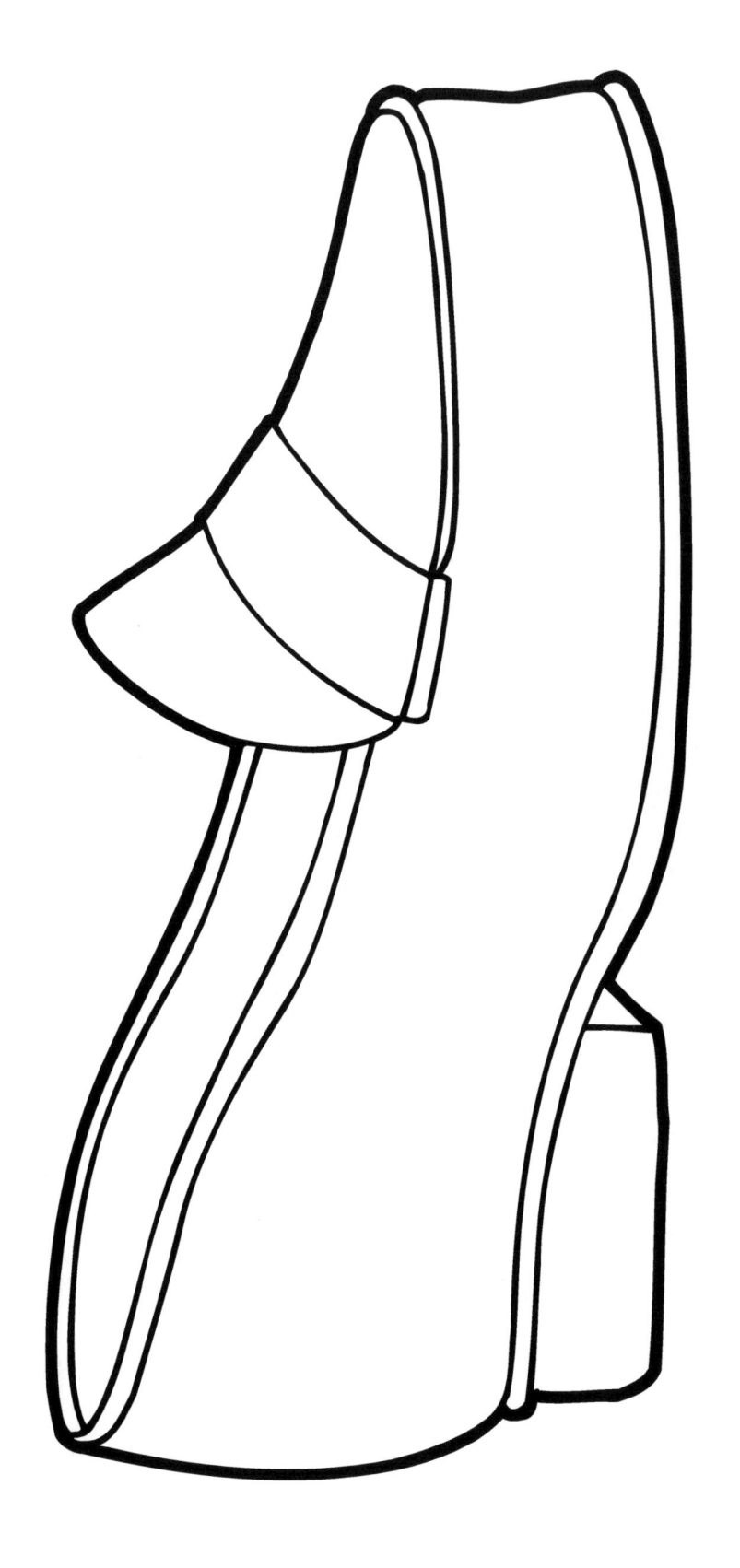

shopping bag

shrew

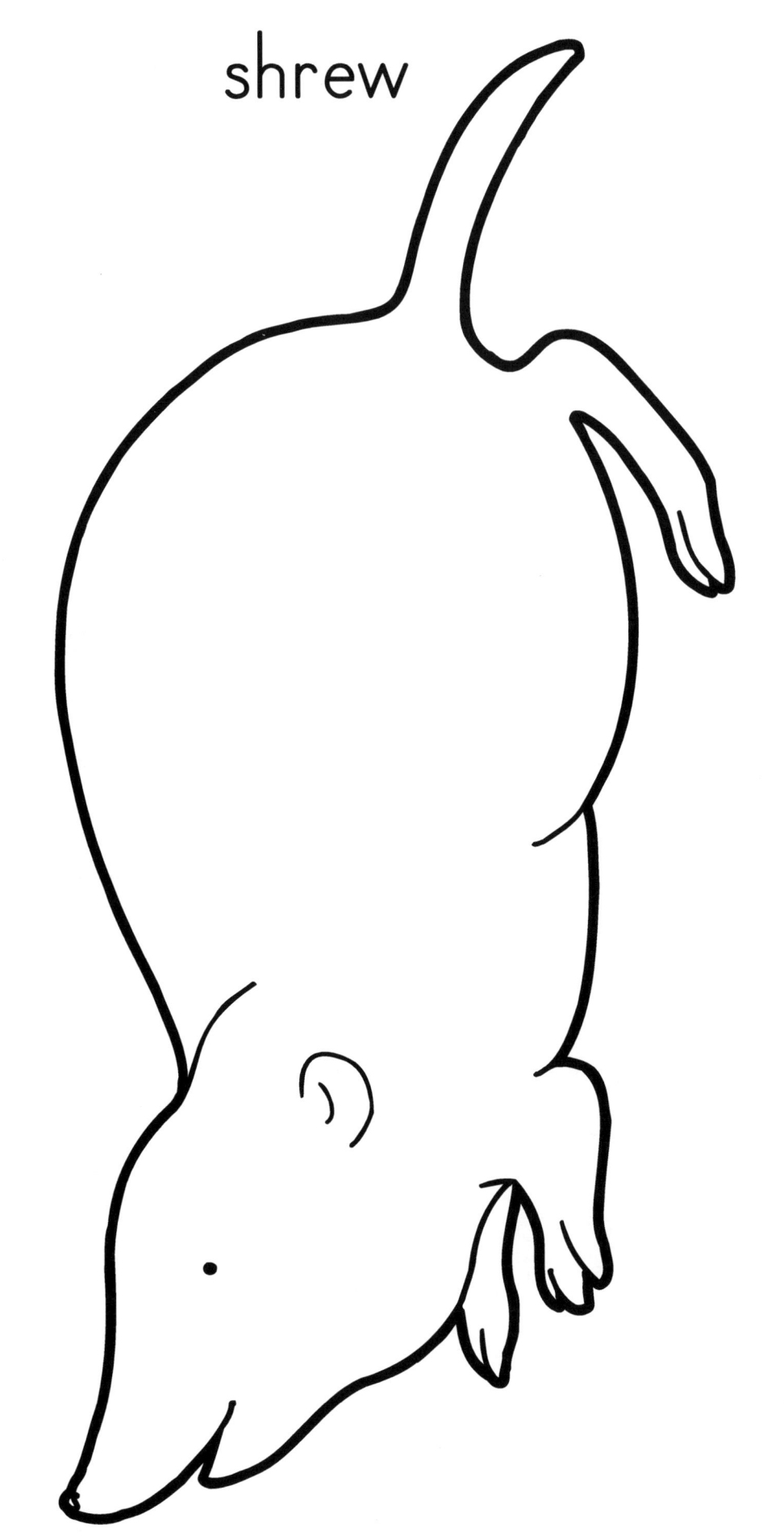

shuttlecock

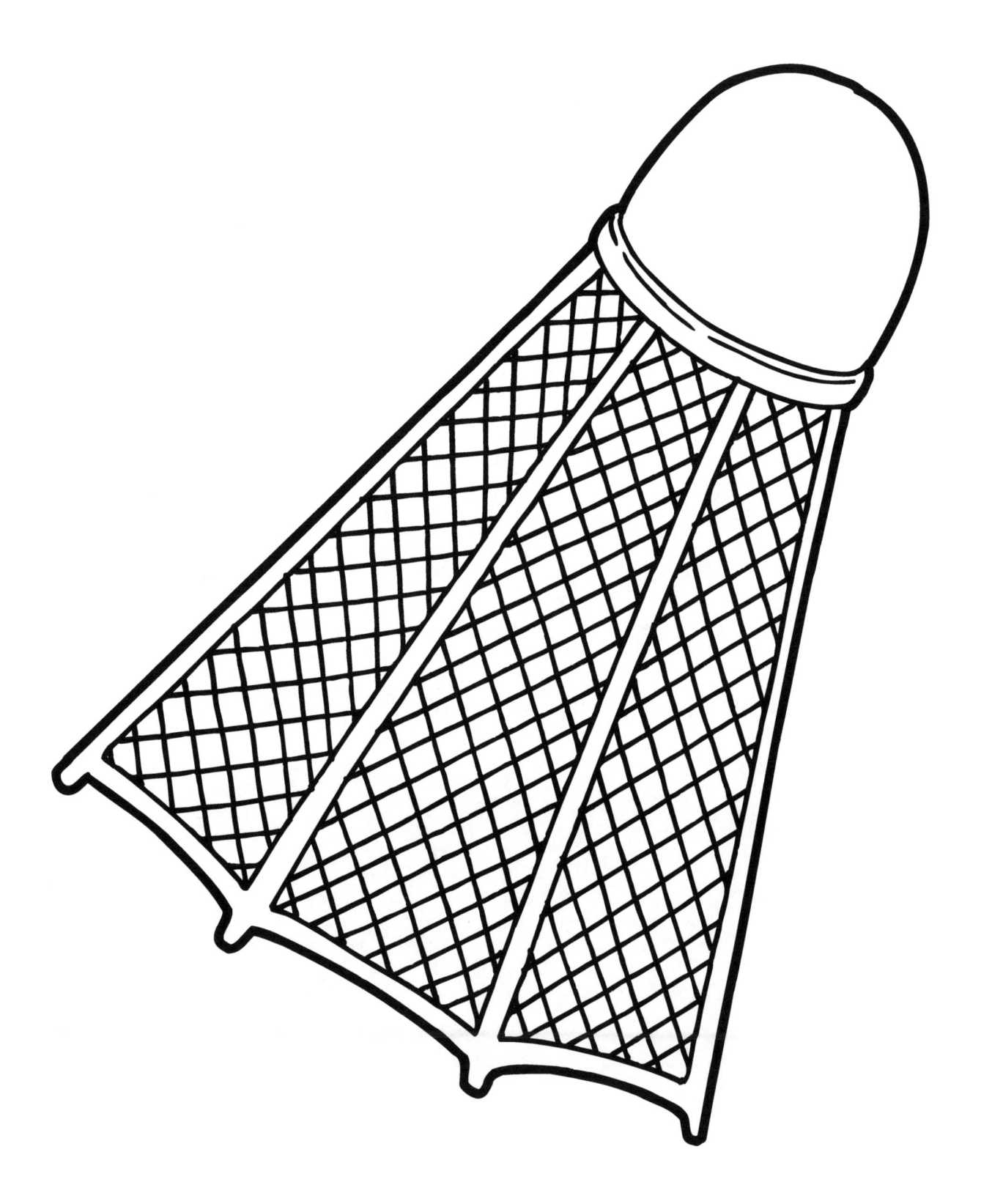

silver (crayon)

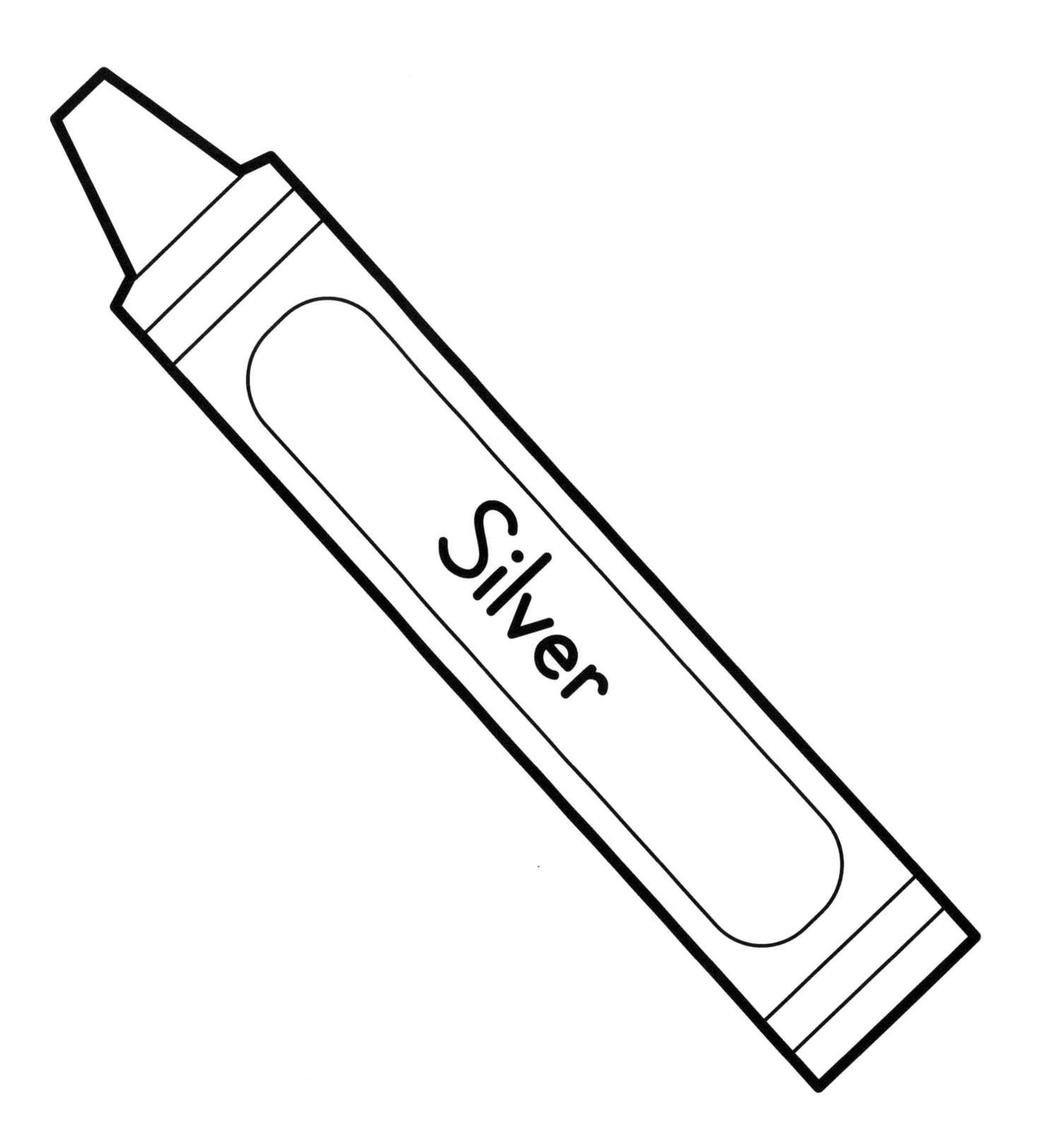

skeleton

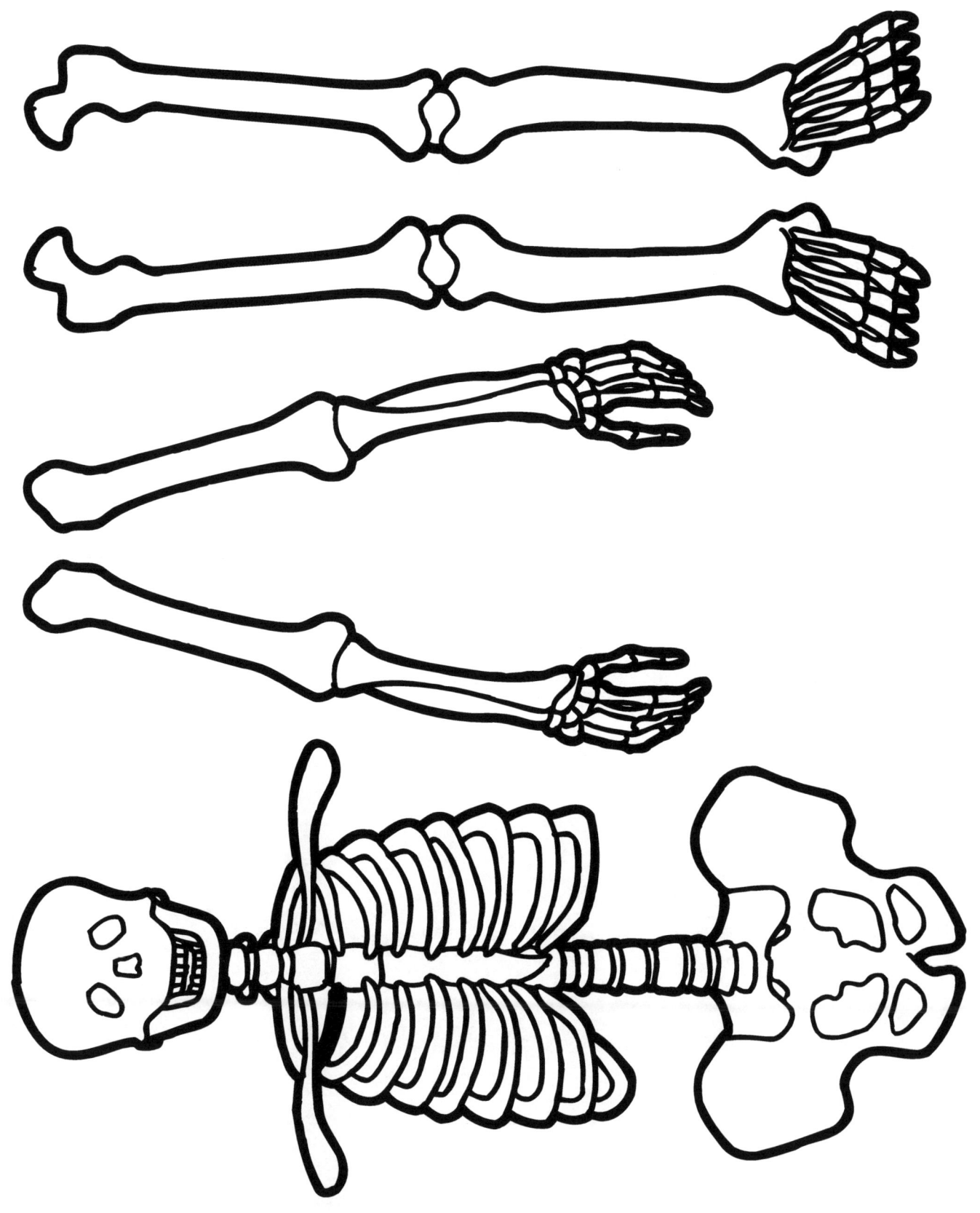

skirt (pleated)

skunk

snail (animated)

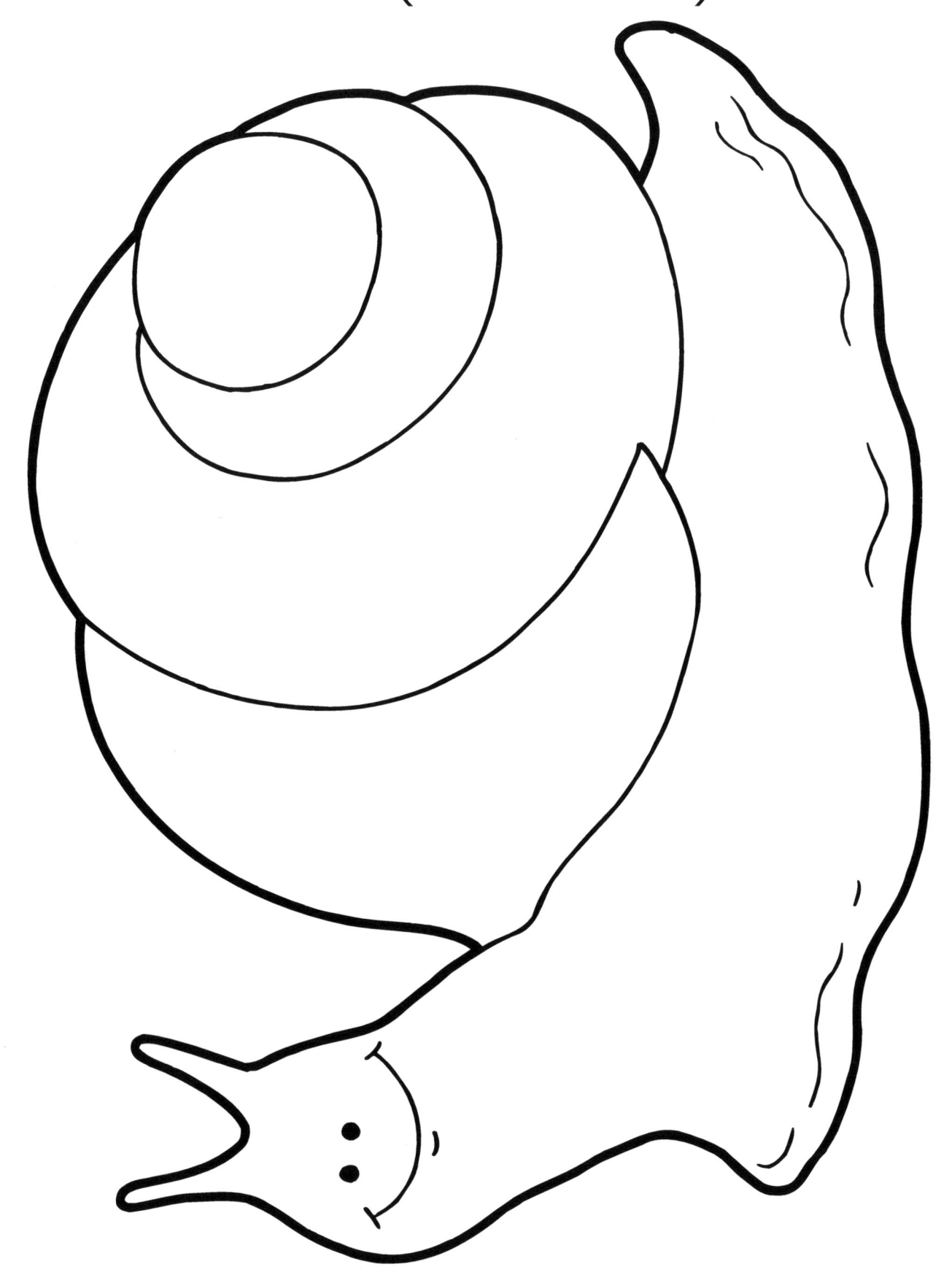

snail (oultine)

snail (stylized)

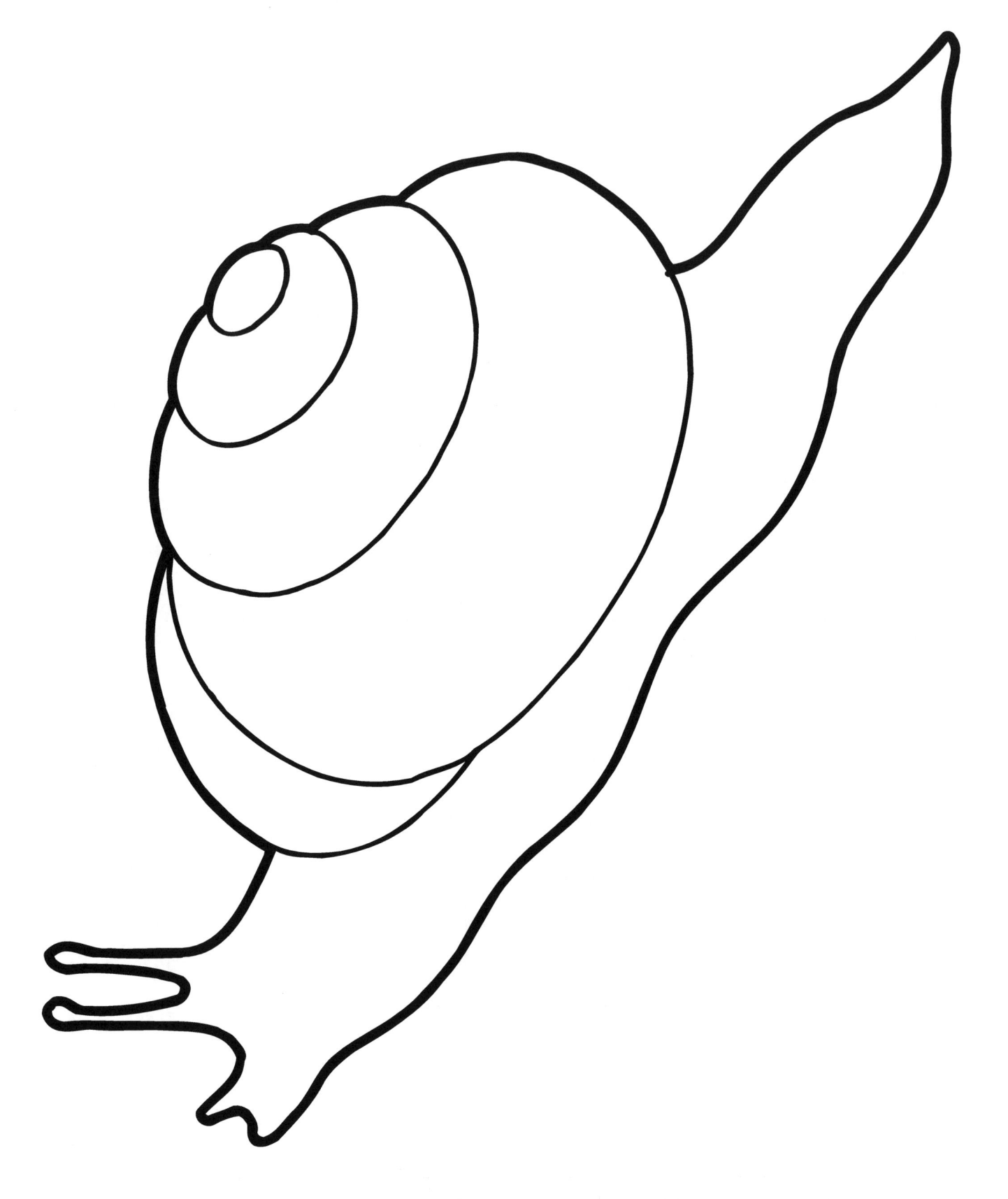

snake

sneaker (left-high top)

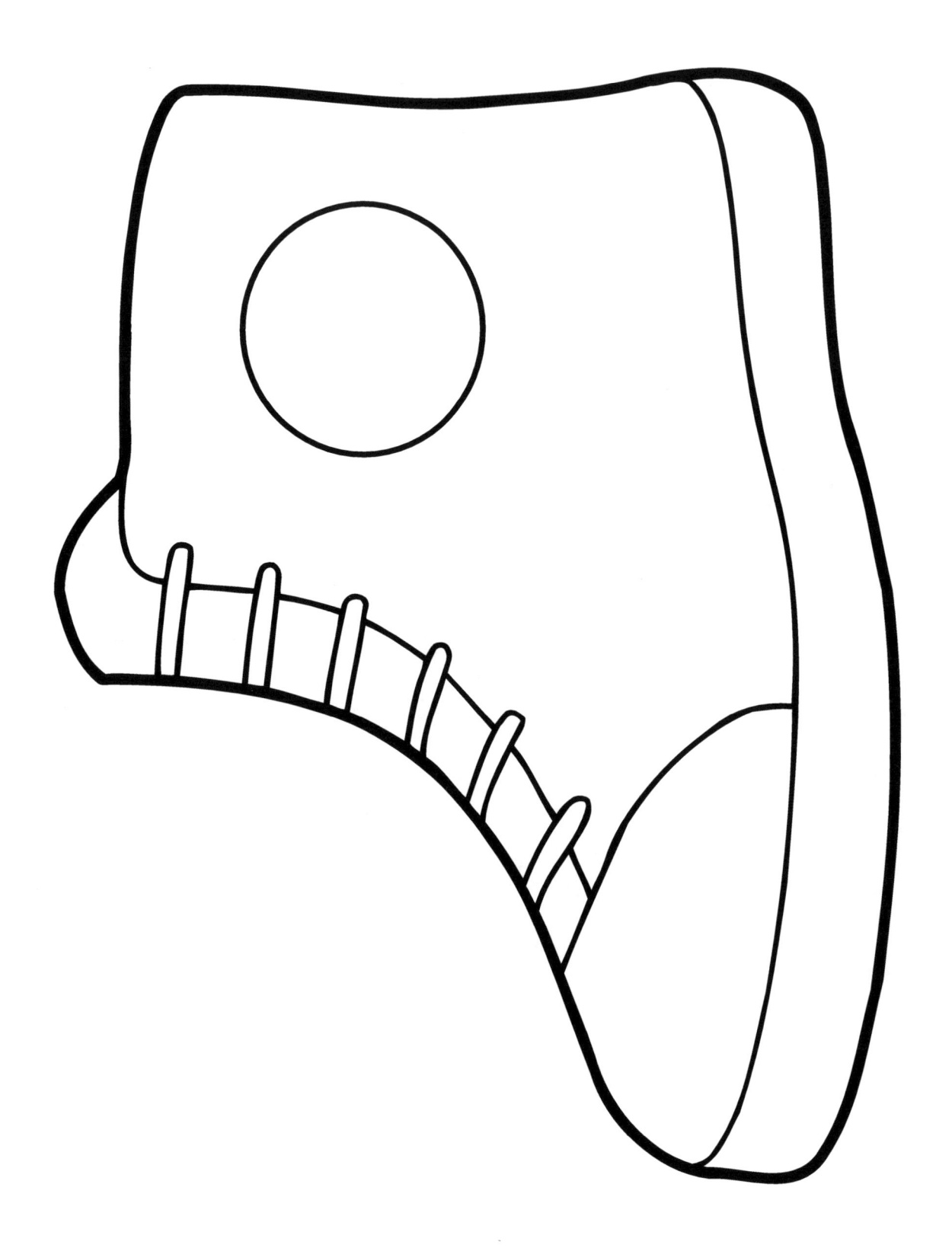

sneaker (right-high top)

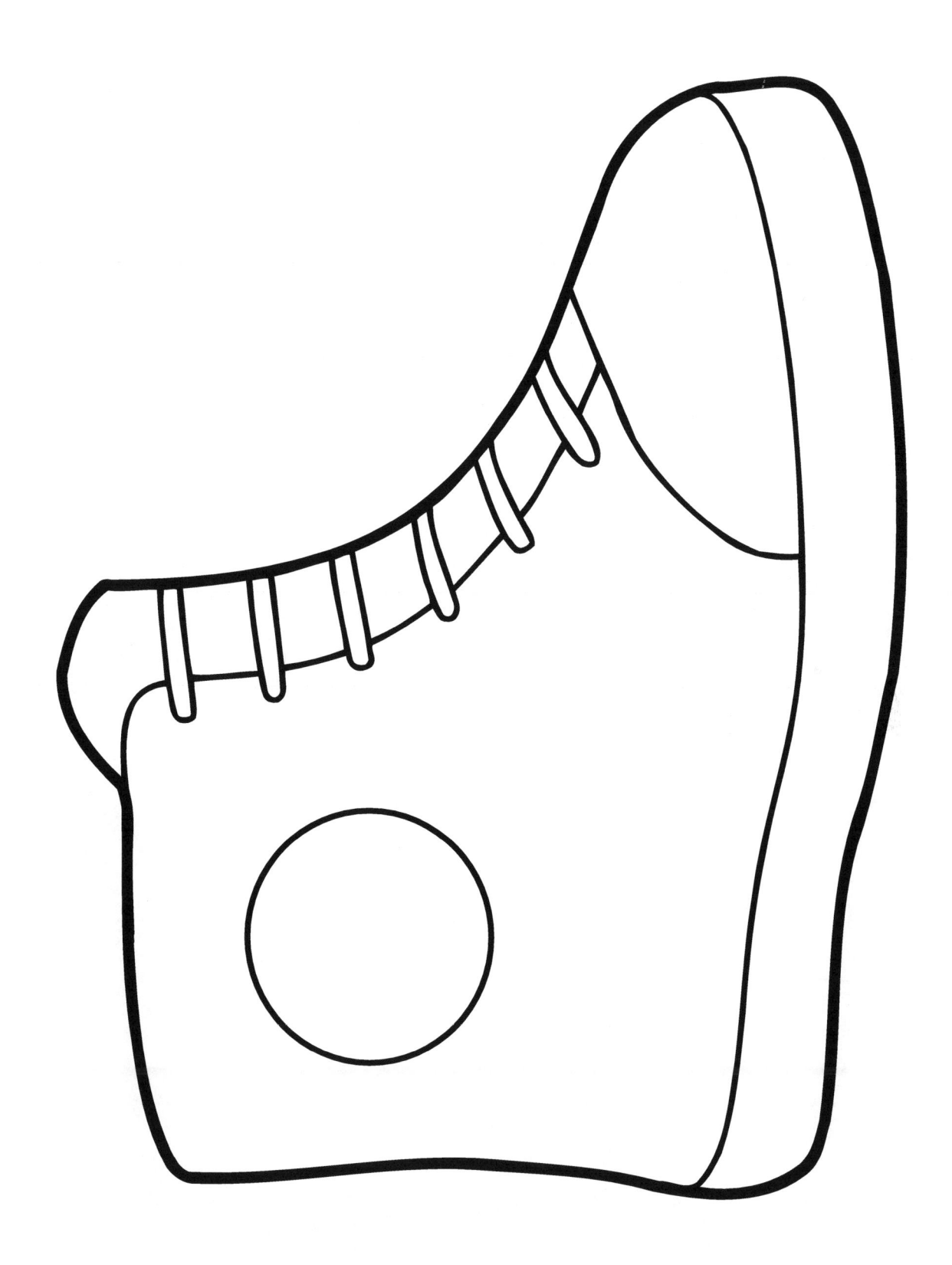

sneaker (outline-high top)

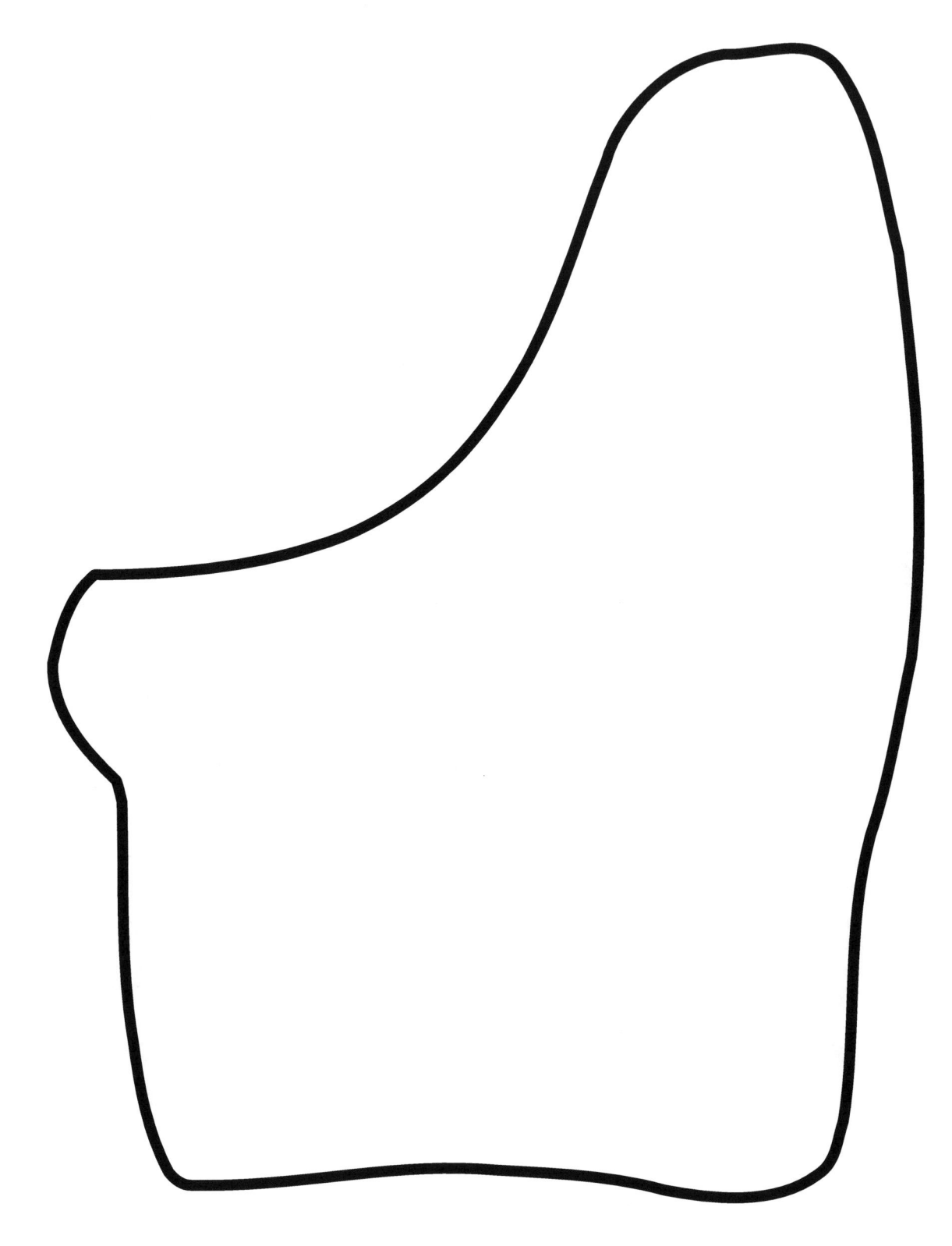

snipe

snowflake

snowman

snowman (waving)

sock (left)

sock (right)

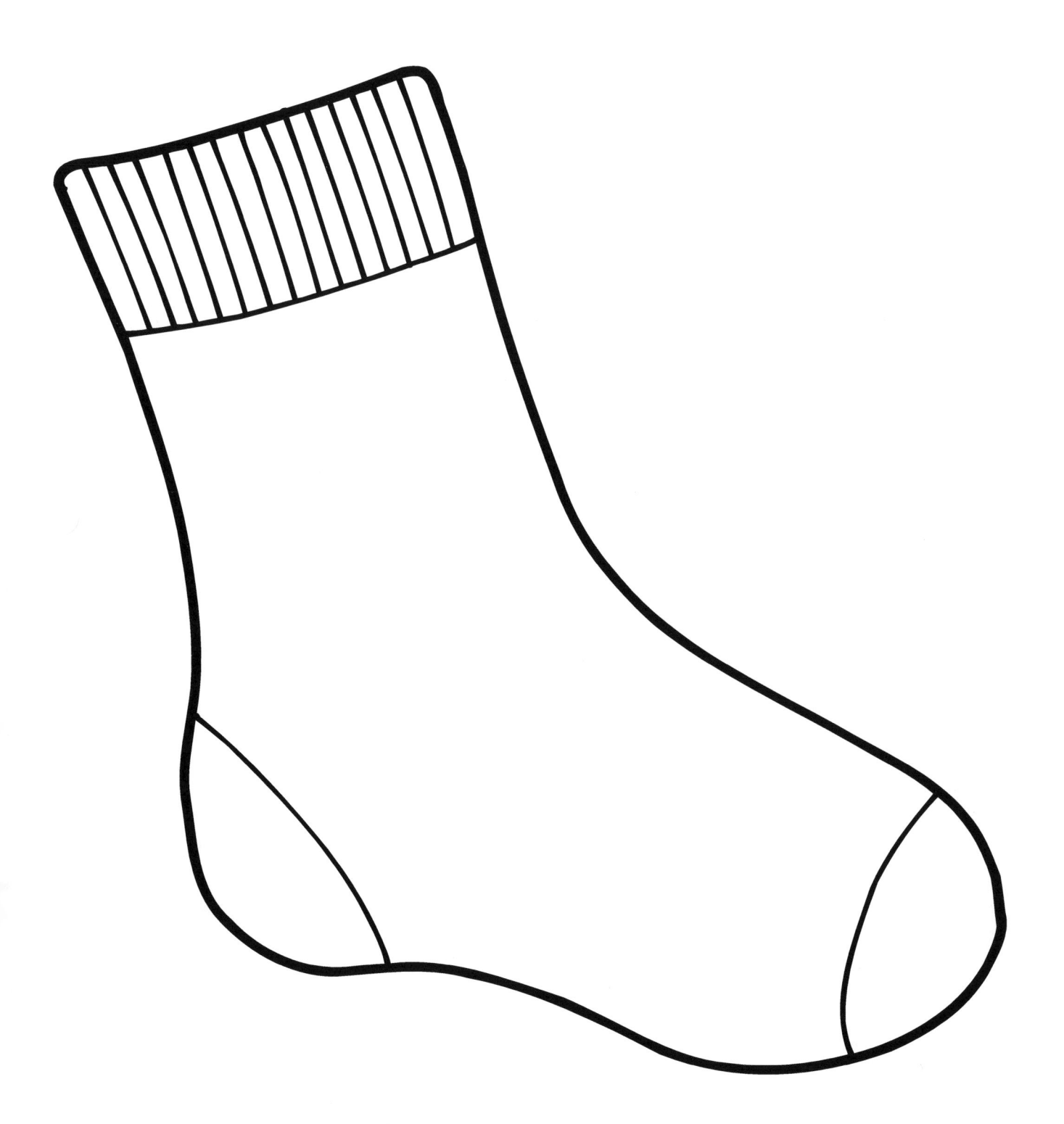

sofa

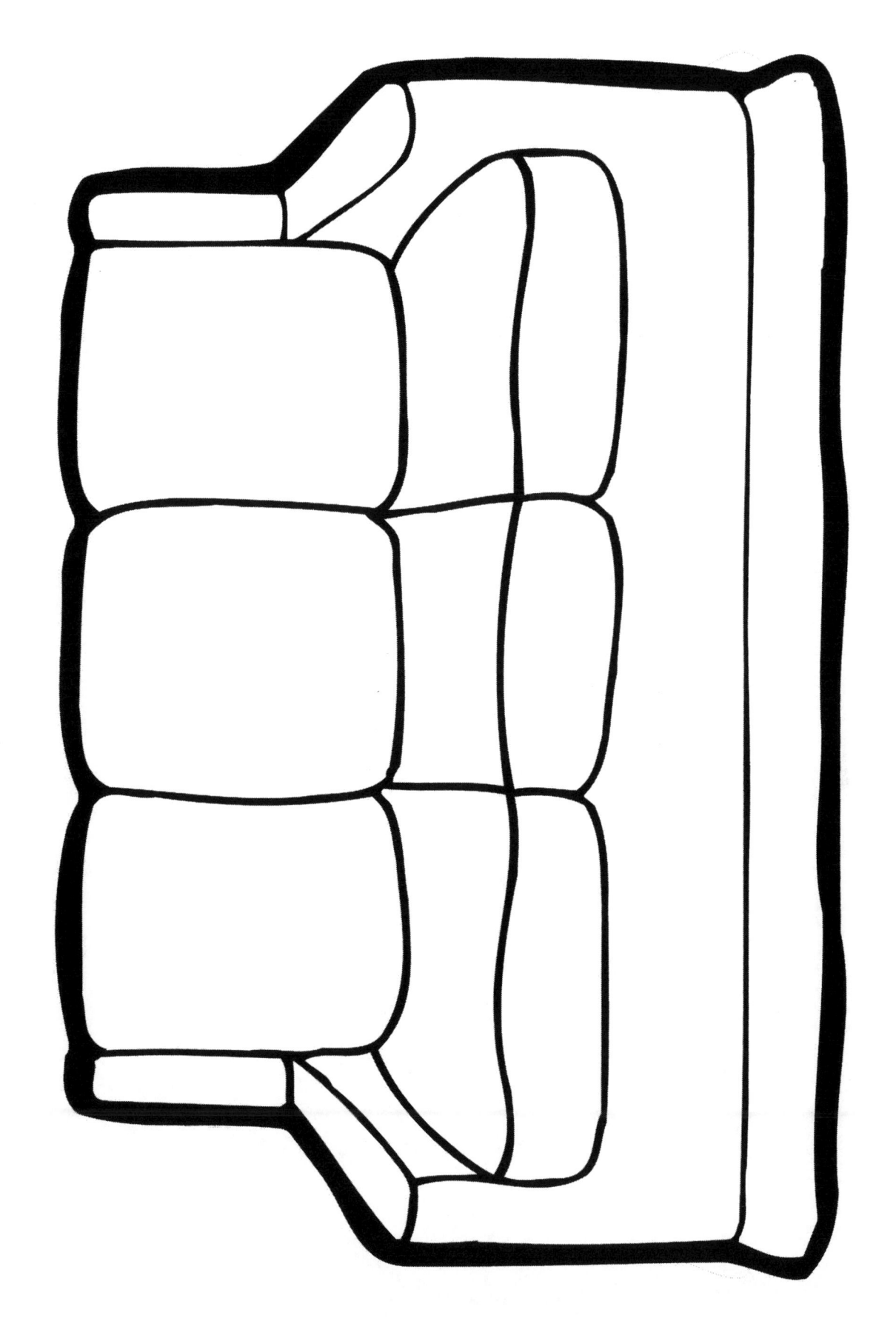

sombrero

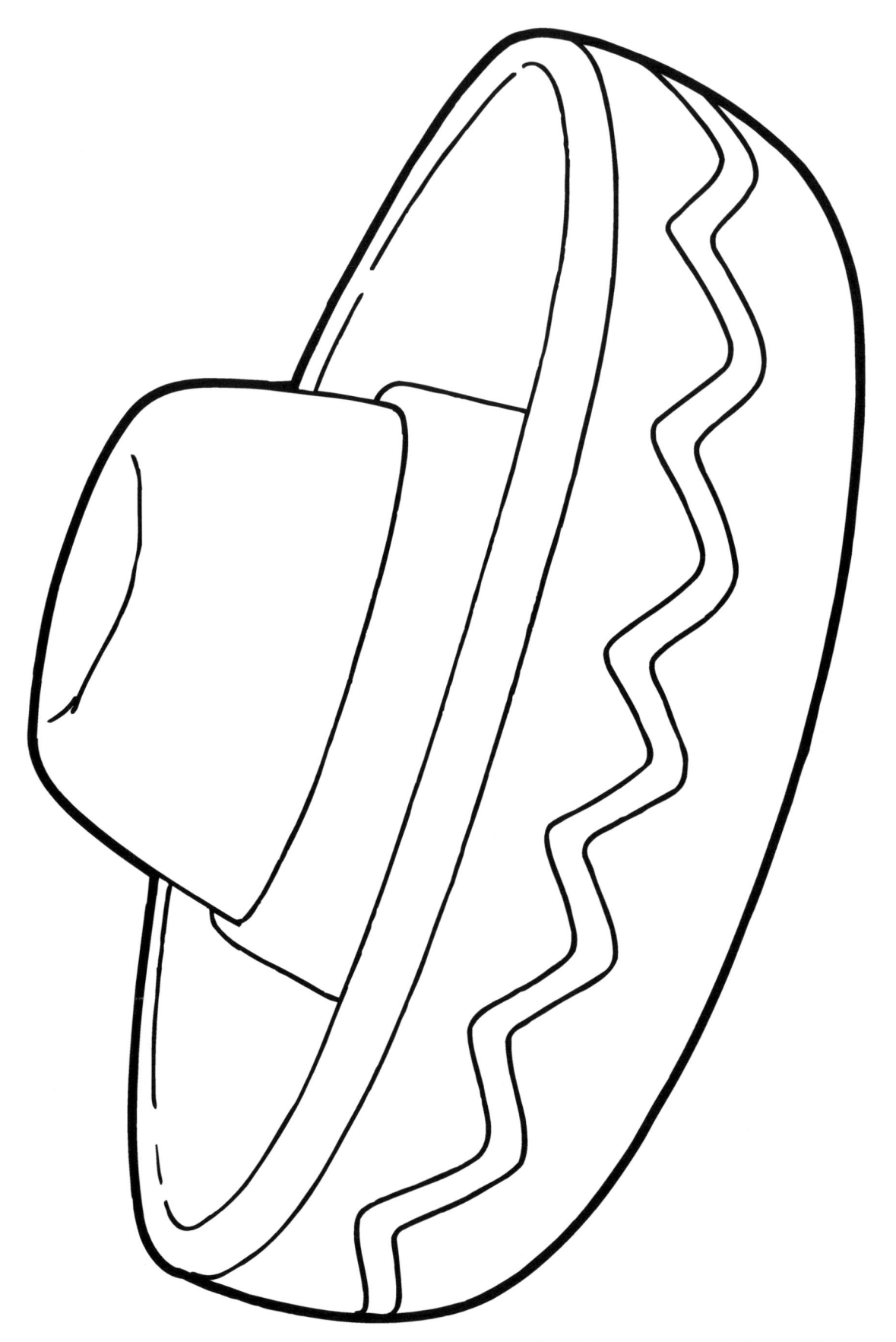

South America

South Carolina, USA

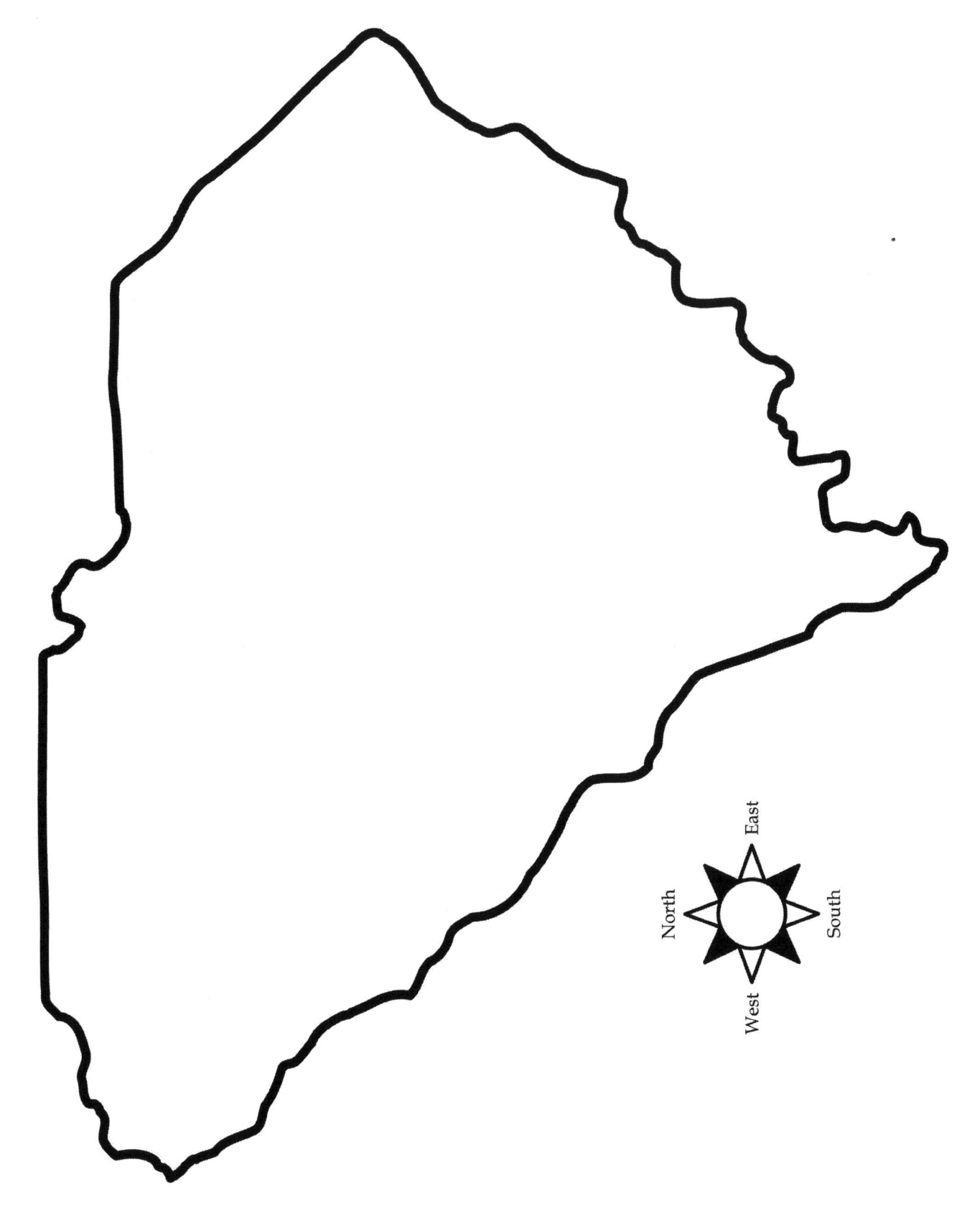

North / East / South / West

Maps are representations and boundaries are not exact.

South Dakota, USA

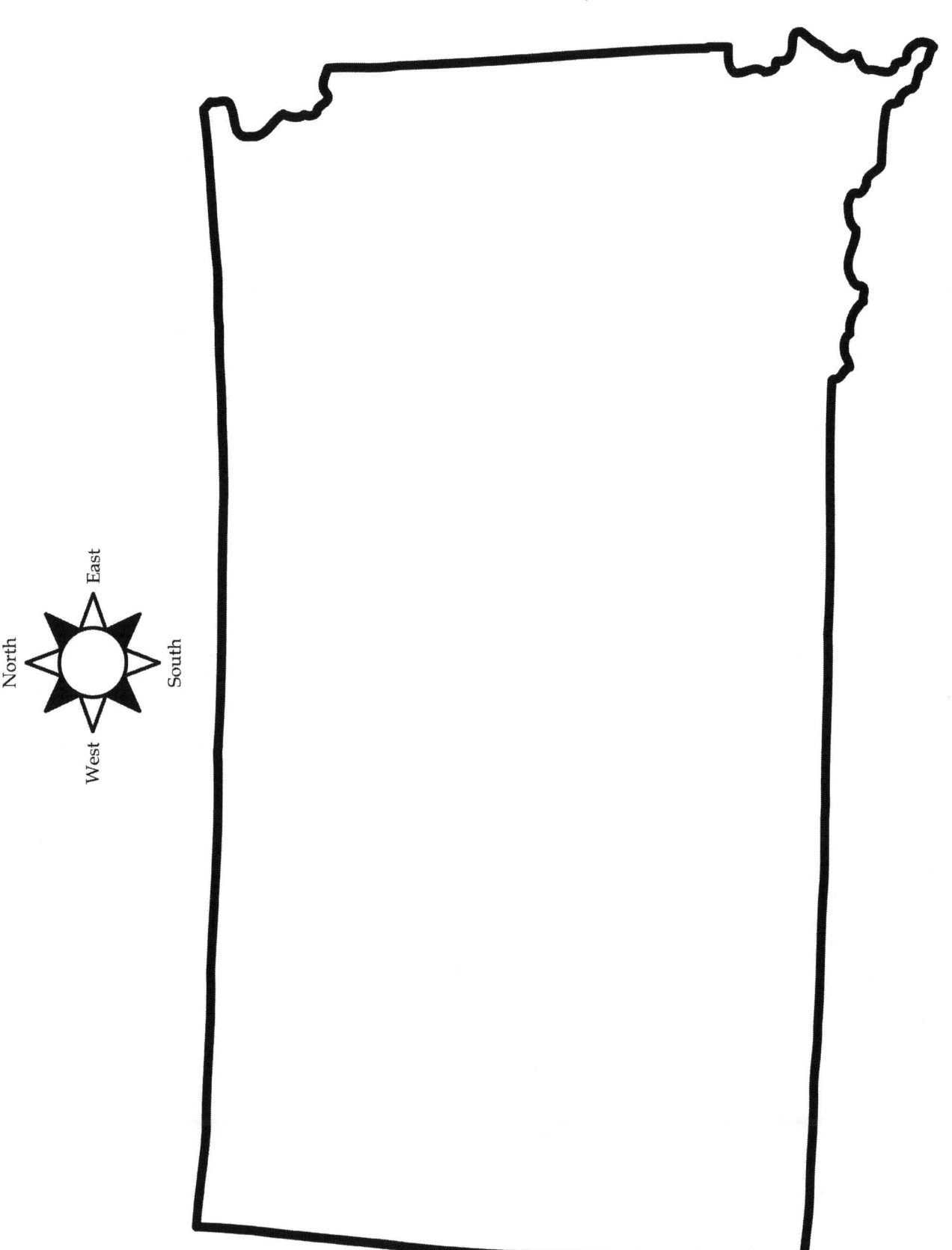

space shuttle

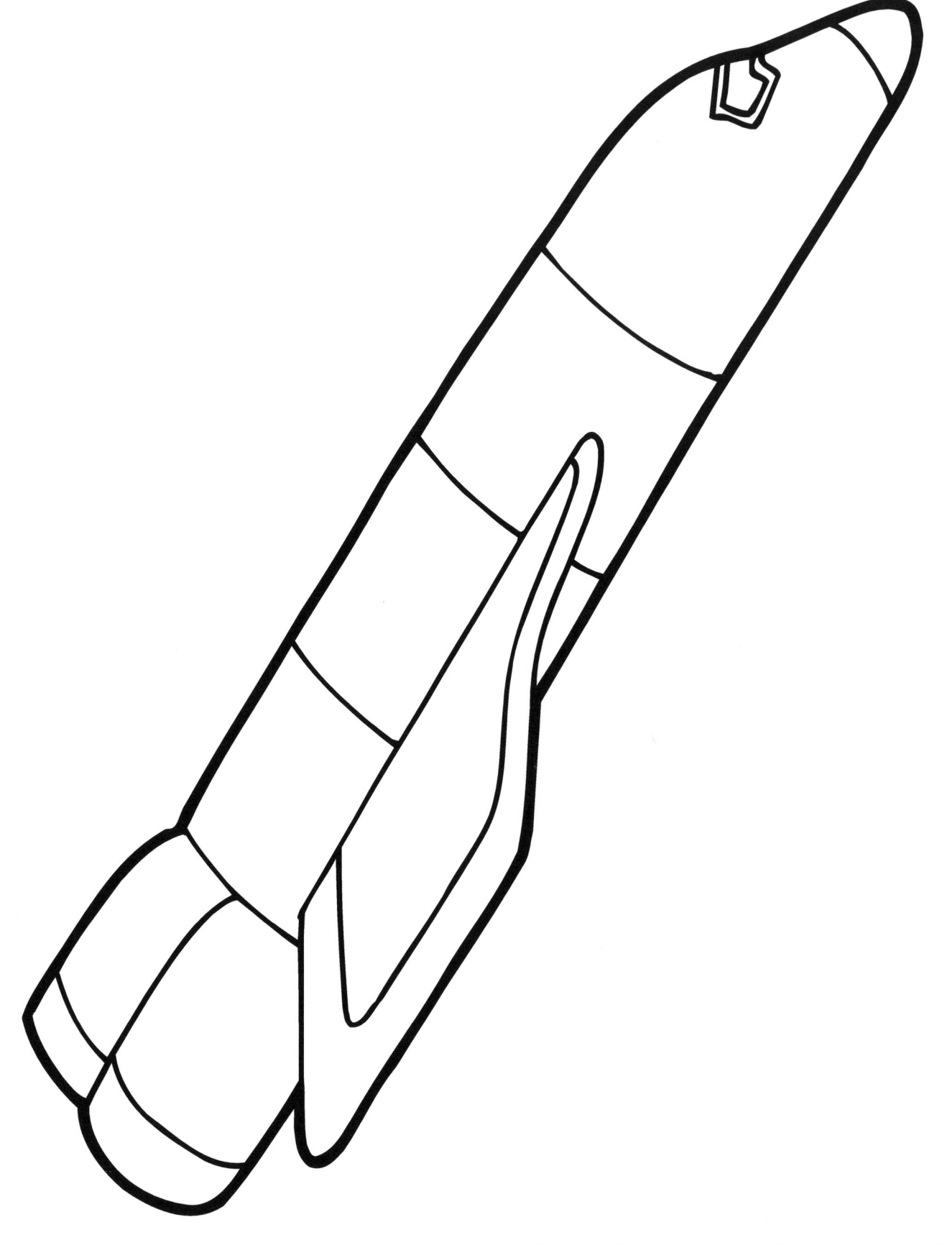

space shuttle (in flight)

spade (symbol)

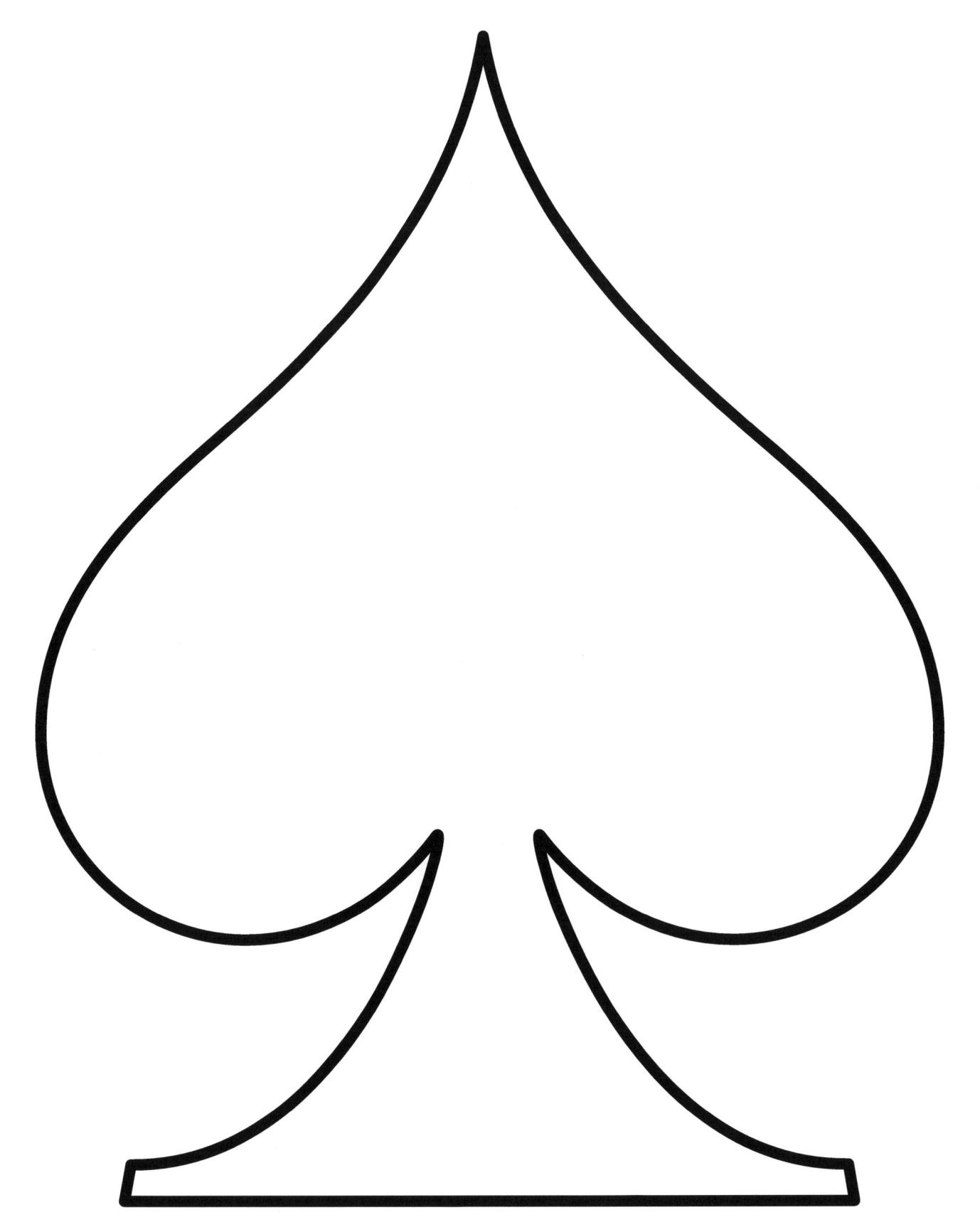

spade (tool)

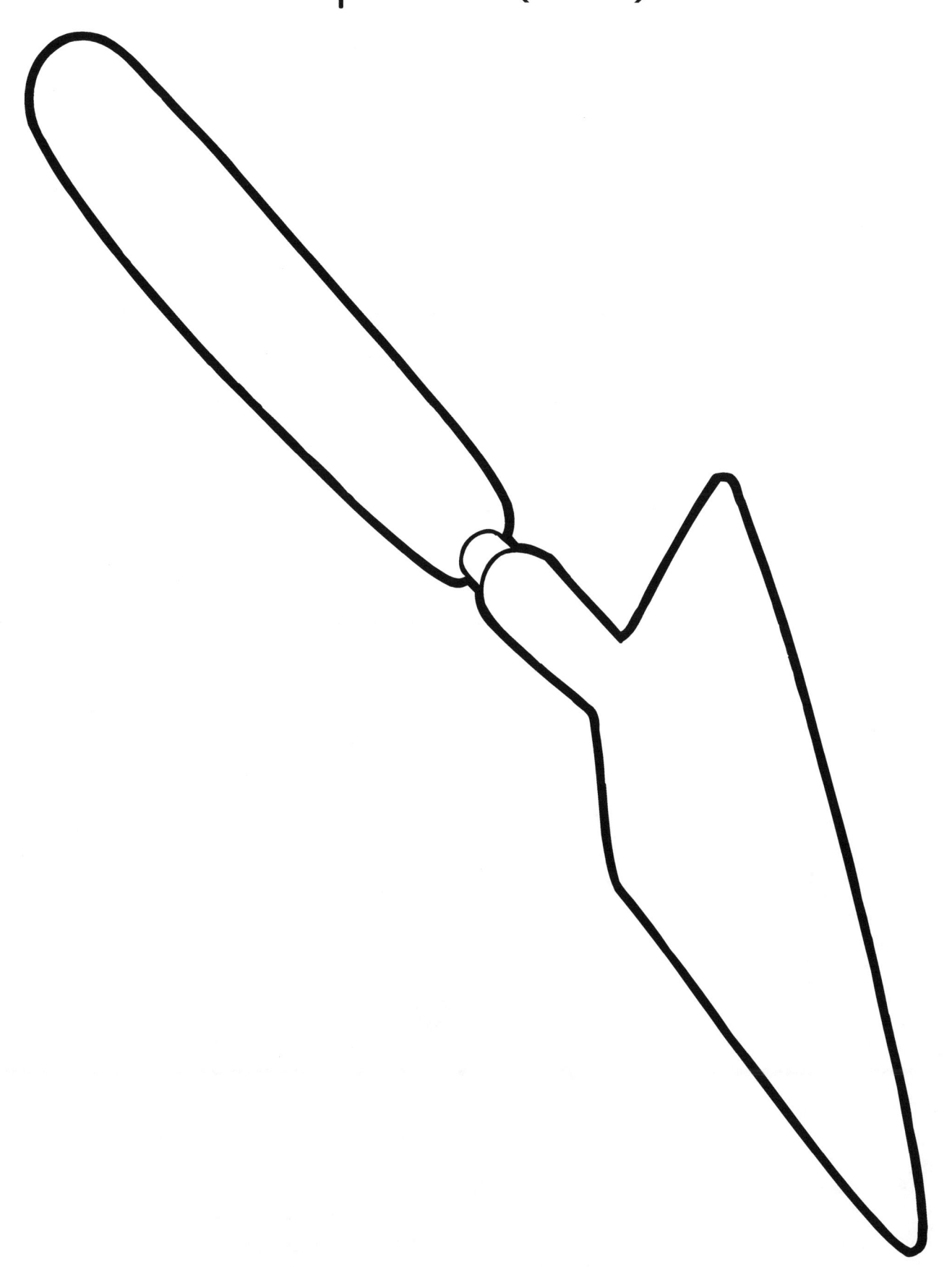

sphinx

spider

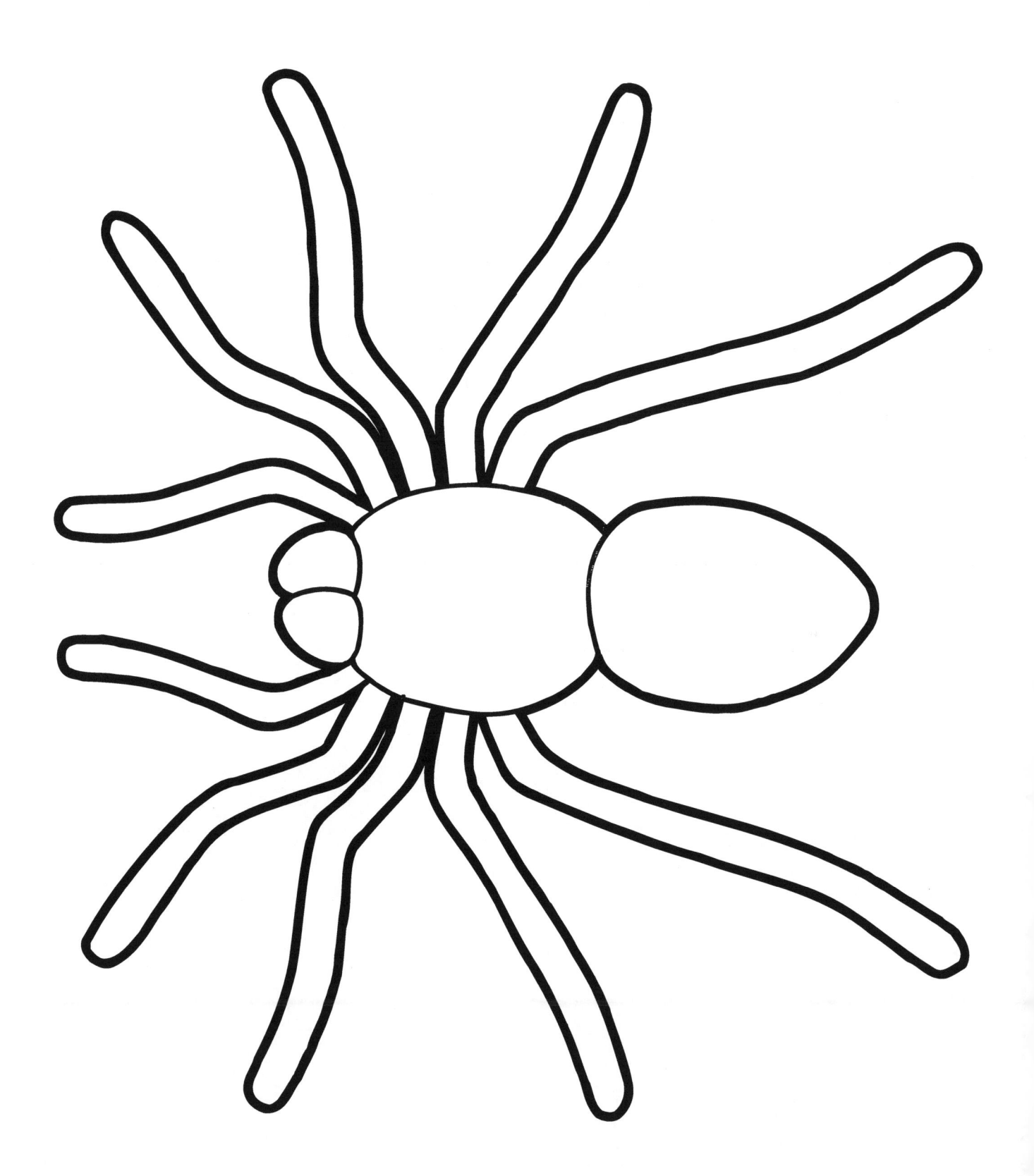

Spirit of St. Louis

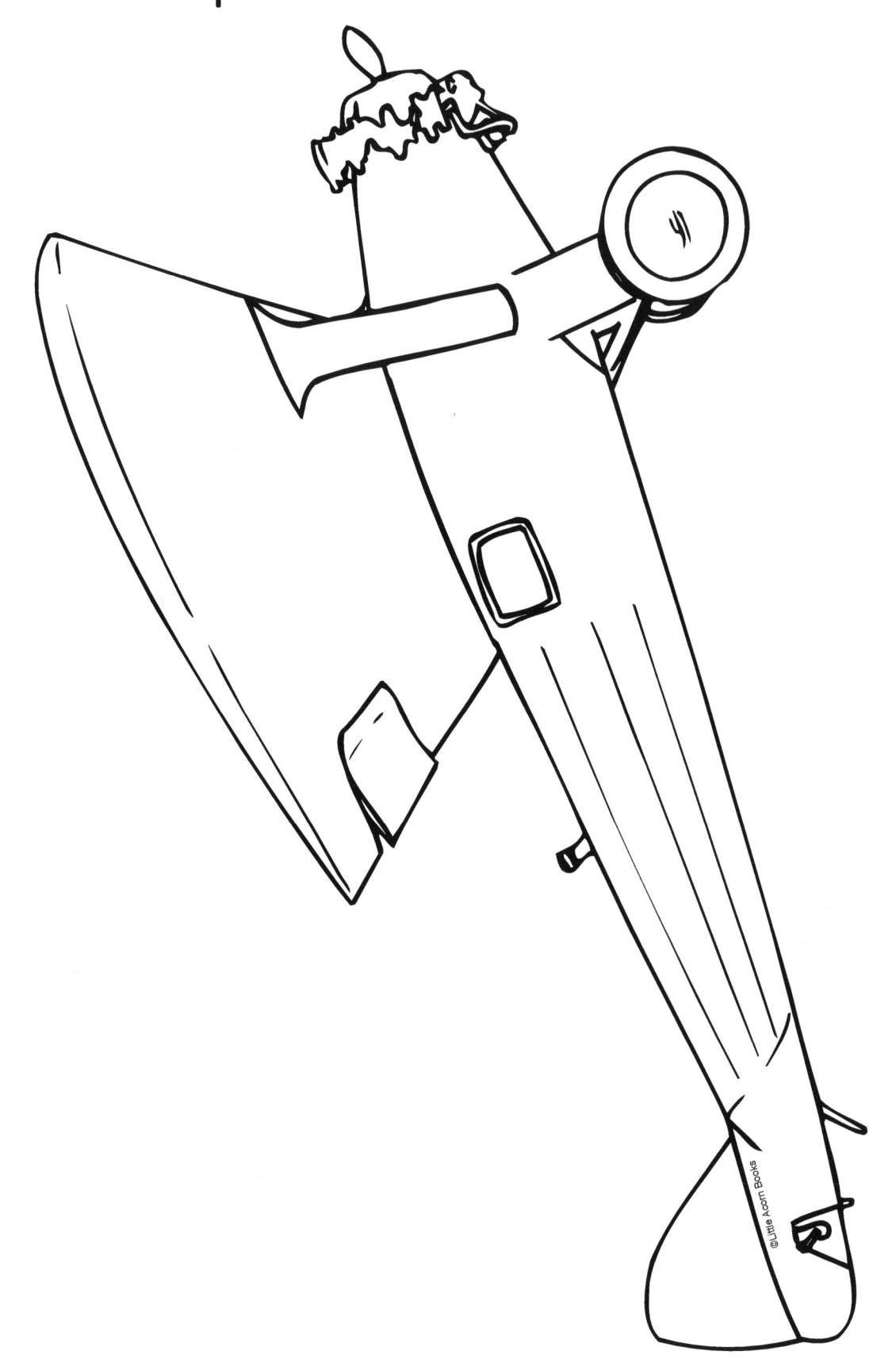

spool

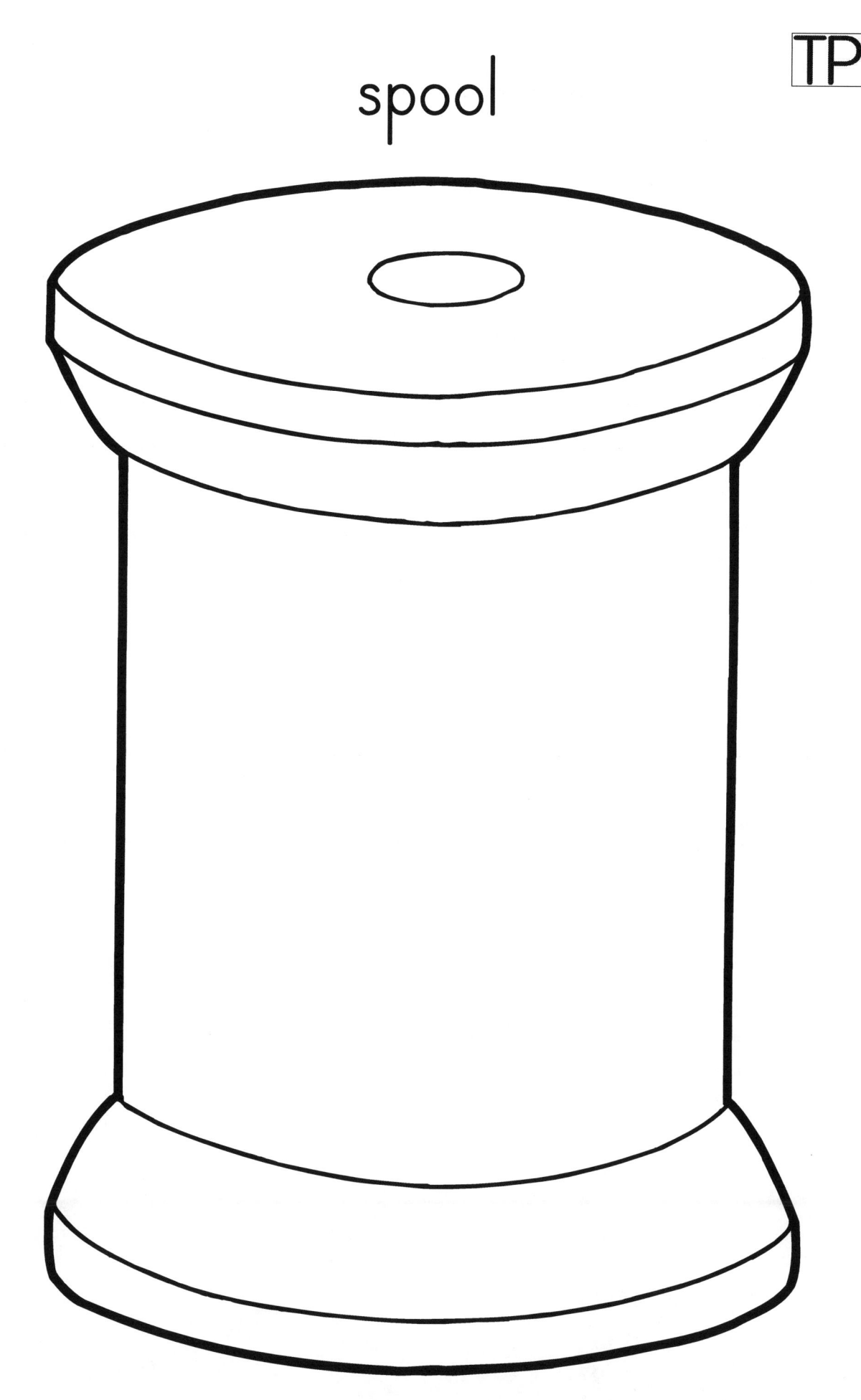

spoon (flat)

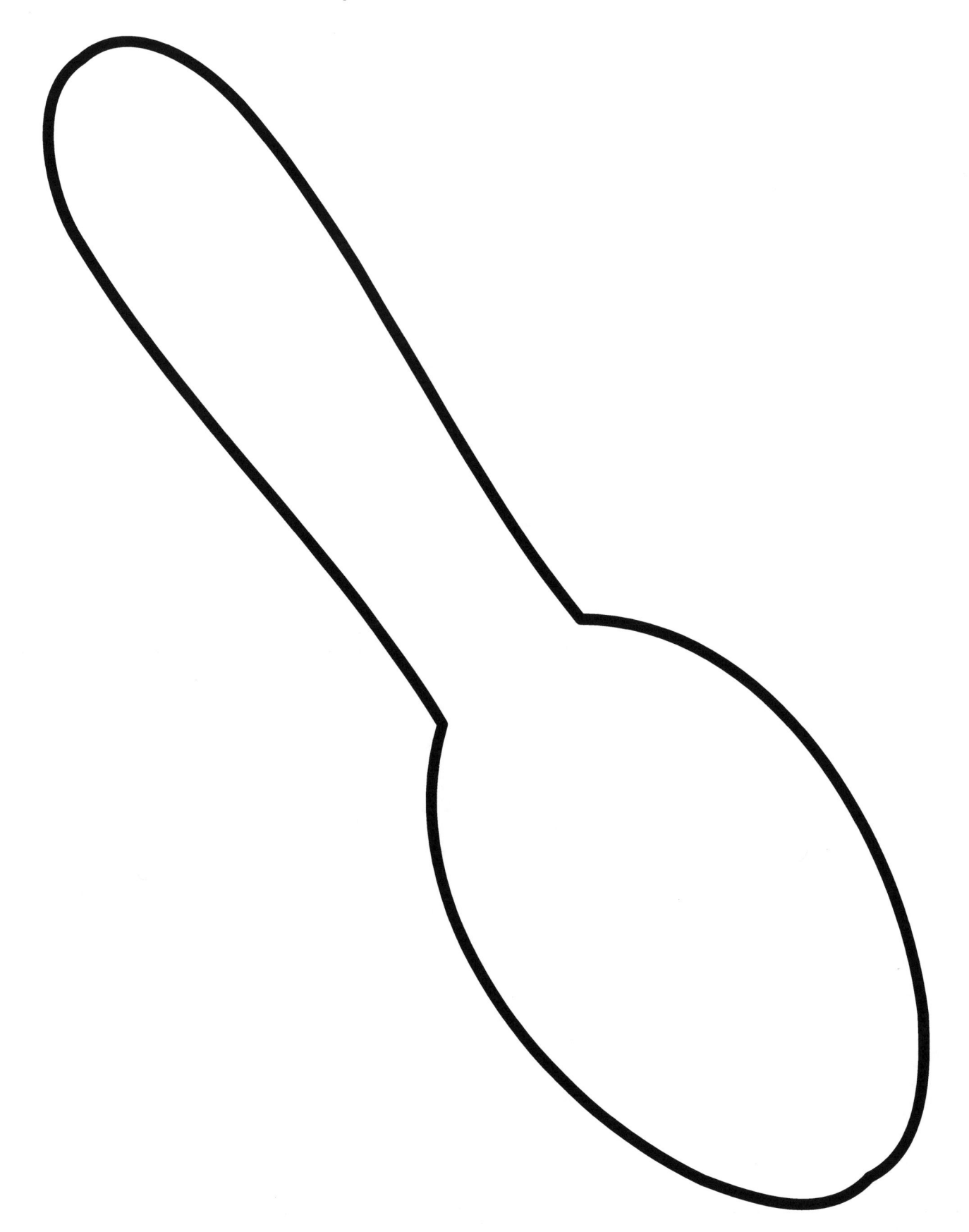

spoon

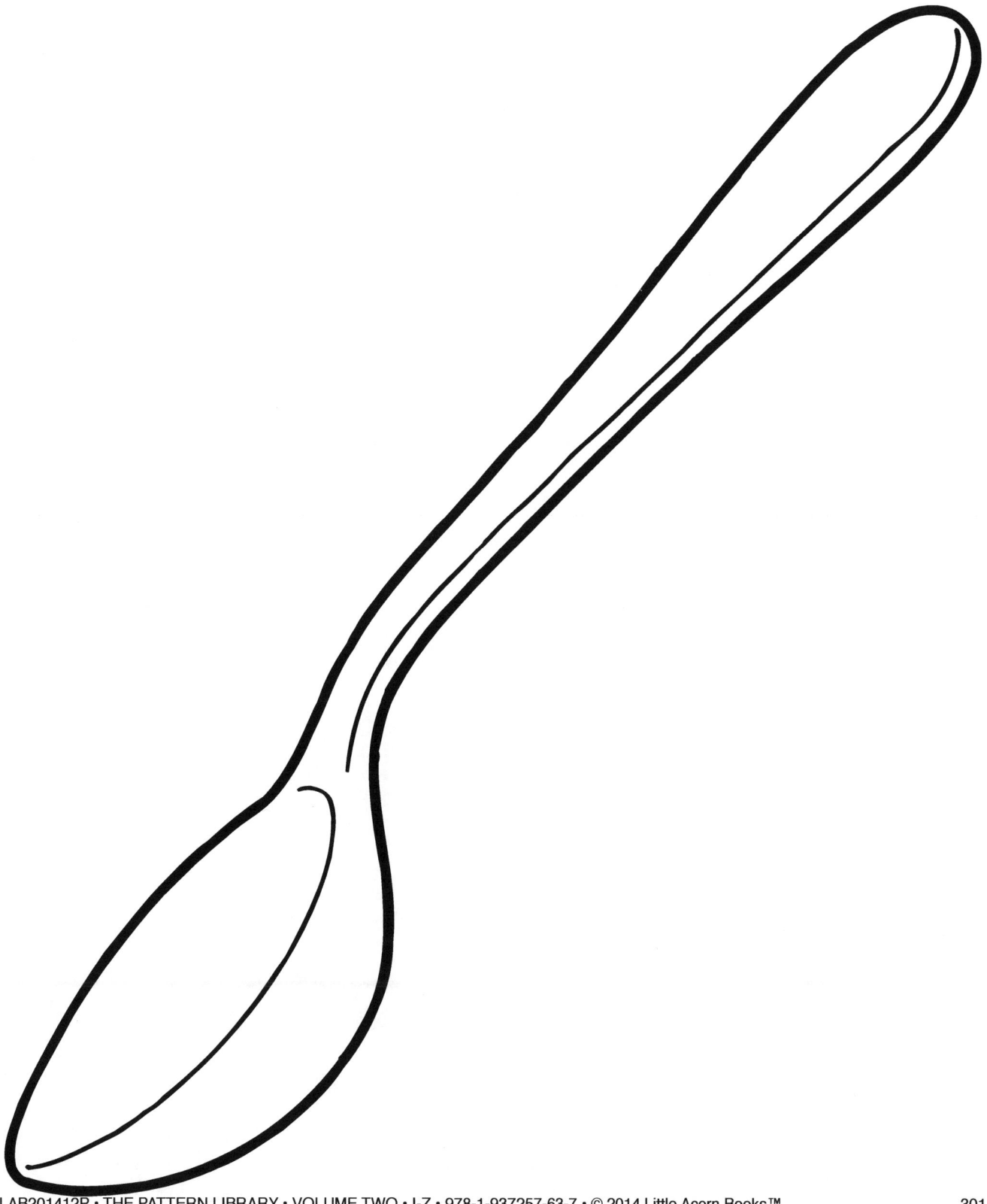

squirrel (animated)

squirrel (stylized)

squirrel (wearing sweater)

stage

stagecoach

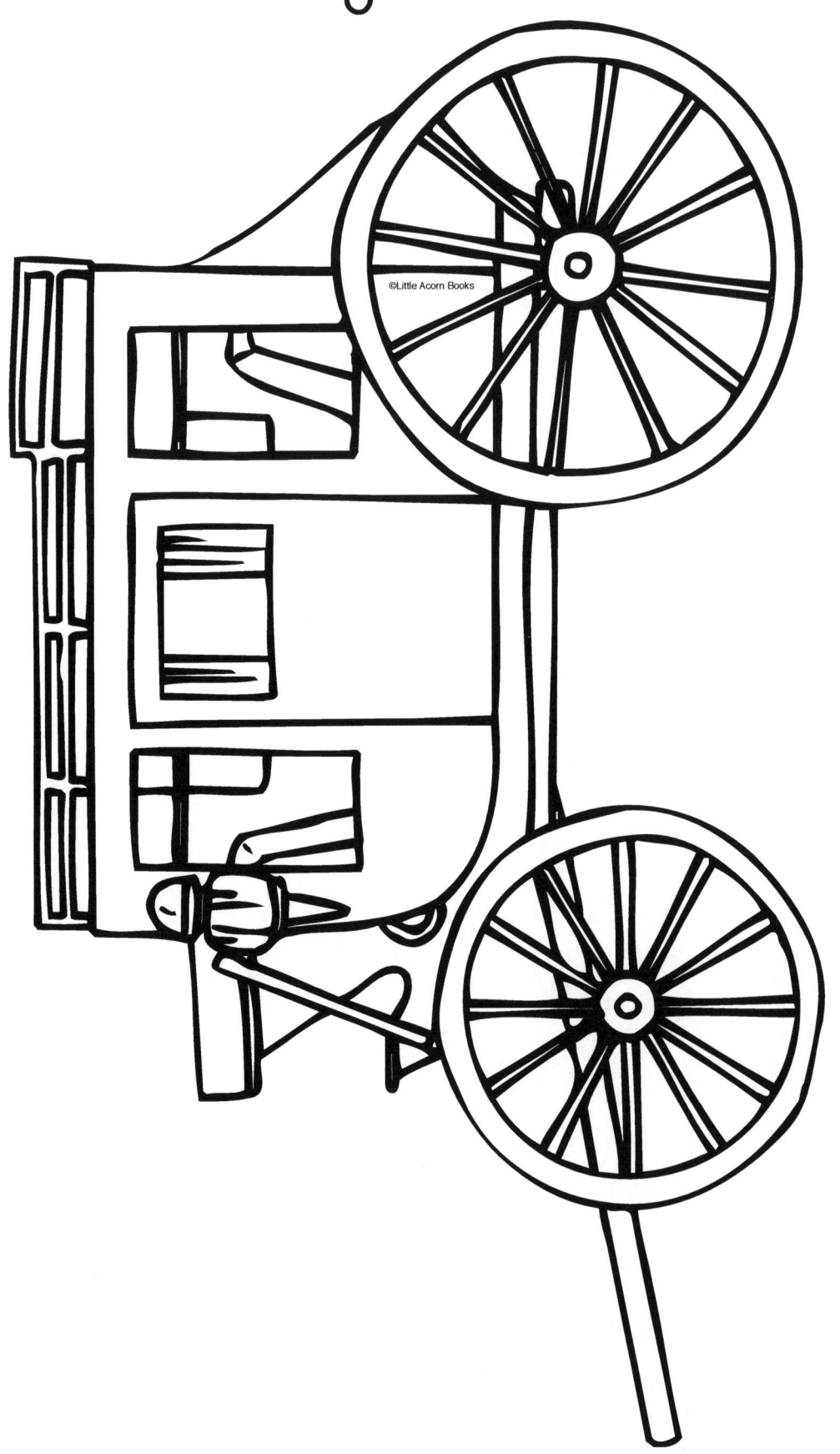

stapler

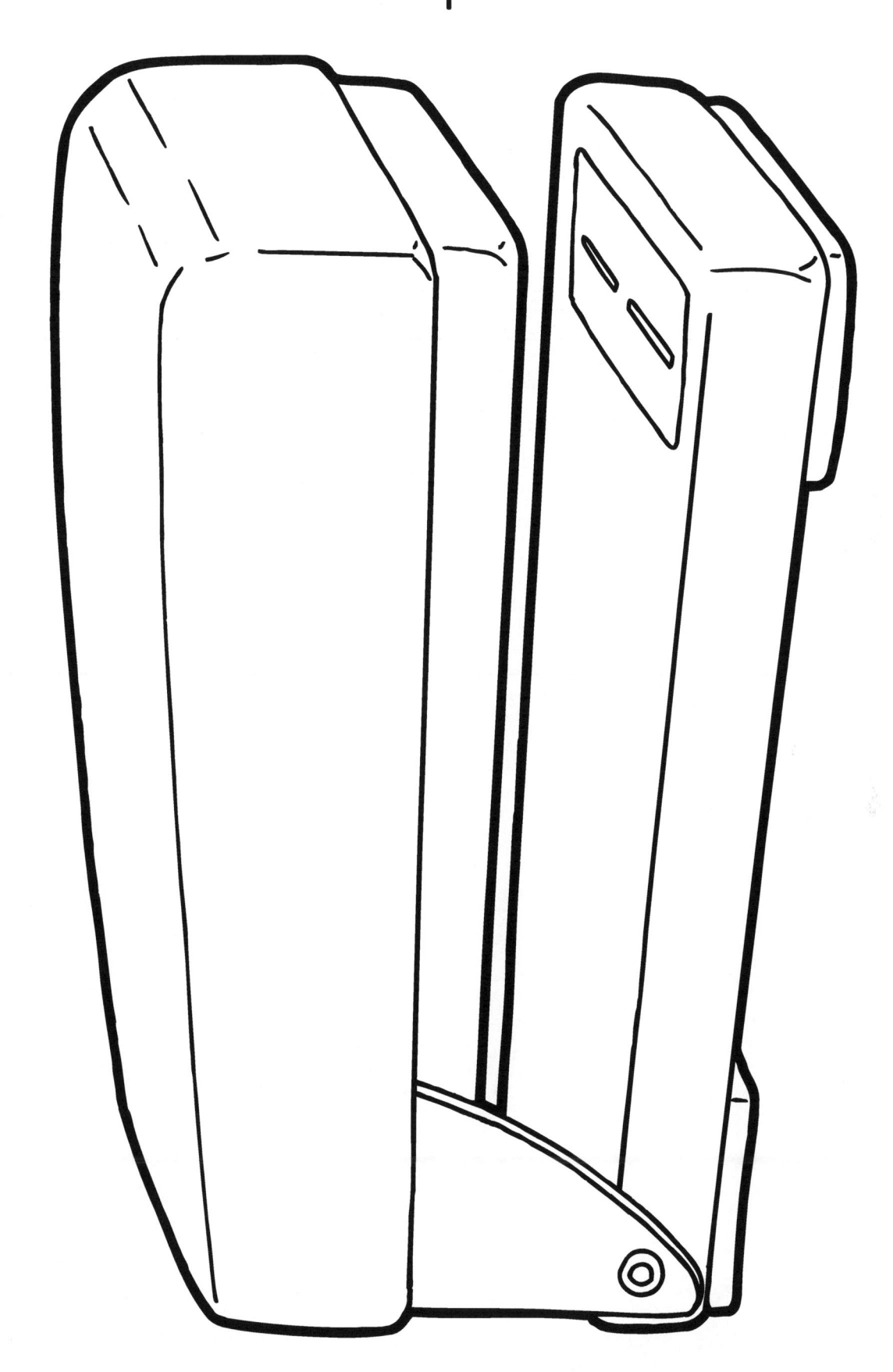

star (five points)

star (six points)

starfish

stocking (outline)

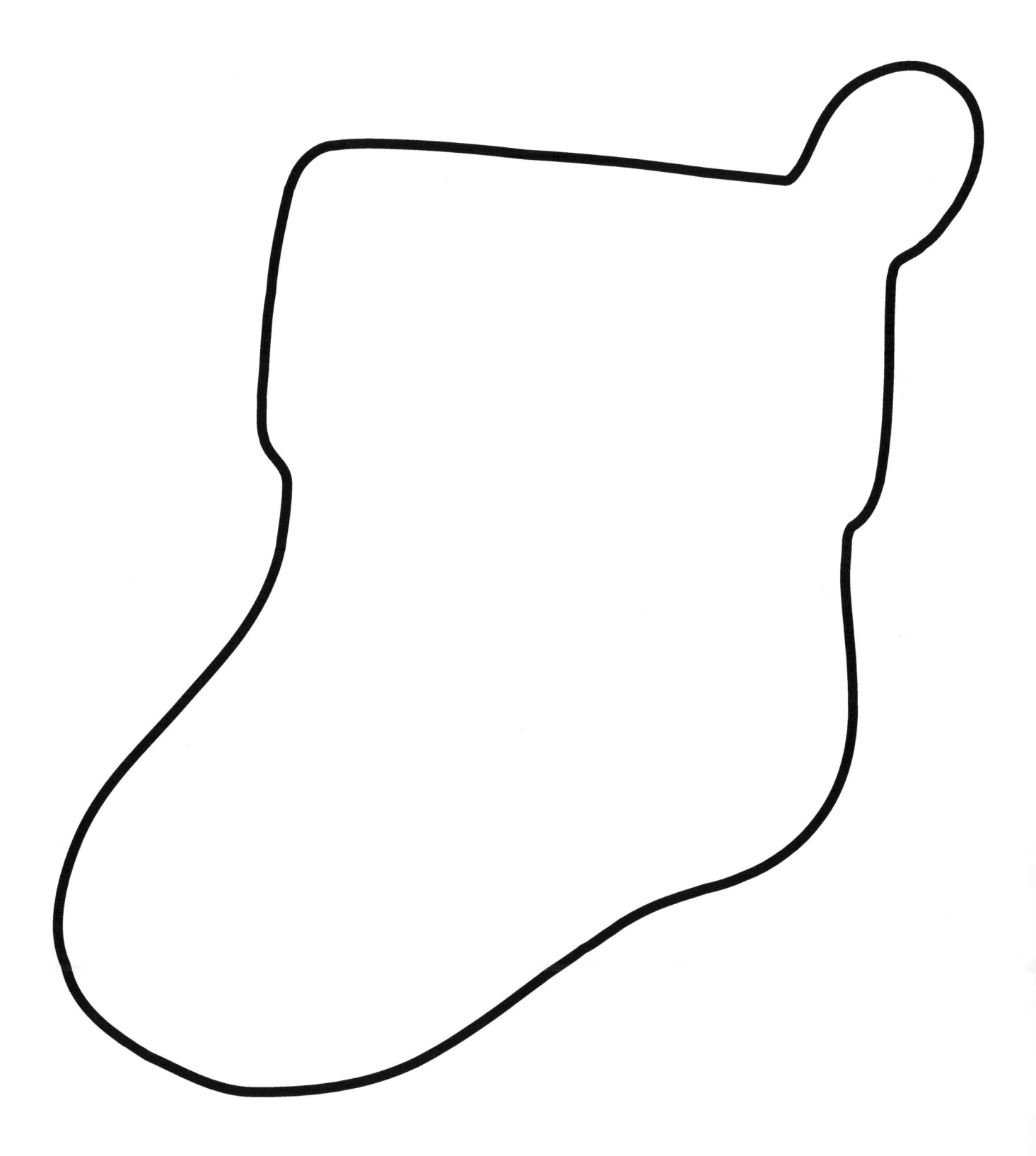

stomach

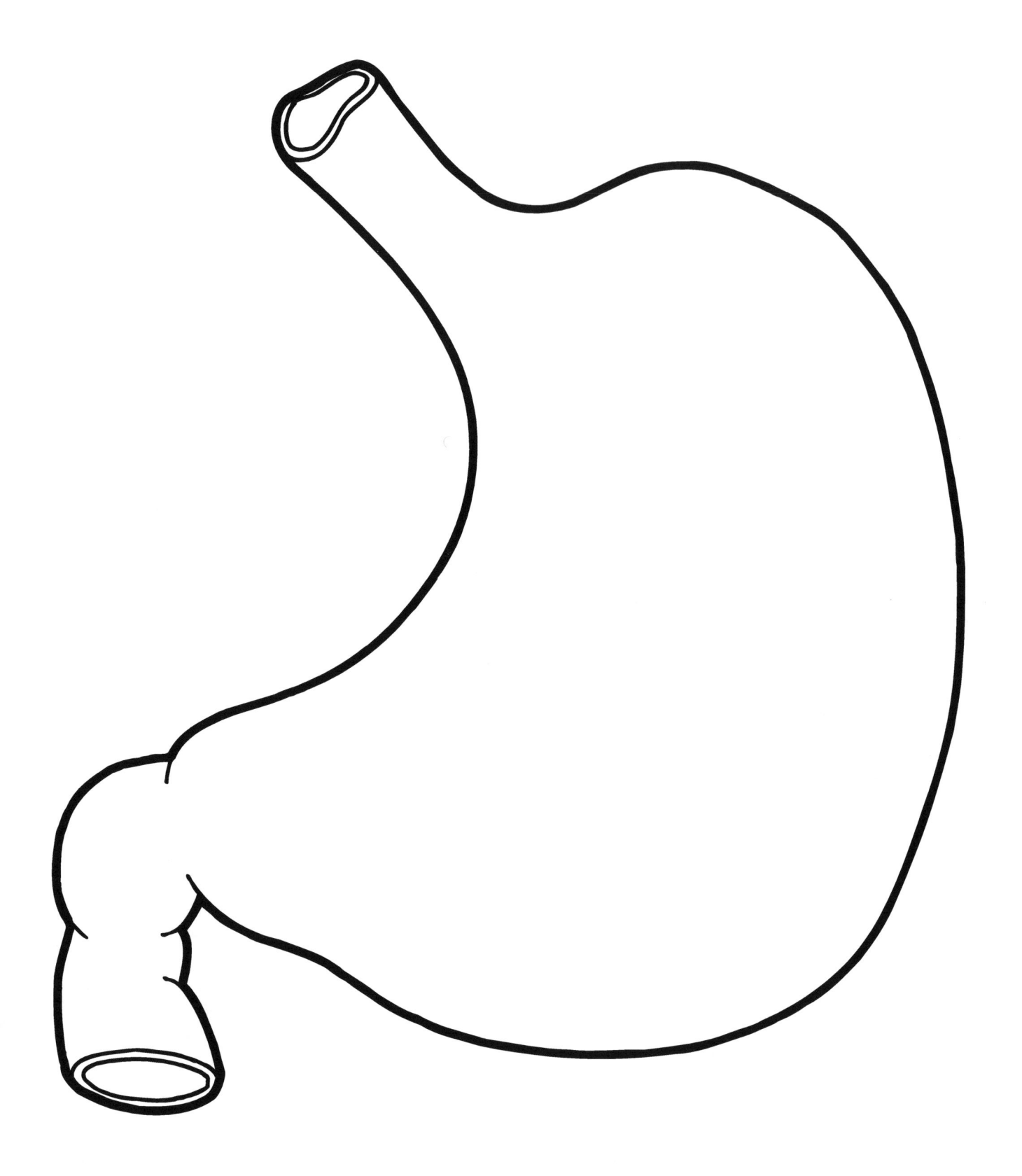

strawberries

submarine (1898)

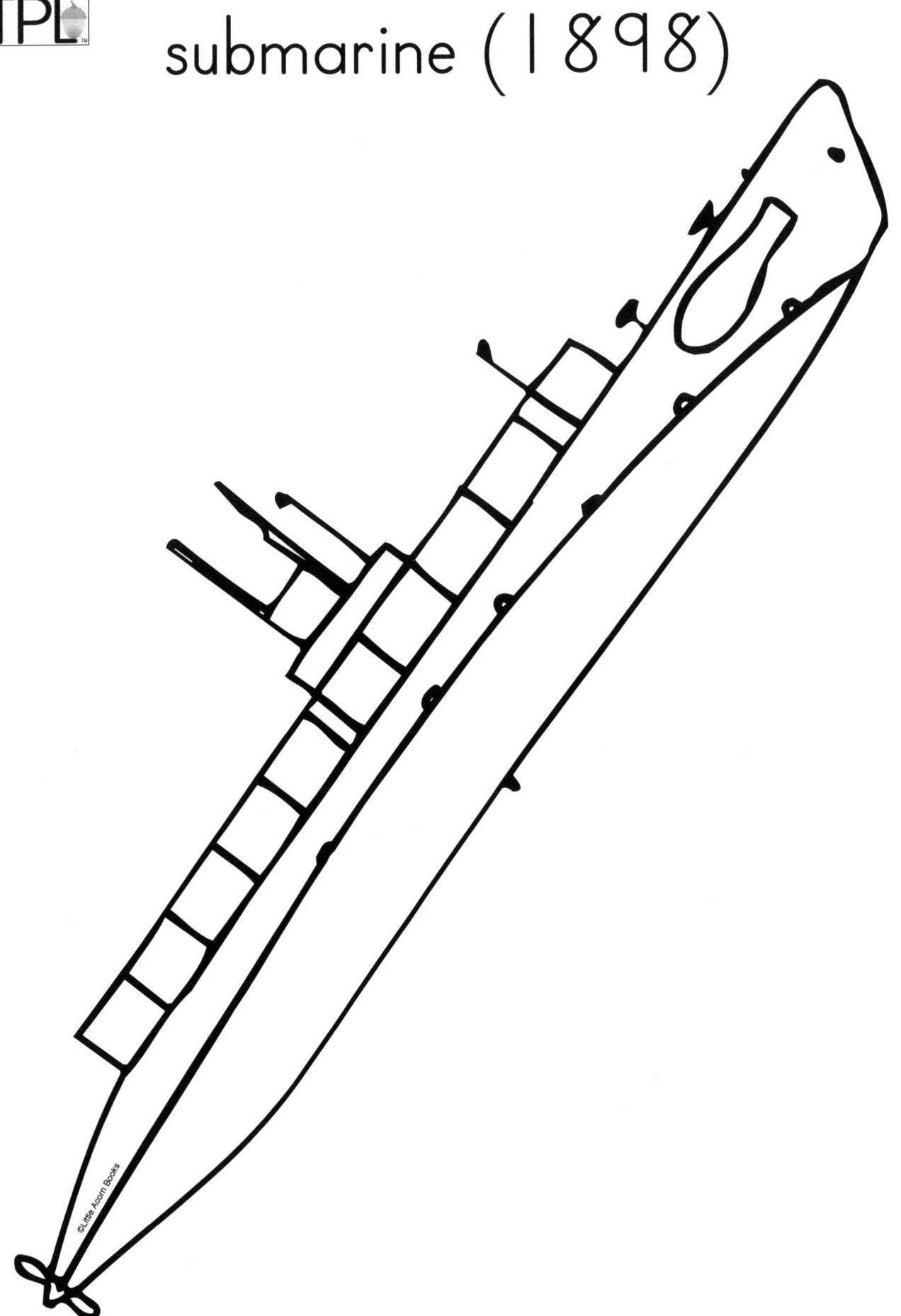

submarine

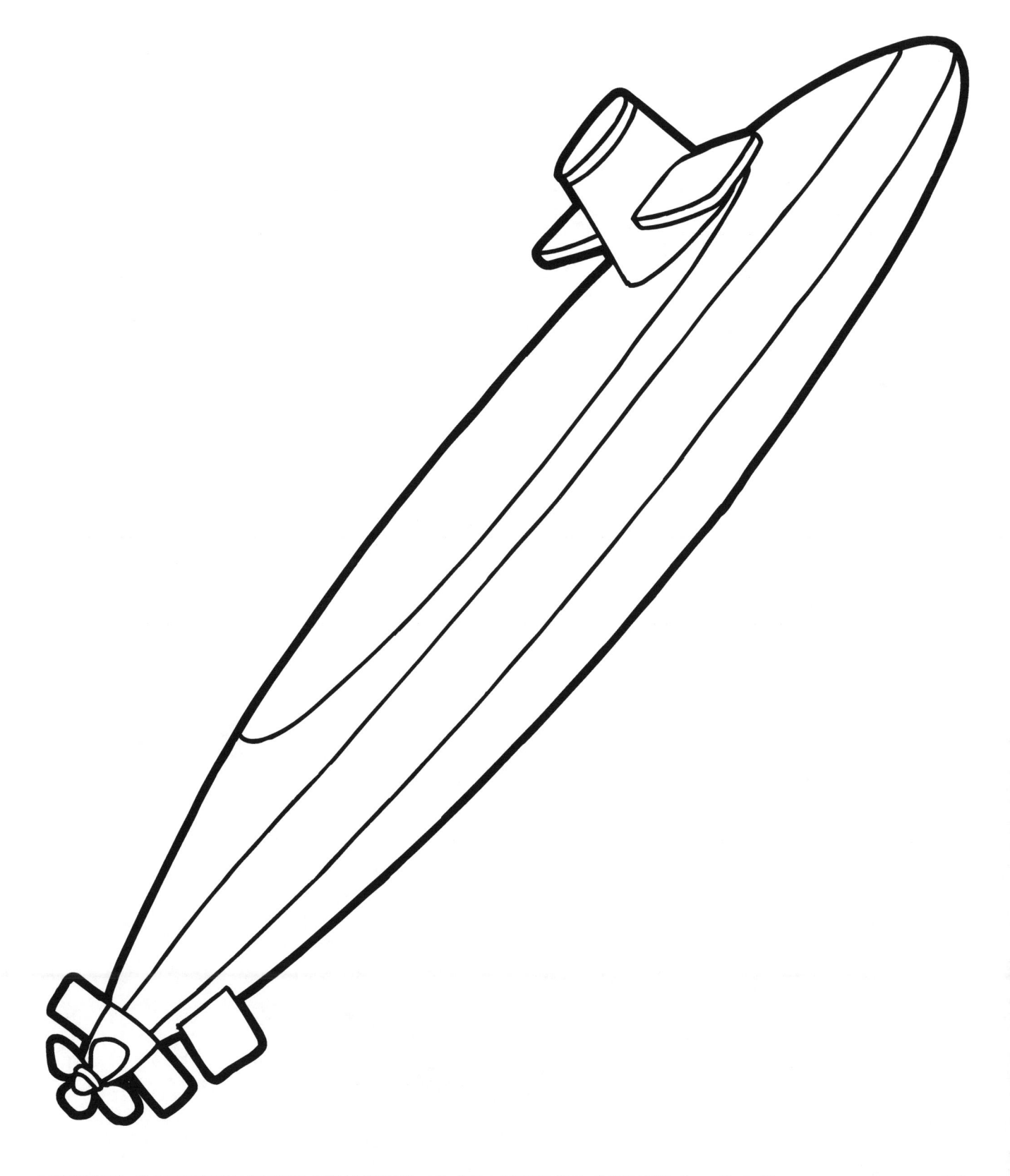

suitcase

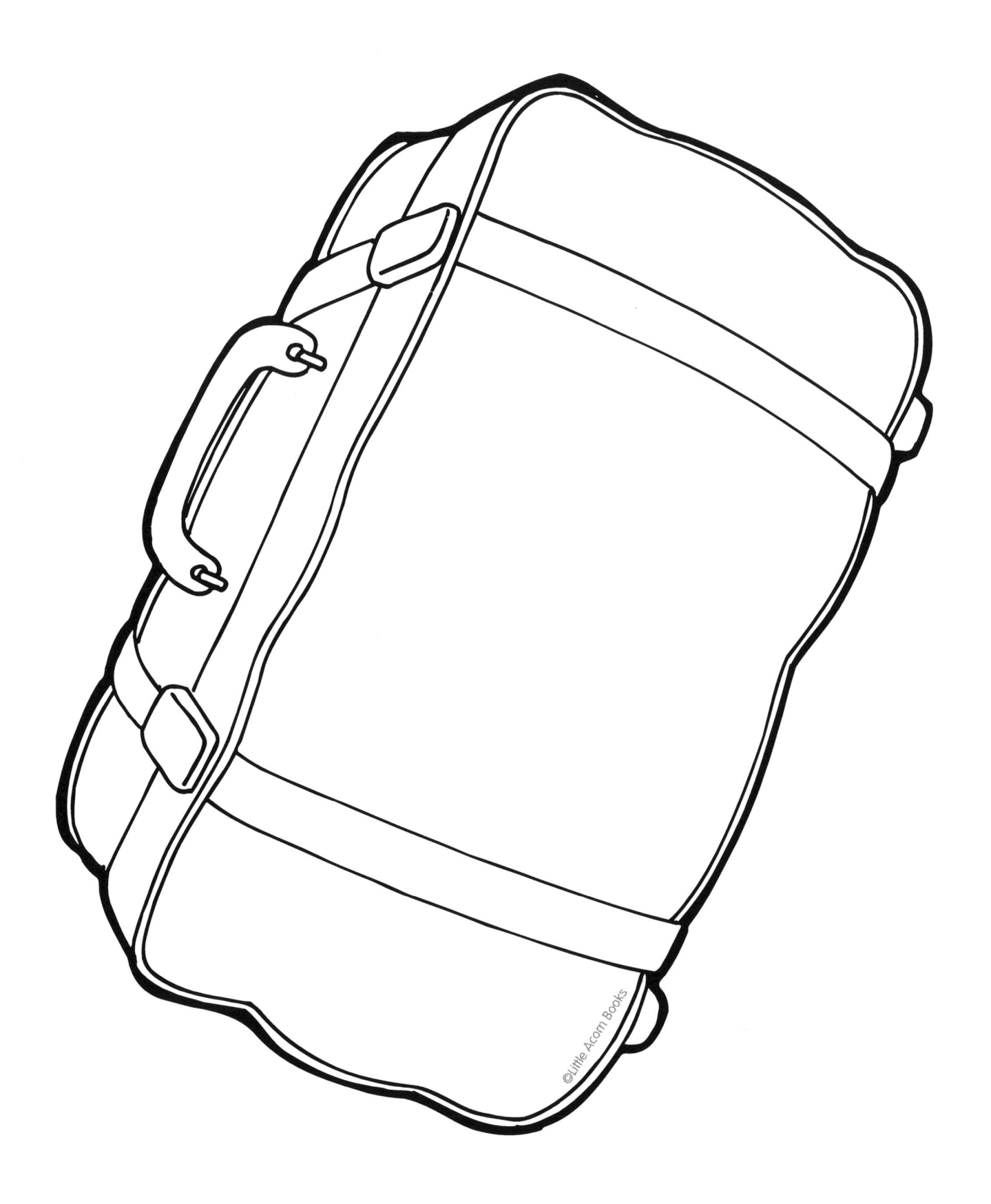

sun (animated)

swan

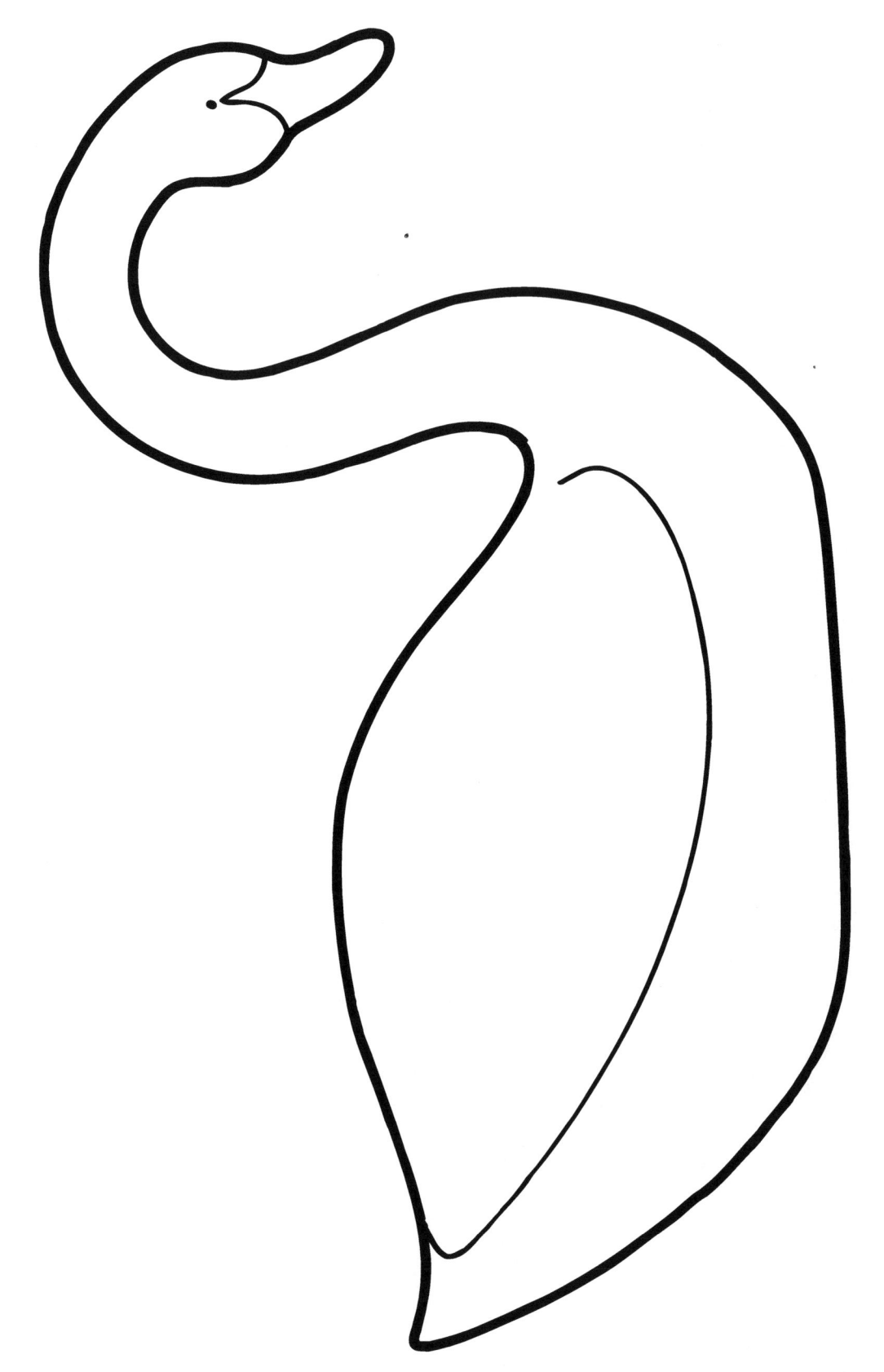

tadpole

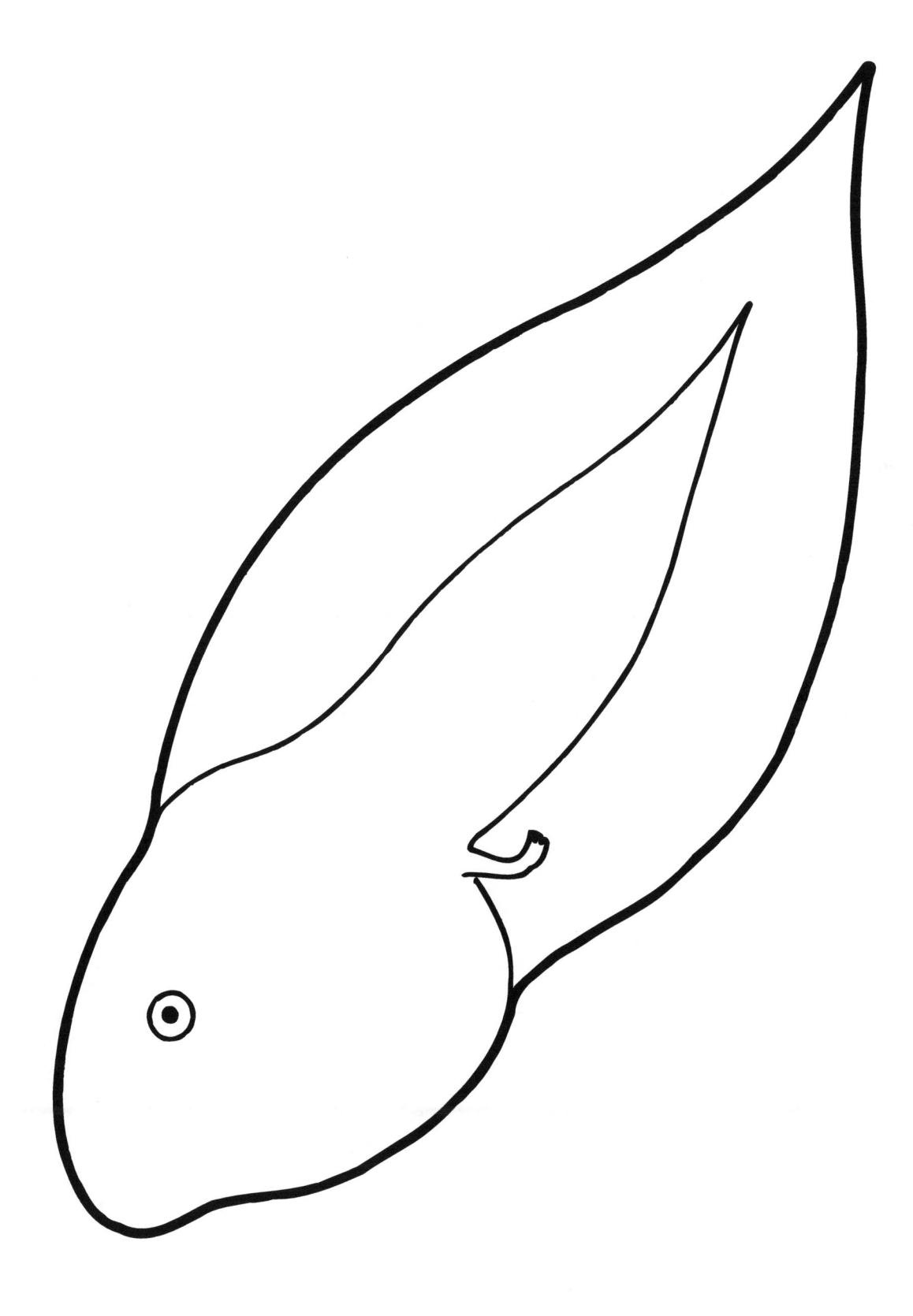

tamborine

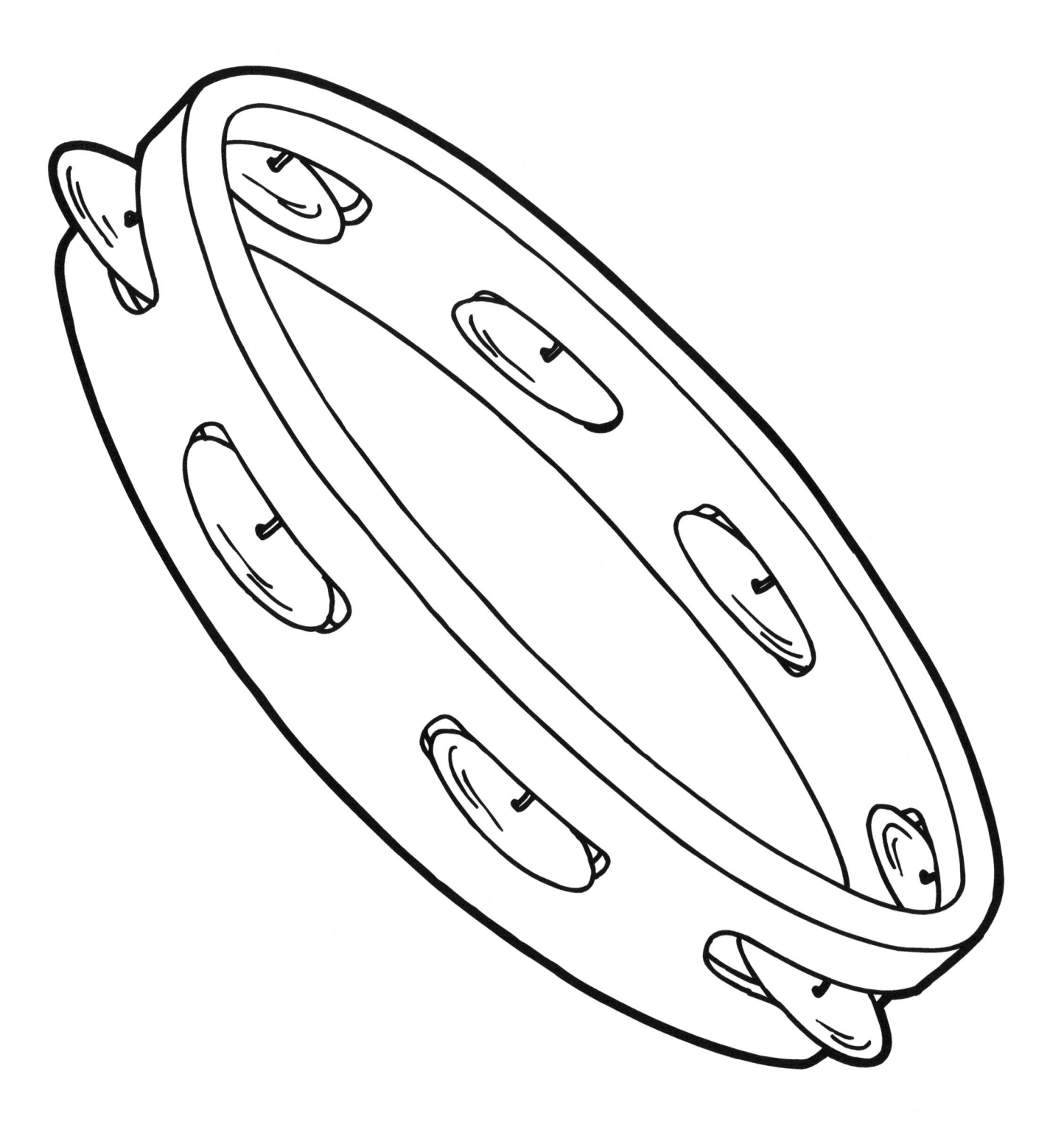

tan (crayon)

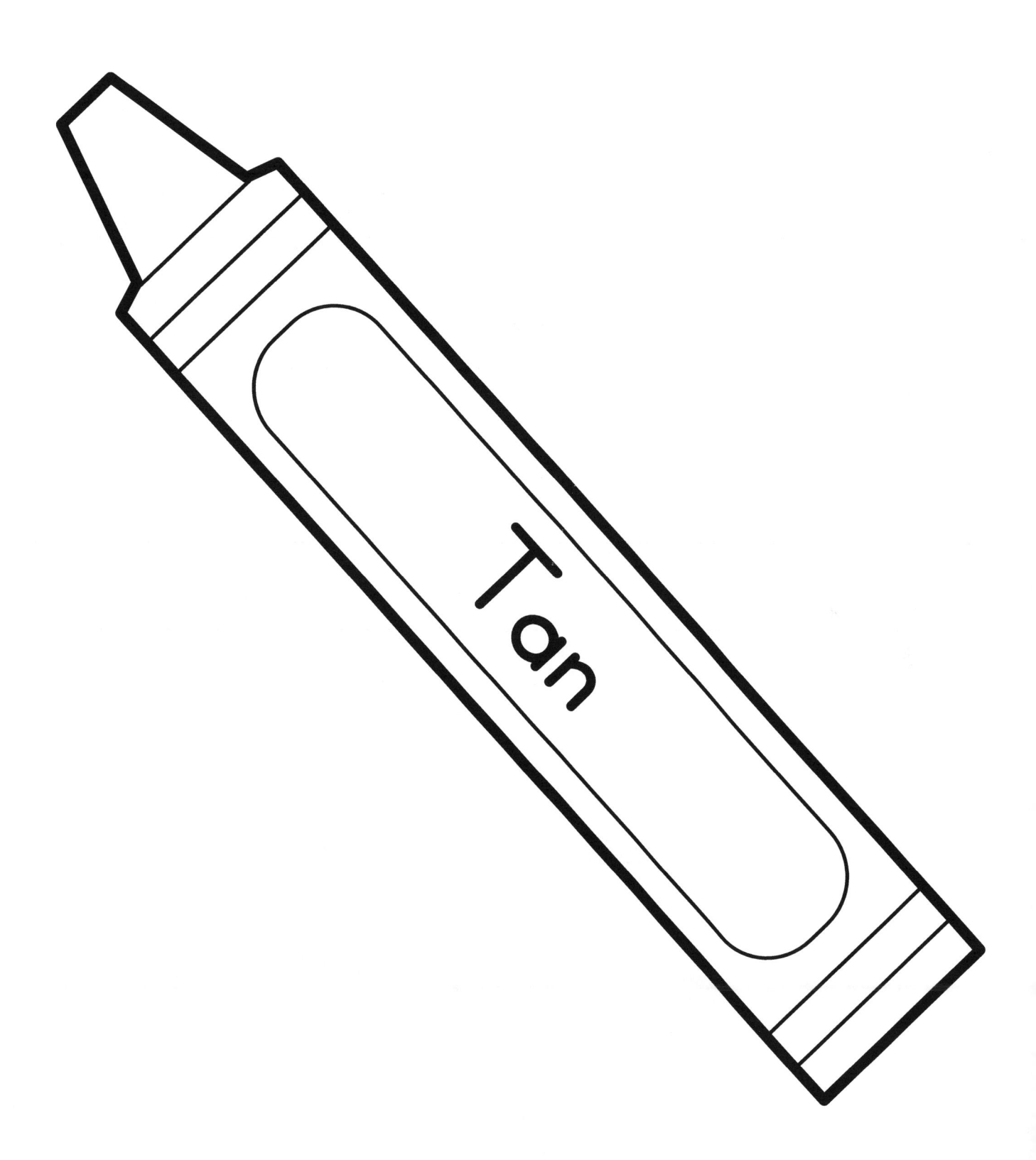

teacup

teacup and saucer

teapot

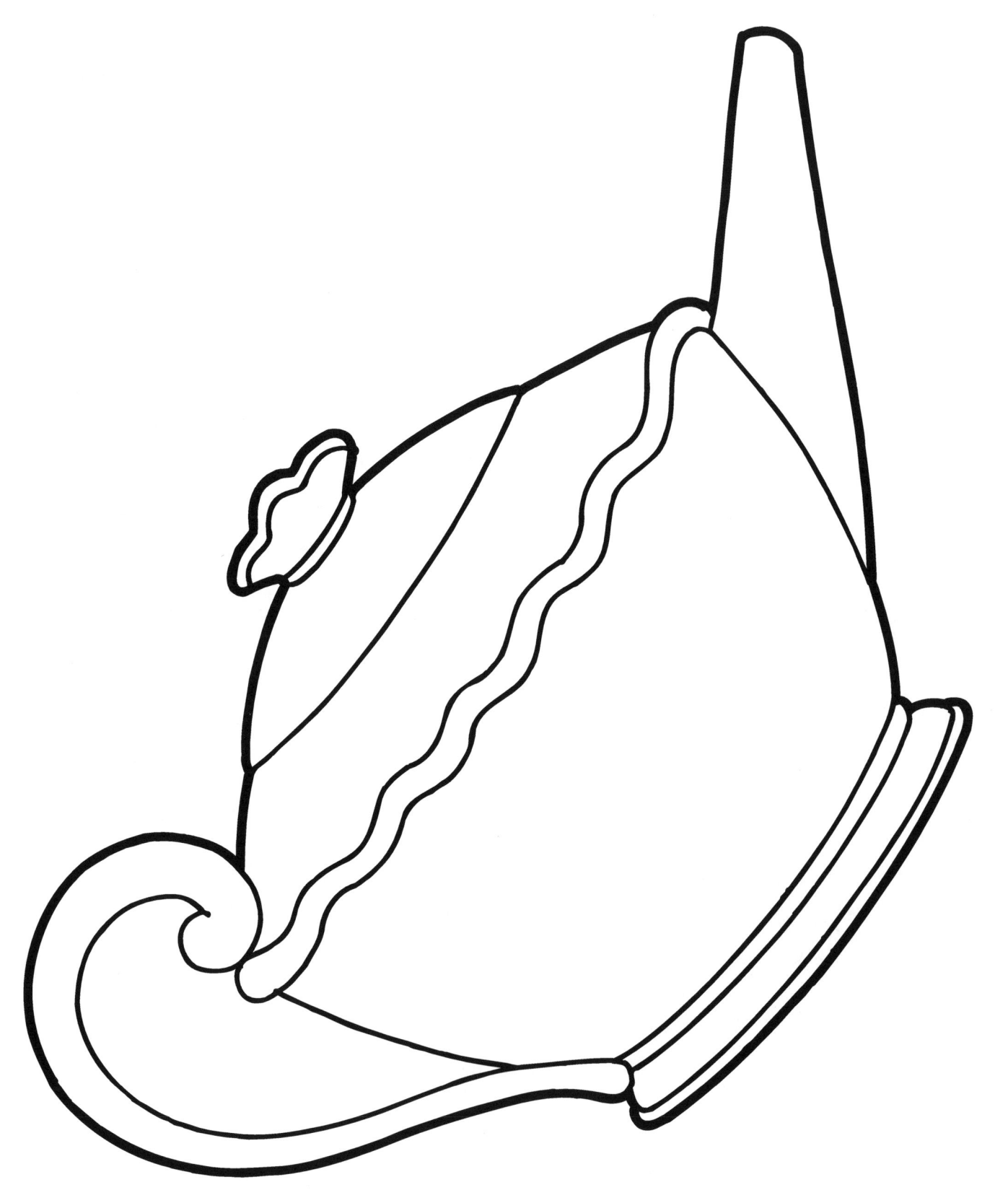

telephone (1940s)

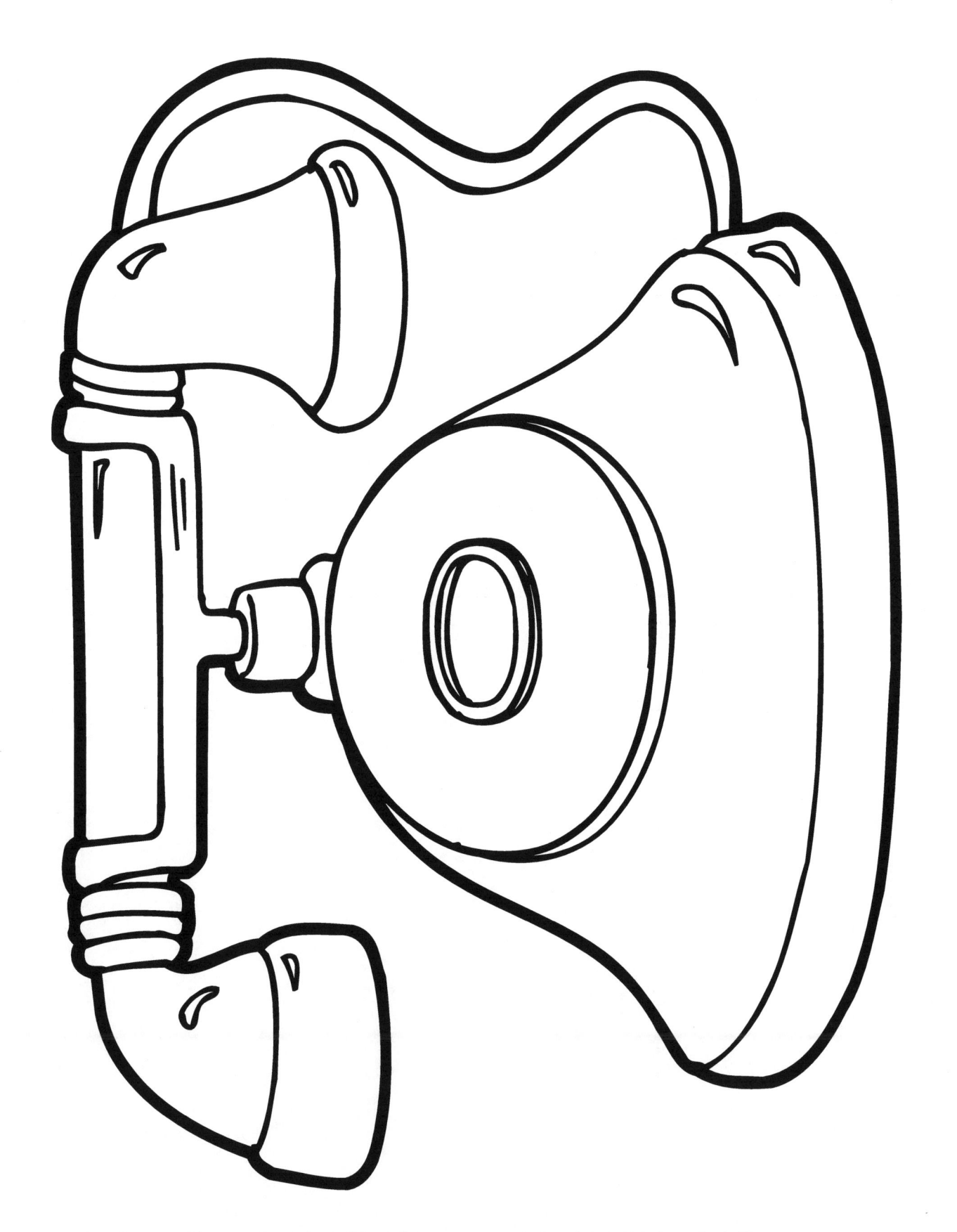

telephone (push buttons)

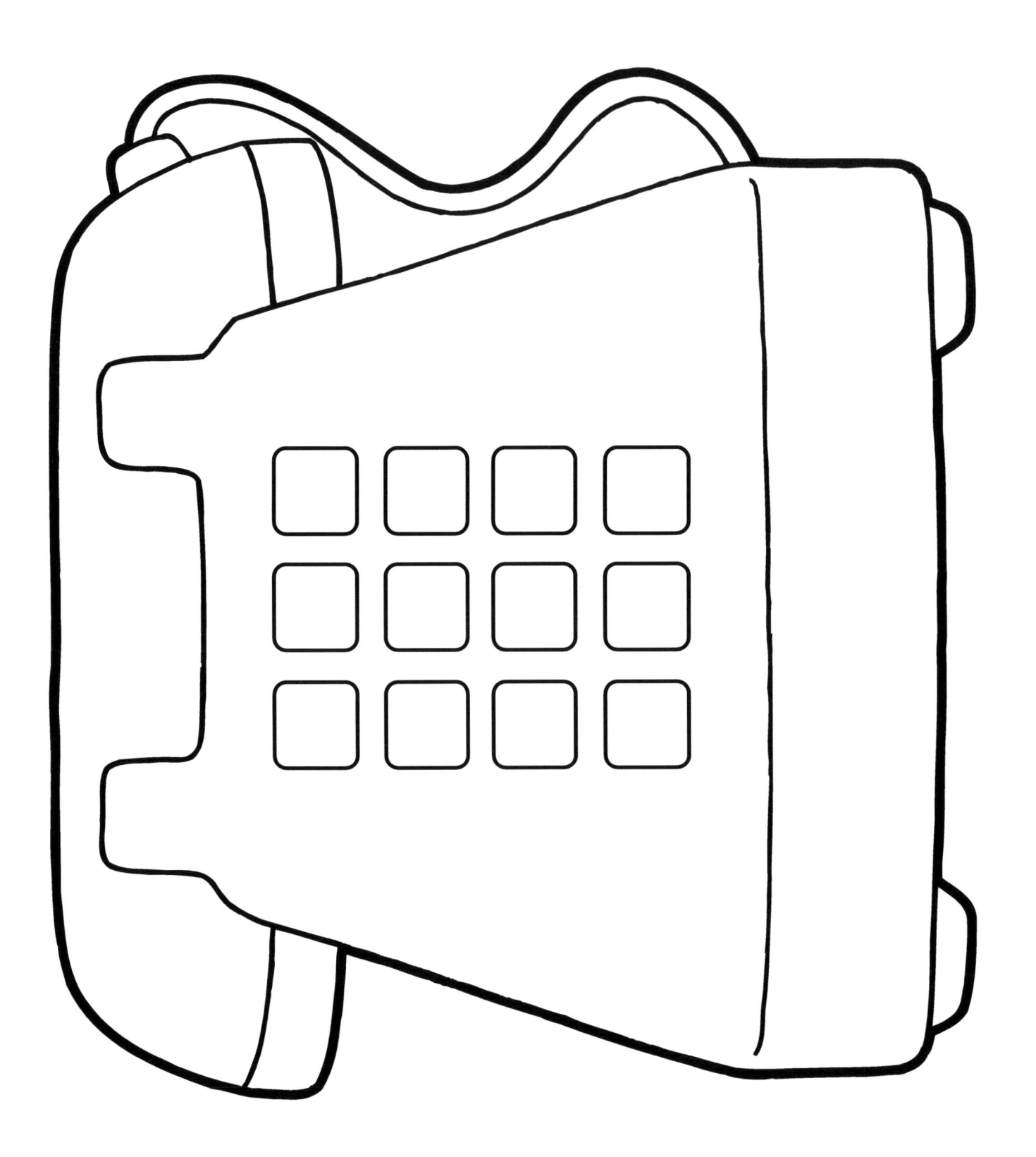

telephone (cordless)

telephone (first)

telephone (rotary dial)

telephone (slimline)

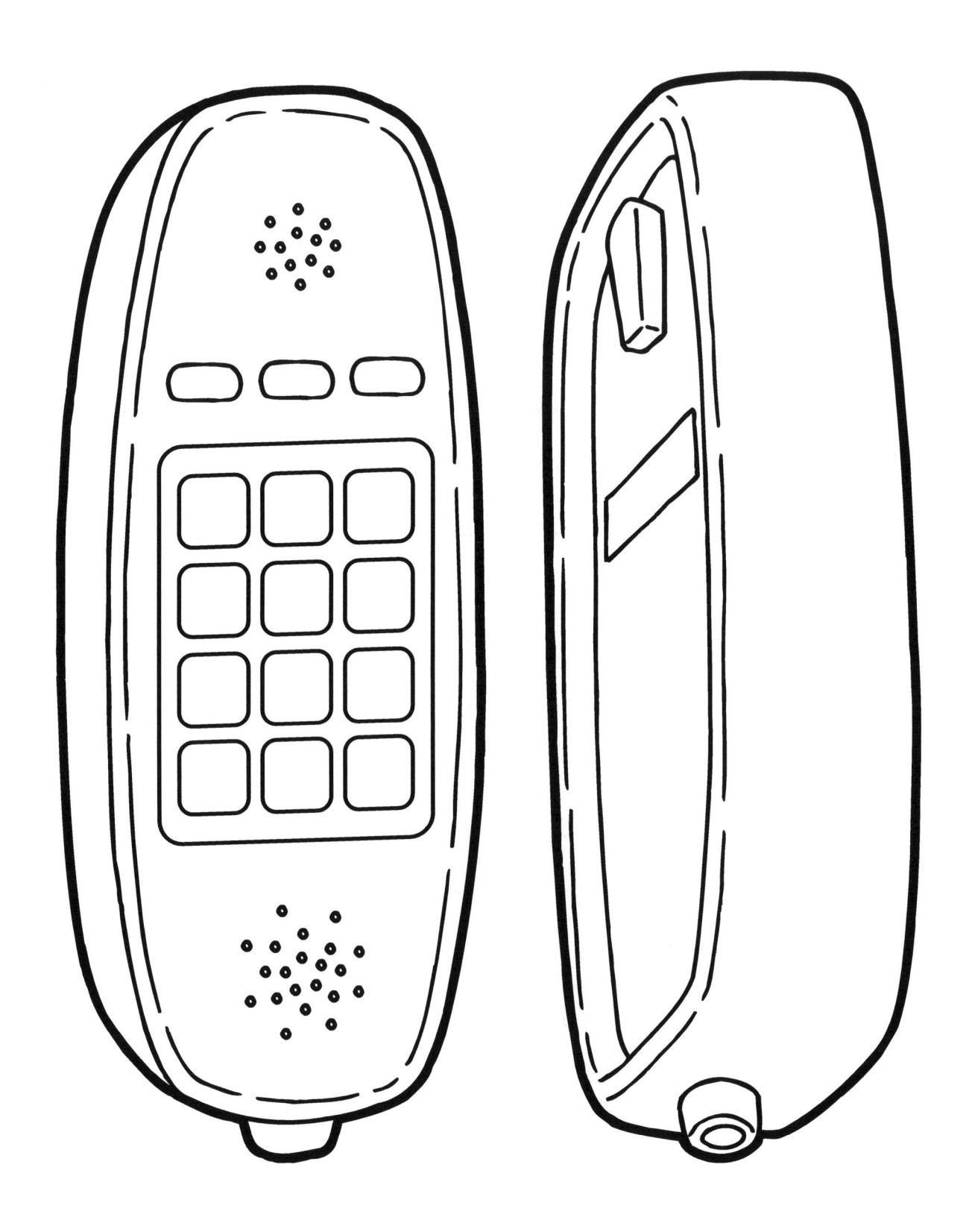

Tennessee, USA

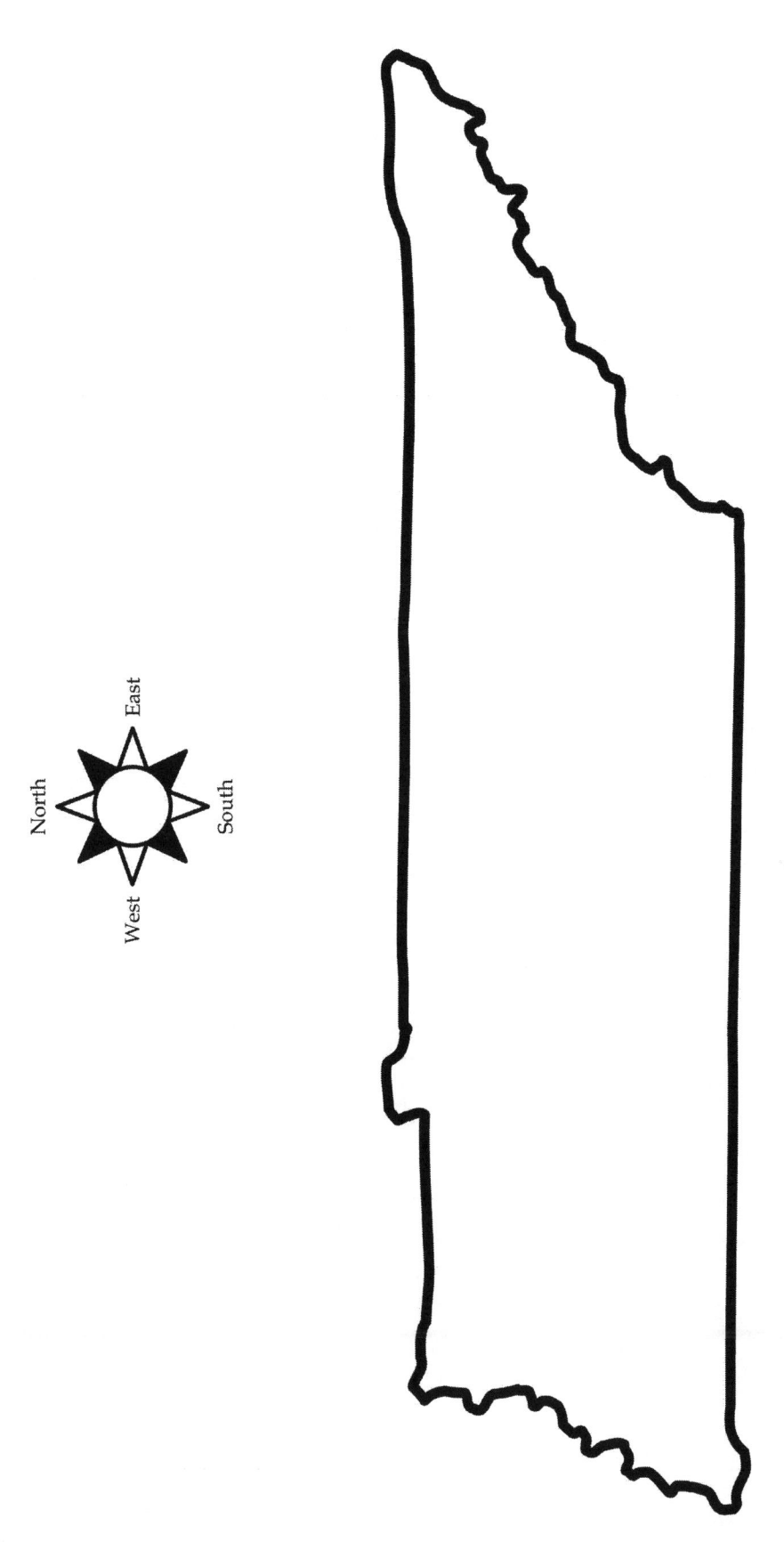

Maps are representations and boundaries are not exact.

Texas, USA

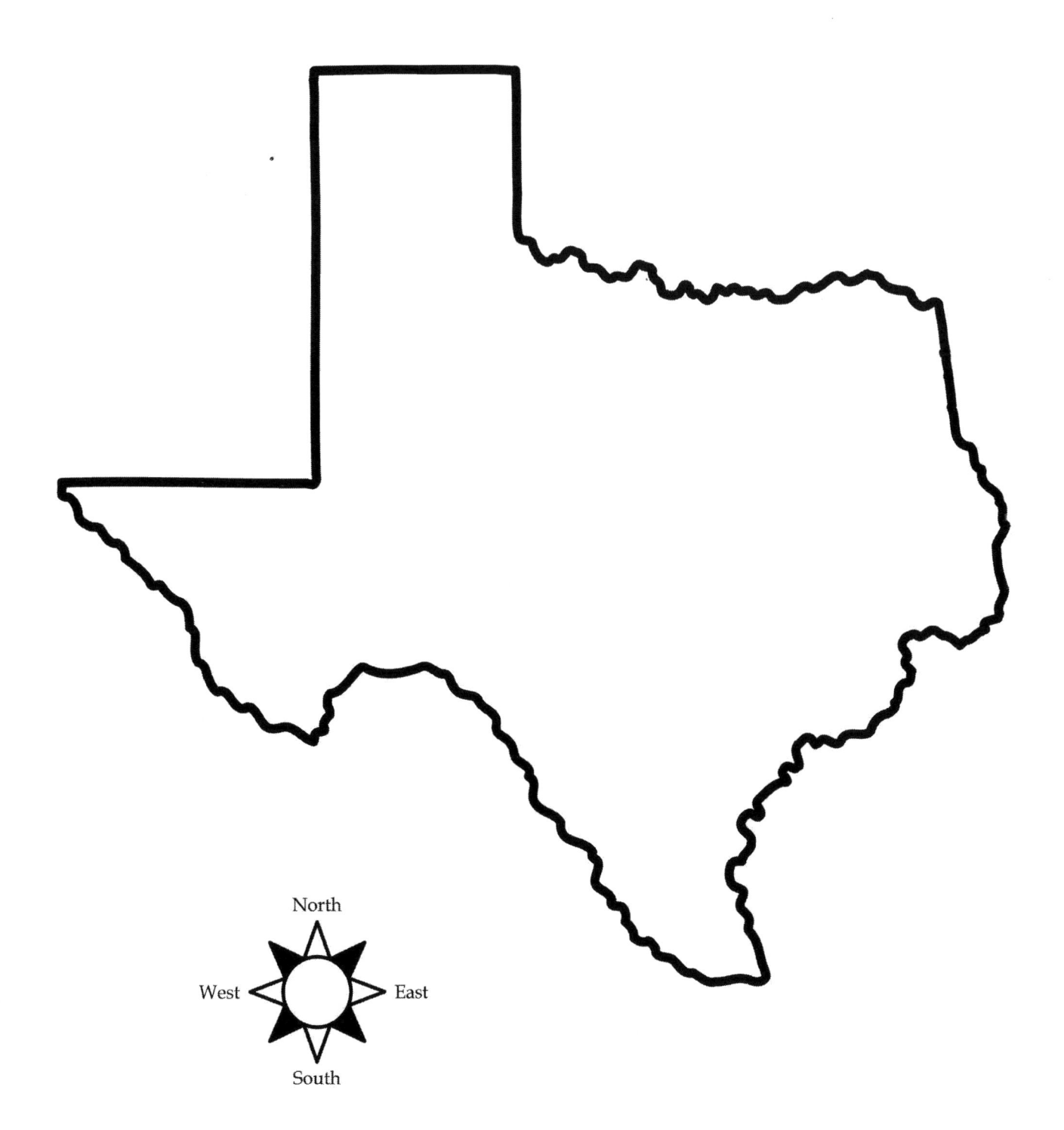

thimble

tiger

tire

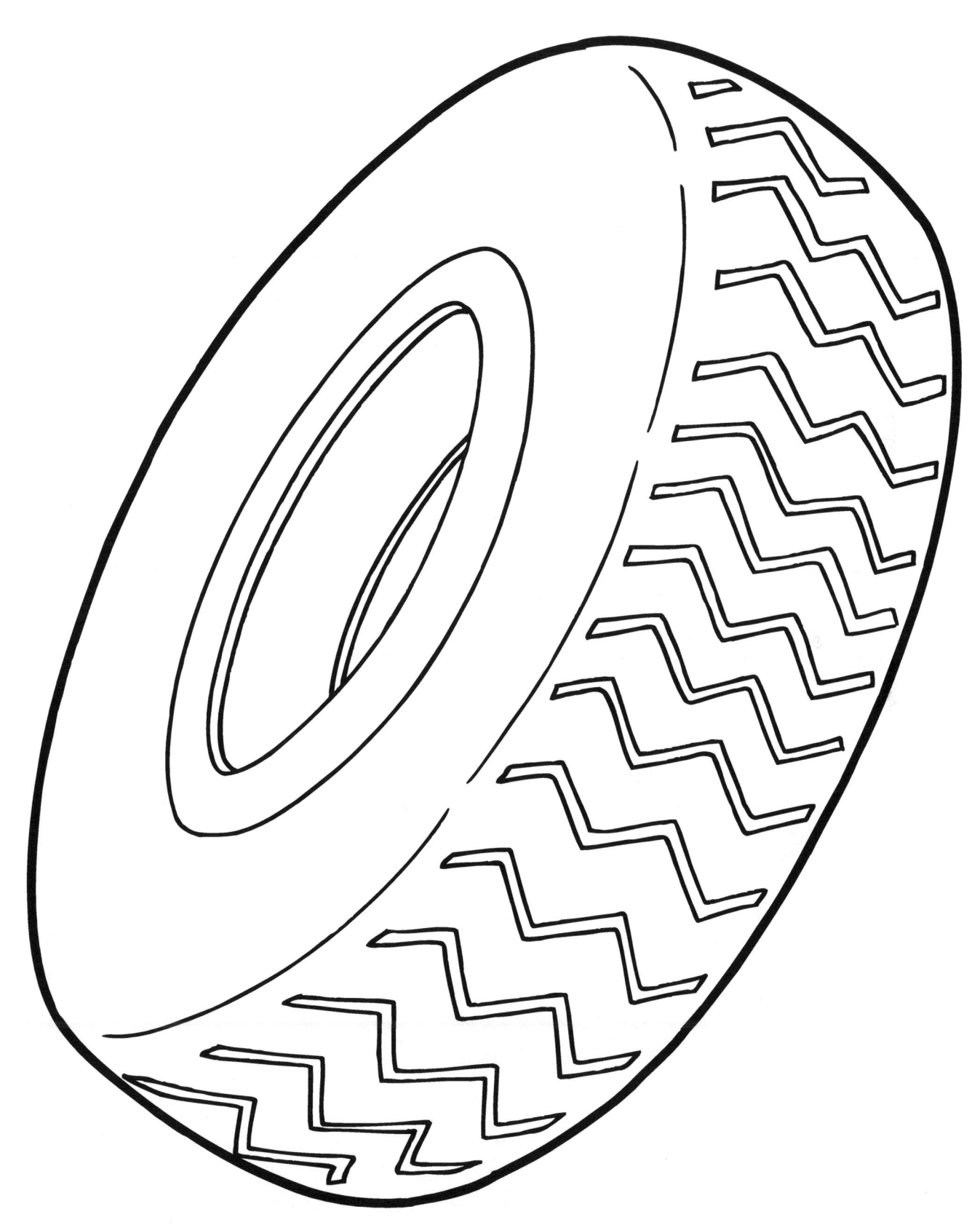

tire

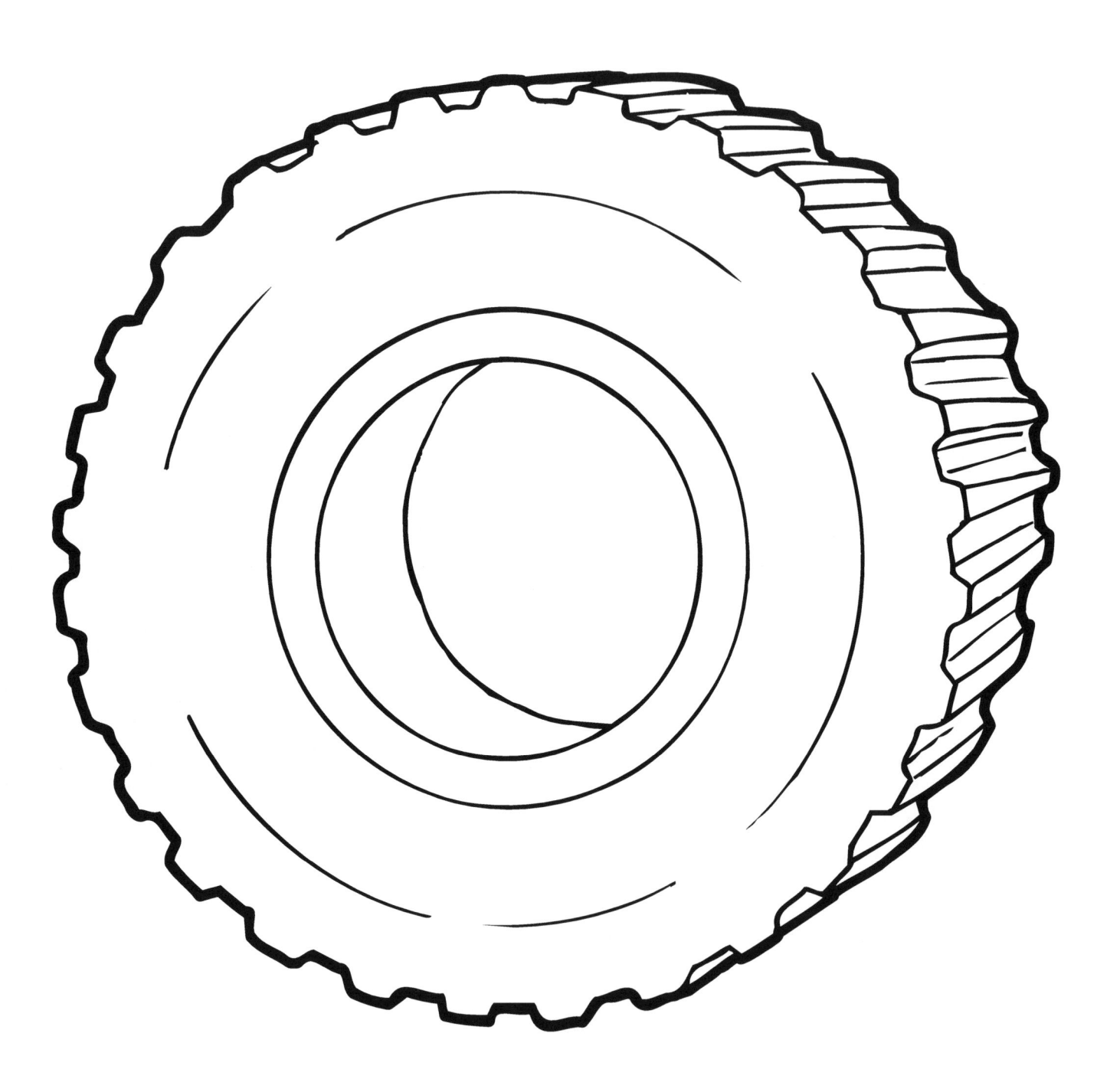

tomato

tooth

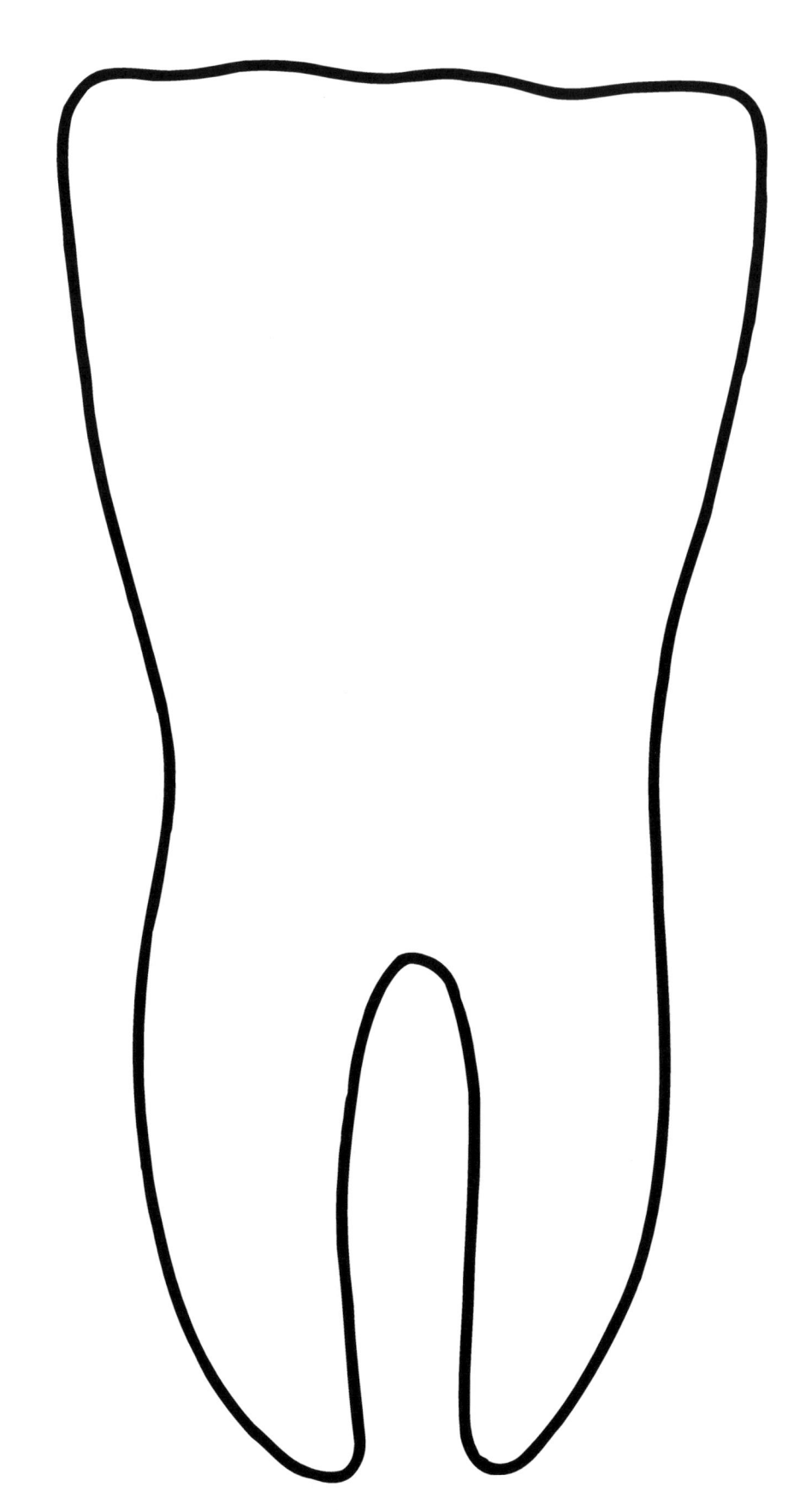

tooth (molar)

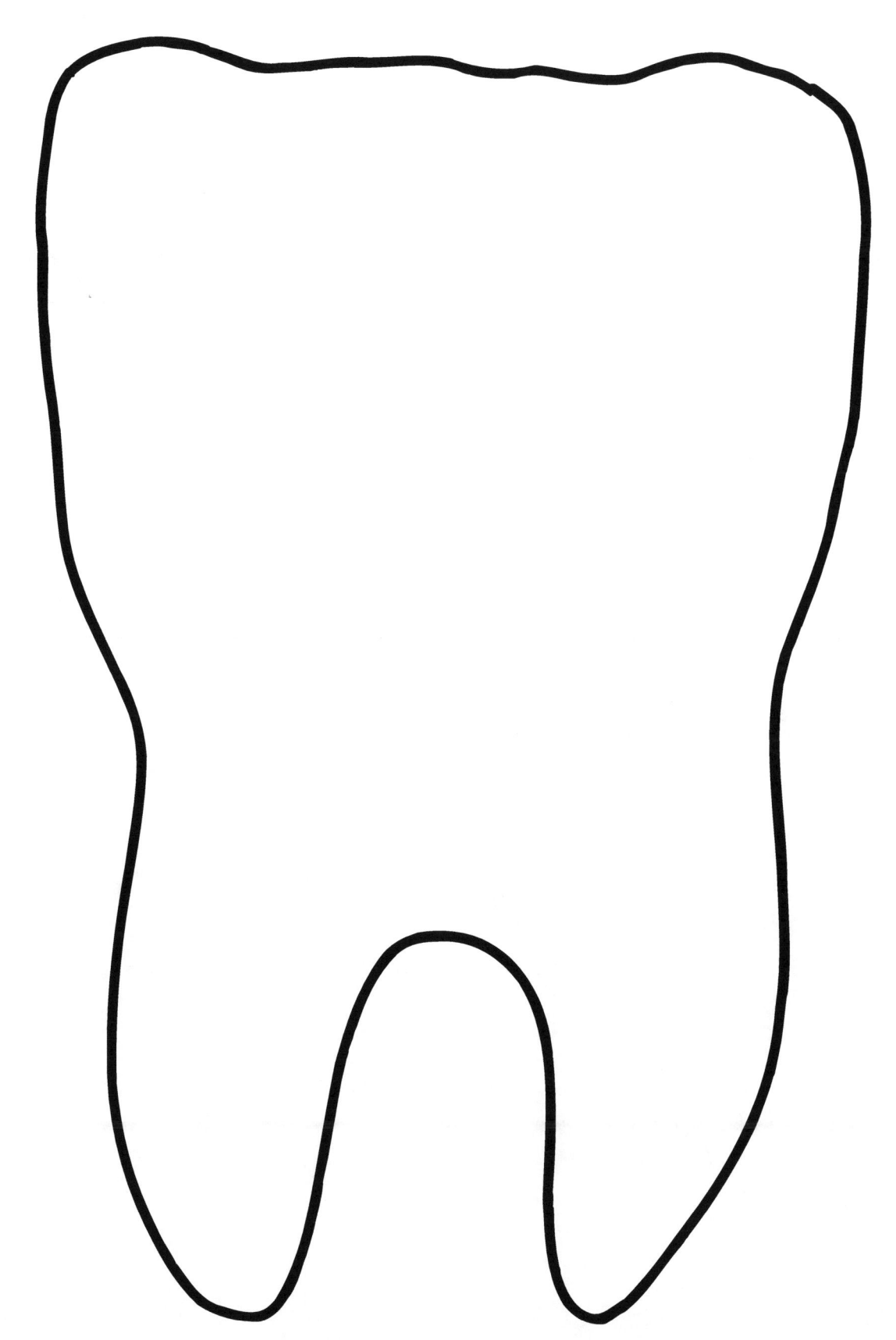

toothbrush

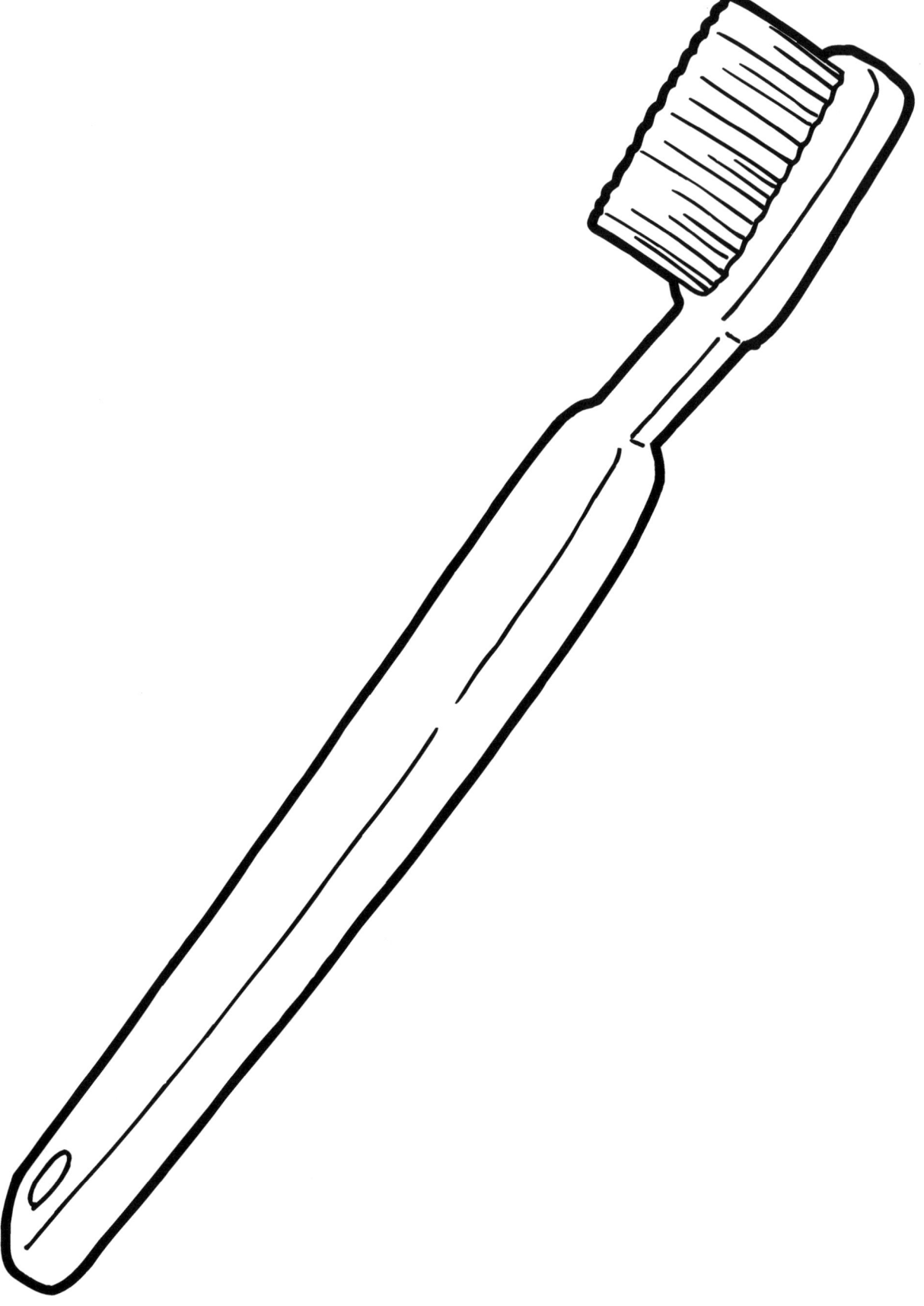

toothpaste

toucan

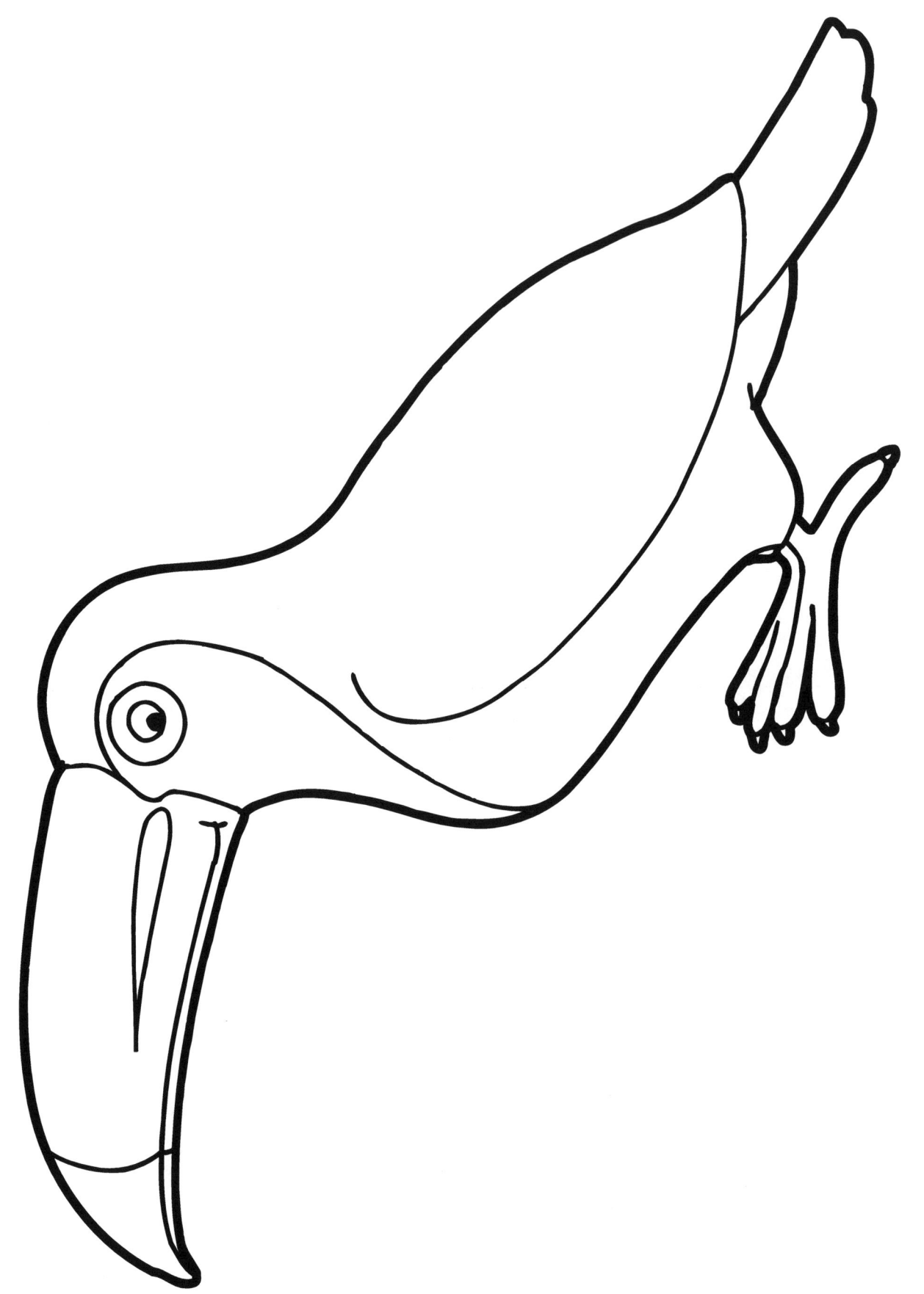

toucan (outline)

tractor

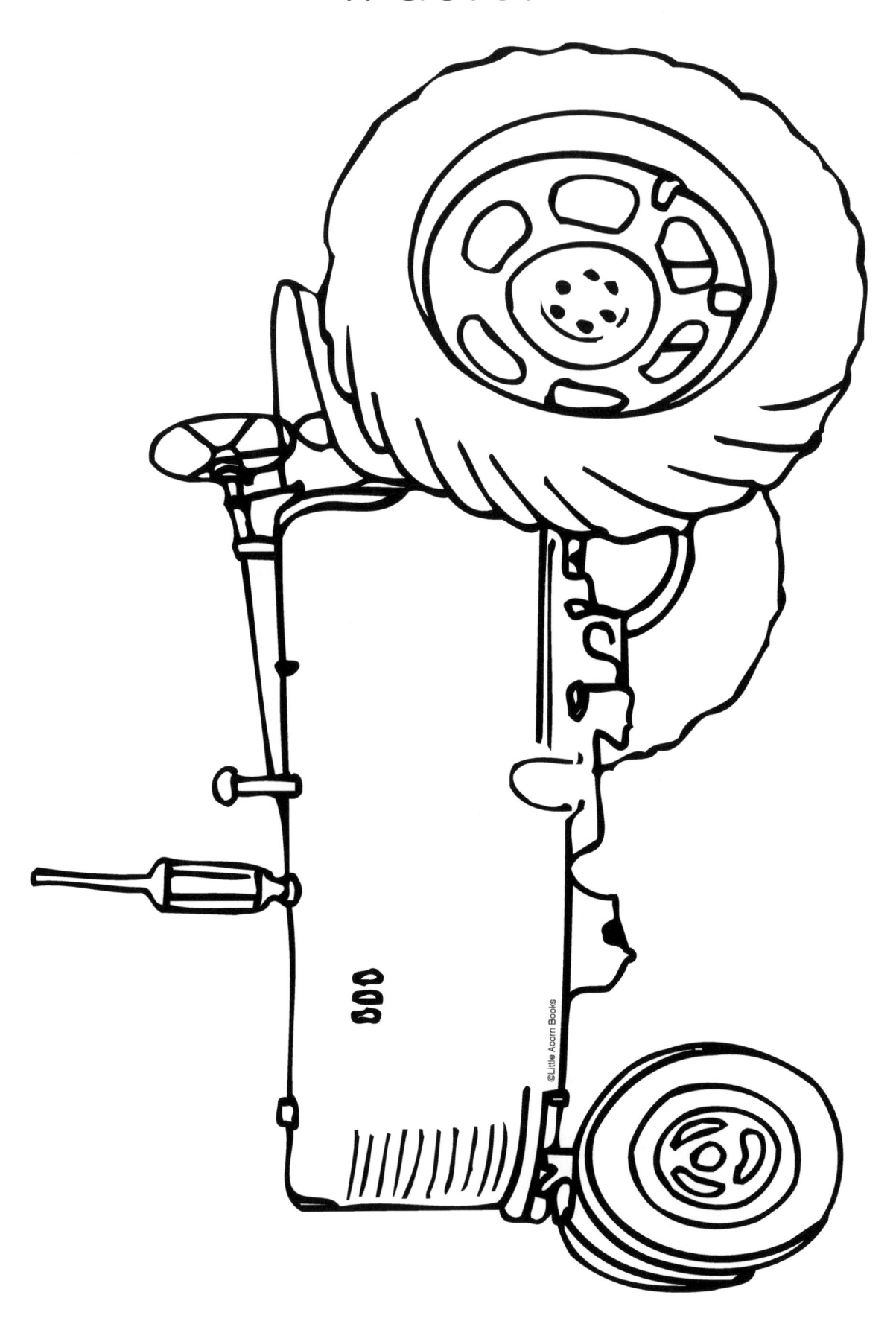

traffic signal

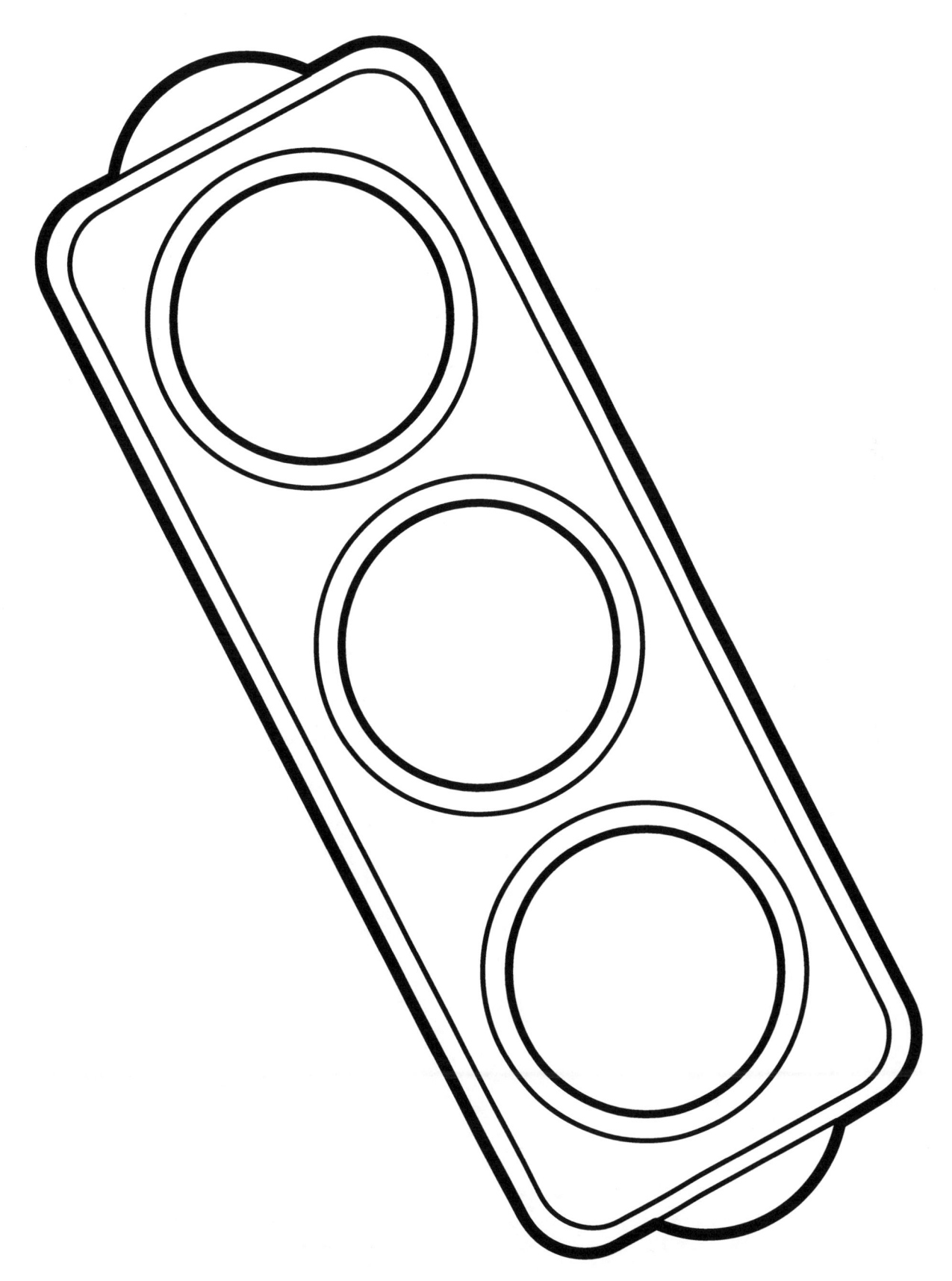

tree

tree (pine)

triangle

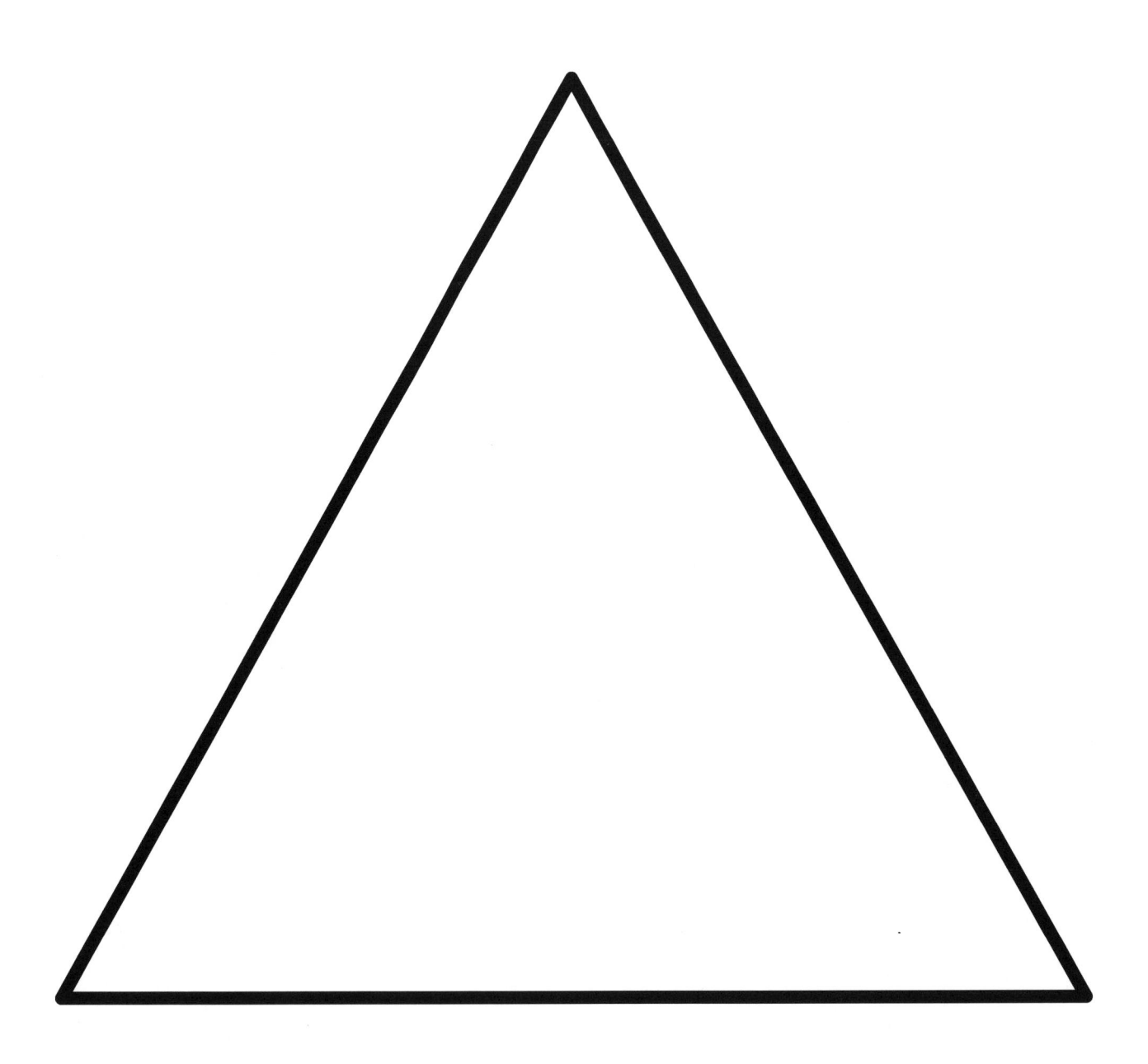

tricycle

trowel

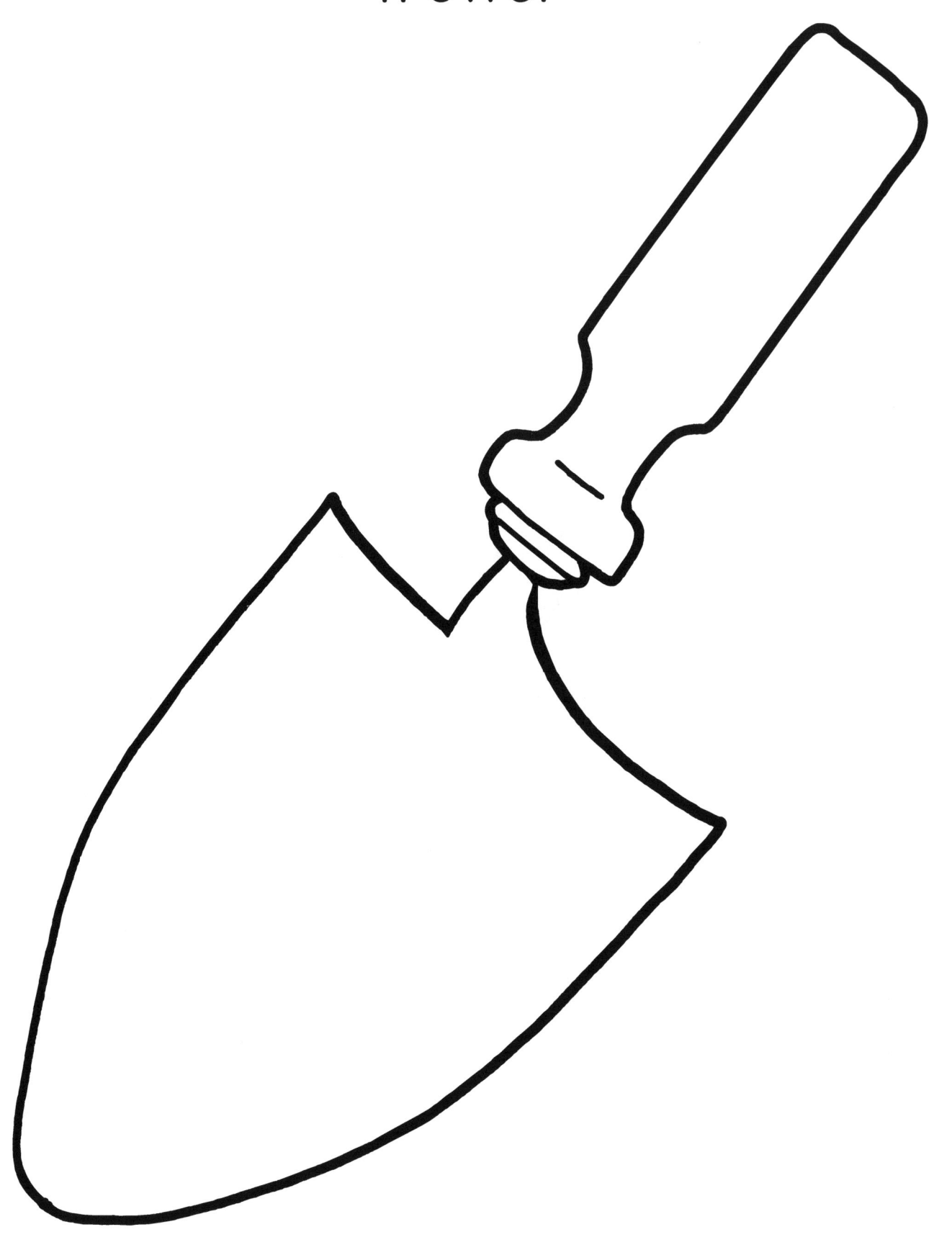

truck

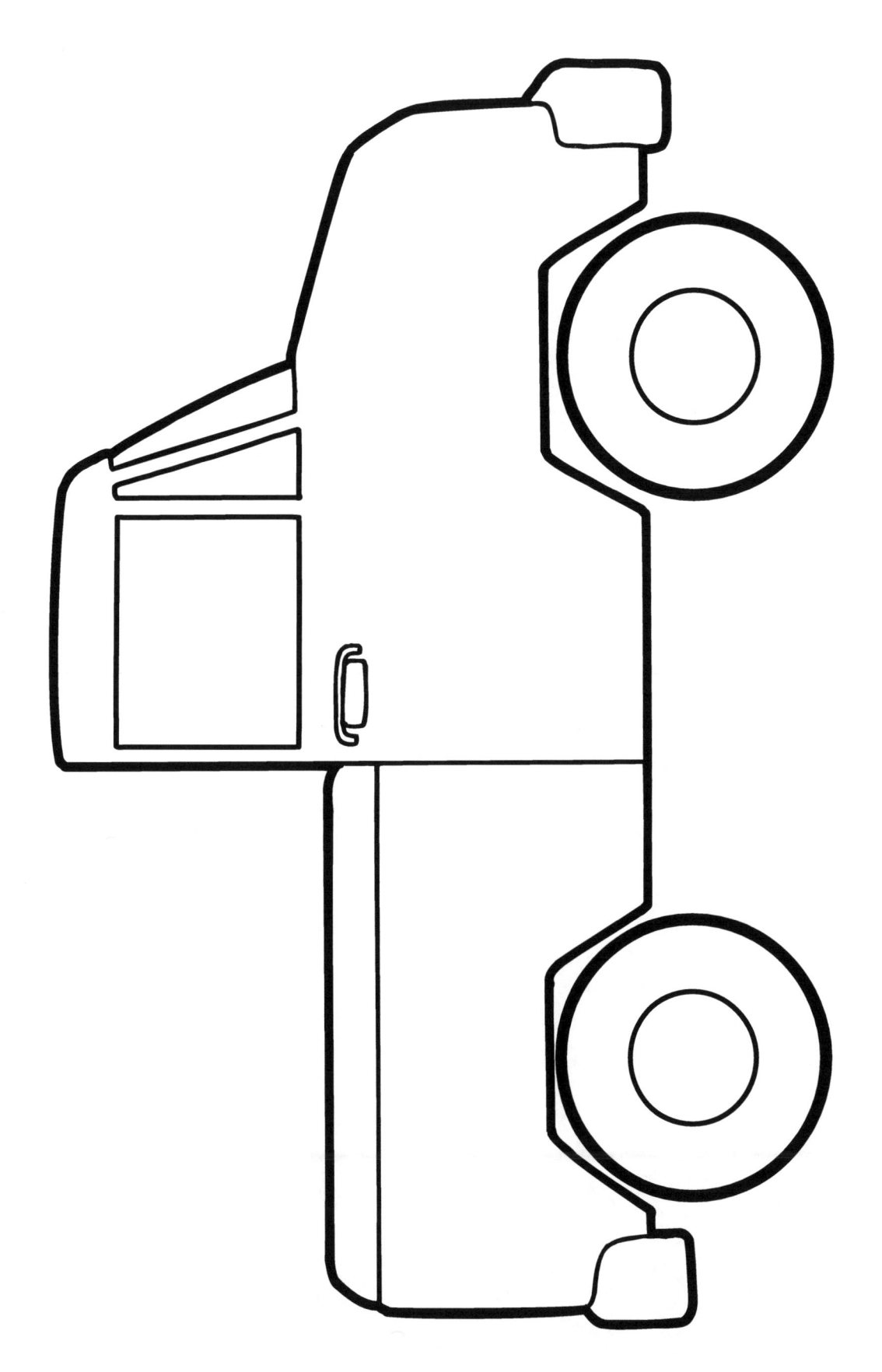

trunk (storage)

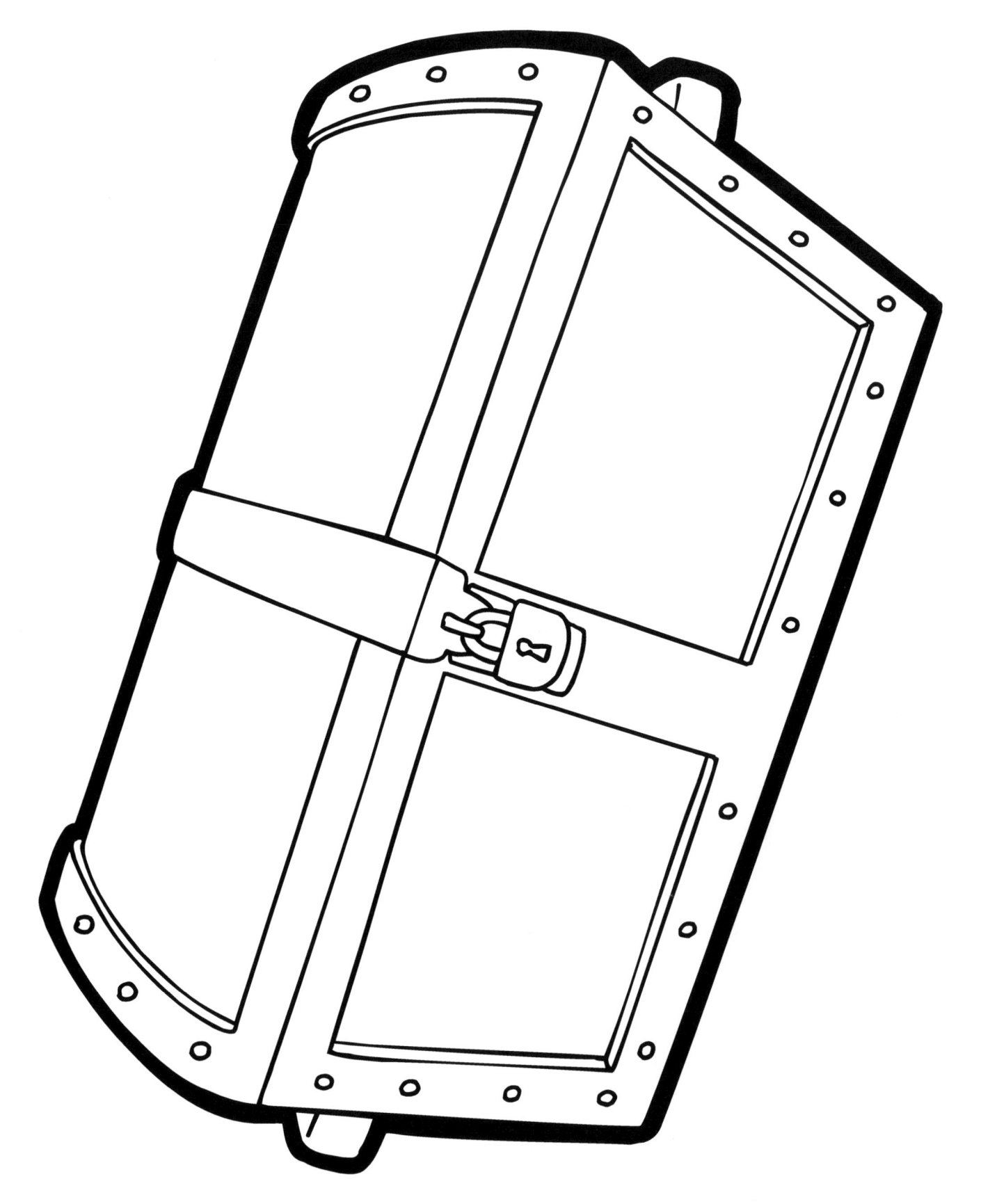

trunk (tree)

tub

tube (cardboard)

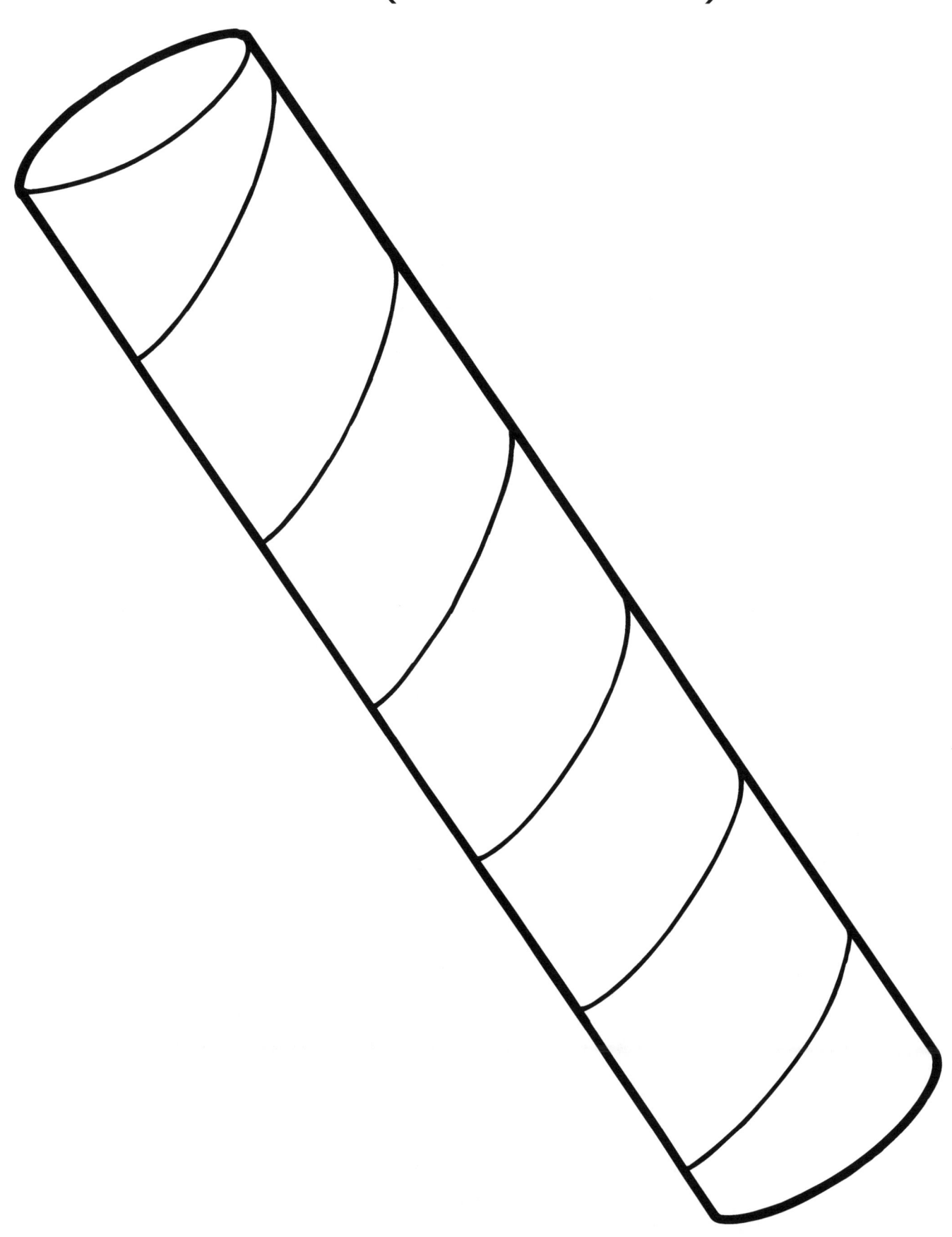

tulip

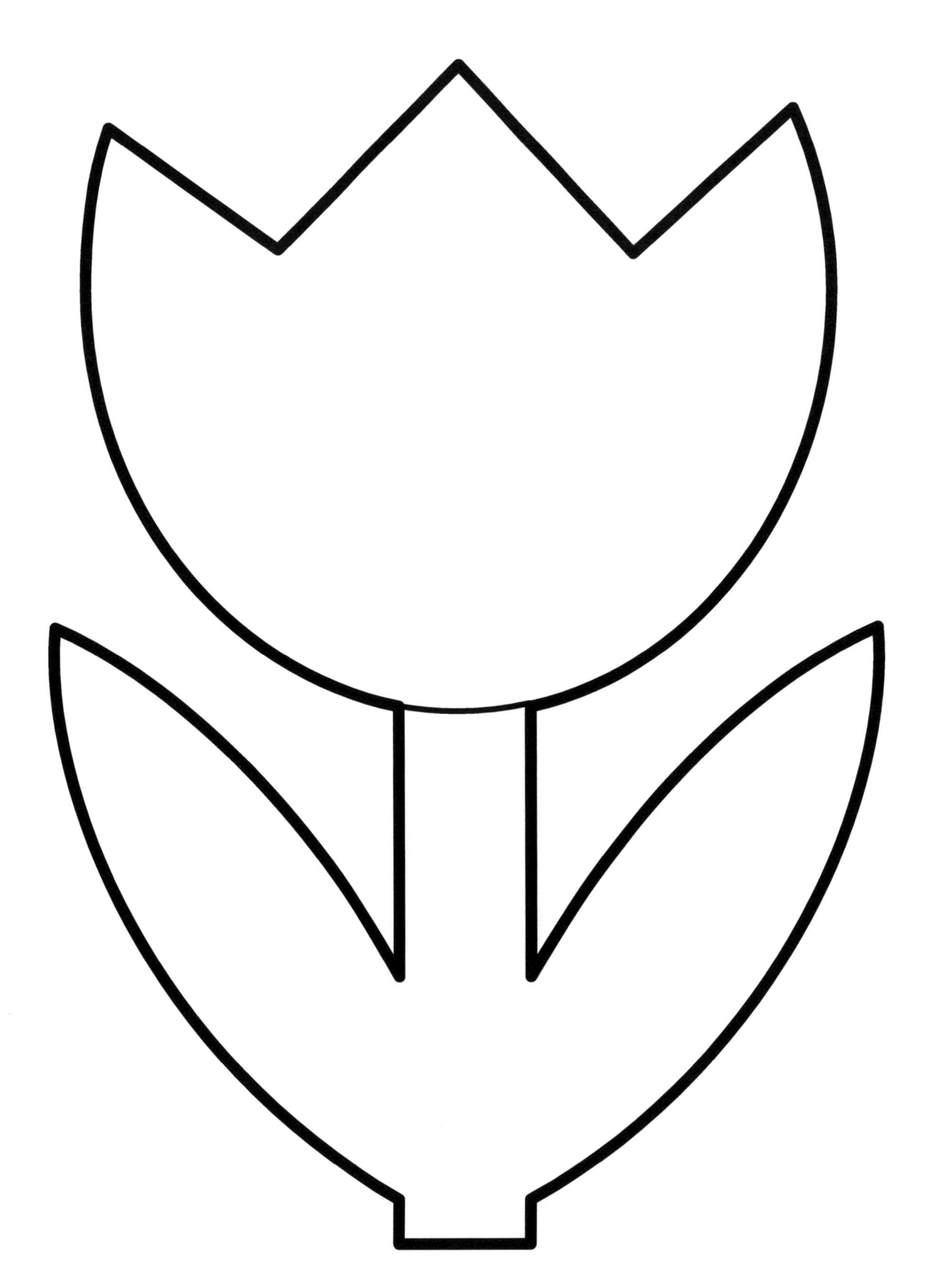

tuna

turkey

turkey (hen)

turkey (outline)

turkey (tom)

tuquoise (crayon)

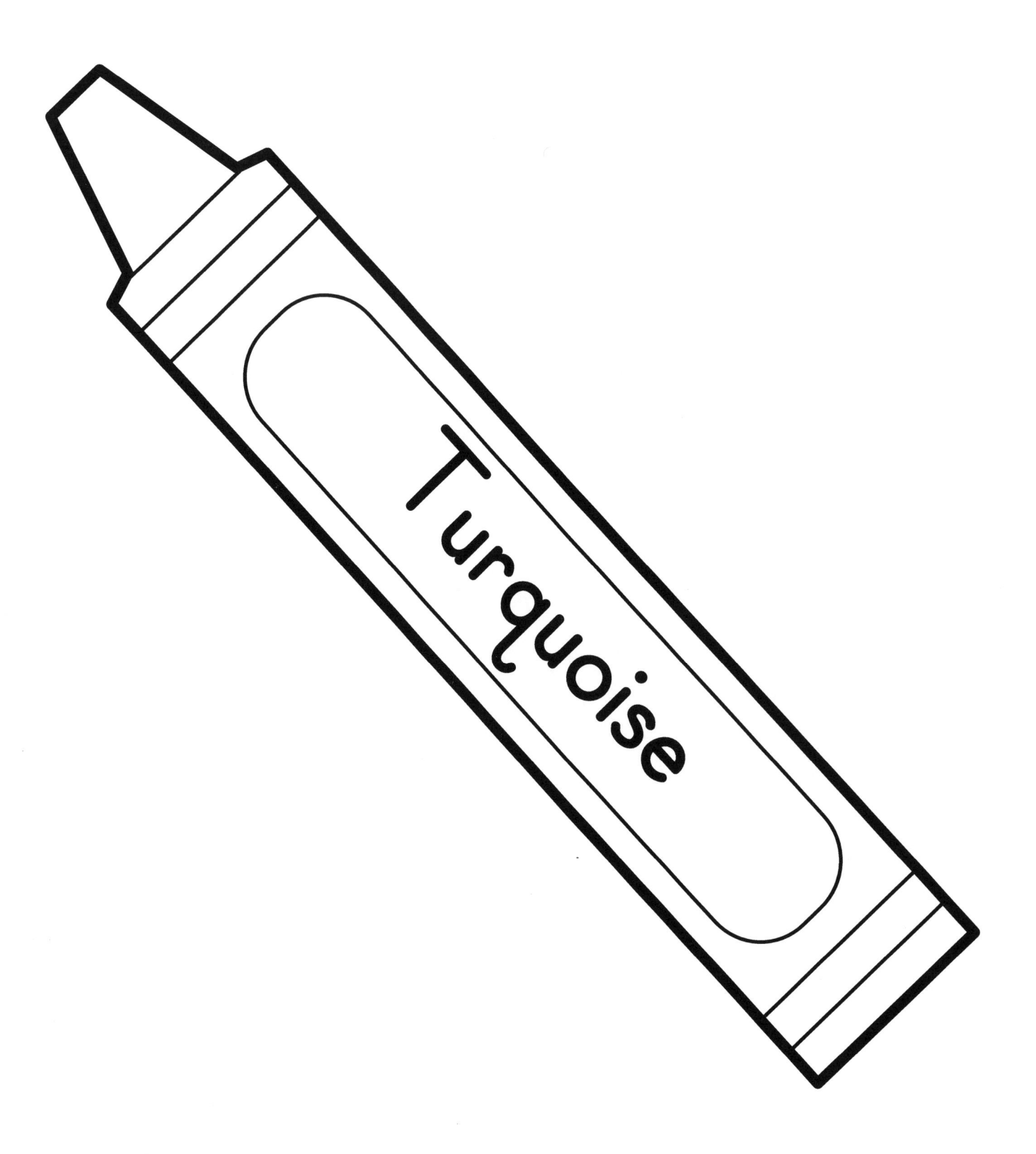

turtle (animated)

turtle (animated with hat)

turtle (loggerhead)

turtle (outline)

turtle (pet)

turtledove

typewriter (1867)

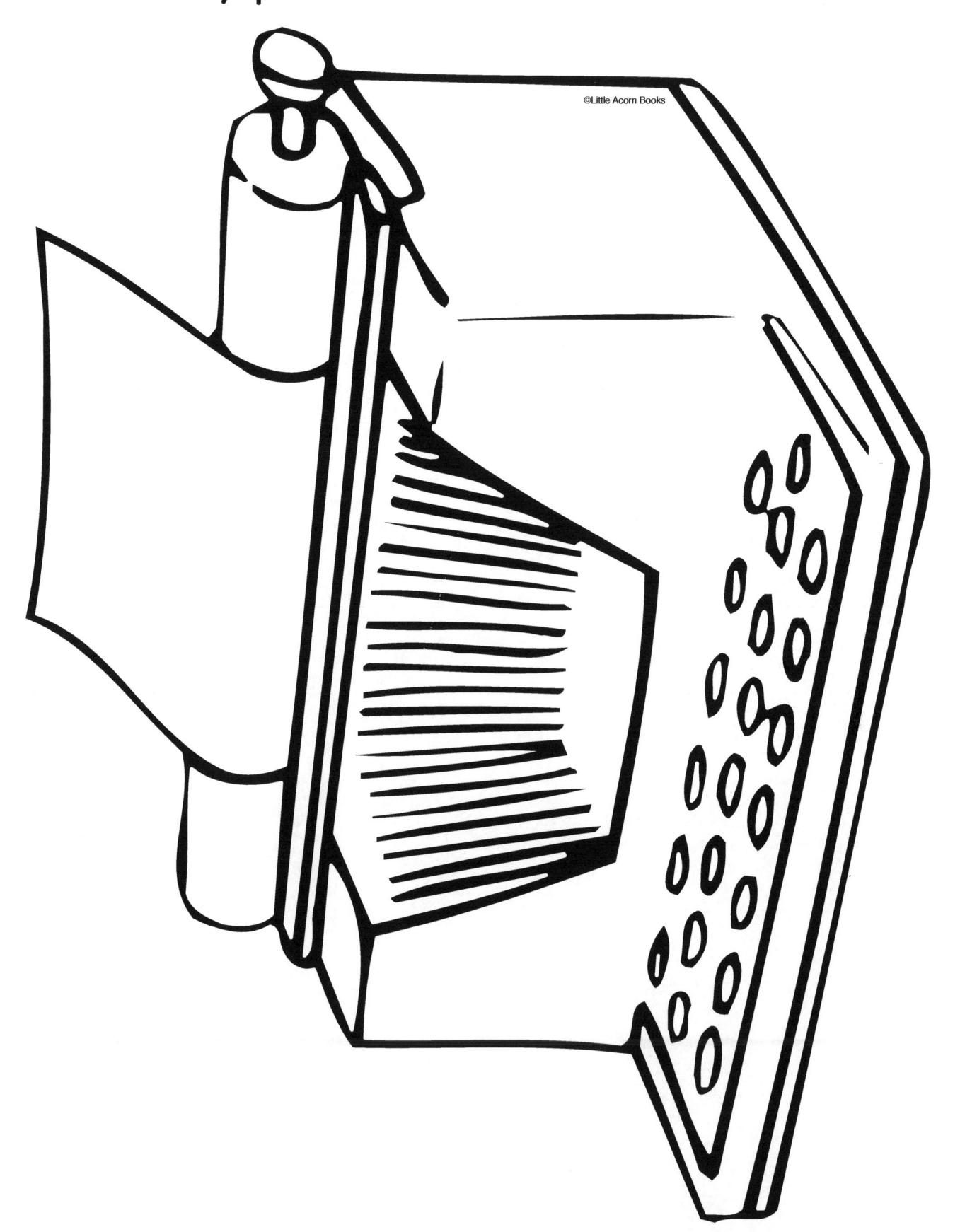

umbrella (beach)

umbrella (outline)

umbrella (rain)

umpire

underwear

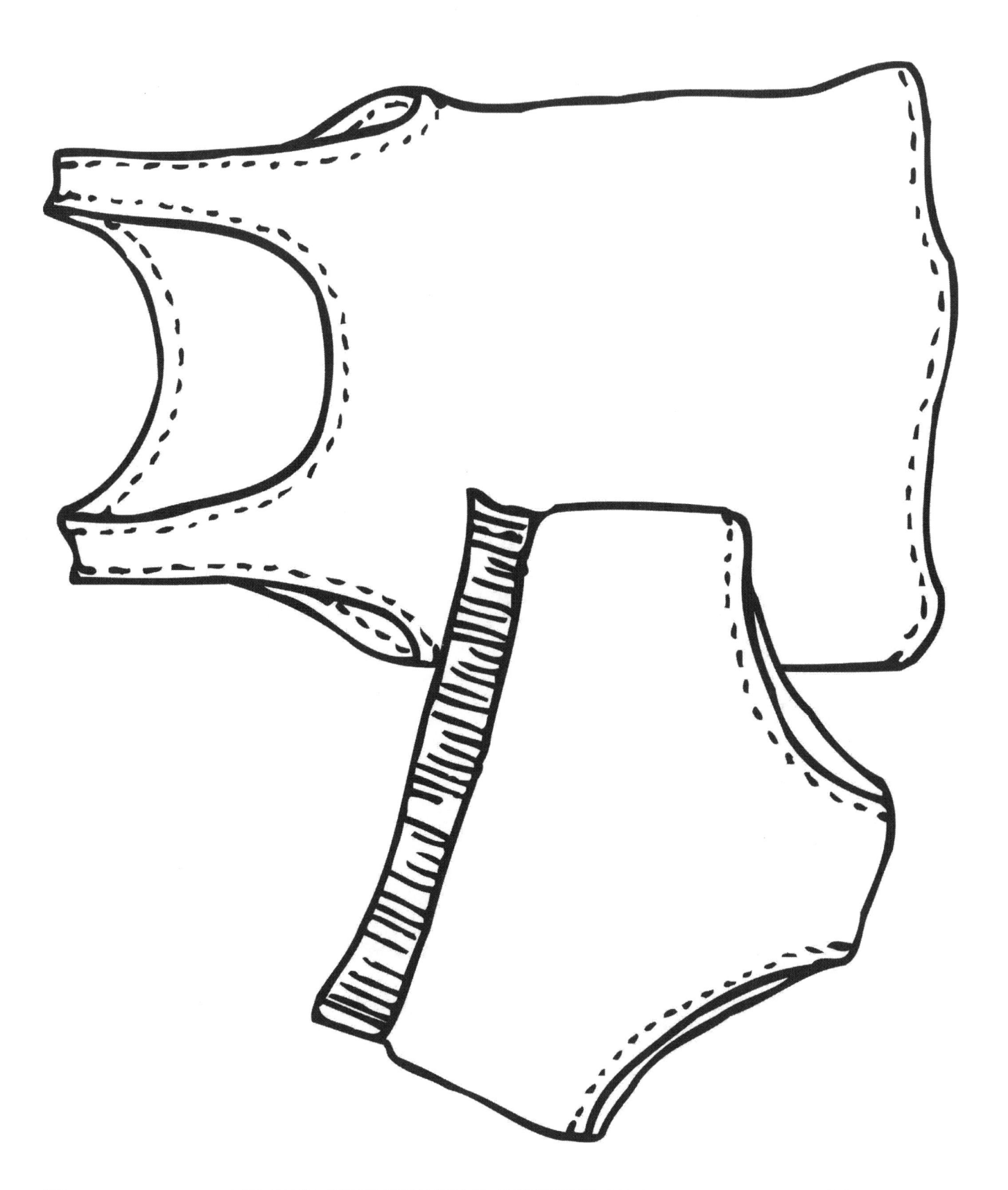

unicycle

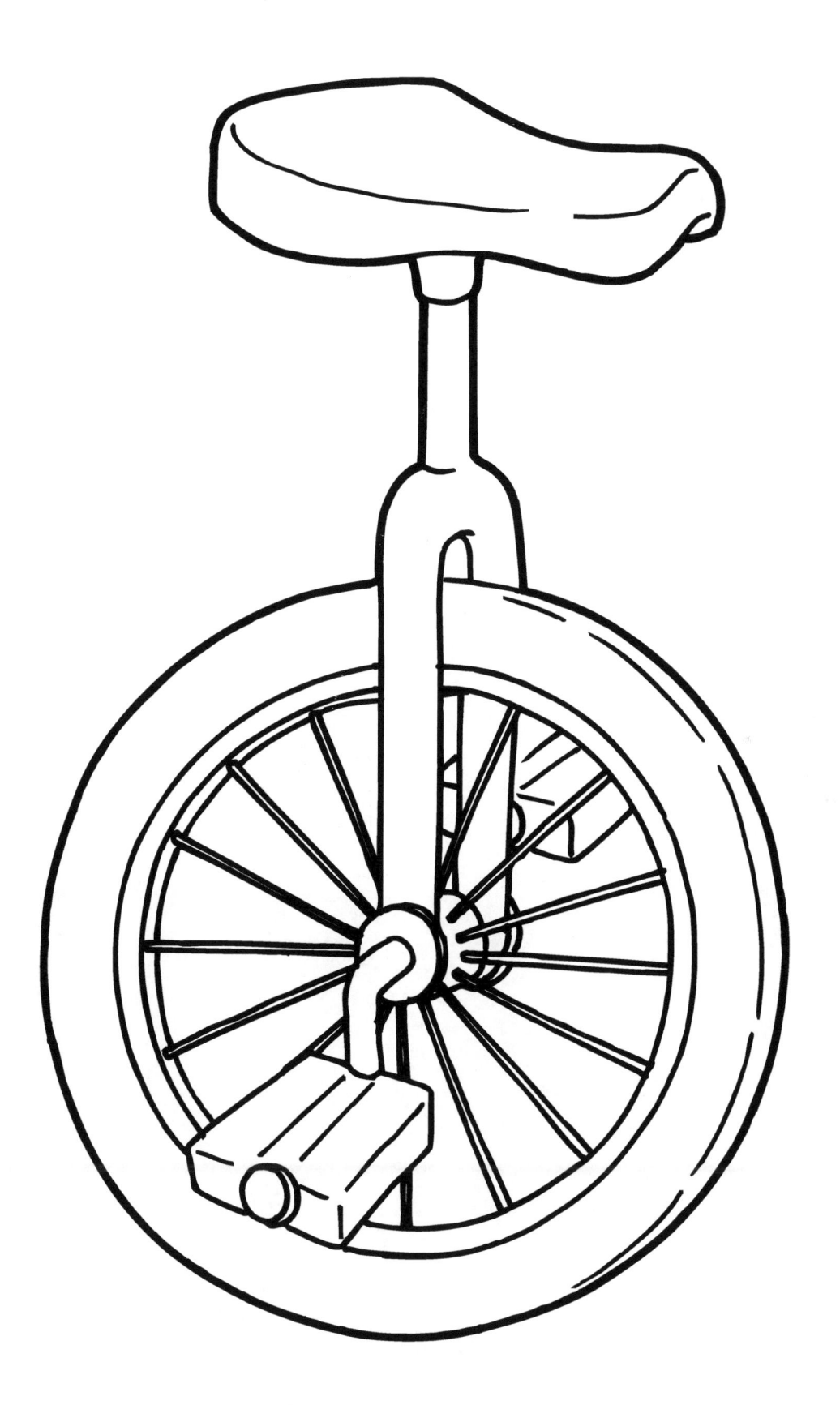

United Kingdom

North
West
East
South

Maps are representations and boundaries are not exact.

United States of America

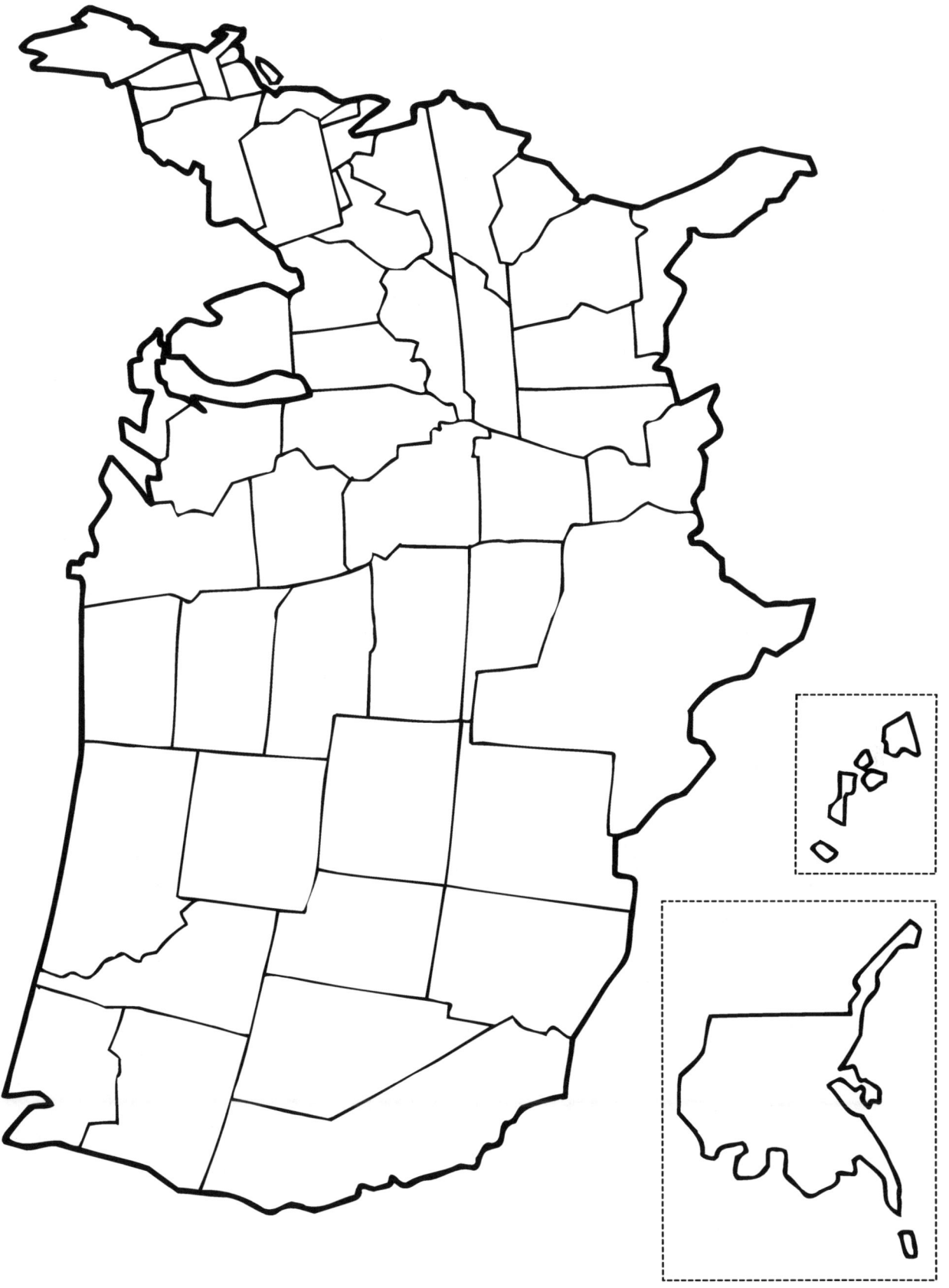

Maps are representations and boundaries are not exact.

USS Constitution

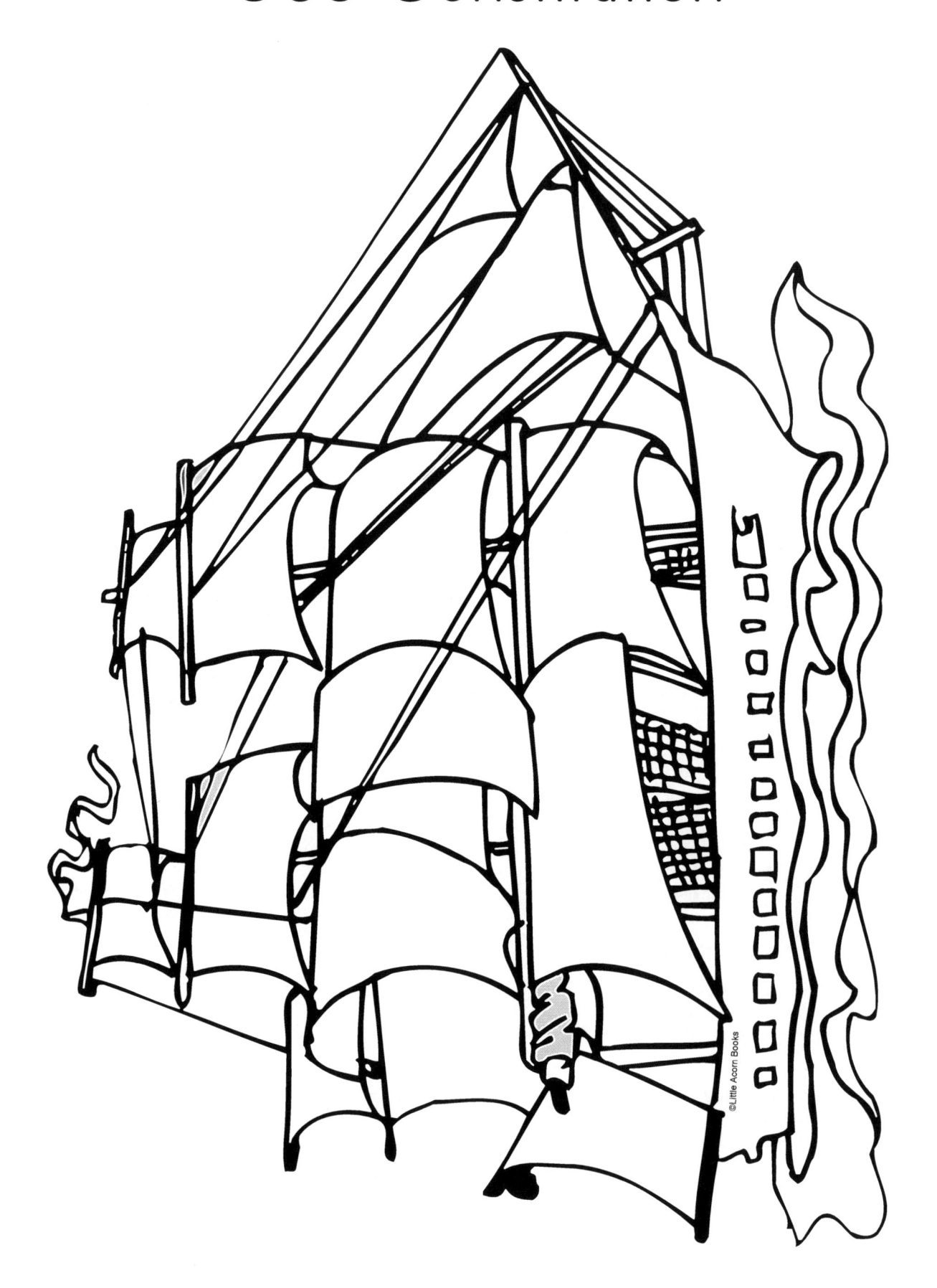

urchin

Utah, USA

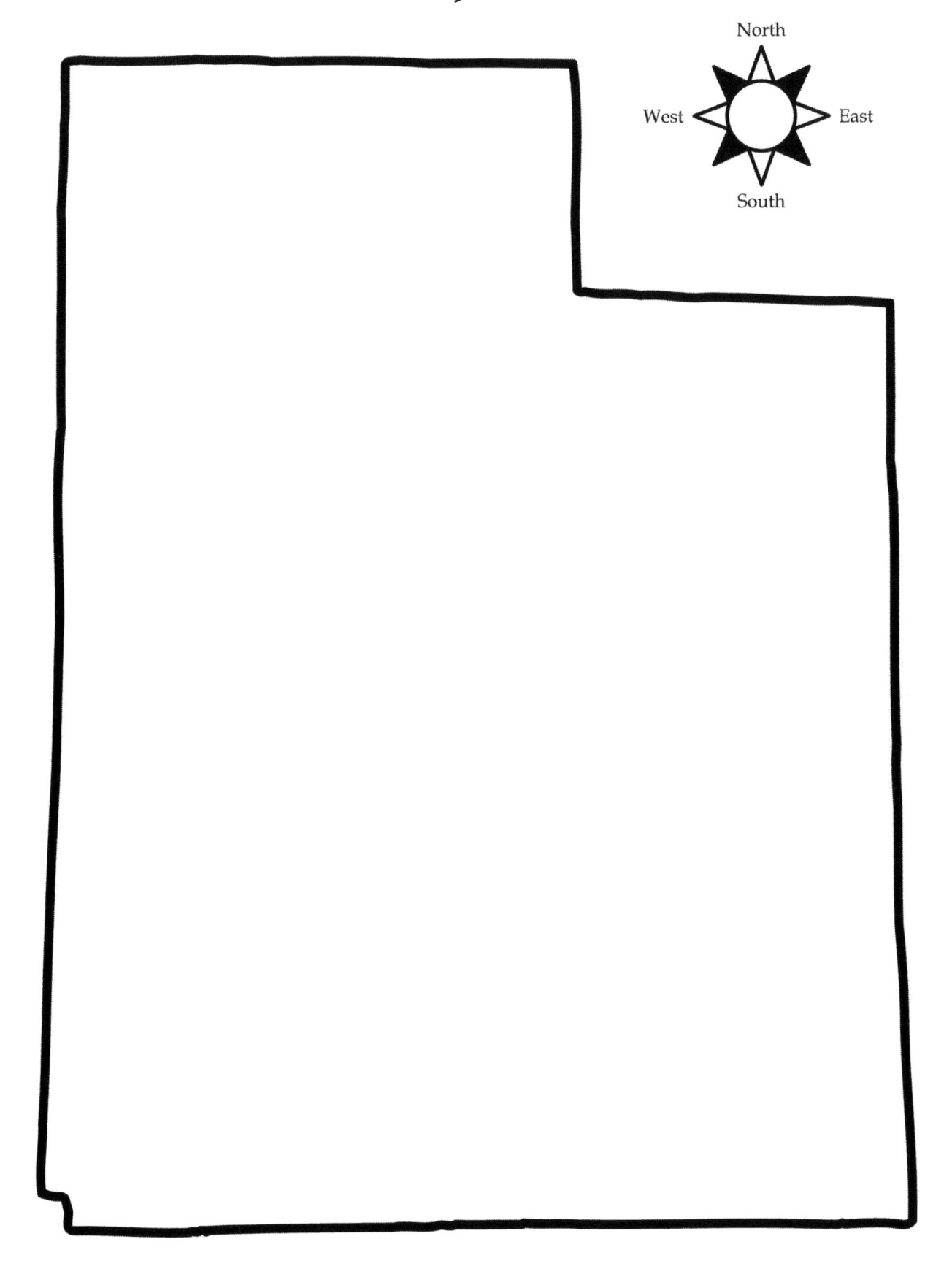

North
West East
South

Maps are representations and boundaries are not exact.

vacuum cleaner (1908)

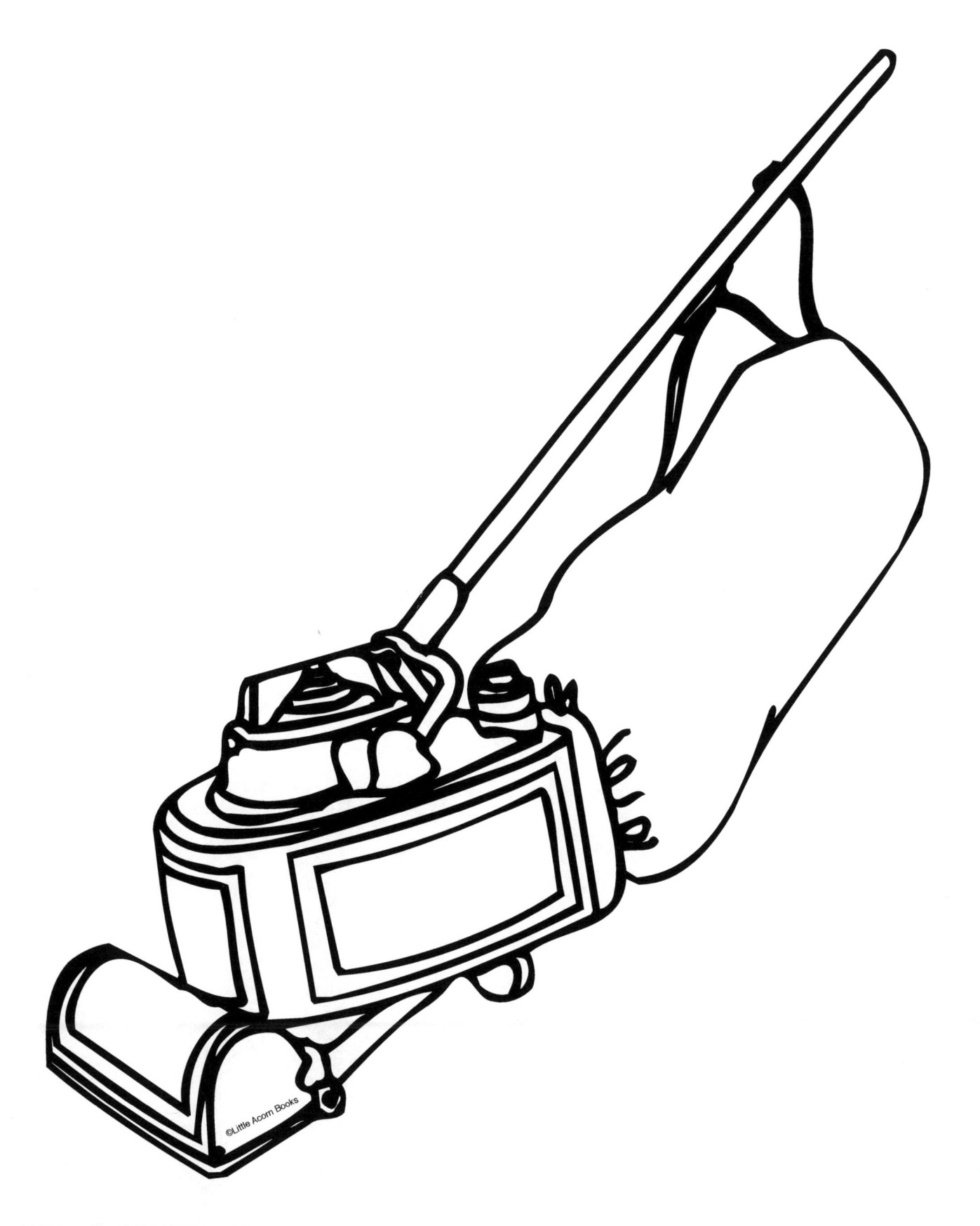

vacuum cleaner (upright)

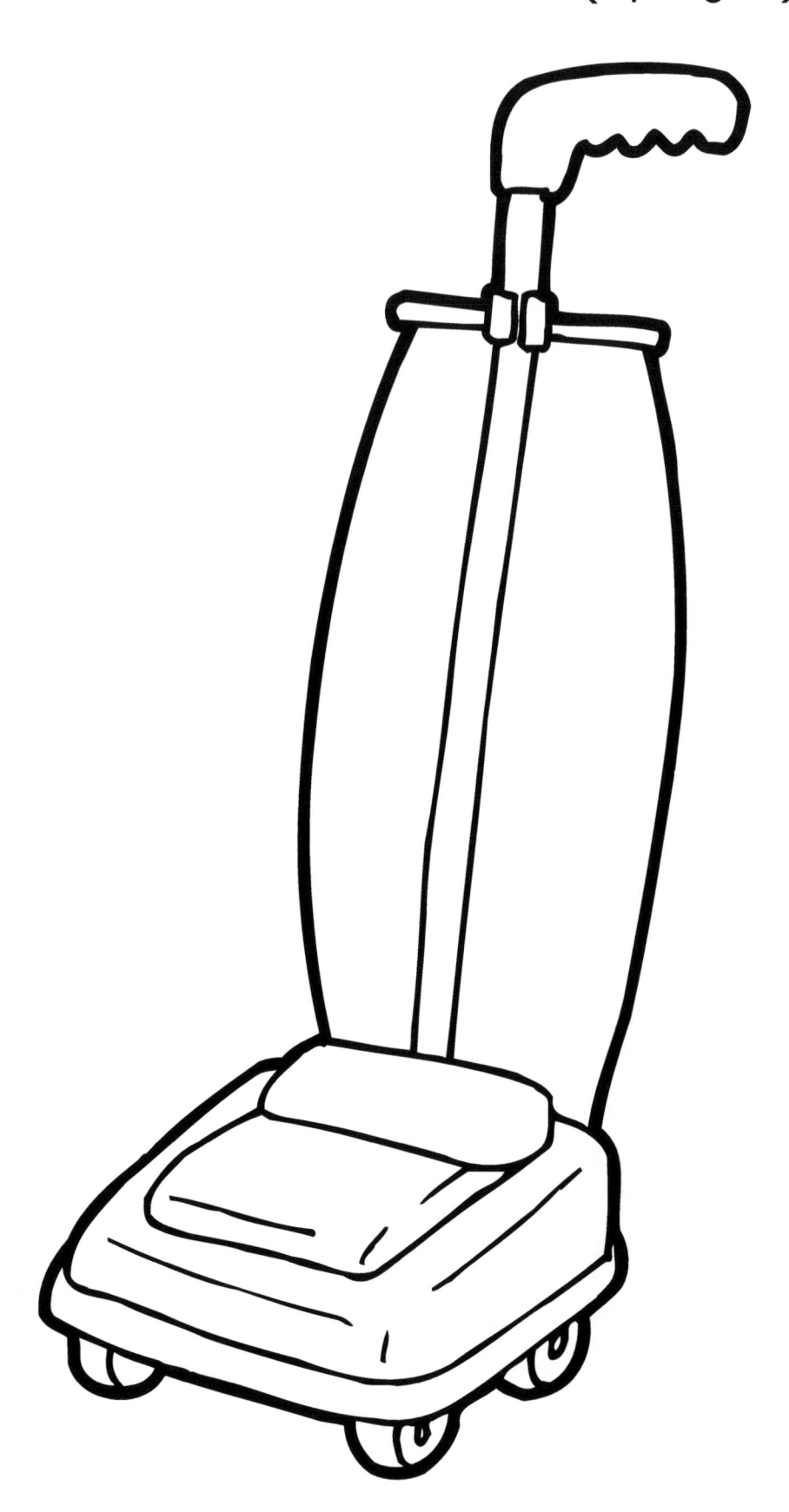

Valentine candy box

van

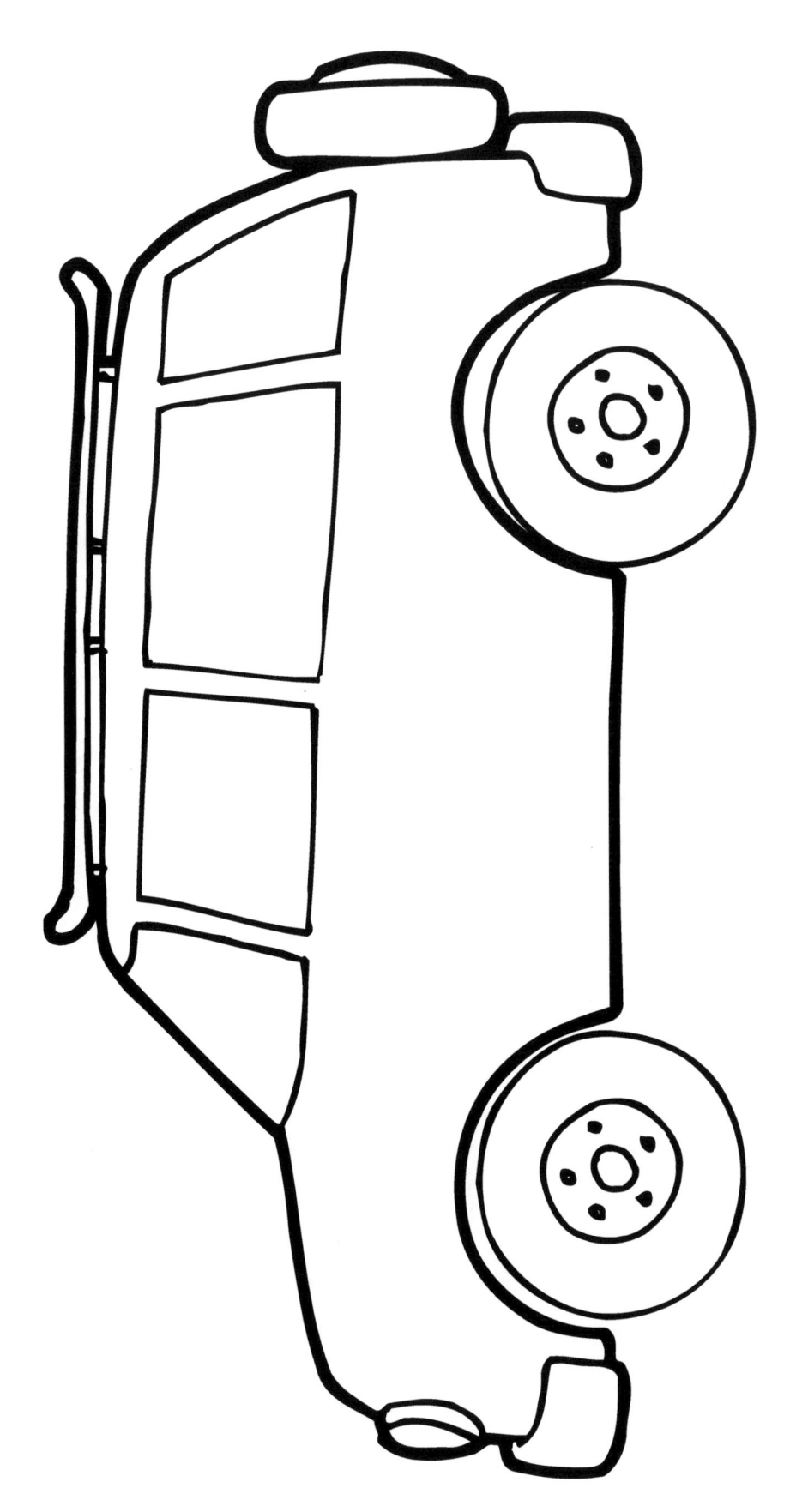

vase

venus flytrap

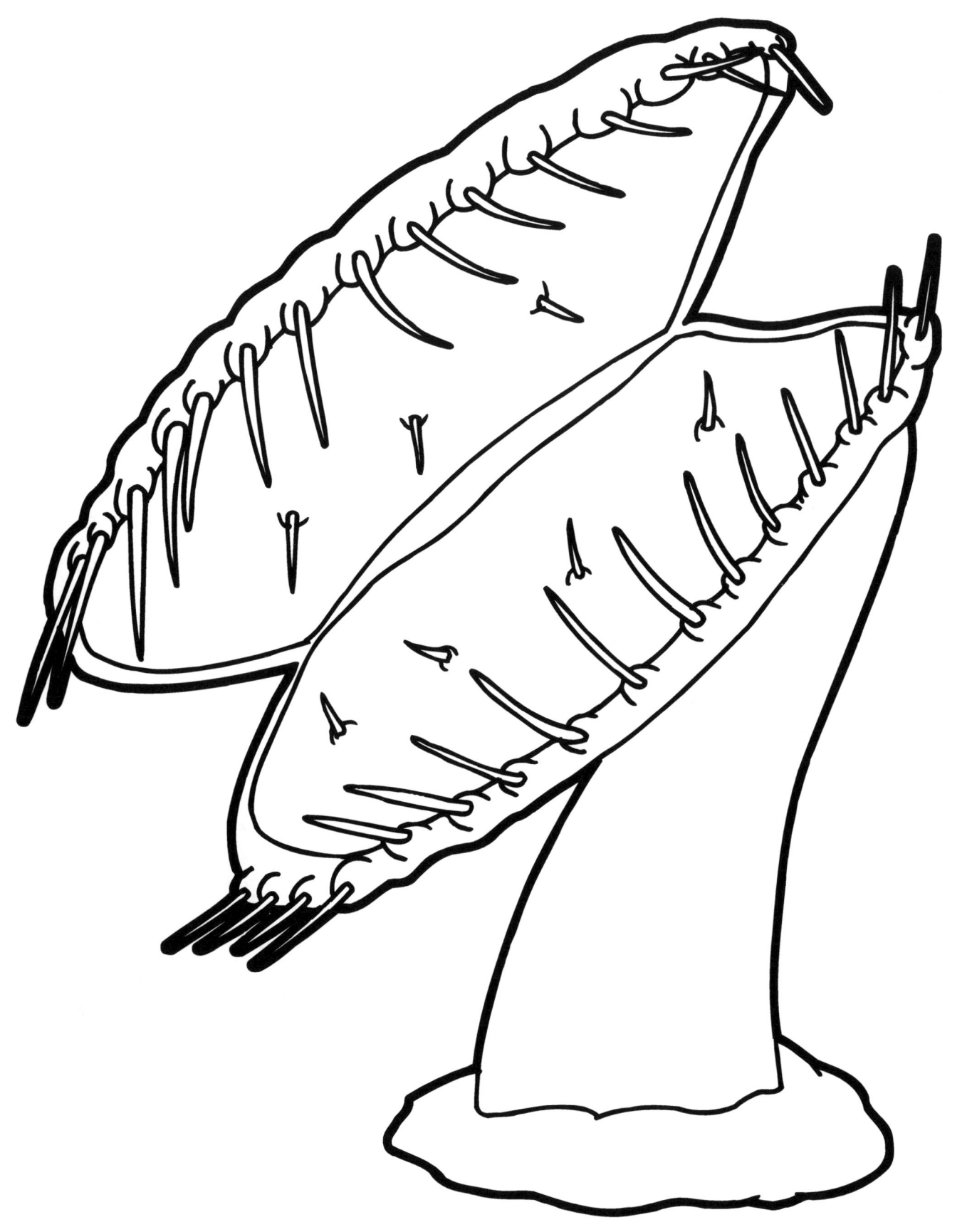

Vermont, USA

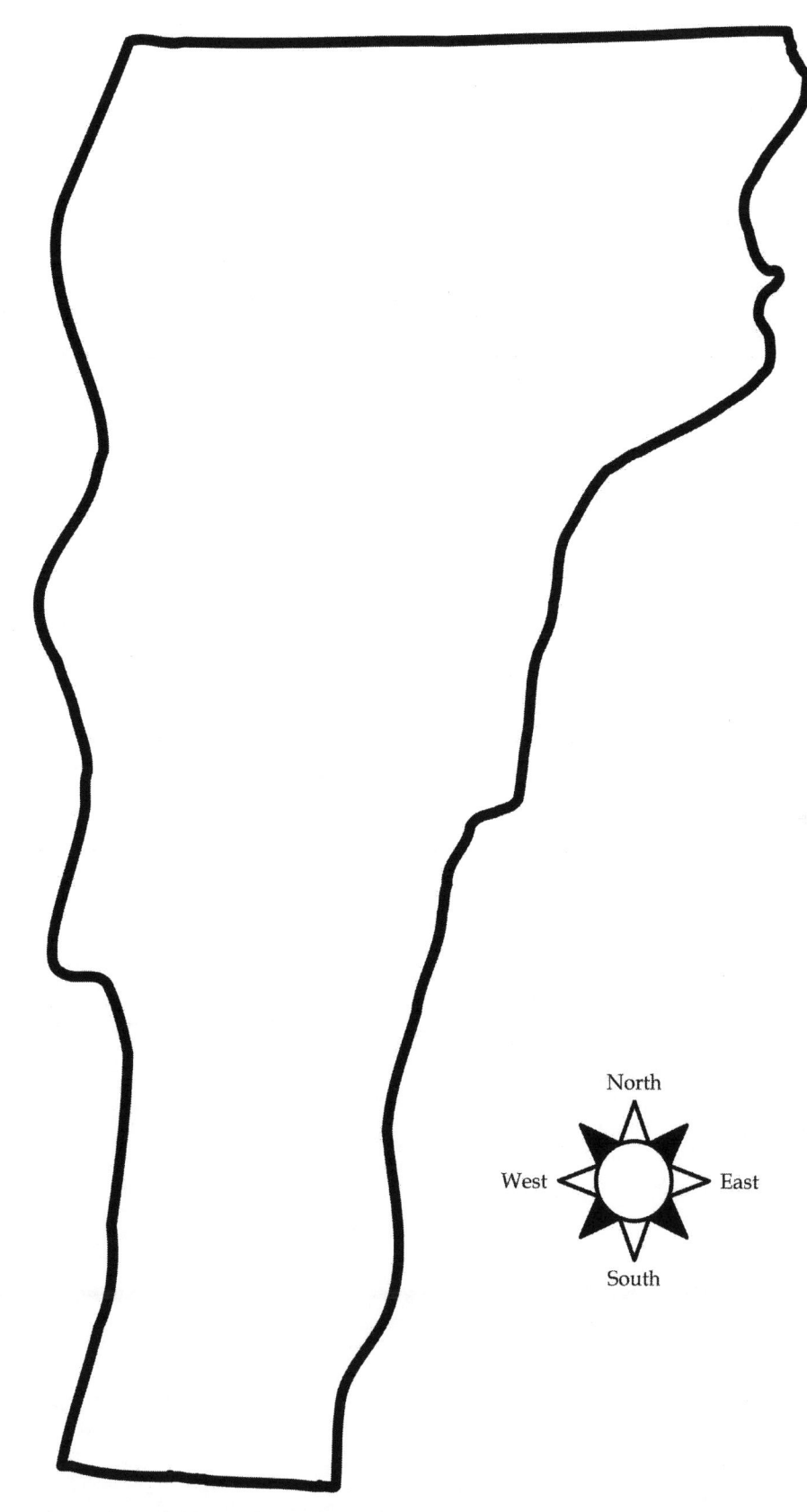

vest

vicuña

viking

violin

Virginia, USA

Maps are representations and boundaries are not exact.

visor

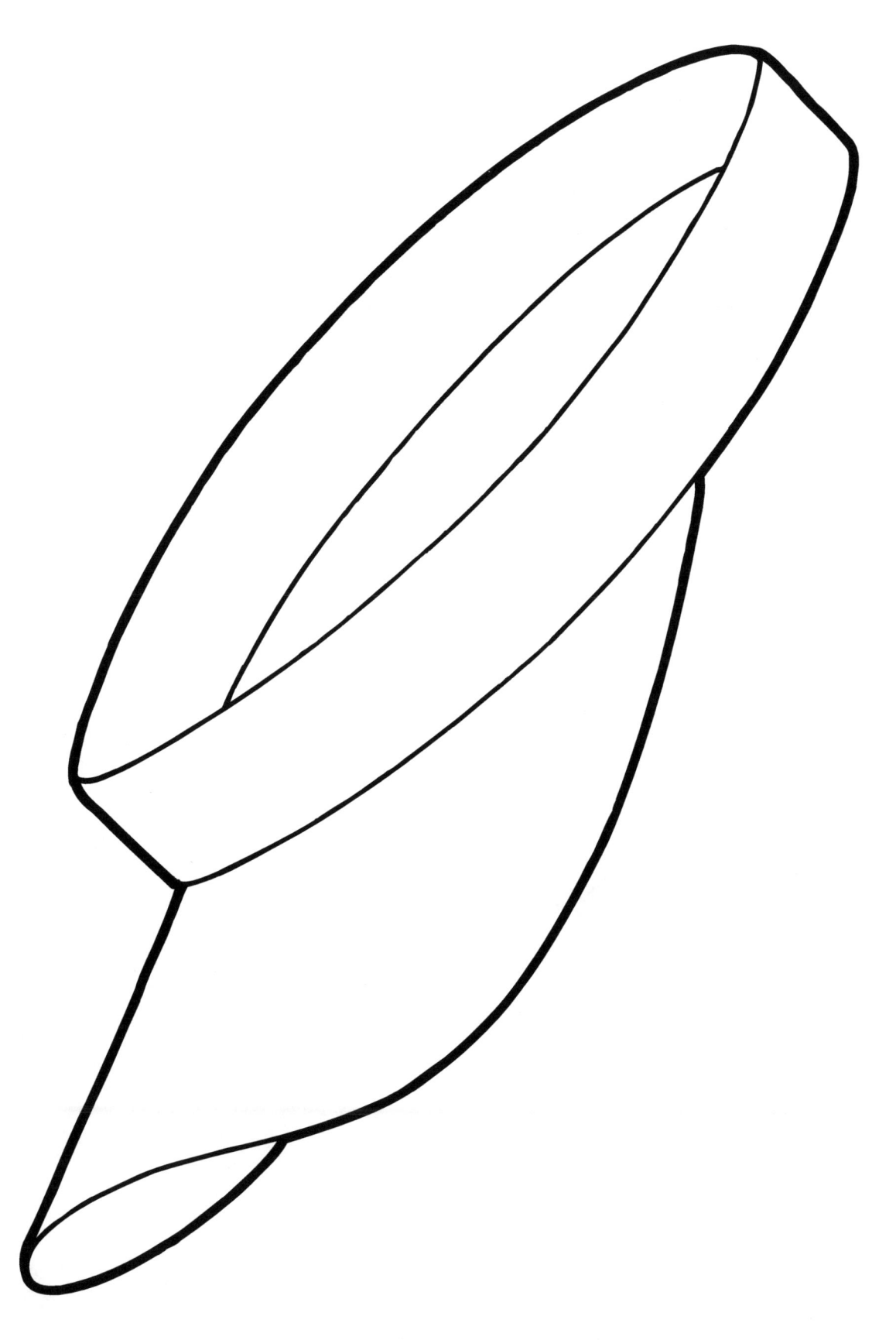

volcano

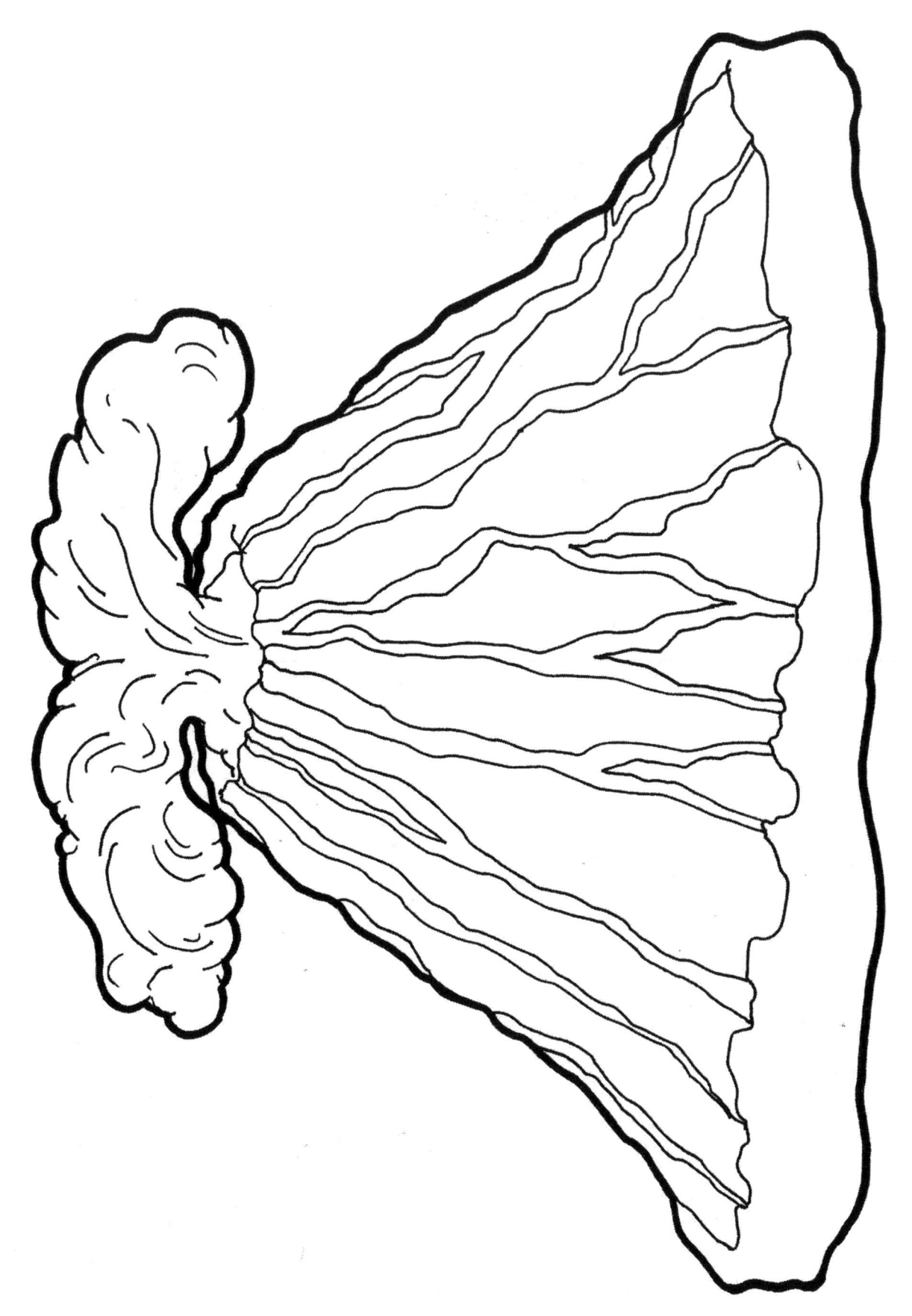

vole

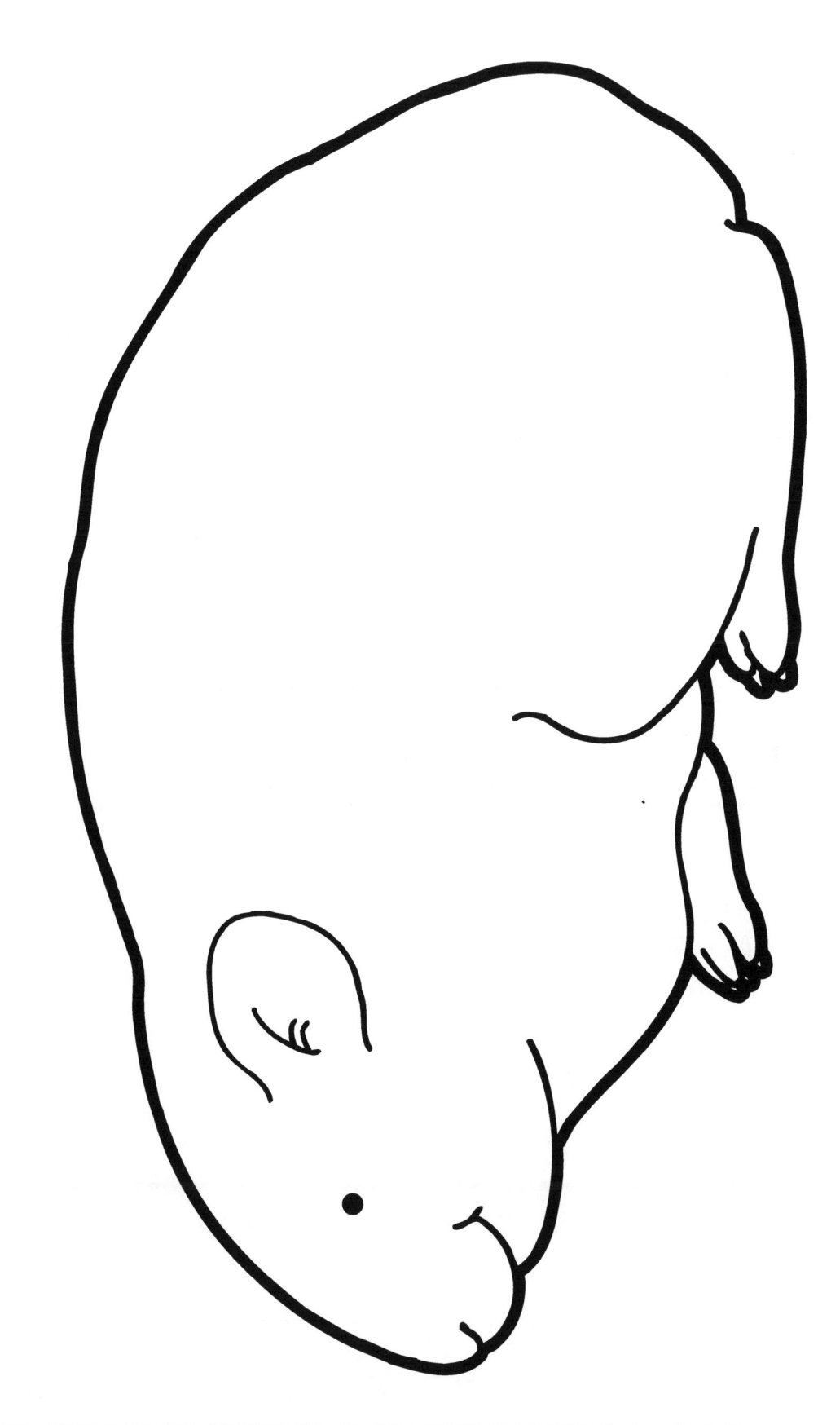

volley ball

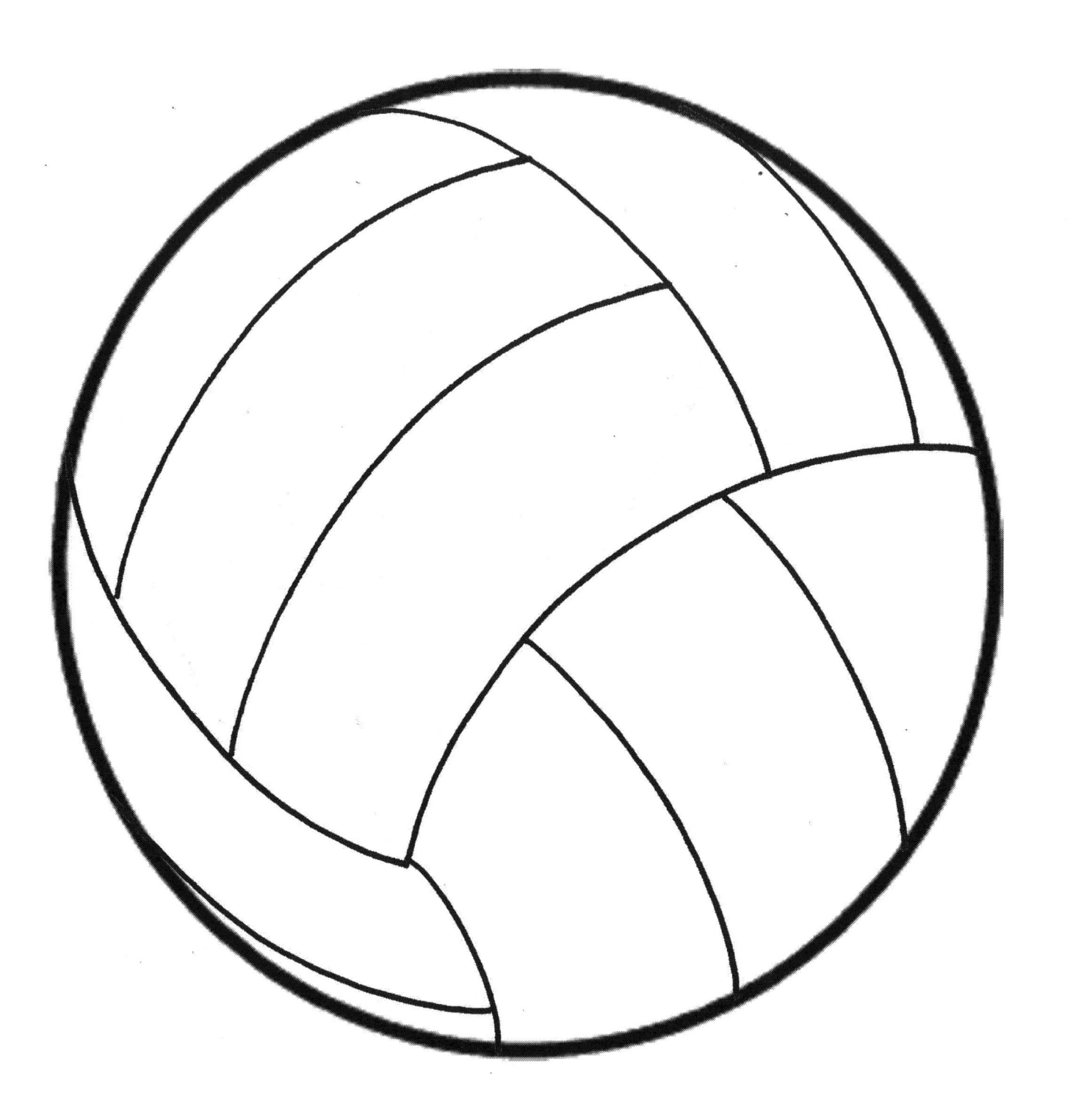

vulture

wagon (covered)

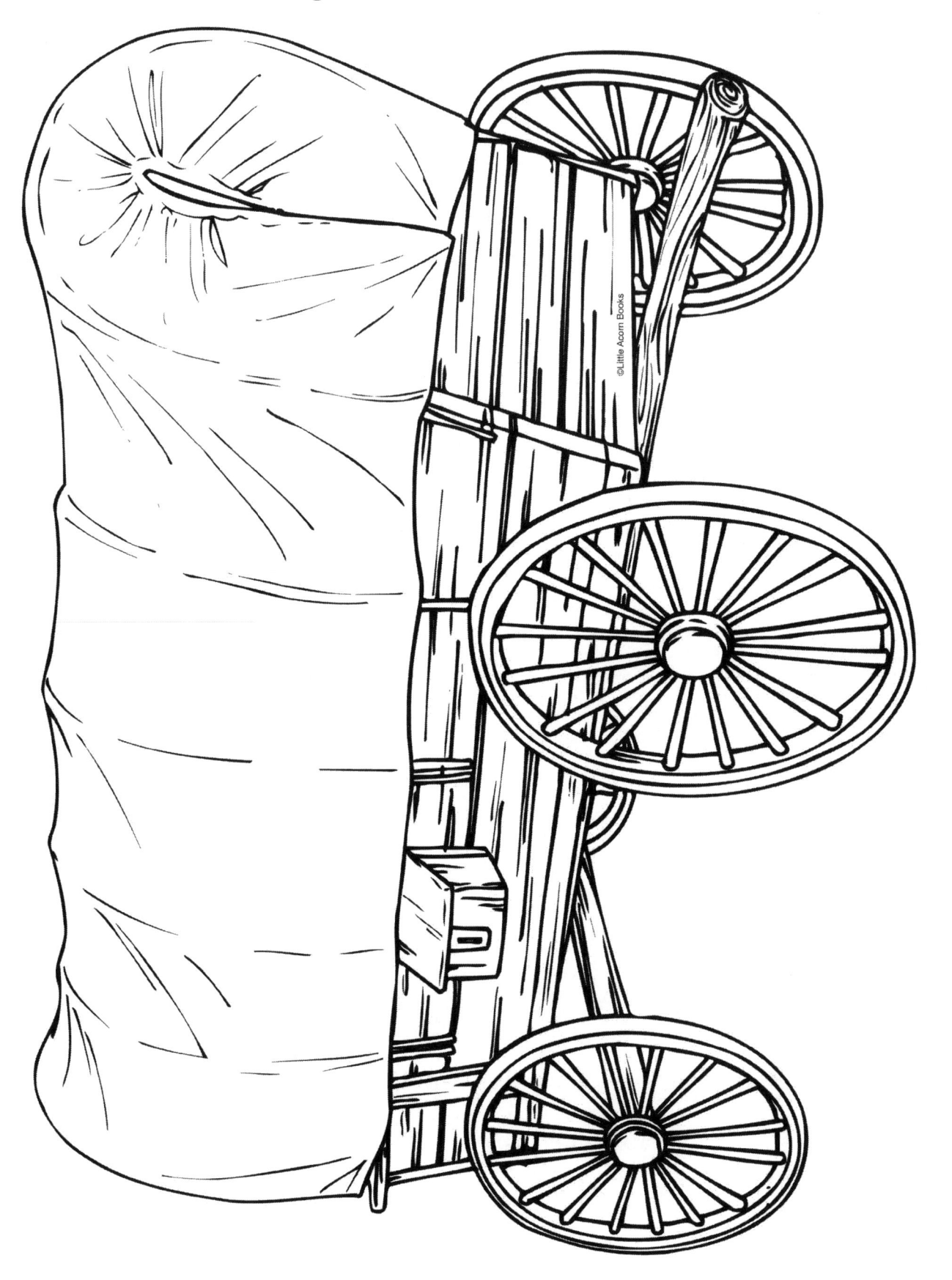

wagon (toy)

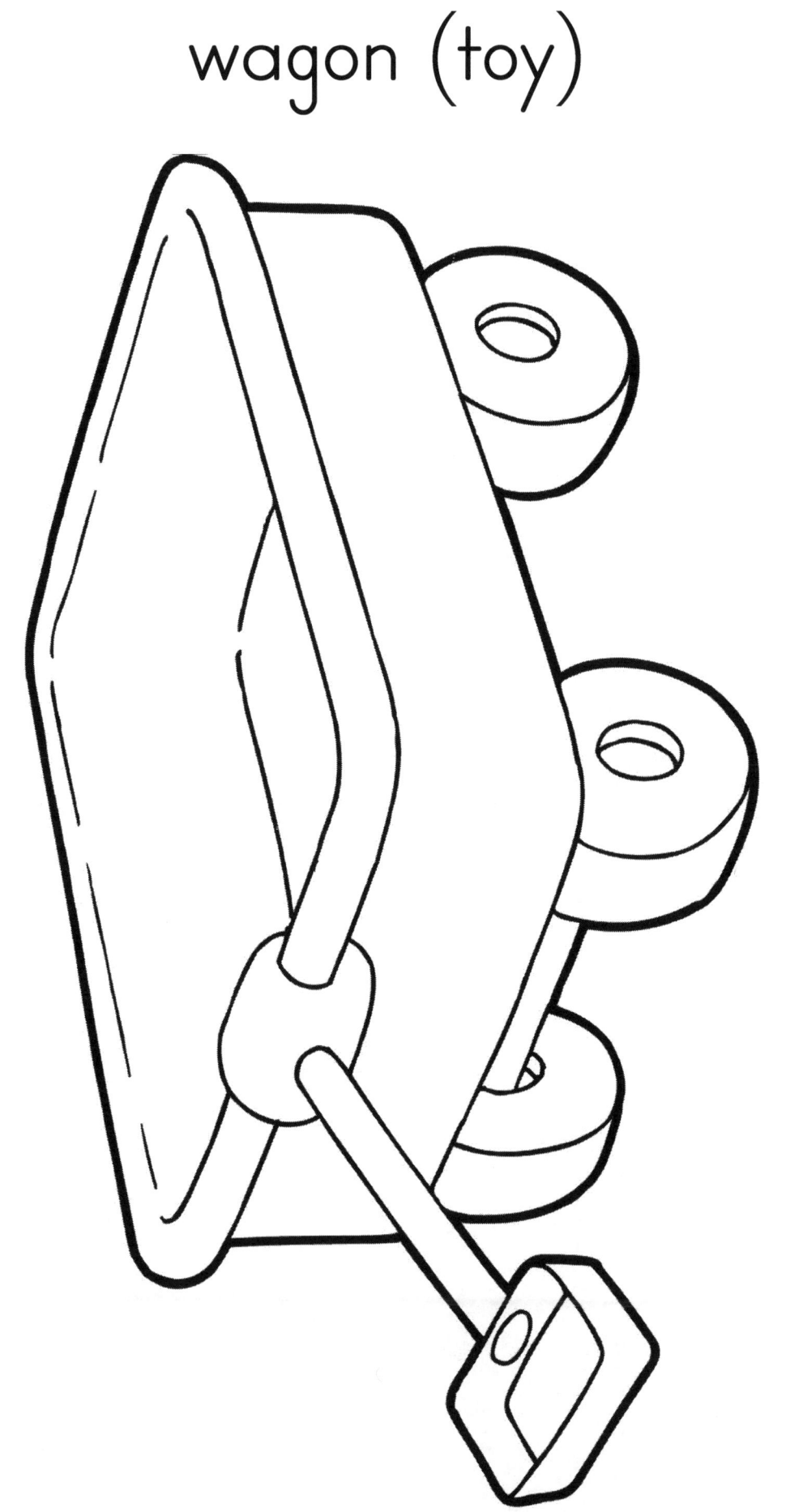

walrus

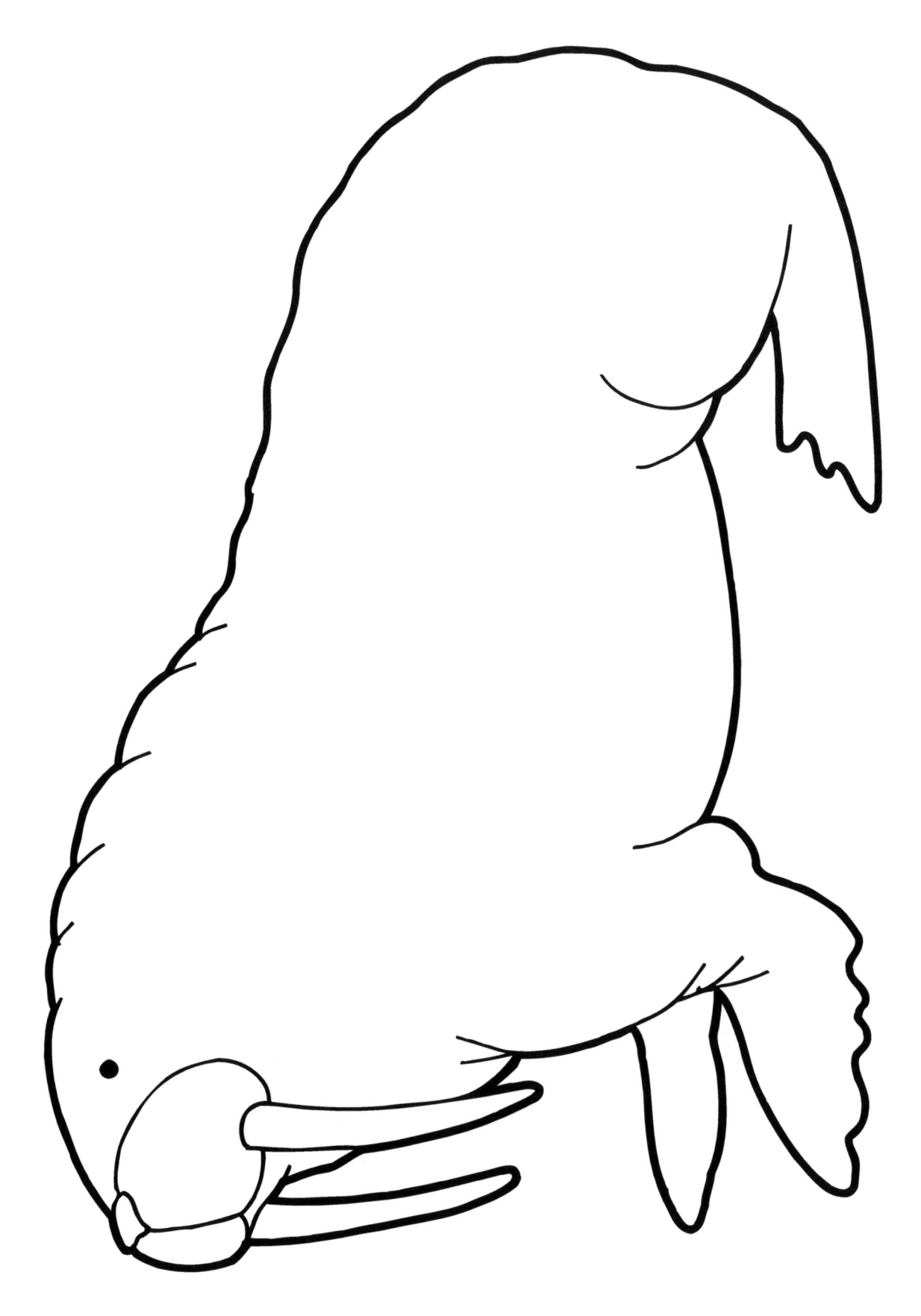

Washington, USA

North
West — East
South

Maps are representations and boundaries are not exact.

Washington, DC
(District of Columbia, USA)

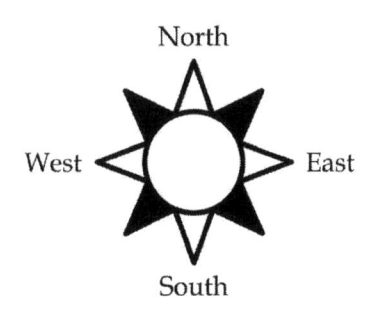

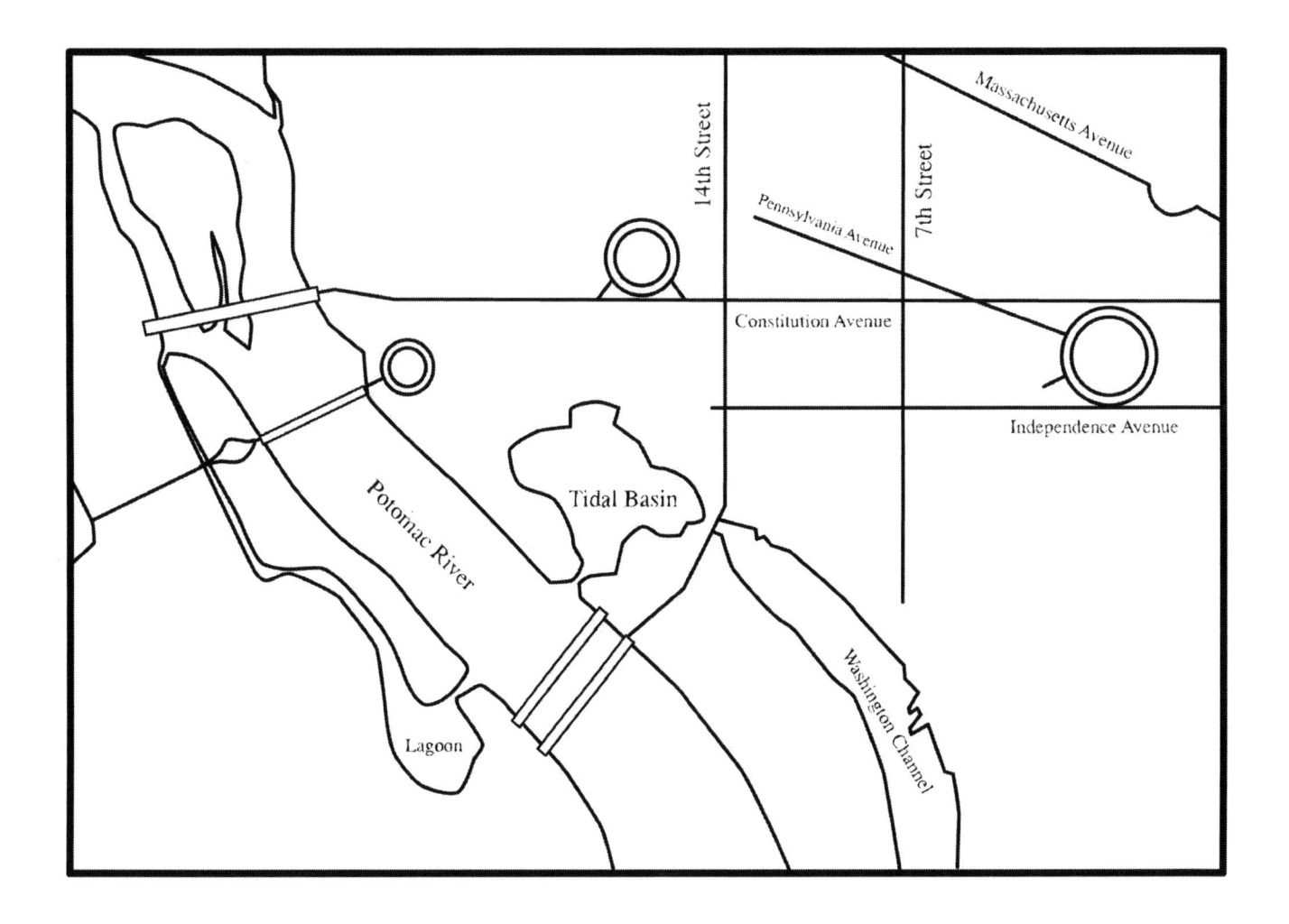

watermelon (wedge)

watermelon (whole)

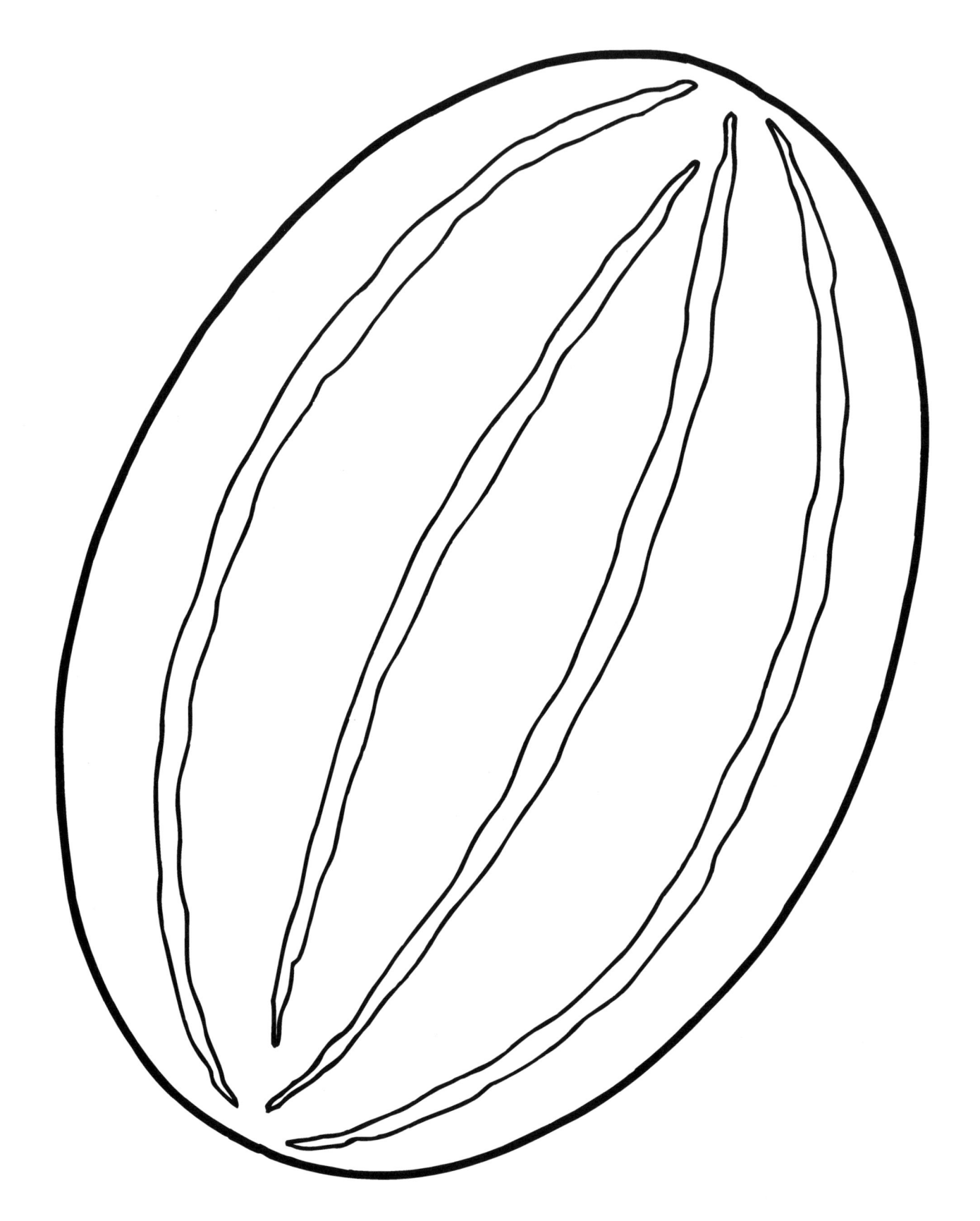

weasel

web (spider)

West Virginia, USA

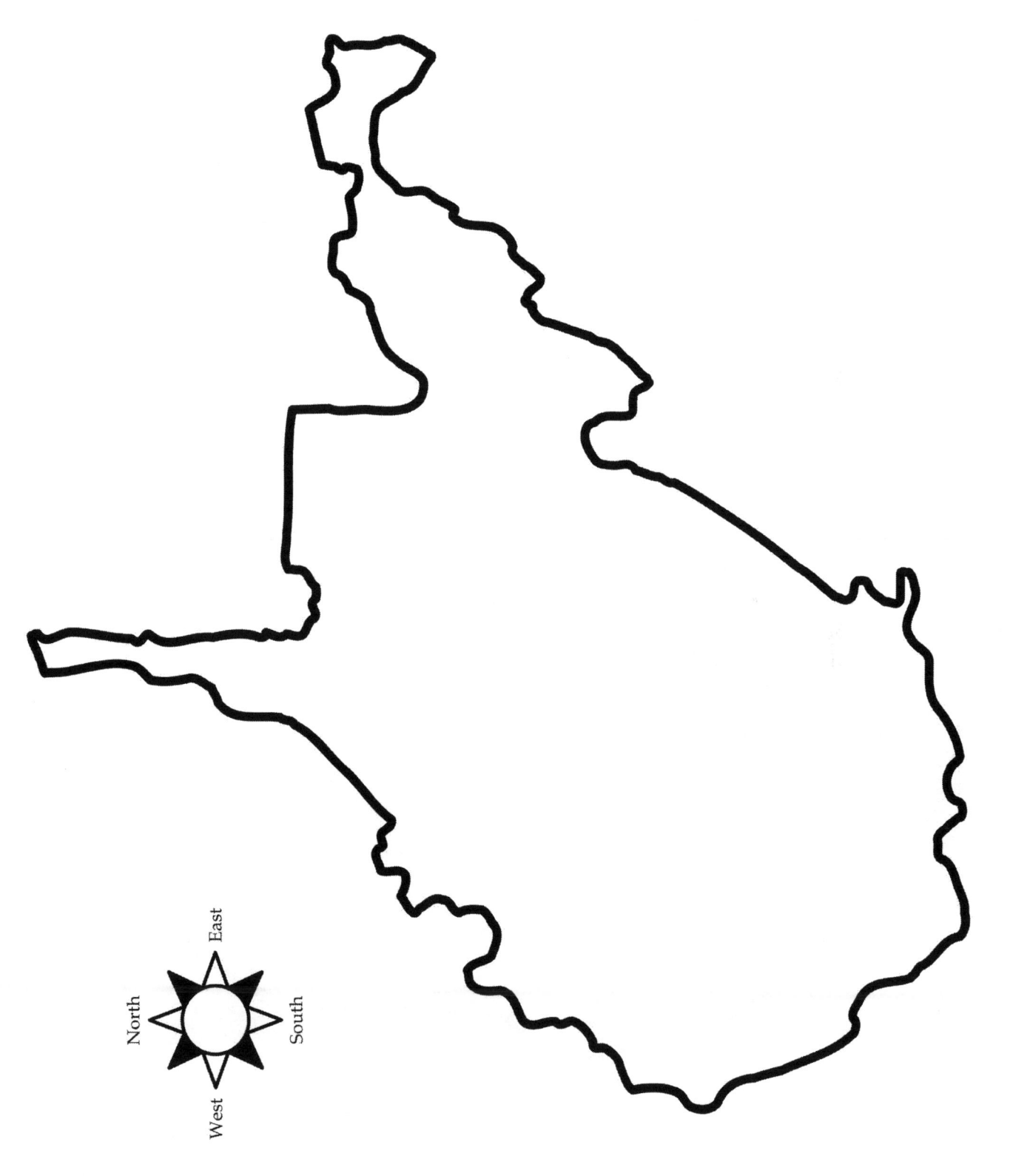

Maps are representations and boundaries are not exact.

Western hemisphere

Maps are representations and boundaries are not exact.

whale (animated)

whale (humpback)

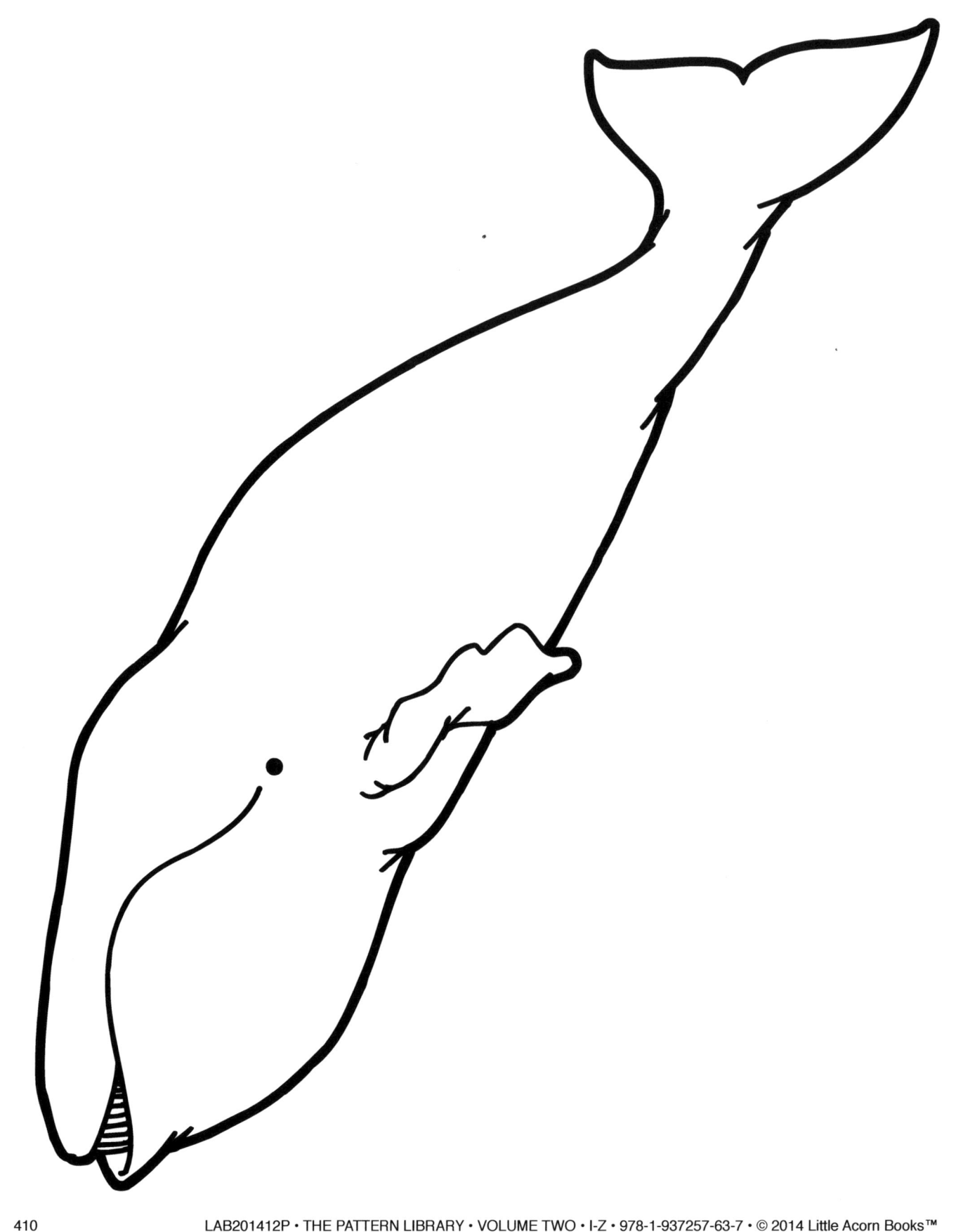

whale (outline)

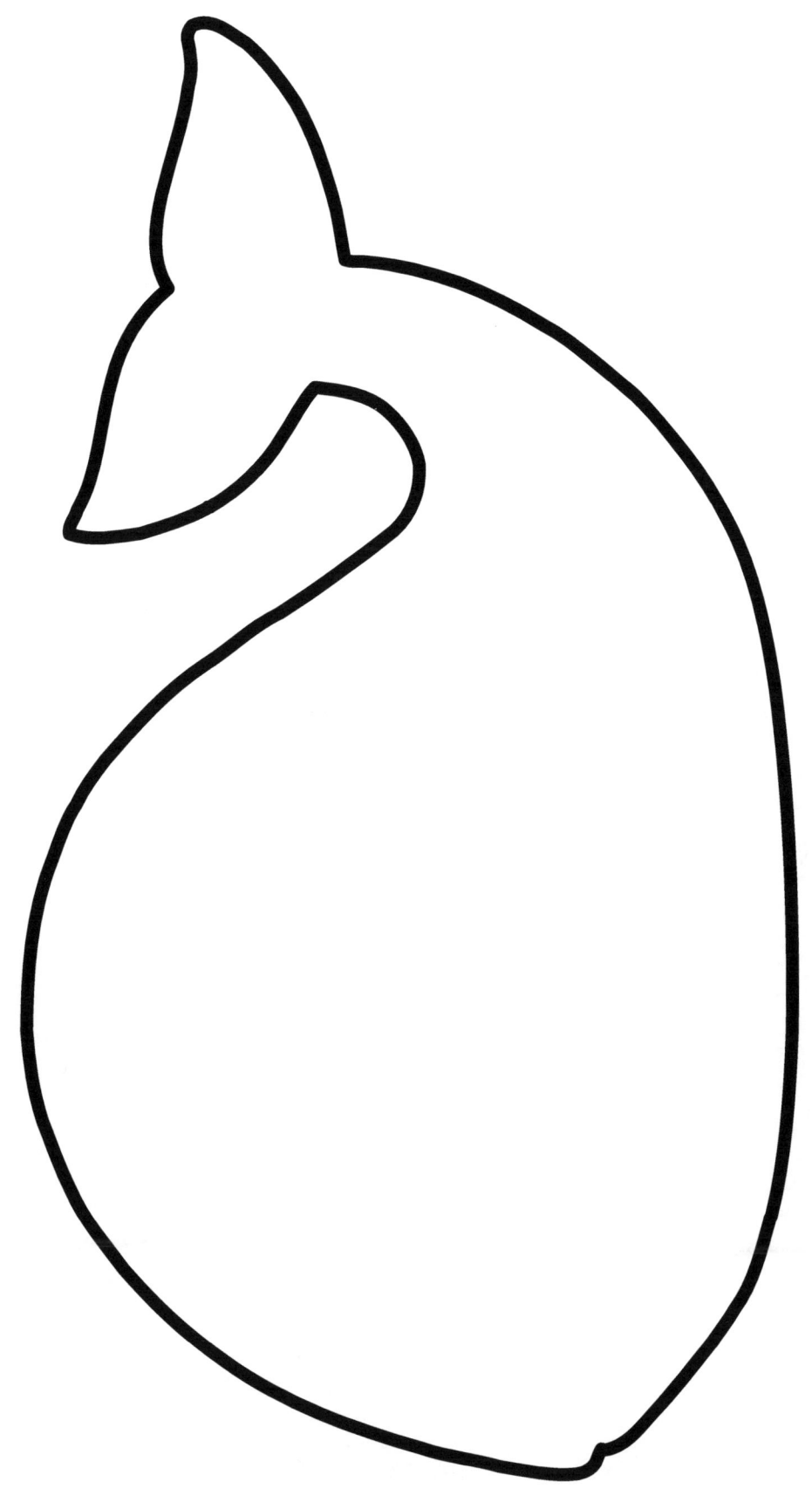

wheel (spoked)

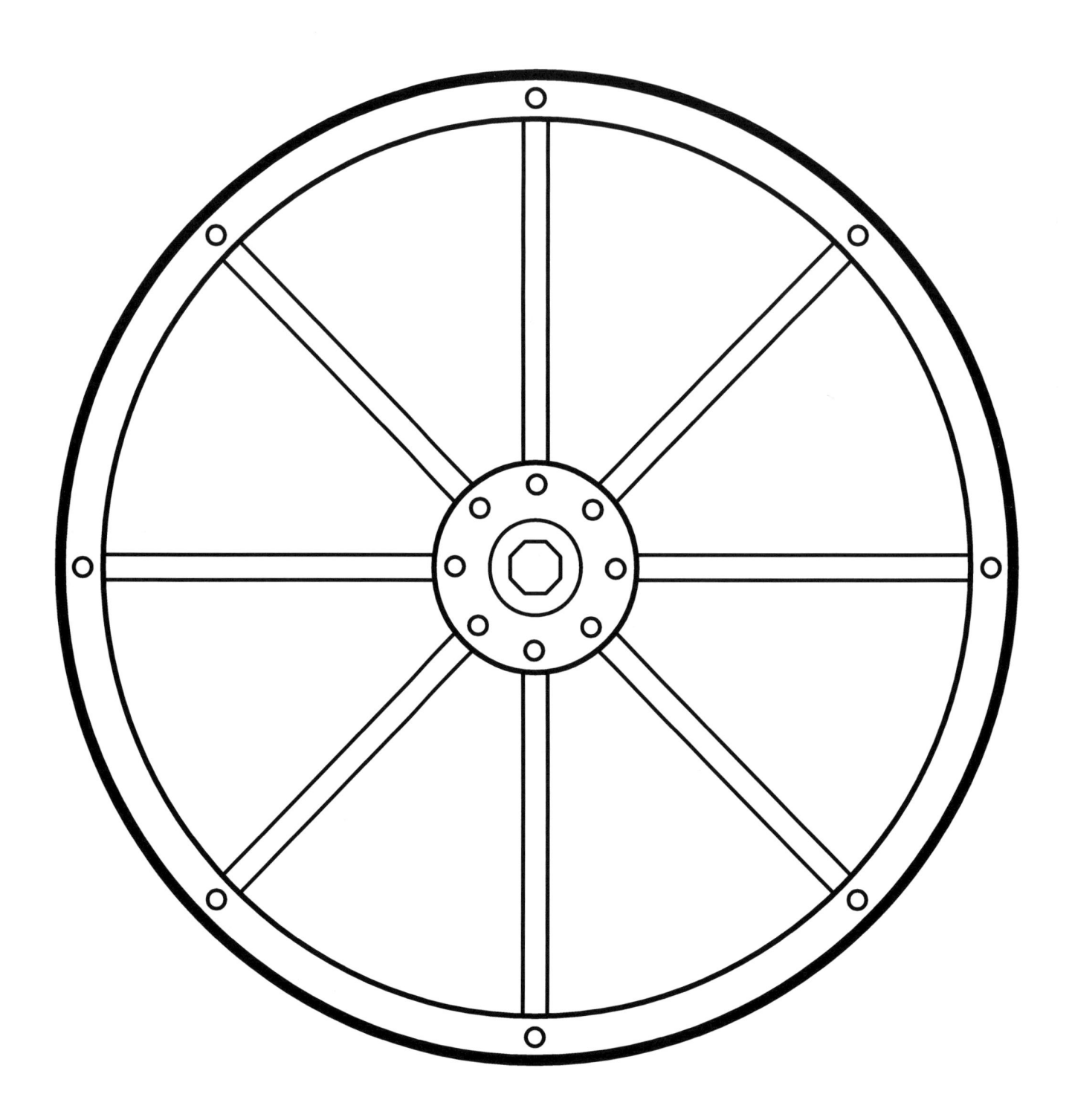

wheelbarrow

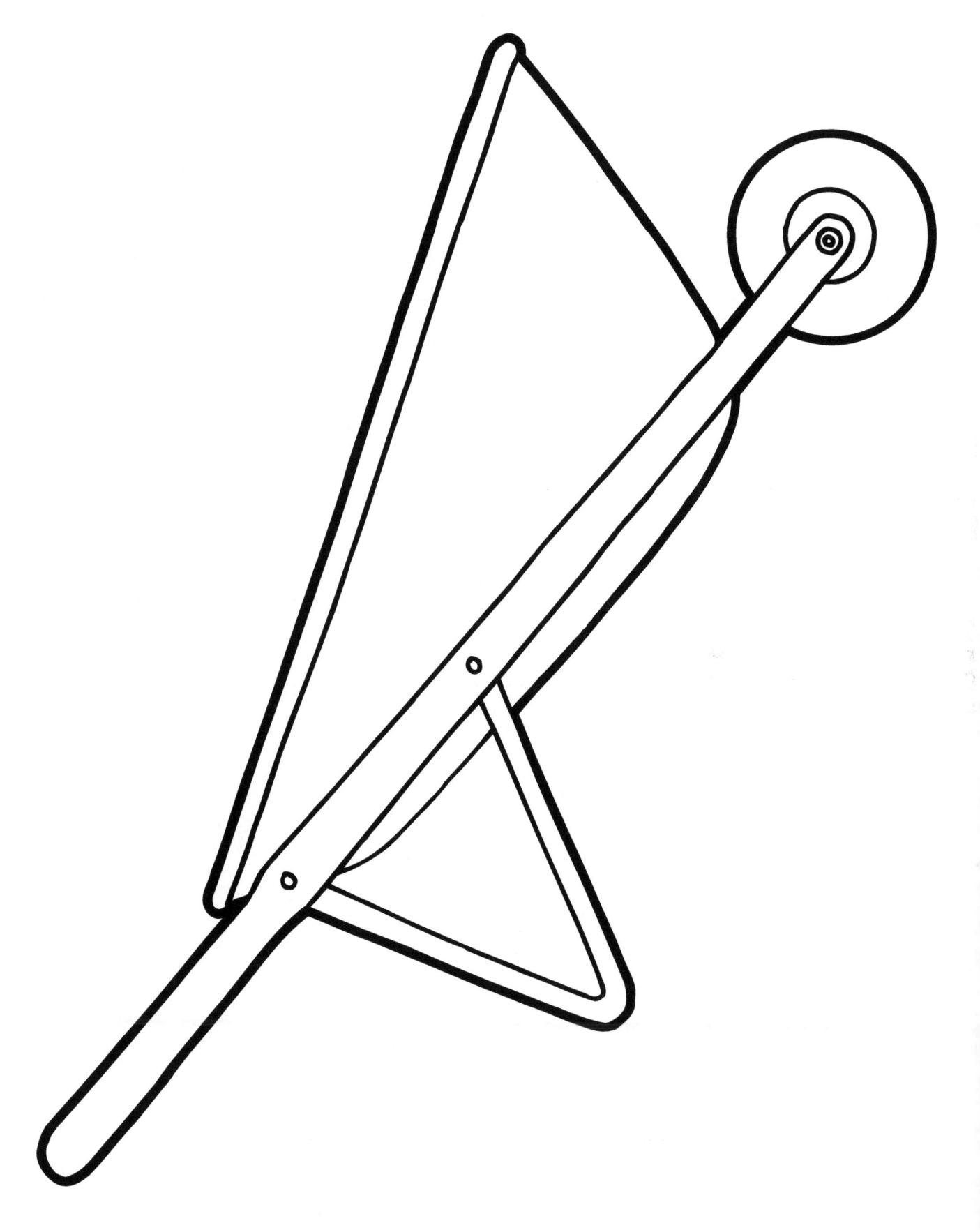

whip

whisk

whistle

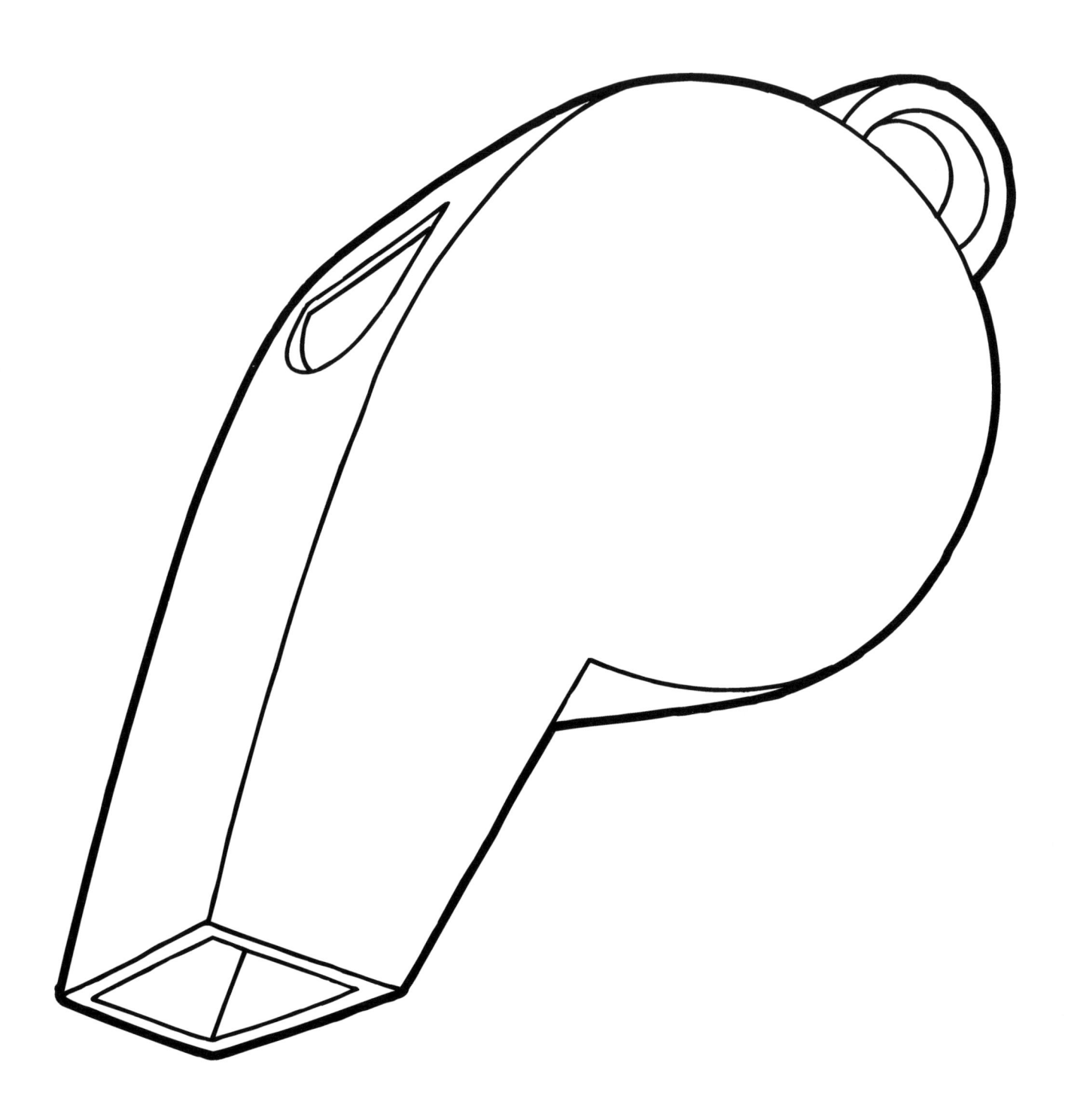

White House, The, USA

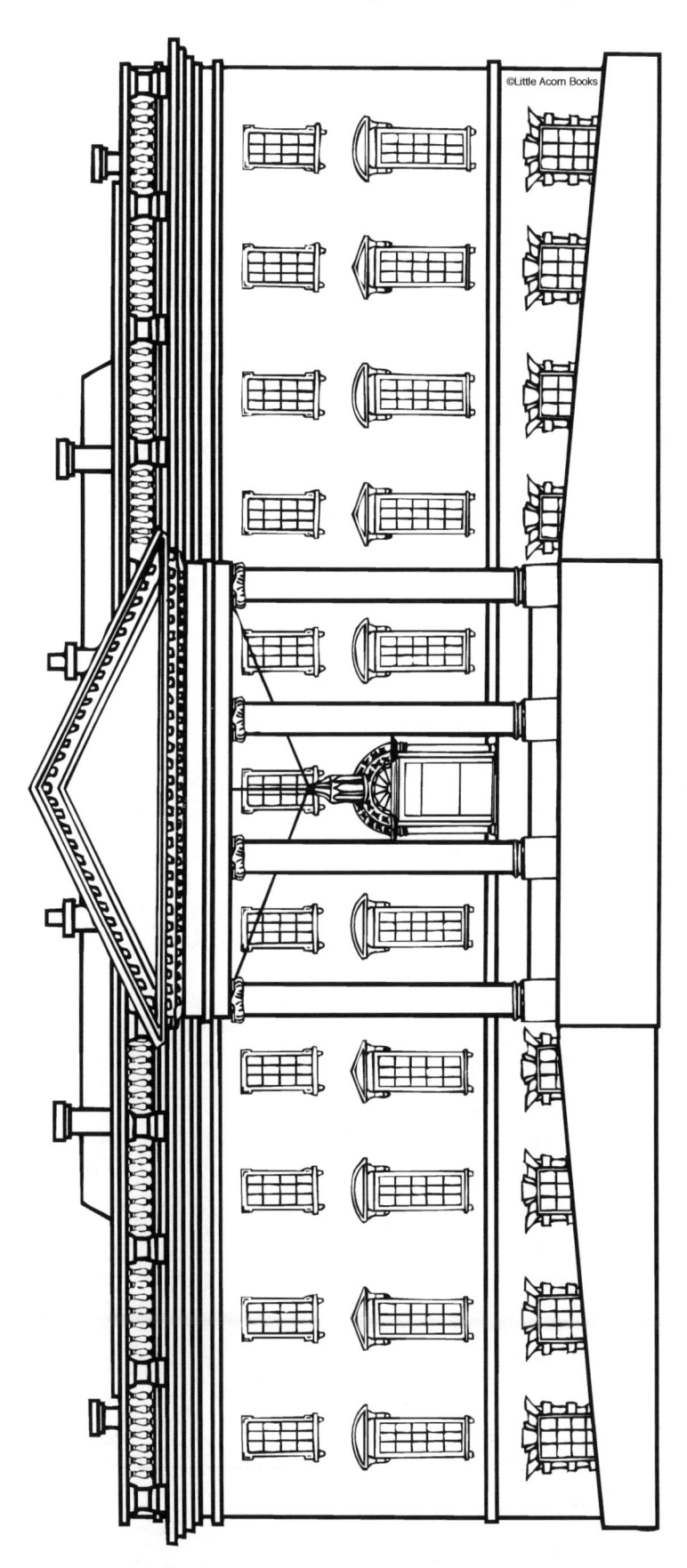

wig

window

Wisconsin, USA

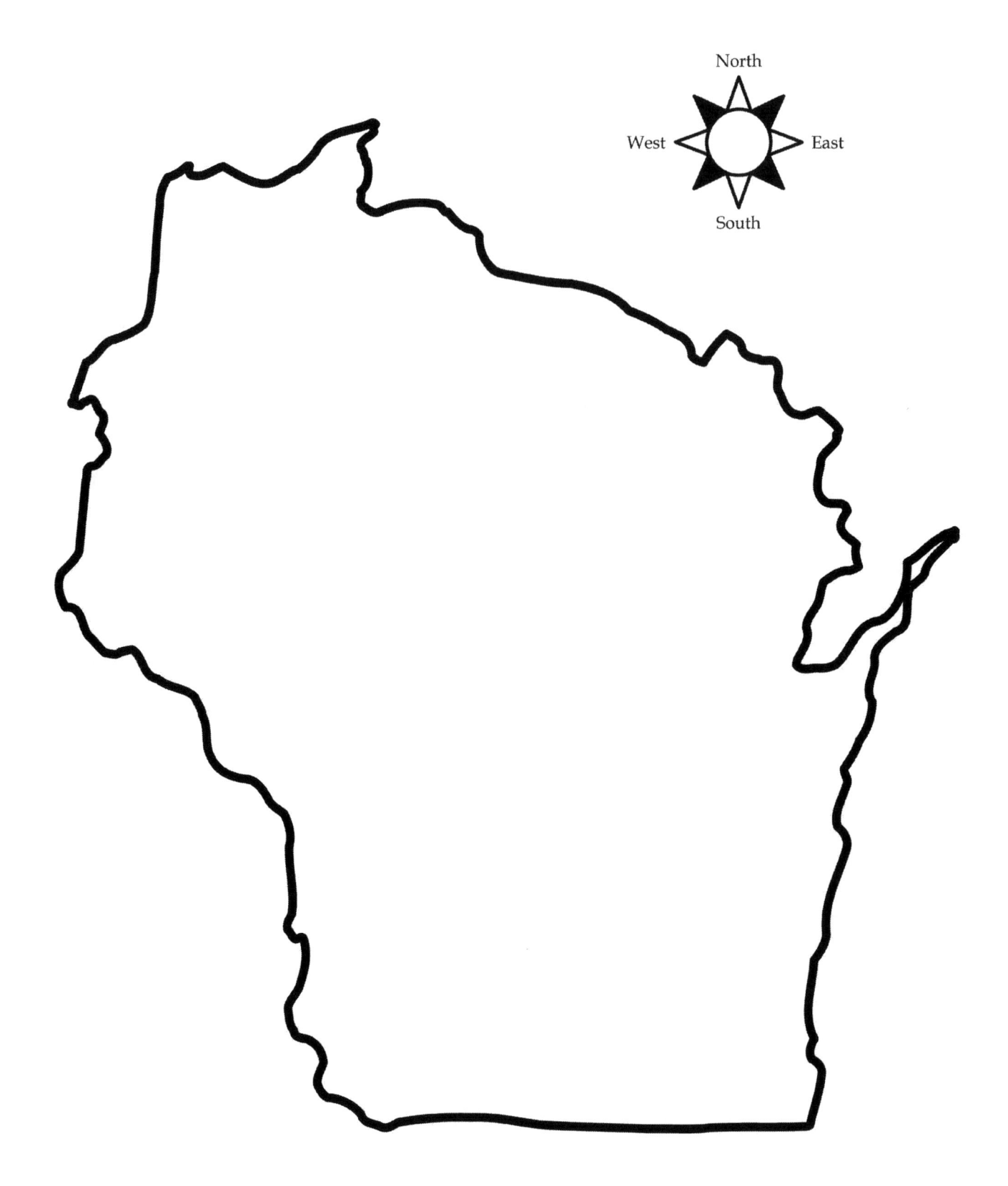

North
West East
South

Maps are representations and boundaries are not exact.

wolf (running)

wolf (standing)

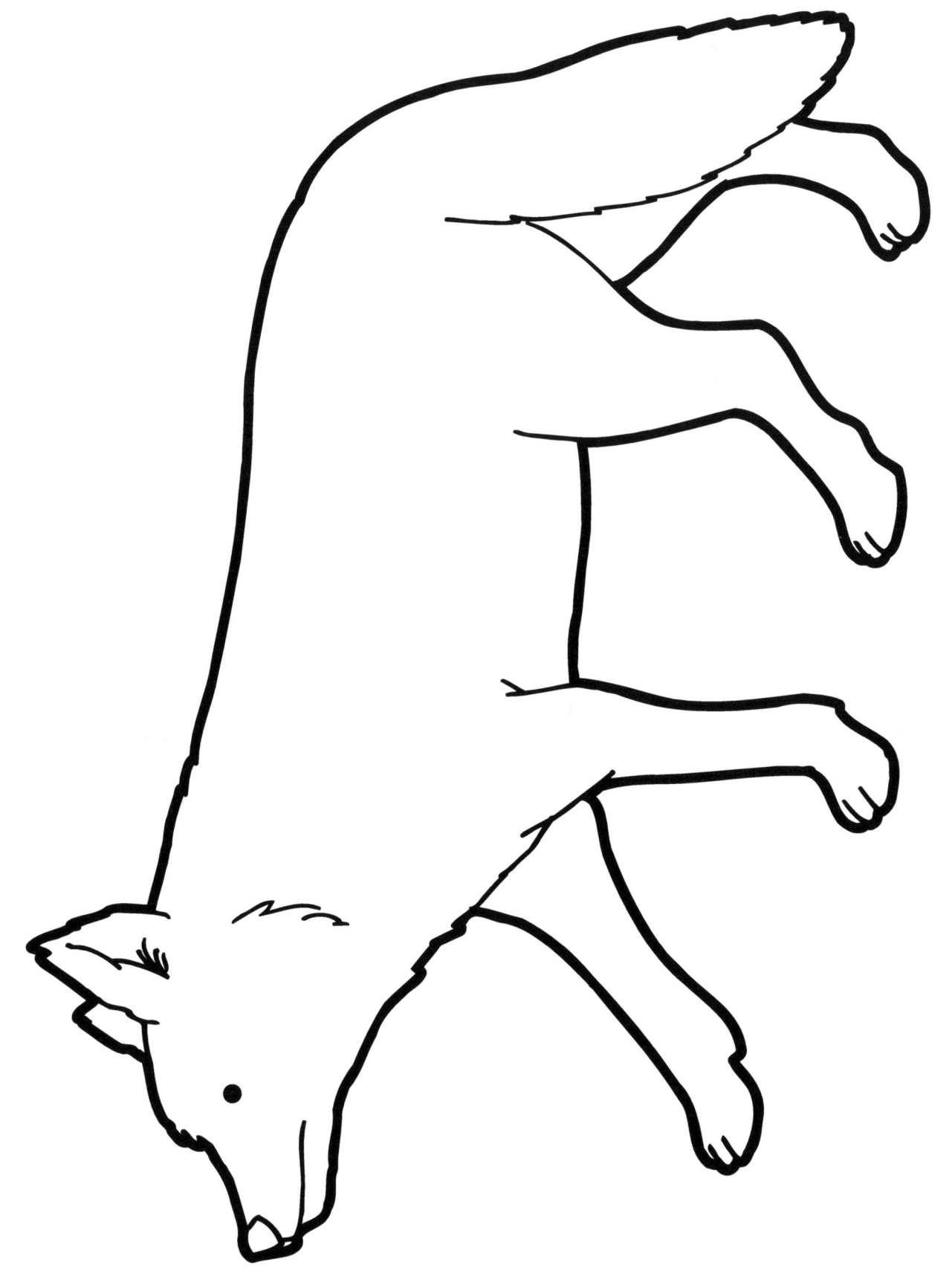

wood (cut logs)

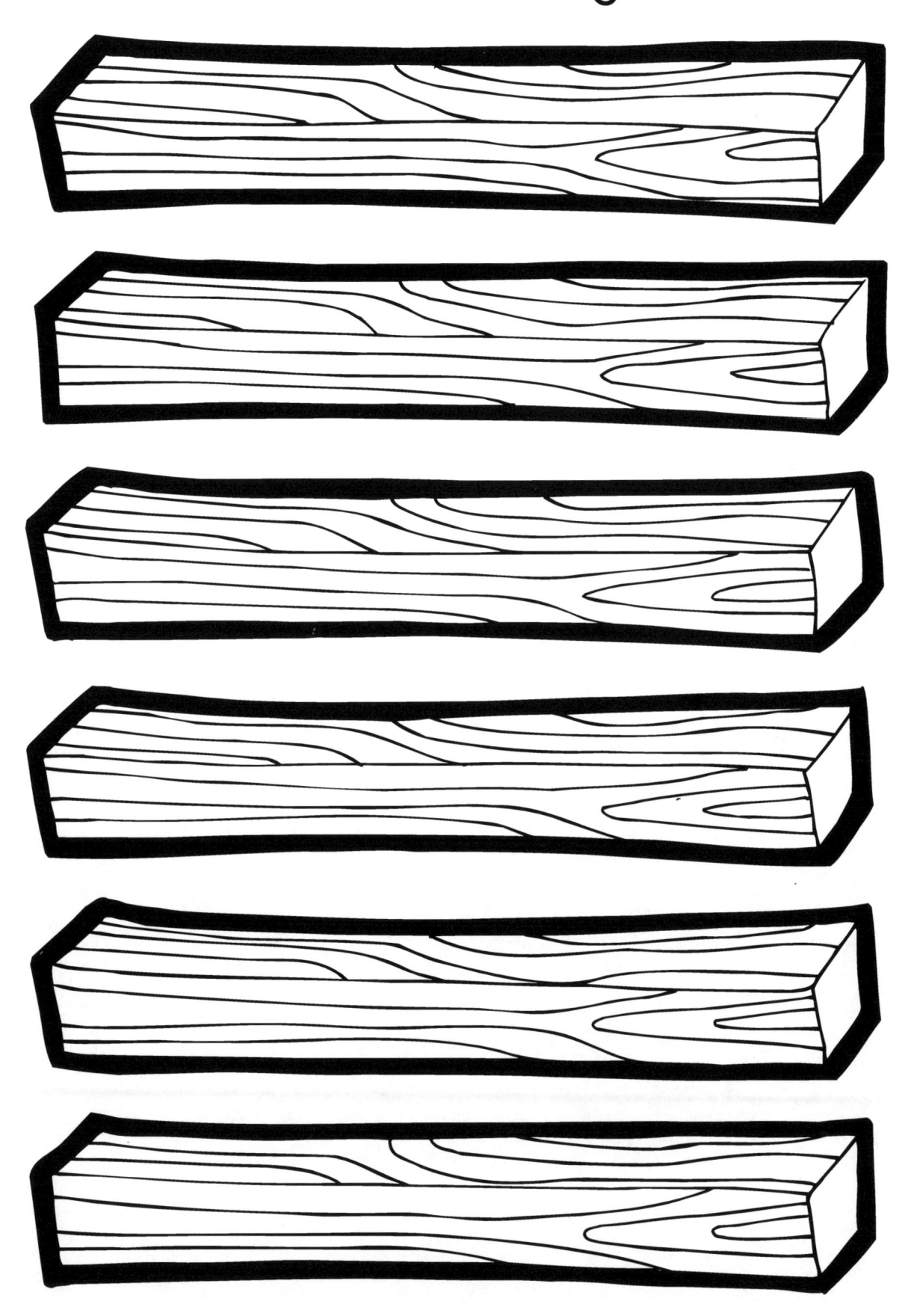

wreath (detailed)

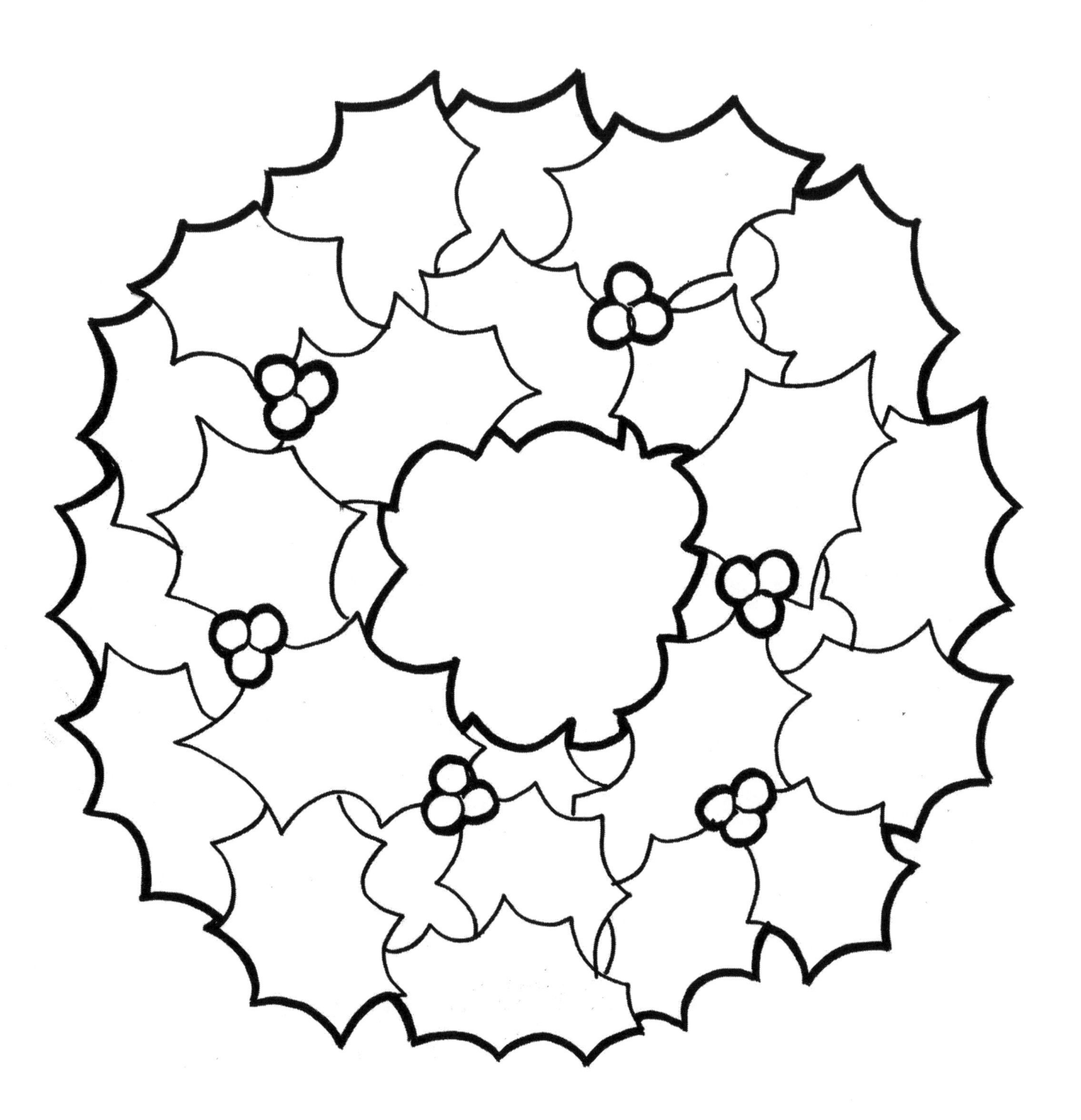

wreath (plain)

Wyoming, USA

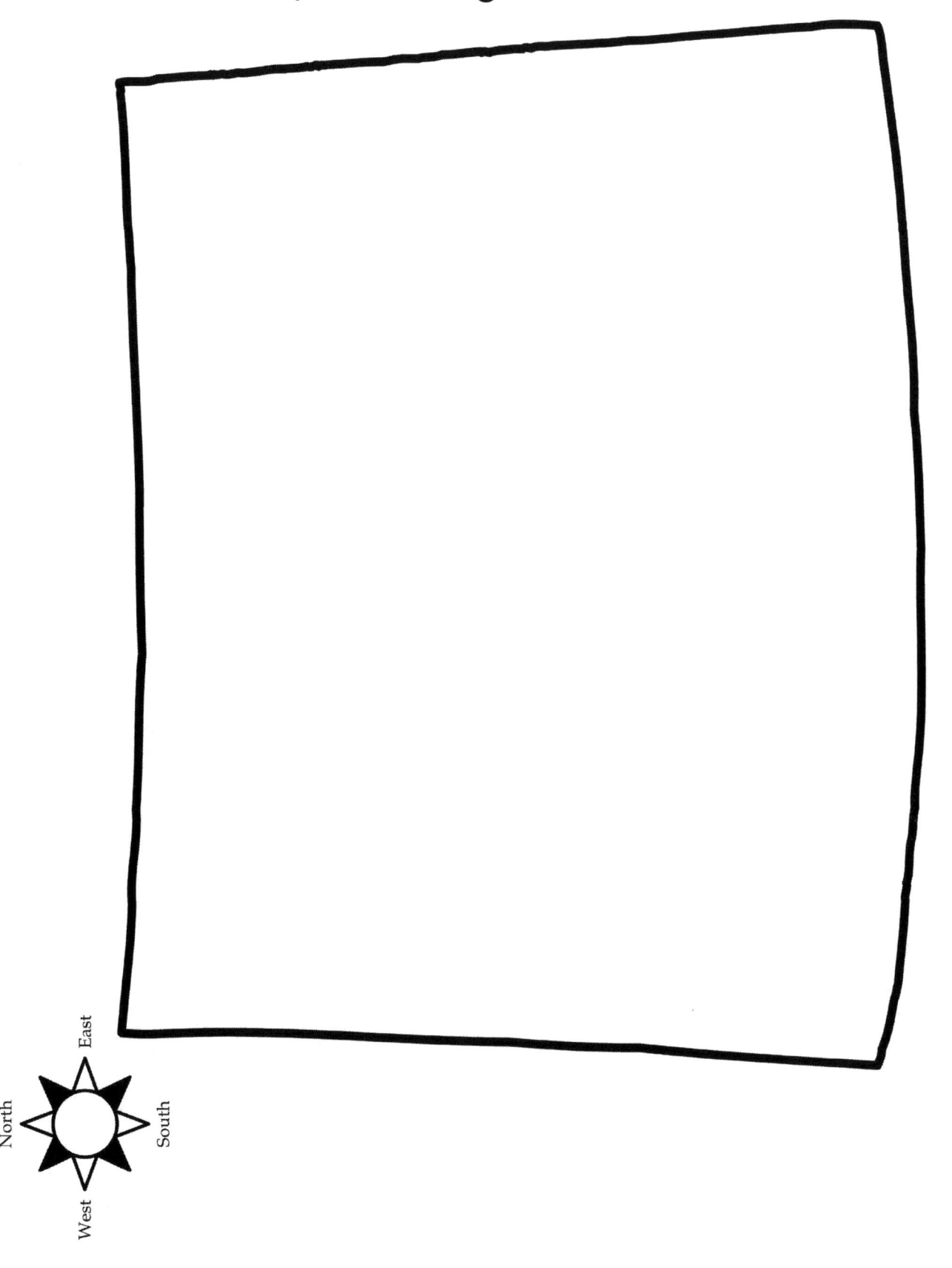

North · East · South · West

Maps are representations and boundaries are not exact.

x-ray

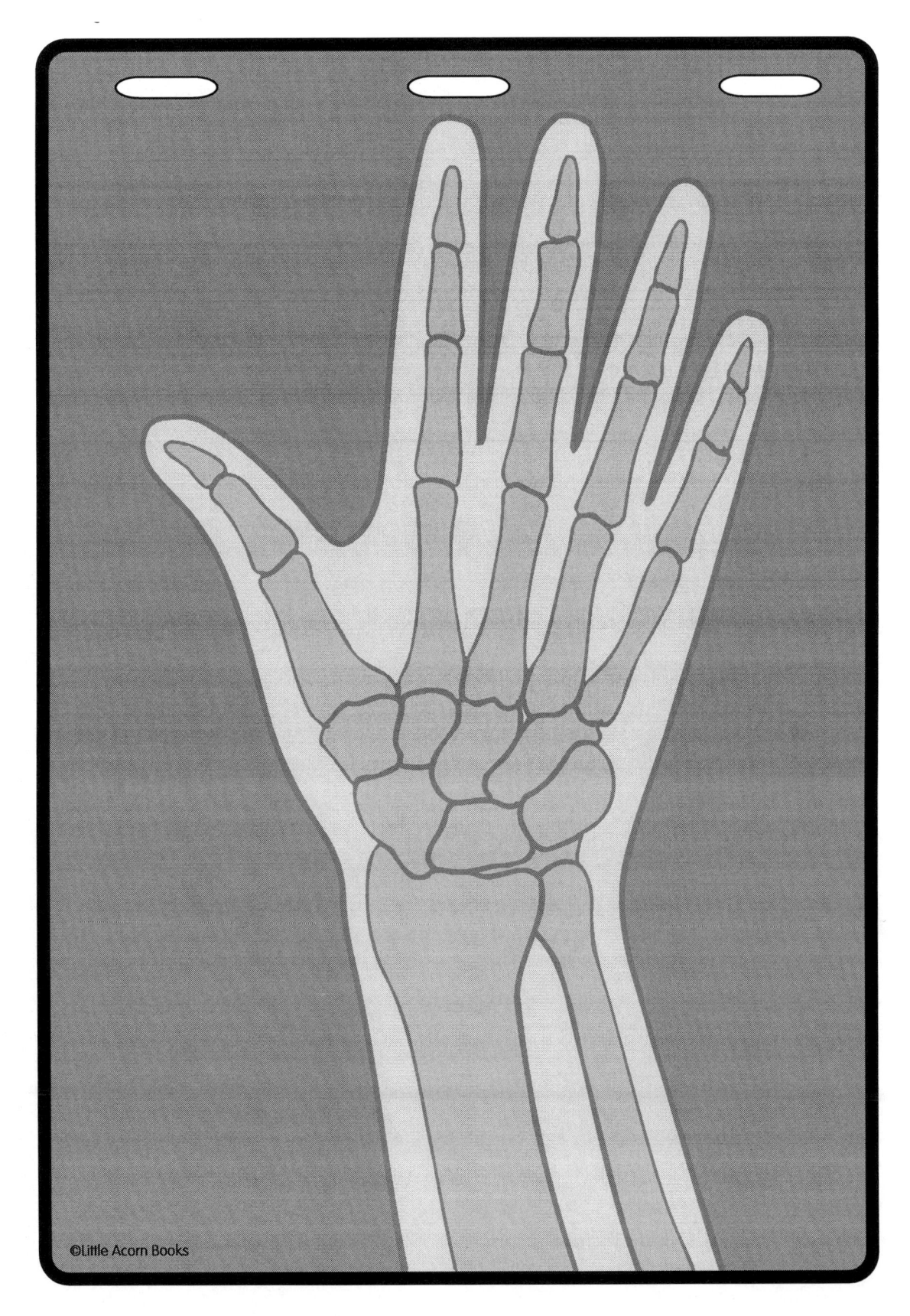

xantusia

letter Xx

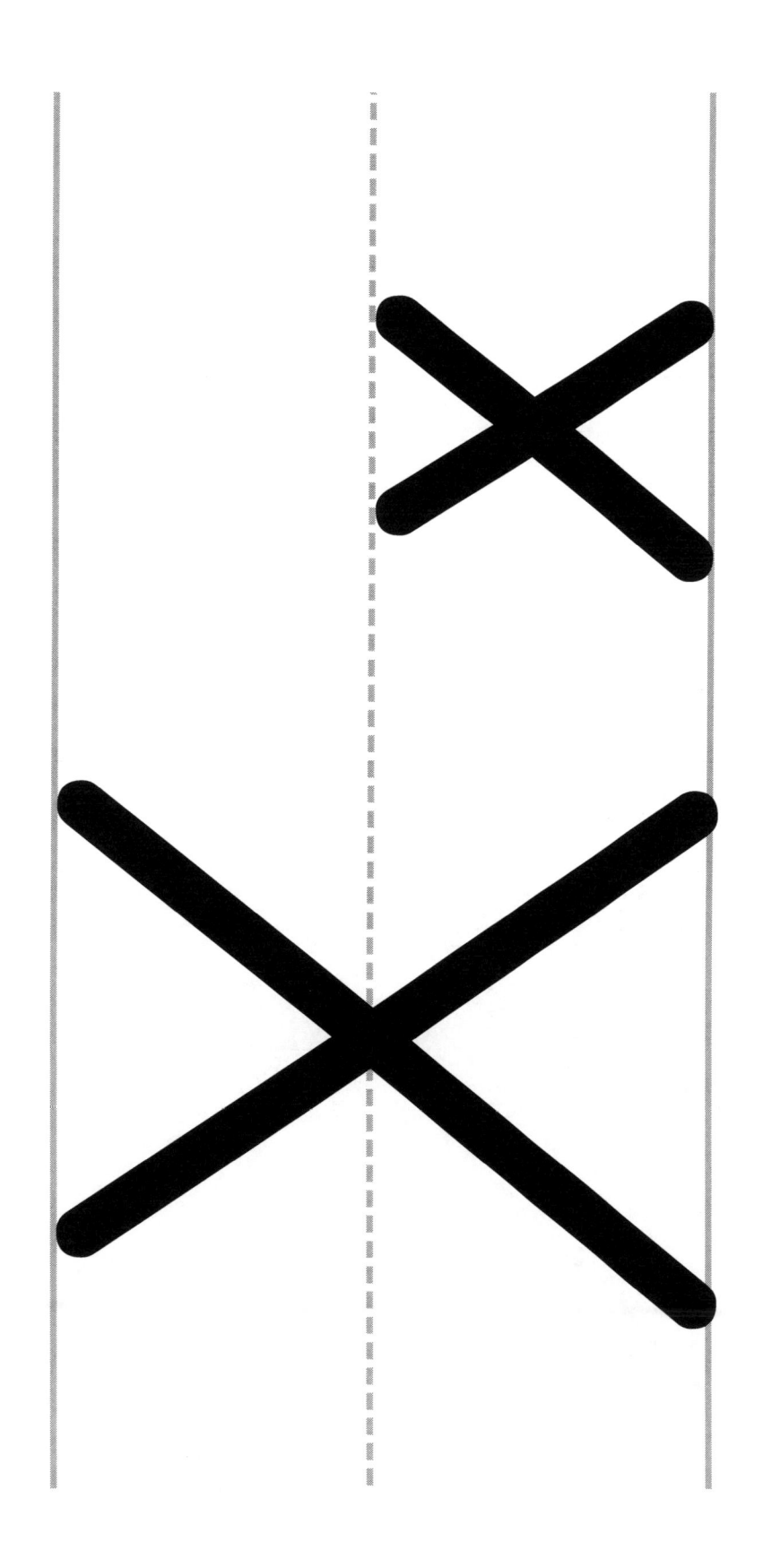

xylophone

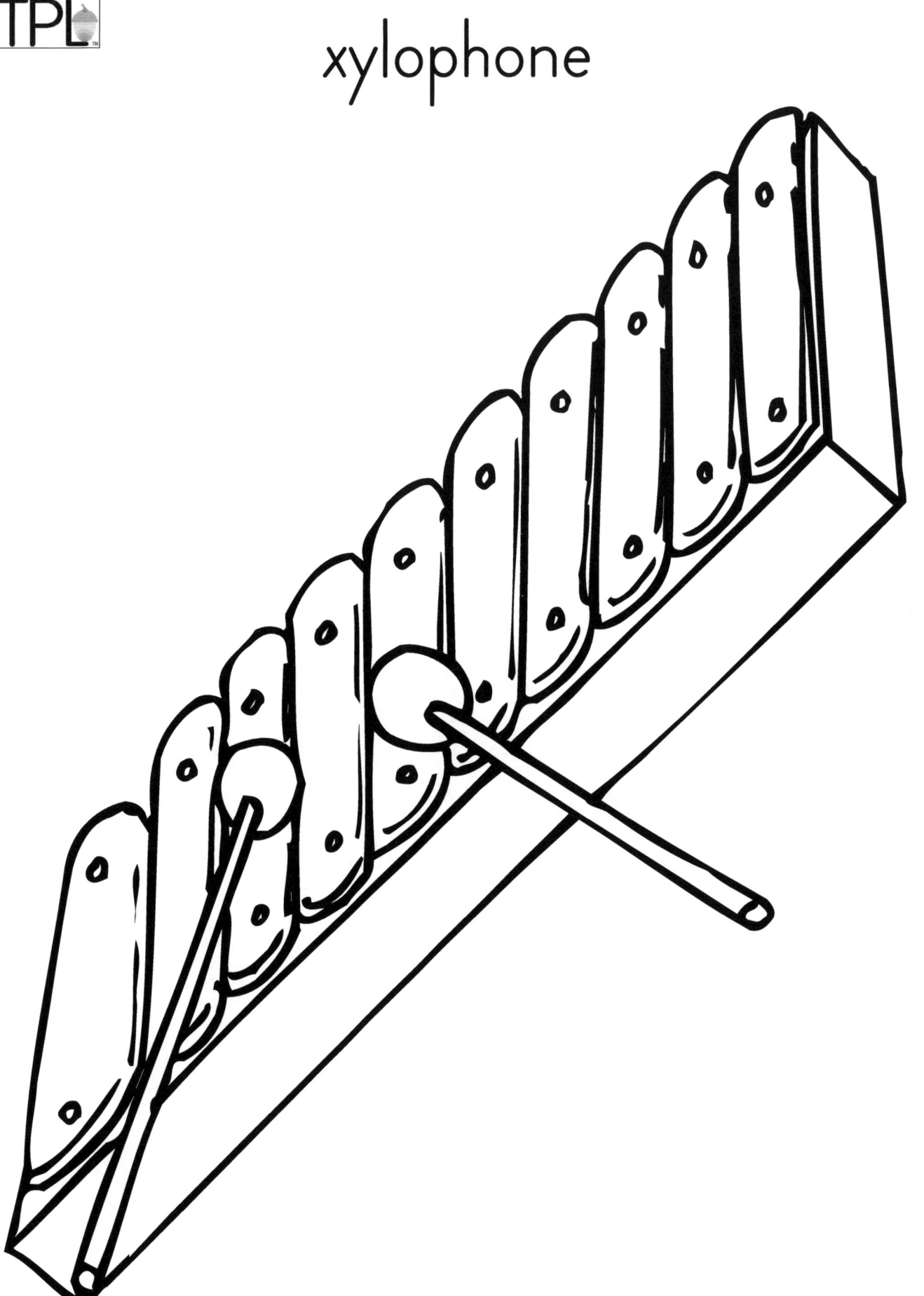

yak

yarn ball

yawn

yo-yo

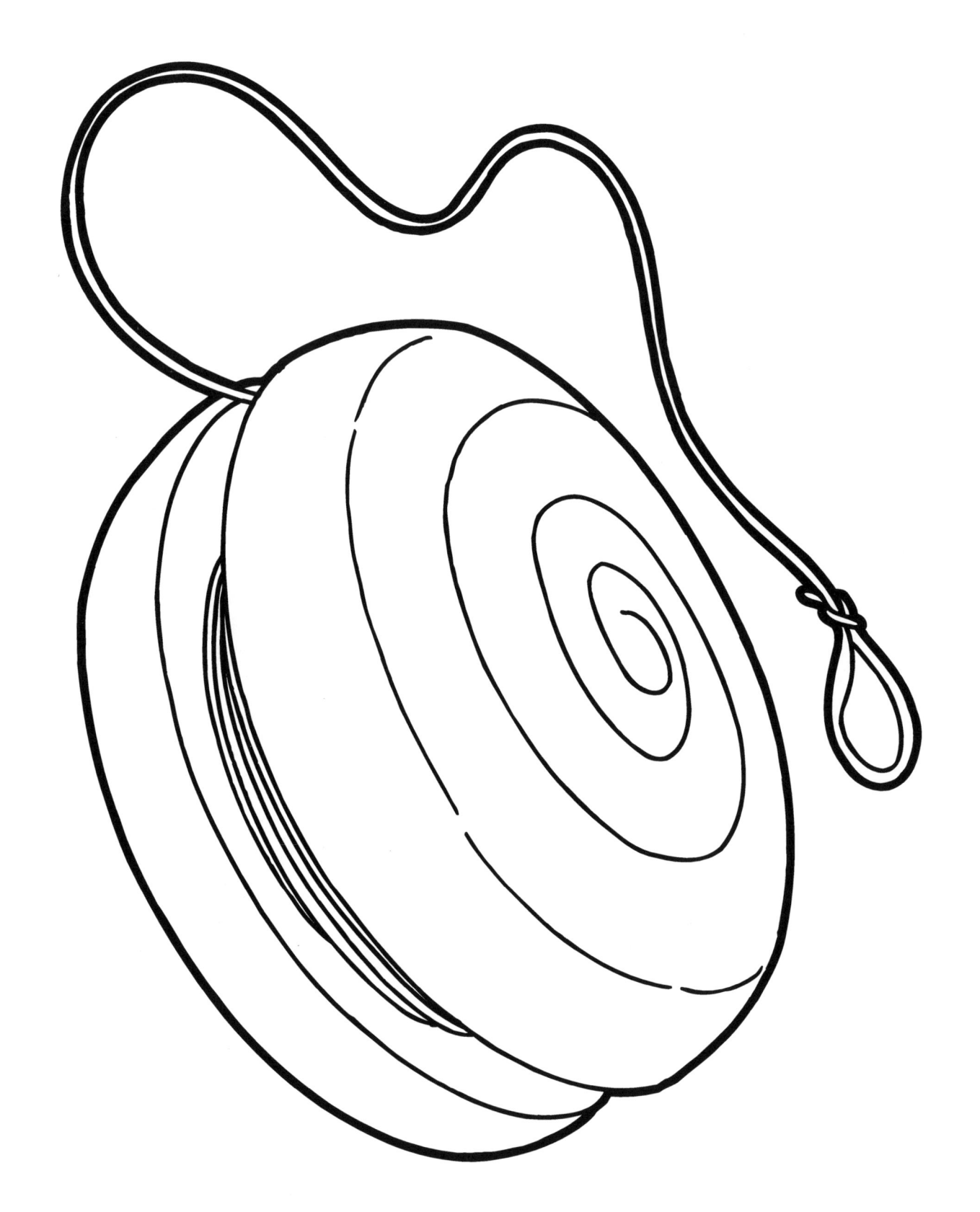

Yukon, Canada

North
West East
South

Maps are representations and boundaries are not exact.

zebra

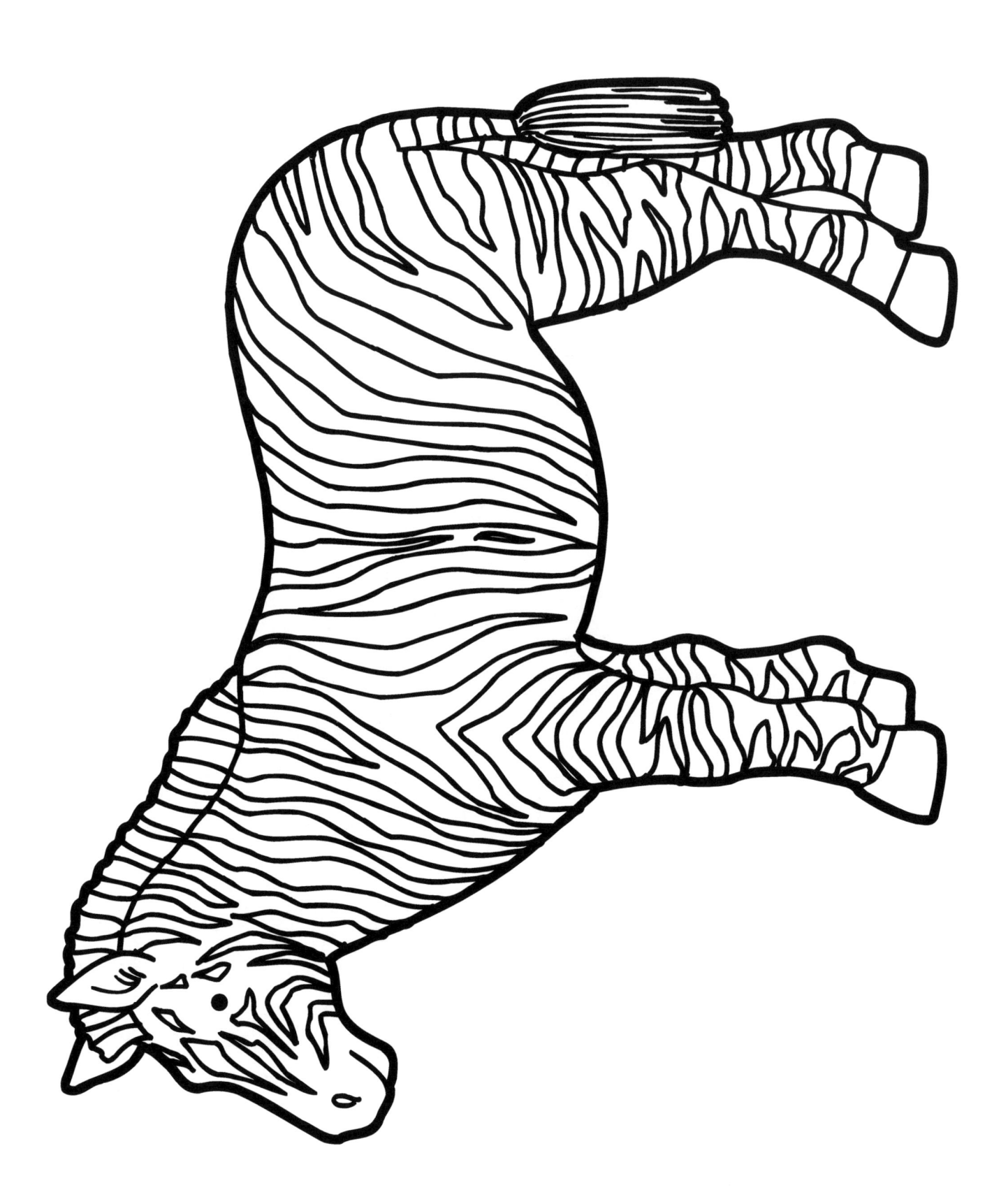

zebu

zipper

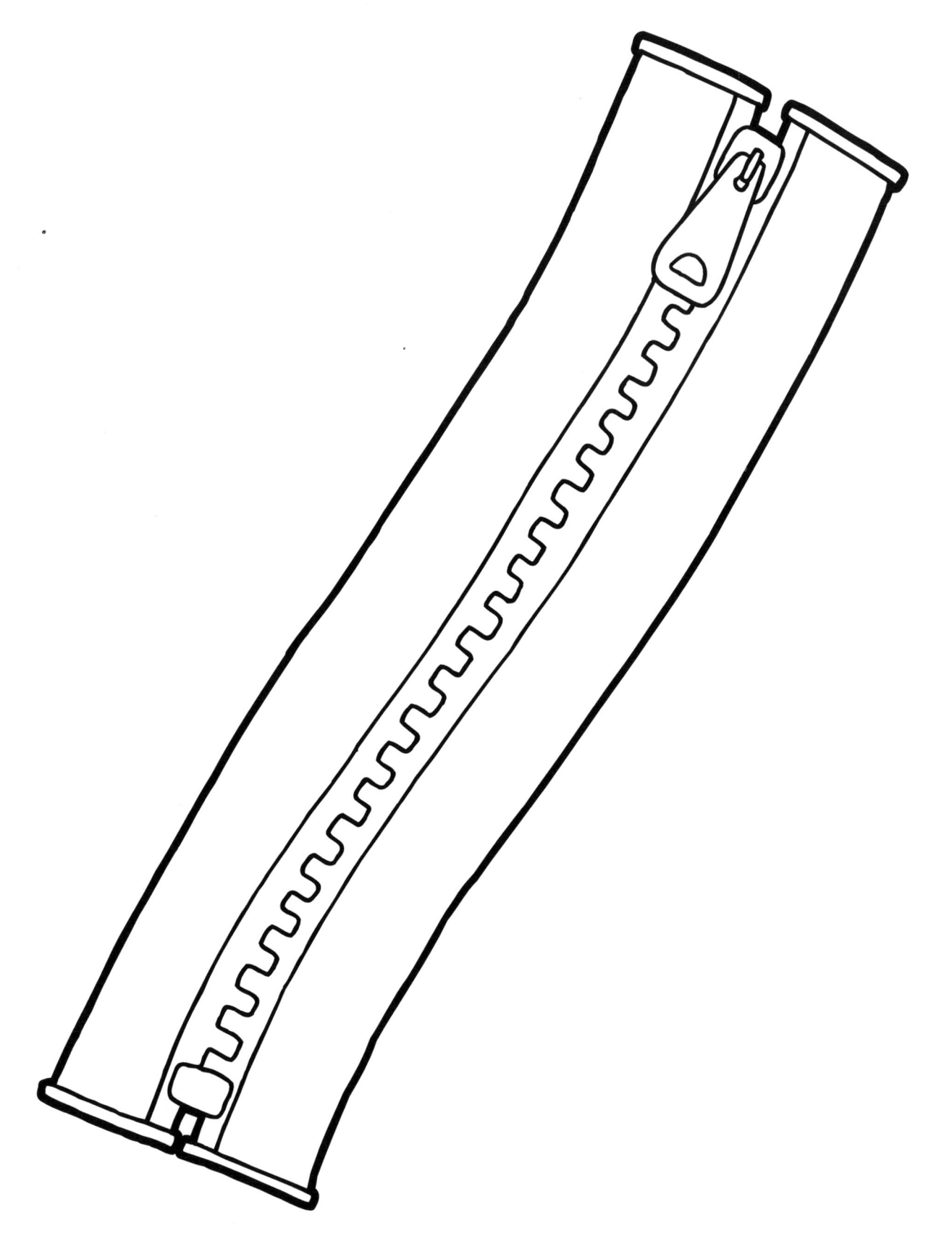

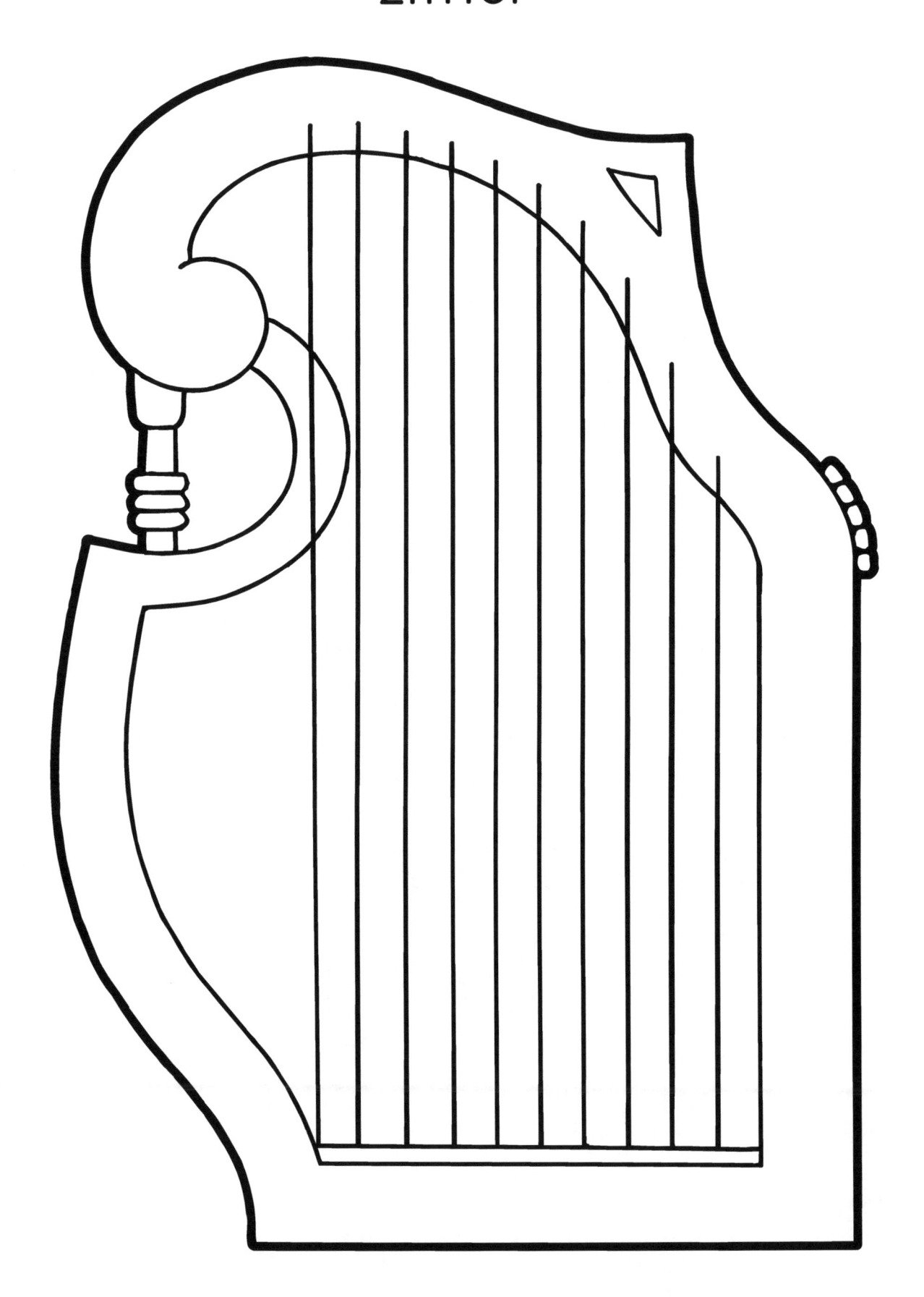

zither

Little Acorn Books™

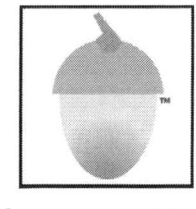

Promoting Early Skills for a Lifetime™

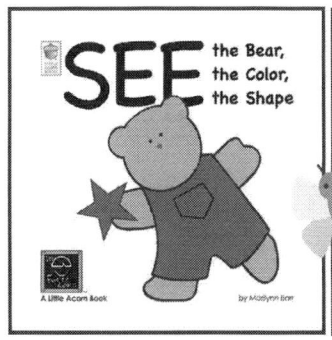

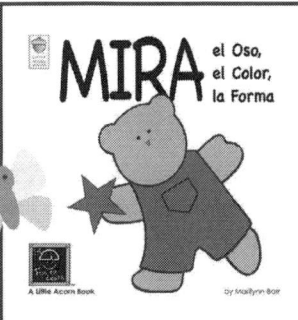

SEE the Bear, the Color, the Shape

MIRA el Oso, el Color, la Forma

CUENTA los Osos

COUNT the Bears

A Hands-on Picture Book Series • Infancy–Age 4

Using Crayons, Scissors, & Glue for Crafts
Preschool–Grade 1

Miss Pitty Pat & Friends
Preschool–Grade 1

Mookie's Christmas Tree
For All Ages and Not Just for Christmas

It's Fun to Learn

Little Acorn Books™
Visit our web site:
www.littleacornbooks.com

Made in the USA
Lexington, KY
11 June 2016